U•X•L ENCYCLOPEDIA OF

NATIVE AMERICAN TRIBES

U•X•L ENCYCLOPEDIA OF NATIVE AMERICAN TRIBES

VOLUME

4

California
Pacific Northwest

Sharon Malinowski, Anna Sheets
& Linda Schmittroth, *Editors*

AN IMPRINT OF THE GALE GROUP

DETROIT · SAN FRANCISCO · LONDON
BOSTON · WOODBRIDGE, CT

U•X•L Encyclopedia of Native American Tribes

Sharon Malinowski, Anna Sheets, and Linda Schmittroth, *Editors*

Staff

Sonia Benson, *U•X•L Senior Editor*
Carol DeKane Nagel, *U•X•L Managing Editor*
Thomas L. Romig, *U•X•L Publisher*
Jeffrey Lehman, *Editor*
Melissa Walsh Doig, *Editor*
Dorothy Maki, *Manufacturing Manager*
Evi Seoud, *Assistant Production Manager*
Rita Wimberley, *Senior Buyer*
Cynthia Baldwin, *Product Design Manager*
Barbara Yarrow, *Graphic Services Director*
Michelle DiMercurio, *Senior Art Director*
Keasha Jack-Lyles, *Permissions Associate*
LM Design, *Typesetter*

Library of Congress Cataloging-in-Publication Data

U•X•L Encyclopedia of Native American Tribes / Sharon Malinowski, Anna Sheets, and Linda Schmittroth, editors
p. cm.

Includes bibliographical references.

Contents: v. 1. The Northeast and Southeast – v. 2. The Great Basin and Southwest – v. 3. The Arctic, Subarctic, Great Plains, and Plateau – v. 4. California and the Pacific Northwest.

ISBN 0-7876-2838-7 (set).

ISBN 0-7876-2839-5 (volume 1) ISBN 0-7876-2841-7 (volume 3)

ISBN 0-7876-2840-9 (volume 2) ISBN 0-7876-2842-5 (volume 4)

1. Indians of North America – Encyclopedias, Juvenile. [1. Indians of North America – Encyclopedias.] I. Malinowski, Sharon. II. Sheets, Anna J. (Anna Jean), 1970– . III. Schmittroth, Linda. IV. Title: Encyclopedia of Native American tribes.

E76.2.U85 1999
970'.003—dc21

98-54353

CIP
AC

Contents

VOLUME 1

VOLUME 2

VOLUME 3

VOLUME 4

Tribes Alphabetically

First numeral signifies volume number. The numeral after the colon signifies page number. For example, **3:871** *means Volume 3, page 871.*

A

B

C

Reader's Guide

Long before the Vikings, Spaniards, and Portuguese made landfall on North American shores, the continent already had a rich history of human settlement. The *U•X•L Encyclopedia of Native American Tribes* opens up for students the array of tribal ways in the United States and Canada past and present. Included in these volumes, readers will find the stories of:

- the well-known nineteenth century Lakota hunting the buffalo on the Great Plains
- the contemporary Inuit of the Arctic, who have recently won their battle for Nunavut, a vast, self-governing territory in Canada
- the Seminole in Florida, drawing tourists with their alligator wrestling shows
- the Haida of the Pacific Northwest, whose totem poles have become a familiar adornment of the landscape
- the Anasazi in the Southwest, who were building spectacular cities long before Europeans arrived
- the Mohawk men in the Northeast who made such a name for themselves as ironworkers on skyscrapers and bridges that they have long been in demand for such projects as the World Trade Center and the Golden Gate Bridge
- the Yahi of California, who became extinct when their last member Ishi died in 1916.

The *U•X•L Encyclopedia of Native American Tribes* presents eighty tribes, confederacies, and Native American groups. Among the tribes included are large and well-known nations, smaller communities with their own fascinating stories, and prehistoric peoples. The tribes are grouped in the ten major geographical/cultural areas of North America in which tribes shared environmental and cultural connections. The ten sections, each beginning with an introductory essay on the geographical area and the shared history and culture within it, are arranged in the volumes as follows:

- •Volume 1: Northeast and Southeast
- •Volume 2: The Great Basin and Southwest
- •Volume 3: Arctic, Subarctic, Great Plains, and Plateau
- •Volume 4: California and Pacific Northwest

The *U•X•L Encyclopedia of Native American Tribes* provides the history of each of the tribes featured and a fascinating look at their ways of life: how families lived in centuries past and today, what people ate and wore, what their homes were like, how they worshiped, celebrated, governed themselves, and much more. A student can learn in depth about one tribe or compare aspects of many tribes. Each detailed entry is presented in consistent rubrics that allow for easy access and comparison, as follows:

- •History
- •Religion
- •Language
- •Government
- •Economy
- •Daily Life
- •Arts
- •Customs
- •Current Tribal Issues
- •Notable People

Each entry begins with vital data on the tribe: name, location, population, language family, origins and group affiliations. A locator map follows, showing the traditional homelands and contemporary communities of the group; regional and migration maps throughout aid in locating the many groups and at different times in history. Brief timelines in each entry chronicle important dates of the tribe's history, while an overall timeline at the beginning of all the volumes outlines key events in history pertinent to all Native Americans. Other sidebars present recipes, oral literature or stories, population statistics, language keys, and background material on the tribe. Black-and-white photographs and illustrations, further reading sections, a thorough subject index, and a glossary are special features that make the volumes easy, fun, and informative to use.

A note on terminology

Throughout the *U•X•L Encyclopedia of Native American Tribes* various terms are used for Native North Americans, such as *Indian, American Indian, Native,* and *aboriginal.* The Native peoples of the Americas have the unfortunate distinction of having been given the wrong name by the Europeans who first arrived on the continent, mistakenly thinking they had arrived in India. The search for a single name, however, has never been entirely successful. The best way to characterize Native North Americans is by recognizing their specific tribal or community identities. In compiling this book, every effort has been made to keep Native tribal and community identities distinct, but by necessity, inclusive terminology is often used. We do not wish to offend anyone, but rather than favor one term for Native North American people, the editors have used a variety of terminology, trying always to use the most appropriate term in the particular context.

Europeans also had a hand in giving names to tribes, often misunderstanding their languages and the relations between different Native communities. Most tribes have their own names for themselves, and many have succeeded in gaining public acceptance of traditional names. The Inuit, for example, objected to the name Eskimo, which means "eaters of raw meat," and in time their name for themselves was accepted. In the interest of clarity the editors of this book have used the currently accepted terms, while acknowledging the traditional ones or the outmoded ones at the beginning of each entry.

The term *tribe* itself is not accepted by all Native groups. The people living in North America before the Europeans arrived had many different ways of organizing themselves politically and relating to other groups around them—from complex confederacies and powerful unified nations to isolated villages with little need for political structure. Groups divided, absorbed each other, intermarried, allied, and dissolved. The epidemics and wars that came with non-Native expansion into North America created a demographic catastrophe to many Native groups and greatly affected tribal affiliations. Although in modern times there are actual rules about what comprises a tribe (federal requirements for recognition of tribes are specific, complicated, and often difficult to fulfill), the hundreds of groups living in the Americas in early times did not have any one way of categorizing themselves. Some Native American peoples today find the word *tribe* misleading. In a study of Indian peoples, it can also be an elusive defining term. But in facing the challenges of maintaining traditions and heritage in modern times, tribal or community identity is acutely important to many Native Americans. Tremendous efforts have been undertaken to preserve native languages, oral traditions, religions, ceremonies, and traditional arts and economies— the things that, put together, make a tribe a cultural and political unit.

Advisors and contributors

For the invaluable contributions, suggestions, and advice on the *U•X•L Encyclopedia of Native American Tribes,* special thanks are due to: Edward D. Castillo, (Cahuilla-Luiseño), Director, Native American Studies Program, Sonoma State University, California; Ned Blackhawk; Elizabeth Hanson, Ph.D., Research Associate to the Dean, The College of Charleston, South Carolina; Daniel Boxberger, Department of Anthropology, Western Washington University; John H. Moore, Ph.D., Anthropology Department, University of Florida, Gainesville; Amanda Beresford McCarthy; George Cornell, Ph.D., Associate Professor, History and American Studies, Michigan State University; Brian Wescott, Athabascan/Yup'ik; Gordon L. Pullar, Director, Department of Alaska Native and Rural Development, College of Rural Alaska,UAF; and Barbara Bigelow.

Comments and suggestions

In this first edition of the *U•X•L Encyclopedia of Native American Tribes* we have presented in-depth information on eighty of the hundreds of tribes of North America. While every attempt was made to include a wide representation of groups, many historically important and interesting tribes are not covered in these volumes. We welcome your suggestions for tribes to be featured in future editions, as well as any other comments you may have on this set. Please write: Editors, *U•X•L Encyclopedia of Native American Tribes,* U•X•L, 27500 Drake Road, Farmington Hills, Michigan 48331–3535; call toll-free 1-800-347-4253; or fax: 313-699-8066; or send e-mail via http://www.galegroup.com.

Words to Know

A

Aboriginal: native, or relating to the first or earliest group living in a particular area.

Activism: taking action for or against a controversial issue; political and social activists may organize or take part in protest demonstrations, rallies, petitioning the government, sit-ins, civil disobedience, and many other forms of activities that draw attention to an issue and/or challenge the authorities to make a change.

Adobe: (pronounced *uh-DOE-bee*) a brick or other building material made from sun-dried mud, a mixture of clay, sand, and sometimes ashes, rocks, or straw.

Alaska Native Claims Settlement Act (ANCSA): an act of Congress passed in 1971 that gave Alaska Natives 44 million acres of land and $962.5 million. In exchange, Alaska Natives gave up all claim to other lands in Alaska. The ANCSA also resulted in the formation of 12 regional corporations in Alaska in charge of Native communities' economic development and land use.

Allotment: the practice of dividing and distributing something into individual lots. In 1887 the U.S. Congress passed the Dawes Act, or the General Allotment Act, which divided Indian reservations into privately owned parcels (pieces) of land. Under allotment, tribes could no longer own their lands in common (as a group) in the traditional way. Instead, the head of a family received a lot, generally 160 acres. Land not allotted was sold to non-Natives.

American Indian Movement (AIM): an activist movement founded in 1966 to aggressively press for Indian rights. The movement was formed to improve federal, state, and local social services to Native Americans in urban neighborhoods. AIM sought the reorganization of the Bureau of Indian Affairs to make it more responsive to Native

American needs and fought for the return of Indian lands illegally taken from them.

Anthropology: the study of human beings in terms of their populations, cultures, social relations, ethnic characteristics, customs, and adaptation to their environment.

Archaeology: the study of the remains of past human life, such as fossil relics, artifacts, and monuments, in order to understand earlier human cultures.

Arctic: relating to the area surrounding the North Pole.

Assimilate: to absorb, or to be absorbed, into the dominant society (those in power, or in the majority). U.S. assimilation policies were directed at causing Native Americans to become like European-Americans in terms of jobs and economics, religion, customs, language, education, family life, and dress.

B

Band: a small, loosely organized social group composed of several families. In Canada, the word *band* originally referred to a social unit of nomadic (those who moved from place to place) hunting peoples, but now refers to a community of Indians registered with the government.

Boarding school: a live-in school.

Breechcloth: a garment with front and back flaps that hang from the waist. *Breechcloths* were one of the most common articles of clothing worn by many Native American men and sometimes women in pre-European/American settlement times.

Bureau of Indian Affairs (BIA): the U.S. government agency that oversees tribal lands, education, and other aspects of Indian life.

C

Census: a count of the population.

Ceremony: a special act or set of acts (such as a wedding or a funeral) performed by members of a group on important occasions, usually organized according to the group's traditions and beliefs.

Clan: a group of related house groups and families that trace back to a common ancestor or a common symbol or totem, usually an animal such as the bear or the turtle. The *clan* forms the basic social and political unit for many Indian societies.

Colonialism: a state or nation's control over a foreign territory.

Colonize: to establish a group of people from a mother country or state in a foreign territory; the colonists set up a community that remains tied to the mother country.

Confederacy: a group of people, states, or nations joined together for mutual support or for a special purpose.

Convert: (as verb) to cause a person or group to change their beliefs or practices. A *convert* (noun) is a person who has been *converted* to a new belief or practice.

Coup: (pronounced *COO*) a feat of bravery, especially the touching of an enemy's body during battle without causing or receiving injury. To *count coup* is to count the number of such feats of bravery.

Cradleboard: a board or frame on which an infant was bound or wrapped by some Native American peoples. It was used as a portable carrier or for carrying an infant on the back.

Creation stories: sacred myths or stories that explain how the Earth and its beings were created.

Culture: the set of beliefs, social habits, and ways of surviving in the environment that are held by a particular social group.

D

Dentalium: (pronounced *den-TAIL-ee-um*; from the Latin word for tooth). Dentalia (plural) are the tooth-like shells that some tribes used as money. The shells were rubbed smooth and strung like beads on strands of animal skin.

Depletion: decreasing the amount of something; *depletion* of resources such as animals or minerals through overuse reduces essential elements from the environment.

Dialect: (pronounced *DY-uh-lect*) a local variety of a particular language, with unique differences in words, grammar, and pronunciation.

E

Economy: the way a group obtains, produces, and distributes the goods it needs; the overall system by which it supports itself and accumulates its wealth.

Ecosystem: the overall way that a community and its surrounding environment function together in nature.

Epidemic: the rapid spread of a disease so that many people in an area have it at the same time.

Ethnic group: a group of people who are classed according to certain aspects of their common background, usually by tribal, racial, national, cultural, and language origins.

Extended family: a family group that includes close relatives such as mother, father, and children, plus grandparents, aunts and uncles, and cousins.

F

Federally recognized tribes: tribes with which the U.S. government maintains official relations as established by treaty, executive order, or act of Congress.

First Nations: one of Canada's terms for its Indian nations.

Five Civilized Tribes: a name given to the Cherokee, Choctaw, Chickasaw, Creek, and Seminole during the mid-1800s. The tribes were given this name by non-Natives because they had democratic constitutional governments, a high literacy rate (many people who could read and write), and ran effective schools.

Formal education: structured learning that takes place in a school or college under the supervision of trained teachers.

G

Ghost Dance: a revitalization (renewal or rebirth) movement that arose in the 1870s after many tribes moved to reservations and were being encouraged to give up their traditional beliefs. Many Native Americans hoped that, if they performed it earnestly, the Ghost Dance would bring back traditional Native lifestyles and values, and that the buffalo and Indian ancestors would return to the Earth as in the days before the white settlers.

Great Basin: an elevated region in the western United States in which all water drains toward the center. The *Great Basin* covers part of Nevada, California, Colorado, Utah, Oregon, and Wyoming.

Guardian spirit: a sacred power, usually embodied in an animal such as a hawk, deer, or turtle, that reveals itself to an individual, offering help throughout the person's lifetime in important matters such as hunting or healing the sick.

H

Haudenosaunee: (pronounced *hoo-dee-noh-SHAW-nee*) the name of the people often called Iroquois or Five Nations. It means "People of the Longhouse."

Head flattening: a practice in which a baby was placed in a cradle, and a padded board was tied to its forehead to mold the head into a desired shape. Sometimes the effect of flattening the back of the head was achieved by binding the infant tightly to a cradleboard.

I

Immunity: resistance to disease; the ability to be exposed to a disease with less chance of getting it, and less severe effects if infected.

Indian Territory: an area in present-day Kansas and Oklahoma where the U.S. government once planned to move all Indians, and, eventually, to allow them to run their own province or state. In 1880 nearly one-third of all U.S. Indians lived there, but with the formation of the state of Oklahoma in 1906, the promise of an Indian state dissolved.

Indigenous: (pronounced *in-DIJ-uh-nus*) native, or first, in a specific area. Native Americans are often referred to as *indigenous* peoples of North America.

Intermarriage: marriage between people of different groups, as between a Native American and a non-Native, or between people from two different tribes.

K

Kachina: (pronounced *kuh-CHEE-nuh*) a group of spirits celebrated by the Pueblo Indians; the word also refers to dolls made in the image of *kachina* spirits.

Kiva: (pronounced *KEE-va*) among the Pueblo, a circular (sometimes rectangular) underground room used for religious ceremonies.

L

Lacrosse: a game of Native American origin in which players use a long stick with a webbed pouch at the end for catching and throwing a ball.

Language family: a group of languages that are different from one another but are related. These languages share similar words, sounds, or word structures. The languages are alike either because they have borrowed words from each other or because they originally came from the same parent language.

Legend: a story or folktale that tells about people or events in the past.

Life expectancy: the average number of years a person may expect to live.

Linguistics: the study of human speech and language.

Literacy: the state of being able to read and write.

Longhouse: a large, long building in which several families live together; usually found among Northwest Coast and Iroquois peoples.

Long Walk of the Navajo: the enforced 300-mile walk of the Navajo people in 1864, when they were being removed from their homelands to the Bosque Redondo Reservation in New Mexico.

M

Matrilineal: tracing family relations through the mother; in a *matrilineal* society, names and inheritances are passed down through the mother's side of the family.

Medicine bundle: a pouch in which were kept sacred objects believed to have powers that would protect and aid an individual, a clan or family, or a community.

Midewiwin Society: the Medicine Lodge Religion, whose main purpose was to prolong life. The society taught morality, proper conduct, and a knowledge of plants and herbs for healing.

Migration: movement from one place to another. The *migrations* of Native peoples were often done by the group, with whole nations moving from one area to another.

Mission: an organized effort by a religious group to spread its beliefs to other parts of the world; *mission* refers either to the project of spreading a belief system or to the building(s)—such as a church—in which this takes place.

Mission school: a school established by missionaries to teach people religious beliefs, as well as other subjects.

Myth: a story passed down through generations, often involving supernatural beings. *Myths* often express religious beliefs or the values of a people. They may attempt to explain how the Earth and its beings were created, or why things are as they are. They are not always meant to be taken as factual.

N

Natural resources: the sources of supplies provided by the environment for survival and enrichment, such as animals to be hunted, land for farming, minerals, and timber.

Neophyte: (pronounced *NEE-oh-fite*) beginner; often used to mean a new convert to a religion.

Nomadic: traveling and relocating often, usually in search of food and other resources or a better climate.

Nunavut: a new territory in Canada as of April 1, 1999, with the status of a province and an Inuit majority. It is a huge area, covering most of Canada north of the treeline. *Nunavut* means "Our Land" in Inuktitut (the Inuit language).

O

Oral literature: oral traditions that are written down after enjoying a long life in spoken form among a people.

Oral traditions: history, mythology, folklore, and other foundations of a culture that have been passed by spoken word, often in the form of stories, from generation to generation within a culture group.

P

Parent language: a language that is the common source of two or more languages that came into being at a later time.

Per capita income: *per capita* is a Latin phrase that means "for each person." Per capita income is the average personal income per person.

Petroglyph: a carving or engraving on rock; a common form of ancient art.

Peyote: (pronounced *pay-OH-tee*) a substance obtained from cactus that some Indian groups use as part of their religious practice. After eating the substance, which stimulates the nervous system, a person may go into a trance state and see visions. The Peyote Religion features the use of this substance.

Pictograph: a simple picture representing a historical event.

Policy: the overall plan or course of action issued by the government, establishing how it will handle certain situations or people and what its goals are.

Post-European contact: relating to the time and state of Native Americans and their lands after the Europeans arrived. Depending on the part of the country in which they lived, Native groups experienced contact at differing times in the history of white expansion into the West.

Potlatch: a feast or ceremony, commonly held among Northwest Coast groups; also called a "giveaway." During a *potlatch,* goods are given to guests to show the host's generosity and wealth. Potlatches are used to celebrate major life events such as birth, death, or marriage.

Powwow: a celebration at which the main activity is traditional singing and dancing. In modern times, the singers and dancers at powwows come from many different tribes.

Province: a district or division of a country (like a state in the United States).

R

Raiding: entering into another tribe or community's territory, usually by stealth or force, and stealing their livestock and supplies.

Rancheria: a small Indian reservation, usually in California.

Ratify: to approve or confirm. In the United States, the U.S. Senate *ratified* treaties with the Indians.

Red Power: a term used to describe the Native American activism movement of the 1960s, in which people from many tribes came together to protest the injustices of American policies toward Native Americans.

Removal Act: an act passed by the U.S. Congress in 1830 that directed all Indians to be moved to Indian Territory, west of the Mississippi River.

Removal Period: the time, mostly between 1830 and 1860, when most Indians of the eastern United States were forced to leave their homelands and relocate west of the Mississippi River.

Reservation: land set aside by the U.S. government for the use of a group or groups of Indians.

Reserve: in Canada, lands set aside for specific Indian bands. *Reserve* means in Canada approximately what *reservation* means in the United States.

Revitalization: the feeling or movement in which something seems to come back to life after having been quiet or inactive for a period of time.

Ritual: a formal act that is performed in basically the same way each time; rituals are often performed as part of a ceremony.

Rural: having to do with the country; opposite of urban.

S

Sachem: the chief of a confederation of tribes.

Shaman: (can be pronounced either *SHAY-mun* or *SHAH-mun*) a priest or medicine person in many Native American groups who understands and works with supernatural matters. *Shamans* traditionally performed in rituals and were expected to cure the sick, see the future, and obtain supernatural help with hunting and other economic activities.

Smallpox: a very contagious disease that spread across North America and killed many thousands of Indians. Survivors had skin that was badly scarred.

Subsistence economy: an economic system in which people provide themselves with the things they need for survival and their way of life rather than working for money or making a surplus of goods for trade.

Sun Dance: a renewal and purification (cleansing) ceremony performed by many Plains Indians such as the Sioux and Cheyenne. A striking aspect of the ceremony was the personal sacrifice made by some men. They undertook self-torture in order to gain a vision that might provide spiritual insight and knowledge beneficial to the community.

Sweat lodge: an airtight hut containing hot stones that were sprinkled with water to make them steam. A person remained inside until he or she was perspiring. The person then usually rushed out and plunged into a cold stream. This treatment was used before a ceremony or for the healing of physical or spiritual ailments. *Sweat lodge* is also the name of a sacred Native American ceremony involving the building of the lodge and the pouring of water on the stones, usually by a medicine person, accompanied by praying and singing. The ceremony has many purposes, including spiritual cleansing and healing.

T

Taboo: a forbidden thing or action. Many Indians believe that the sacred order of the world must be maintained if one is to avoid illness or other misfortunes. This is accomplished, in part, by observing a large assortment of taboos.

Termination: the policy of the U.S. government during the 1950s and 1960s to end the relationships set up by treaties with Indian nations.

Toloache: a substance obtained from a plant called jimsonweed. When consumed, the drug causes a person to go into a trance and see visions. It is used in some religious ceremonies.

Totem: an object that serves as an emblem or represents a family or clan, usually in the form of an animal, bird, fish, plant, or other natural object. A *totem pole* is a pillar built in front of the homes of Natives in the Northwest. It is painted and carved with a series of totems that show the family background and either mythical or historical events.

Trail of Tears: a series of forced marches of Native Americans of the Southeast in the 1830s, causing the deaths of thousands. The marches were the result of the U.S. government's removal policy, which ordered Native Americans to be moved to Indian Territory (now Oklahoma).

Treaty: an agreement between two parties or two nations, signed by both, usually defining the benefits to both parties that will result from one side giving up title to a territory of land.

Tribe: a group of Natives who share a name, language, culture, and ancestors; in Canada, called a band.

Tribelet: a community within an organization of communities in which one main settlement was surrounded by a few minor outlying settlements.

Trickster: a common culture hero in Indian myth and legend. *Tricksters* generally have supernatural powers that can be used to do good or harm, and stories about them take into account the different forces of the universe, such as good and evil or night and day. The Trickster takes different forms among various groups; for example, Coyote in the Southwest; Ikhtomi Spider in the High Plains, and Jay or Wolverine in Canada.

Trust: a relationship between two parties (or groups) in which one is responsible for acting in the other's best interests. The U.S. government has a *trust* relationship with tribal nations. Many tribes do not own their lands outright; according to treaty, the government owns the land "in trust" and tribes are given the use of it.

U

Unemployment rate: the percentage of the population that is looking for work but unable to find any. (People who have quit looking for work are not included in *unemployment* rates.)

Urban: having to do with cities and towns; the opposite of rural.

V

Values: the ideals that a community of people shares.

Vision quest: a sacred ceremony in which a person (often a teenage boy) goes off alone and fasts, living without food or water for a period of days. During that time, he hopes to learn about his spiritual side and to have a vision of a guardian spirit who will give him help and strength throughout his life.

W

Wampum: small cylinder-shaped beads cut from shells. Long strings of *wampum* were used for many different purposes. Indians believed that the exchange of wampum and other goods established a friendship, not just a profit-making relationship.

Wampum belt: a broad woven belt of wampum used to record history, treaties among the tribes, or treaties with colonists or governments.

Weir: a barricade used to funnel fish toward people who wait to catch them.

Timeline

25,000–11,000 B.C.E. Groups of hunters cross from Asia to Alaska on the Bering Sea Land Bridge, which was formed when lands now under the waters of the Bering Strait were exposed for periods of time, according to scientists.

1400 B.C.E. People who live along the lower Mississippi River are building large burial mounds and living in planned communities.

1 C.E. Small, permanent villages of the Hohokam tradition emerge in the Southwest.

400 Anasazi communities emerge in the Four Corners region of the Southwest. Anasazi eventually design communities in large multiroomed apartment buildings, some with more than 1,200 rooms. The Anasazi are farmers and skilled potters.

900 The Mississippian mound-building groups form complex political and social systems, and participate in long-distance trade and an elaborate and widespread religion.

1000–1350 The Iroquois Confederacy is formed among the Mohawk, Oneida, Onondaga, Cayuga, and Seneca nations. The Five Nations of the Haudenosaunee are from this time governed by chiefs from the 49 families who were present at the origin of the confederation.

Anasazi ruins at Pueblo del Arroyo, Chaco Canyon, New Mexico.

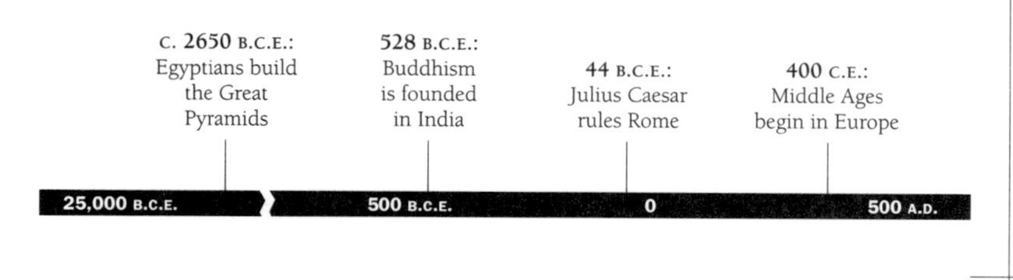

1040: Pueblos (towns) are flourishing in New Mexico's Chaco Canyon. The pueblos are connected by an extensive road system that stretches many miles across the desert.

1350 Moundville, in present-day Alabama, one of the largest ceremonial centers of the Mound Builders, thrives. With 20 great mounds and a village, it is probably the center of a chiefdom that includes several other related communities.

1494: Christopher Columbus begins the enslavement of American Indians, capturing over 500 Taino of San Salvador and sending them to Spain to be sold.

1503 French explorer Jacques Cartier begins trading with Native Americans along the East Coast.

1539–43 Spanish explorers Hernando de Soto and Francisco Coronado traverse the Southeast and Southwest, bringing with them disease epidemics that kill thousands of Native Americans.

1609 The fur trade begins when British explorer Henry Hudson, sailing for the Netherlands, opens trade in New Netherland (present-day New York) with several Northeast tribes.

The attack on the Pequot fort in 1637.

1634–37 An army of Puritans, Pilgrims, Mohican, and Narragansett attacks and sets fire to the Pequot fort, killing as many as 700 Pequot men, women, and children.

1648–51 The Iroquois, having exhausted the fur supply in their area, attack other tribes in order to get a new supply. The Beaver Wars begin, and many Northeast tribes are forced to move west toward the Great Lakes area.

1660 The Ojibway, pushed west by settlers and Iroquois expansion, invade Sioux territory in Minnesota. After fighting the Ojibway, many Sioux groups move to the Great Plains.

1760–63 The Delaware Prophet tells Native Americans in the Northeast that they must drive Europeans out of North America and return to the customs of their ancestors. His message influences the Ottawa leader Pontiac, who uses it to unite many tribes against the British.

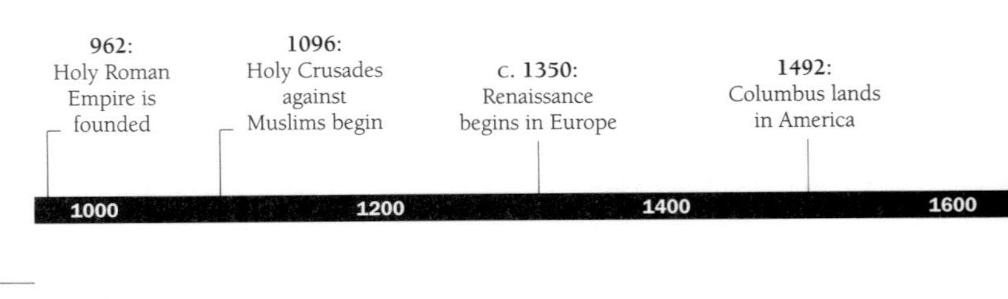

1763 England issues the Proclamation of 1763, which assigns all lands west of the Appalachian Mountains to Native Americans, while colonists are allowed to settle all land to the east. The document respects the aboriginal land rights of Native Americans. It is not popular with colonists who want to move onto Indian lands and becomes one of the conflicts between England and the colonies leading to the American Revolution.

Franciscan priest with an Indian child at a Spanish mission, California.

1769 The Spanish build their first mission in California. There will be 23 Spanish missions in California, which are used to convert Native Californians to Christianity, but also reduces them to slave labor.

c. 1770 Horses, brought to the continent by the Spanish in the sixteenth century, spread onto the Great Plains and lead to the development of a new High Plains Culture.

1778 The treaty-making period begins, when the first of 370 treaties between Indian nations and the U.S. government is signed. The treaty-making period ends in 1871.

1786 The first federal Indian reservations are established.

1789 The Spanish establish a post at Nootka Sound on Vancouver Island, the first permanent European establishment in the territory of the Pacific Northwest Coast tribes.

Sacajawea points out the way to Lewis and Clark.

1805–06 Explorers Meriwether Lewis and William Clark, led by Sacajawea, travel through the Plateau area, encountering the Cayuse, Nez Perce, Walla Walla, Wishram, and Yakima.

1830 The removal period begins when the U.S. Congress passes the Indian Removal Act. Over the course of the next 30 years many tribes from the Northeast and Southeast are removed to Indian Territory in present-day Oklahoma and Kansas, often forcibly and at great expense in human lives.

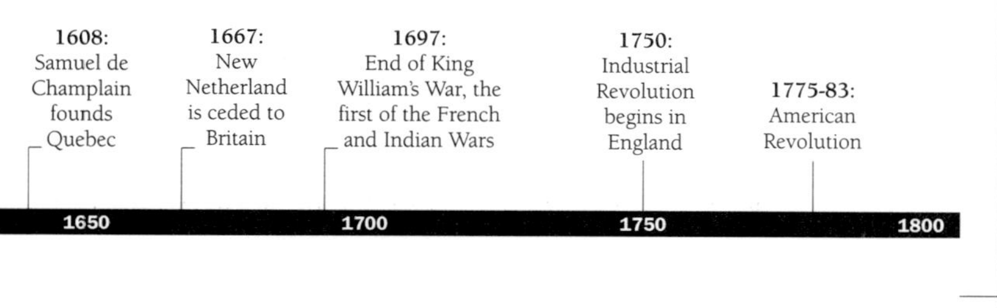

1851 Early reservations are created in California to protect the Native population from the violence of U.S. citizens. These reservations are inadequate and serve only a small portion of the Native Californians, while others endure continued violence and hardship.

1870 The First Ghost Dance Movement begins when Wodzibwob, a Paiute, learns in a vision that a great earthquake will swallow the Earth, and that all Indians will be spared or resurrected within three days of the disaster. Thus, their world will return to its state before the Europeans had arrived.

1870–90 The Peyote Religion spreads through the Great Plains. Peyote (obtained from a cactus plant) brings on a dreamlike feeling that followers believe moves them closer to the spirit world. Tribes develop their own ceremonies, songs, and symbolism, and vow to be trustworthy, honorable, and community-oriented and to follow the Peyote Road.

1876 The Indian Act in Canada establishes an Indian reserve system, in which reserves were governed by voluntary elected band councils. The Act does not recognize Canadian Indians' right to self-government. With the passage of the act, Canadian peoples in Canada are divided into three groups: status Indian, treaty Indian, and non-status Indian. The categories affect the benefits and rights Indians are given by the government.

Preparing for a potlatch ceremony in the Pacific Northwest.

1880s The buffalo on the Great Plains are slaughtered until there are almost none left. Without adequate supplies of buffalo for food, the Plains Indians cannot survive. Many move to reservations.

1884 Potlatches are banned by the Canadian government. The elaborate gift-giving ceremonies have long been a vital part of Pacific Northwest Indian culture.

1887 The Dawes Act, or the General Allotment Act, is passed by Congress. The act calls for the allotment (or parceling out) of tribal lands. Tribes are no longer to own their lands in common in the traditional way. Instead, the land is to be assigned to

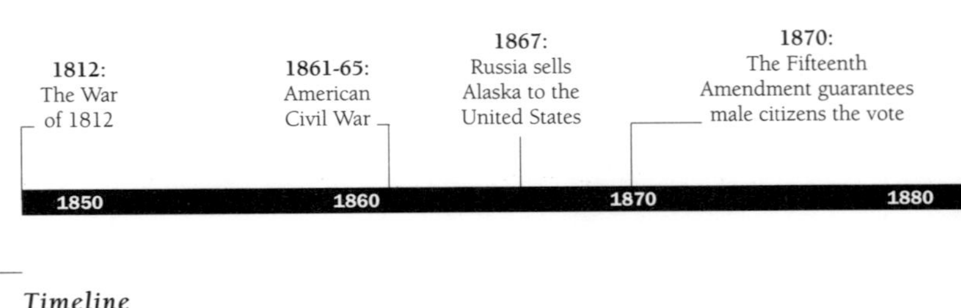

individuals. The head of a family receives 160 acres, and other family members get smaller pieces of land. Many Native Americans, unable to make a living from their land, end up having to sell their parcels. All Indian lands that are not allotted are sold to settlers. Millions of acres of Indian lands are lost.

1889 The Oklahoma Land Runs open Indian Territory to non-Natives. (Indian Territory had been set aside solely for Indian use.) At noon on April 22, an estimated 50,000 people line up at the boundaries of Indian Territory. They claim two million acres of land. By nightfall, tent cities, banks, and stores are doing business there.

The day school at the Sac and Fox Agency in Indian Territory, between 1876 and 1896.

1890 The second Ghost Dance movement is initiated by Wovoka, a Paiute. It includes many Paiute traditions. In some versions, the dance is performed in order to help bring back to Earth many dead ancestors and exterminated game. Ghost Dance practitioners hope the rituals in the movement will restore Indians to their former state, before the arrival of the non-Native settlers.

1912 The Alaska Native Brotherhood is formed to promote civil rights issues, such as the right to vote, access to public education, and civil rights in public places. The organization also fights court battles to win land rights.

1920 The Canadian government amends the Indian Act to allow for compulsory, or forced, enfranchisement, the process by which Indians have to give up their tribal loyalties to become Canadian citizens. Only 250 Indians had voluntarily become enfranchised between 1857 and 1920.

1924 All Indians are granted U.S. citizenship. This act does not take away rights that Native Americans had by treaty or the Constitution.

1928 Lewis Meriam is hired to investigate the status of Indian economies, health, and education, and the federal adminis-

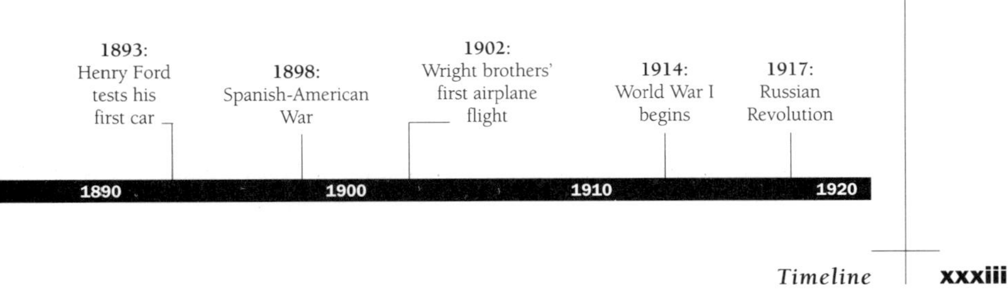

tration of Indian affairs. His report describes the terrible conditions under which Indians are forced to live, listing problems with health care, education, poverty, malnutrition, and land ownership.

1934 U.S. Congress passes the Indian Reorganization Act (IRA), which ends allotment policies and restores some land to Native Americans. The IRA encourages tribes to govern themselves and set up tribal economic corporations, but with the government overseeing their decisions. The IRA also provides more funding to the reservations.

1946 The Indian Lands Commission (ICC) is created to decide land claims filed by Indian nations. Many tribes expect the ICC to return lost lands, but the ICC chooses to award money instead, and at the value of the land at the time it was lost.

1951 A new Indian Act in Canada reduces the power of the Indian Affairs Office, makes it easier for Indians to gain the right to vote, and helps Indian children enter public schools. It also removes the ban on potlatch and Sun Dance ceremonies.

1952 In an all out effort to make Native Americans "blend in" or assimilate with the rest of society, the U.S. government begins a policy of moving Indians from reservations to cities. The government hopes that Native Americans will find jobs in the city and adopt an "American" lifestyle. Then the government will be able to "terminate" the tribes and eliminate the reservations.

1954–62 The U.S. Congress carries out its policy of "termination." At the same time laws are passed giving states and local governments control over tribal members, taking away the tribes' authority to govern themselves. Under the policy of termination, Indians lose their special privileges and are treated as any other U.S. citizens. The tribes that are terminated face extreme poverty and the threat of loss of their

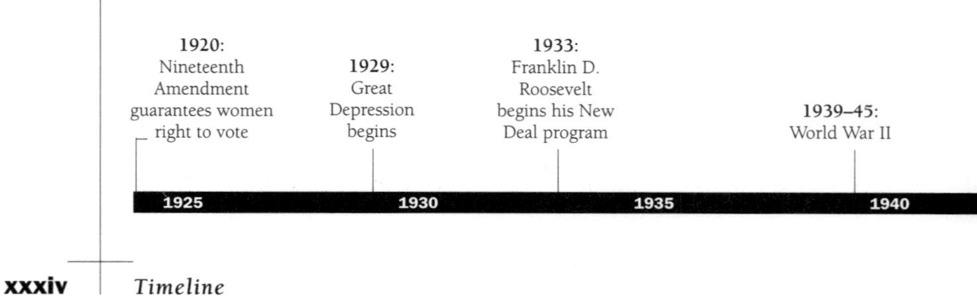

community and traditions. By 1961 the government begins rethinking this policy because of the damage it is causing.

The Menominee tribe was terminated by the U.S. government but after much protest, won back federal recognition.

1955 The Indian Health Service (IHS) assumes responsibility for Native American health care. The IHS operates hospitals, health centers, health stations, clinics, and community service centers.

1960 The queen of England approves a law giving status Indians the right to vote in Canada.

1965 Under the new U. S. government policy, the Self-Determination policy, federal aid to reservations is given directly to Indian tribes and not funneled through the Bureau of Indian Affairs.

1968 The American Indian Movement (AIM) is founded in Minneapolis, Minnesota, by Dennis Banks (Ojibway) and Russell Means (Lakota). AIM is formed to improve federal, state, and local social services to urban neighborhoods and to prevent harassment of Indians by the local police.

1969 Eighty-nine Native Americans land on Alcatraz Island, a former penitentiary in San Francisco Bay in California. The group, calling itself "Indians of All Tribes," claims possession of the island under an 1868 treaty that gave Indians the right to unused federal property on Indian land. Indians of All Tribes occupies the island for 19 months while negotiating with federal officials. They do not win their claim to the island but draw public attention to their cause.

1971 The Alaska Native Claims Settlement Act (ANCSA) is signed into law. With the act, Alaska Natives give up any claim to nine-tenths of Alaska. In return, they are given $962 million and clear title to 44 million acres of land.

1972 Five hundred Indians arrive in Washington, D.C., on a march called the Trail of Broken Treaties to protest the government's policies toward Native Americans. The protestors occupy the Bureau of Indian Affairs building for a week,

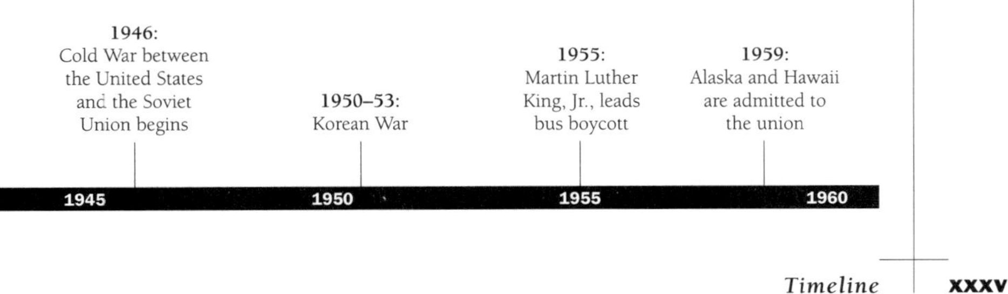

causing considerable damage. They present the government with a list of reforms, but the administration rejects their demands.

The armed takeover of Wounded Knee in 1973.

1973 After a dispute over Oglala Sioux (Lakota) tribal chair Robert Wilson and his strong-arm tactics at Pine Ridge Reservation, AIM leaders are called in. Wilson's supporters and local authorities arm themselves against protestors, who are also armed, and a ten-week siege begins in which hundreds of federal marshals and Federal Bureau of Investigation (FBI) agents surround the Indian protestors. Two Native American men are shot and killed.

1974 After strong protests and "fish-ins" bring attention to the restrictions on Native American fishing rights in the Pacific Northwest, the U.S. Supreme Court restores Native fishing rights in the case *Department of Game of Washington v. Puyallup Tribe et al.*

1978 U.S. Congress passes legislation providing support for additional tribal colleges, schools of higher education designed to help Native American students achieve academic success and eventually transfer to four-year colleges and universities. Tribal colleges also work with tribal elders and cultural leaders to record languages, oral traditions, and arts in an effort to preserve cultural traditions.

1978 The American Religious Freedom Act is signed. Its stated purpose is to "protect and preserve for American Indians their inherent right of freedom to believe, express, and exercise their traditional religions."

1978 The Bureau of Indian Affairs publishes regulations for the new Federal Acknowledgment Program. This program is responsible for producing a set of "procedures for establishing that an American Indian group exists as an Indian tribe." Many tribes will later discover that these requirements are complicated and difficult to establish.

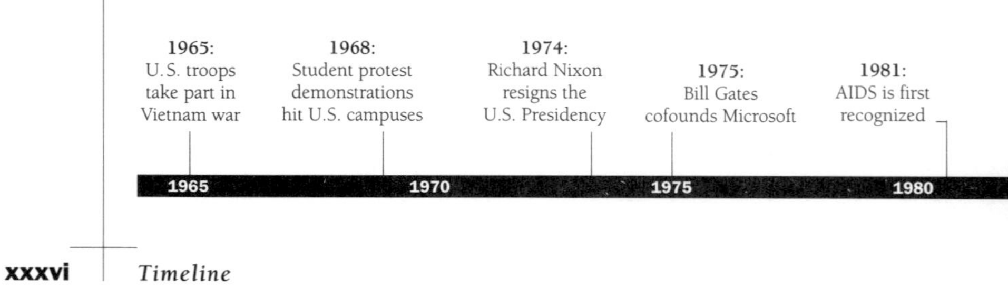

1982 Canada constitutionally recognizes aboriginal peoples in its new Constitution and Charter of Rights and Freedoms. The Constitution officially divides Canada's aboriginal nations into three designations: the Indian, the Inuit, and the Métis peoples. Native groups feel that the new Constitution does not adequately protect their rights, nor does it give them the right to govern themselves.

Chinook Winds Casino, Oregon, 1997.

1988 The Federal Indian Gambling Regulatory Act of 1988 allows any tribe recognized by the U.S. government to engage in gambling activities. With proceeds from gaming casinos, some tribes pay for health care, support of the elderly and sick, housing, and other improvements, while other tribes buy back homelands, establish scholarship funds, and create new jobs.

1989 U.S. Congress approves a bill to establish a National Museum of the American Indian under the administration of the Smithsonian Institution in Washington, D.C. (As of 1999, the Museum has not been built.)

1990 Two important acts are passed by U.S. Congress. The Native American Languages Act is designed to preserve, protect, and promote the practice and development of Indian languages. The Graves Protection and Repatriation Act provides for the protection of American Indian grave sites and the repatriation (return) of Indian remains and cultural artifacts to tribes.

1992 Canadians vote against a new Constitution (the Charlottetown Accord) that contains provisions for aboriginal self-government.

1999 A new territory called Nunavut enters the federation of Canada. Nunavut is comprised of vast areas taken from the Northwest Territories and is populated by an Inuit majority. The largest Native land claim in Canadian history, Nunavut is one-fifth of the landmass of Canada, or the size of the combined states of Alaska and Texas. Meaning "Our Land" in the Inukitut (Inuit) language, Nunavut will be primarily governed by the Inuit.

After many years of struggle, the Inuit celebrate the establishment of a new Canadian territory, Nunavut, or "Our Land," in 1999.

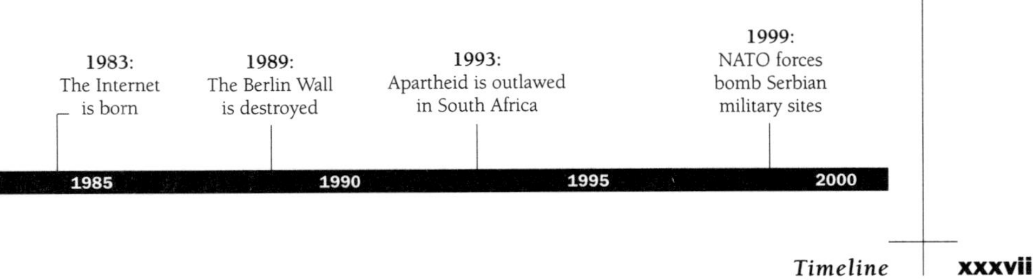

Historic Locations of U.S. Native Groups

Menominee
Sauk
Fox
Dakota
Kickapoo
Winnebago
Potawatomi
Omaha
Peoria
Iowa
Illinois
Oto
Cahokia
Kaskaskia
Kaw (Kansa)
Miami
Erie
Adena
Hopewell
Missouri
Mississippian
Shawnee
Osage
Tonkawa
Waco
Tawakoni
Wichita
Quapaw
Caddo
Hasinai
Kichai
Tunica
Natchez
Houma
Biloxi
Chitimacha
Chickasaw
Choctaw
Alabama
Mobile
Coushatta
Creek
Hitchiti
Yuchi
Etowah
Cherokee
Koasati
Tutelo
Saponi
Lumbee
Catawba
Cheraw
Pedee
Santee
Edisto
Cusabo
Guale
Yamasee
Yazoo
Apalachicola
Apalachee
Seminole
Timucua
Miccosukee
Calusa
Gulf of Mexico
Abenaki
Penobscot
Pennacook
Mohawk
Onondaga
Manhattan
Iroquois
Tuscarora
Oneida
Cayuga
Seneca
Unami
Munsee
Mahican
Wappinger
Mohegan
Nipmuk
Massachuset
Stockbridge
Narraganset
Delaware
Nanticoke
Pequot
Podunk
Wampanoag
Montauk
Shinnecock
Schaghticoke
Susquehanna
Brothertown
Paugussett
Piscataway
Mattaponi
Pamunkey
Monacan
Powhatan
Chickahominy
Rappahannock
Nansemond
Meherrin
Pamlico
Waccamaw
Coharie
Atlantic Ocean

Historic Locations of Canadian Native Groups

Inuit
Inuit
Inuit
Inuit
Inuit
Inuit
Inuit
Inuit
Inuit
Inuit
Inuit
Inuit
Inuit
Inuit
Intuit
Inuit
Beothuk
Inuit
Naskapi
Innu
Cree
Montagnais
Maliseet
Micmac
Passamaquoddy
Ojibwa
Algonkin
Nippissing
Ottawa
Huron
Tobacco
Wenrohronon
Nuetral
Wyandotte

California

California

There are many different California Indian cultures, but among tribes inhabiting specific territories of California—the northwest, the northeast, central California, and southern California—there are some remarkable similarities between groups. The chart on page 973 shows some of the shared features among tribes in different regions. In particular, methods of home construction, tool design, and the technologies used in hunting, trapping, and fishing are shared across tribal lines within territories.

Life in California before Europeans arrived

Over the centuries, the density of Indian populations and the patterns of Indian settlement have been affected by the physical features of the land surrounding them and the availability of water, plants, and animals. Before Europeans arrived, the abundant food supply throughout California allowed Indians to establish villages of up to 1,000 individuals, including craft specialists who produced specific goods for a living. In smaller communities, each family produced all that was necessary for survival.

History of the mission system

California lies on the West Coast of the United States and is bounded on its 700-mile-long western side by the Pacific Ocean. American Indians, the original inhabitants of the area, remained free from European influence until the mid-1500s, when Spanish explorers first laid claim to the region. Spain already had a huge colonial empire in North America, meaning it had established its own governments and settled Spanish people there, before it entered California. Because there had been revolts against the Spanish by the Pueblo Indians in what is now New Mexico in the seventeeth century, the Spanish decided to set up their missions in Alta California (or "Upper" California; the name given to Spanish possessions in what is now the state of California) without immediately sending colonial settlers into the region. Instead of settlers, the missionaries were accompanied by military authorities.

In 1769 the first of 21 coastal missions was organized in San Diego by Franciscan administrator Junípero Serra and military authorities

	NORTHWEST	NORTHEAST	CENTRAL	SOUTHERN
CALIFORNIA TRIBES INCLUDED	Tolowa, Shasta, Karok, Yurok, Hupa, Whilkut, Chilula, Chimariko, and Wiyot.	Modoc, Achumawi, and Atsugewi (Pit River Indians).	Bear River Indians, Mattole, Lassik, Nongatl, Wintun, Yana, Yahi, Maidu, Sinkyone, Wailaki, Cahto, Yuki, Pomo, Lake Miwok, Wappo, Coast Miwok, Interior Miwok, Monache, Yokuts, Costanoan, Esselen, Salinan, and Tubatulabal.	In the North: Chumash, Alliklik, Kitanemuk, Serrano, Luiseño, Gabrieliño, Cahuilla, and Kumeyaay. In the Interior: Serrano, Luiseño, Cahuilla, and Kumeyaay.
ENVIRONMENT	Rain forest environment with villages along rivers, lagoons, bays; dugout canoe main form of transport.	High desert terrain; plateaus.	Vast central valleys and slopes of the Sierra Nevada mountain range.	Terrain and climate varied considerably; included offshore islands, shoreline communities, and drier interior settlements.
RESOURCES AND CRAFTS	Dried ocean food resources, like salmon, shellfish, and abalone. Boats and houses made from great coast Redwoods; basketry popular.	Acorn and salmon in the west; grass seeds, tubers, berries, rabbit, and deer farther east. Tule used for food and weaving. Obsidian, a natural glass, was valued in trade.	Acorn and salmon from the north; also deer, elk, antelope, and rabbit. Basketry was a defining element for Indians in this region.	Shoreline rich in animal/marine resources. Rabbit, deer, acorn, seeds, native grasses in interior; Desert Bighorn at higher elevations. Conical homes made of arrowweed, tule, and croton (a shrub). Basketry; clay storage vessels; carved soapstone; whale bone houses.
TRADITIONS AND POWER STRUCTURE	Elaborate ritual life featuring World Renewal Ceremony to prevent natural catastrophes. Governed by the most wealthy and powerful families; private ownership of food resources.	Independent social/political organization with connections to neighbors by marriage.	Strong adherence to ritual. Semi-underground roundhouses built for elaborate Kuksu Cult dances, held to assure the renewal of the world's plants and animals.	Upper, middle, and lower class within tribe. Led by chieftain and assistant. Great reliance on *shamans*. Ritual use of hallucinogen Jimsonweed primarily in male puberty rituals.

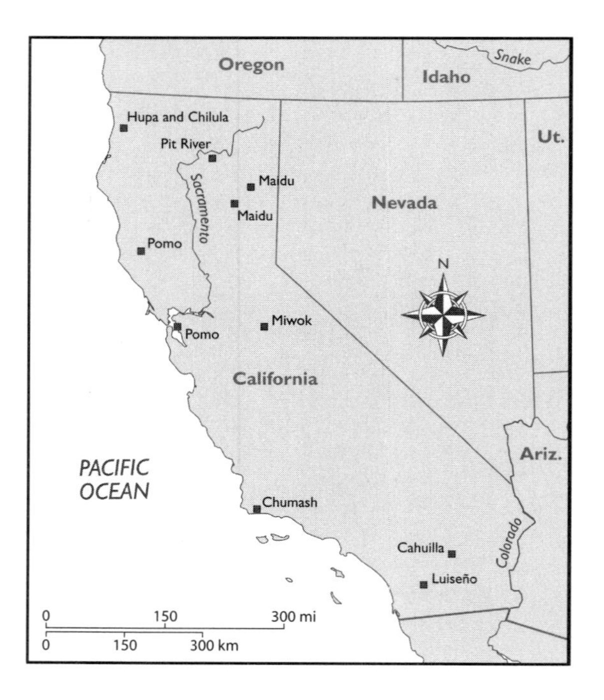

A map showing some contemporary Native American communities in California.

under Gaspar de Portolá. (The Franciscans were a religious order of the Roman Catholic church.)

California missions were essentially labor camps that benefited the Spanish colonizers and proved devastating to the Indians. For the most part, missionaries showed a blatant disregard for Indian tradition, customs, and ritual. Armed Spanish soldiers always accompanied the Franciscans in their missionary efforts, making the presence of Spanish authority quite clear to the local Indians. At the same time, the newcomers introduced domestic stock animals that gobbled up native foods and undermined the tribes' efforts to remain economically independent.

The missions were authorized by the Spanish crown to "convert" the Indians to Christianity in a ten-year period. At that point, control over the missions' livestock, fields, orchards, and buildings was supposed to be surrendered to the Indians. The padres never achieved this goal, though: the lands and wealth of the California Indians ended up in European hands.

Disease and death among California's Indians

Soon after the arrival of Spanish colonists, new diseases appeared among the tribes located near the Spanish missions. The Indians of the Americas did not possess any natural immunities to introduced European diseases. Smallpox, syphilis, diphtheria, chickenpox, and measles caused untold suffering and death among Indians near the Spanish centers of population. Excessive manual labor demands made by the missionaries and poor nutrition probably contributed to the Indians' inability to survive such infections.

Even before the outbreak of these epidemics, though, a general decline in the Mission Indian population was attributed to the unhygienic environment of the neighboring Europeans. The toll was especially high for children. Sadly, the missionary practice of forcibly separating Indian children from their parents and confining children from the age of six in filthy and disease-ridden quarters probably increased the suffering and death from disease. Similarly, all unmarried females from the age of six to the elderly were locked up. For many Indians, faith in their shamans (healers or medicine men) suffered when traditional efforts proved ineffective in stemming the tide

Mission Indians in southern California making baskets and hair ropes.

of misery, suffering, and death that life in the missions caused. Frightened Indian families eventually sought assistance from the European newcomers, who seemed to be immune to the horrible diseases that overwhelmed the Native populations.

The short life expectancy of Mission Indians led missionaries to seek out healthy laborers from interior tribes (those living farther inland from the Pacific Coast).

Native resistance

Clearly, the impact of the mission system on coastal tribal life was devastating. About 100,000—or nearly one-third of the aboriginal population of California—died as a direct consequence of the establishment of missions in California. Missionaries destroyed the traditions of the California Indians, tore their families apart, forced them to abandon their aboriginal (native) territories and live in filthy, disease-ridden work camps, making them perform backbreaking labor.

This harsh treatment sparked several well-documented forms of Indian resistance. More than one out of every 24 Indians successfully escaped the plantation-like mission labor camps. Many Mission Indians viewed the padres (priests) as powerful witches who had to be destroyed. Consequently, several Franciscans were killed in the early 1800s. Widespread armed revolts were organized by Mission Indians against colonial authorities. After 1810, a growing number of guerrilla bands (independent fighting units) evolved in the interior. Mounted on horses and using modern weapons, the Mission Indians began raiding mission livestock and fighting colonial military forces.

Mexican takeover and the collapse of the mission system

In 1823 Mexico gained control of the area that is now the state of California. Little immediate change in Indian policy accompanied the end of Spanish colonial rule. The vast Franciscan mission lands took up about one-sixth of the present territory of the state. Even though Mexico's 1824 Constitution declared Indians to be citizens of Mexico with rights to vote and hold public office, Indians throughout the republic continued to be treated as slaves.

In the mid-1830s the Mexican government finally stripped the Franciscan padres of the power to force the Indians into labor. But Mexico's plans to redistribute mission lands proved worthless to the Mission Indians: the policy was so restrictive that few ex-Mission Indians were eligible for the lands.

After the missions

Once freed from the missions to return to their tribal domains, the liberated Indians of California were faced with the staggering task of reconstructing their devastated communities. Their population had suffered tremendous declines; their tribal lands had become transformed by the introduction of vast herds of horses, cattle, sheep, goats, and hogs; the wild game animals they had previously hunted had been driven off the land.

Outraged Indians banded together and eventually a significant number of these groups formed innovative new conglomerate tribes (bands formed of groups from several different tribes). The new groups began to make systematic efforts to reassert Indian sovereignty (self-government) in the region. The Indians carried out widespread, highly organized campaigns against Mexican ranchers. As resistance to the Mexican government reached its height, interior Mexican ranches were increasingly abandoned because Native stock-raiding activities had caused economic ruin.

Despite these successes in the Indian crusade against non-Native authority, outbreaks of malaria and smallpox severely reduced the Indian population of Mexican California in the 1830s. All tolled, the aboriginal population of approximately 310,000 had been reduced to about 150,000 since the establishment of the first Franciscan mission in San Diego back in 1769.

War and gold: the 1840s and 1850s

The poorly managed Alta California was rapidly overwhelmed by a combination of aggressive Indian raids and the arrival of U.S. military forces in the summer of 1846. For two years Mexico and the United States fought the Mexican-American War (1846–48) over territory that is now part of the southwestern United States. During this struggle, the majority of California Indians sided with the Americans. After the victory of the American forces, however, conditions for Native peoples in the area grew even worse.

With the discovery of gold in the foothills of the Sierra Nevada in the late 1840s, a hoard of 100,000 adventurers from all over the world descended upon the Native peoples of the area with disastrous results. A deadly pattern of violence and murder developed. Groups formed whose principal occupation seems to have been to kill Indians and kidnap their children. There was also widespread random killing of Indians by individual miners. As many as 100,000 Indians were believed to have been murdered in the first two years of the gold rush. The survivors—by this time numbering fewer than 70,000—teetered near the brink of total annihilation.

Treaties made, treaties rejected

In January 1851 three federal officials were sent to San Francisco to iron out the region's land title issues. Over the next year, 18 treaties were negotiated. According to the terms of these treaties, the federal government promised to reserve nearly 7.5 million acres of land for the California Indians. The land would be partitioned into defined areas called tracts; these tracts of land would then be divided among the signatory tribes (tribes that signed the treaties). In addition, the treaties assured the Indians that they would receive cloth, stock animals, seeds, agricultural equipment, and assistance from American farmers, schoolteachers, and blacksmiths. In return, the signatory tribes would surrender their lands to the United States. But there were problems in the way these treaties were created. Many California Indian tribes had not been consulted in the formation of this policy, but they too would be bound by the terms of the treaties. During negotiations prior to making the treaties, most California Indians who attended meetings did not understand the English language spoken at them. Worse still, many important tribes were not contacted at all.

Upon hearing that Indians were to receive millions of acres, most white Americans in California decided they wanted the Indians removed to some other territory or state. On July 8, 1852, the United

States Senate refused to ratify, or validate, the 18 treaties. Around the same time, a congressional commission was established to validate land titles in California. The commission was required by law to inform the Indians that they needed to file claims for their lands and to report upon the nature of these claims. Because no one bothered to inform the Indians of these requirements, no claims were submitted. Through this "error," the complete dispossession of the Indians occured in the eyes of the American government—in other words, in the eyes of the U.S. government, they had no lands.

A harsh state government

Despite entering the union as a free state in 1850, the California legislature rapidly enacted a series of laws legalizing Indian slavery. In the new governor's first address to the legislature, he promised: "A war of extermination will continue to be waged between the races until the Indian race becomes extinct." Despite guarantees in the Treaty of Guadalupe Hidalgo, the 1848 agreement that settled the Mexican War, Indians were denied state citizenship, voting rights, and the right to testify in court. California's Native peoples were left with no legal protection.

The U.S. government decided to establish an Indian policy in California in 1854, but efforts to establish Indian "reserves" and "farms" were largely marred by the corruption and incompetence of the federal government's Indian Affairs workers. The reservations and farms that were formed provided little in the way of support or even minimal refuge for the Native peoples who moved there. They lacked game, suitable agricultural lands, and sufficient water supplies. In time, they were overrun by white squatters, who compounded the Indians' problems by introducing an epidemic of sexually transmitted diseases to the Native population. Most of the early reserves and Indian farms were abandoned in the 1860s due to the state's Indian slavery codes that allowed all able-bodied males, females, and even children to be indentured (bound to work for someone else for a given period of time) to white Americans. A great many reservation residents could not participate in the agricultural and ranching programs because their labor "belonged" to private state citizens.

Adaptation and resistance in the late 1800s

The vast majority of California Indians struggled to survive without government aid or recognition. Many on the verge of actual starvation scattered throughout their old territories and tried to sup-

A Gabrieliño woman photographed c. 1900.

port themselves as farm and ranch hands on the lands now claimed by whites.

Organized Indian resistance was reignited between 1858 and 1872. A series of Indian wars in northwestern California pitted the Yurok, Karok, Hupa, and other tribes against increasingly aggressive Americans who routinely murdered them, stole their children, and burned their villages. This burgeoning racial hatred led white militia groups (small groups of armed forces) to lash out even at nonhostile Indians.

The Indian peoples of California were able to cope with these great hardships because of their deeply held spiritual beliefs. A religious movement called the Ghost Dance religion sprang up in the region around 1870, strengthening Native ties to the spirit world. The movement was triggered in part by a new introduction of Christian missionaries and by the massive decline in California Indian populations. Promising the return of dead relatives and the disappearance of their oppressors, the Ghost Dance religion crossed tribal lines and revitalized intra-tribal religious unity.

Because both state and federal authorities seriously underestimated the number of surviving California Indians, plans to remove all Indians to a handful of reservations proved impractical. Several attempts to place multiple tribes on single reservations resulted in violence, mass murder, and war. None of the California tribes wanted to be relocated outside of its aboriginal territory. Non-Indians could not begin to understand the intensity and depth of the Indians' spiritual attachment to their lands. Not surprisingly, the Bureau of Indian Affairs showed little interest in assisting tribes affected by relocation policies.

Special reports conducted in 1858, 1867, and 1883 clearly document the thorough corruption and inefficiency plaguing government programs for Indians in California. Reservation agents insisted their residents join Christian churches and give up their traditional Native ways. The Dawes Act (1887; also called the General Allotment Act) forcibly divided reservation tribal lands, doling out (or "allotting") small parcels to individual Indians and their families. If the allottees built a house, engaged in farming or ranching, sent their children to government Indian schools, and renounced their tribal allegiance, they would—after 25 years—receive title to their land and U.S. citizenship. Between 1893 and 1930, approximately 2,300 allotments had been carved out of the tiny communal tribal reservation lands of California. The allotment system undermined the Native tribal system, divided populations, and rendered the Indians politically powerless. Widespread opposition to allotment led to the repeal of the law in 1934.

The fight for compensation

Around the turn of the century only 6,536 Indians were "recognized" and living on reservations. Every Indian who survived to see the dawn of the twentieth century had witnessed great suffering and irreplaceable family loss. Some lineages disappeared altogether. According to demographer S. F. Cook, the California Indian population declined to fewer than 16,000 individuals in 1900—an unbelievable descent from over 300,000 in just 131 years of colonization.

The plight of the California Indians following colonization was terrible, but the survivors did not give up the struggle. Several Indian reform groups blossomed before and after the turn of the twentieth century. The efforts of the Northern California Indian Association led to the creation of 36 new reservations and rancherias (pronounced *ranch-uh-REE-uhs*) in 16 Northern California counties. (Rancherias were very tiny parcels of land set aside as homesites for small bands of landless Indians.) However, no rancherias or homesites were made available for landless Southern California Indians.

The impact of politically active tribes and pan-Indian organizations (organizations that advocate reform for all Indian groups) was first felt in the early 1920s. Beginning with the early efforts of the Indian Board of Cooperation, several Indian self-help groups began organizing legal action against the United States. The groups claimed that the U.S. government had failed to compensate California's Indians for the loss of their ancestral lands. In response, Congress passed the Jurisdictional Act of 1928, allowing the region's Indians to sue the federal government and use the state Attorney General's office to represent them. A controversial settlement was eventually reached in 1944. More than $17 million was offered for the failure of the government to deliver the 18 reservations promised to California Indians in treaty negotiations of 1851 and 1852. Less than a third of the money was actually distributed among 36,095 California Indians—that's only about $150 for each surviving Indian. This unfair settlement prompted California Indians to seek further legal compensation and led to the creation of the Federal Indian Claims Commission in 1946. This federal body allowed Indian groups to press for compensation to tribes over the theft of their lands in the nineteenth century. Again, the results were meager. The major problem with the process was that it was *not* a court proceeding and therefore not subject to constitutional protection. The Indians were left with little hope that they would ever have enough money to spark desperately needed economic development in their communities.

Termination

By the 1950s the Bureau of Indian Affairs began plans to end all federal services to California Indians and to transfer all authority over federal Indian reservations to the state. This new policy, called Termination, became law in California under authority of the 1958 Rancheria Act, which allowed tribes to divide communal tribal property into parcels to be distributed to its members. Distributees would receive title to their lands, be free to sell it, and be obliged to pay property tax from that time forward.

The tribes were led to believe that acceptance of Termination would increase their freedom and economic independence. The U.S. government promised to upgrade squalid housing, pave roads, build bridges, improve water supplies, and even provide college scholarships in return for a vote to terminate. Between 1958 and 1970, 23 rancherias and reservations were terminated. Many Bureau of Indian Affairs services like health and education were abruptly ended for all Indians in the state. Chronically high unemployment rates, low educational achievement, and huge medical bills soon forced many Indians to make loans on or sell their lands. The Termination Policy failed miserably to improve the economic and political power of the California Indians. Instead, it stripped small tribes of their ownership of 10,037 acres of land, disrupted tribal institutions and traditions, and left the Indians in the region more desperate and impoverished than ever.

Hope for the future

A new Civil Rights era generation of young, energetic, and highly educated California Indians emerged in the late 1960s. Understandably skeptical of the government, these new leaders were committed to protecting tribal autonomy (freedom from external control). More important, they found great value in tribal traditions and encouraged tribal religious practices, traditional ceremonies, and language retention among California's Native peoples. In recognition of the growing sophistication of California Indians, the state legislature created the Native American Heritage Commission in 1978. This all-Indian commission works as a mediator between state, federal, and tribal governments. To date 17 rancherias and reservations have reversed the disastrous Termination process. Unrecognized tribes—especially the Acagchemem of San Juan Capistrano, the Muwekma of the San Francisco Bay area, and the Coast Miwok (pronounced *MEE-wok*) of Marin County—are vigorously pursuing federal recognition. (Federal recognition of tribes allows the tribes to negotiate as self-governing units and brings much-needed government aid to Native communities.)

By the late 1990s more than 41 reservations and rancherias had established gaming businesses (gambling casinos) on their lands. Some were highly successful; others less so. Few private investors have come forward to work with Indian tribes outside of the gaming industry. Without other options, reservation leaders view gaming as an important step toward greater economic independence and diversification.

The amazing adaptive capabilities of California Indians have demonstrated the resiliency and genius that these misunderstood and hard working tribes can achieve under the most unfavorable of circumstances. We enter the twenty-first century filled with optimism.

FURTHER READING

Heizer, R. F., ed. *Handbook of North American Indians.* Vol. 8: *California.* Washington, DC: Smithsonian Institution, 1978.

Holliday, J. S. *The World Rushed In: California Gold Rush Experience.* New York: Simon & Schuster, 1981.

Kelsey, Harry. "The California Indian Treaty Myth." In *Southern California Quarterly,* 55:3, 1973: 225-38.

Edward D. Castillo
(Cahuilla-Luiseño)
Native American Studies Program
Sonoma State University
Rohnert Park, California

Cahuilla

Name

The name Cahuilla (pronounced *ka-WEE-ya*) is from the word *kawiya,* meaning "powerful ones."

Location

Members of seven bands (groups) of Cahuilla live on or near ten small reservations in inland southern California. They are located in mostly rural areas, although part of the Agua Caliente reservation is located within the limits of the city of Palm Springs. The reservations are located in the area of the tribe's traditional lands, bounded on the north by the San Bernardino Mountains, on the east by the Colorado desert, and on the west by Riverside County and the Palomar Mountains. Nearly two-thirds of traditional Cahuilla territory was desert.

Population

There were about 6,000 Cahuilla at the time of contact with the Spanish. By the 1850s, there were 2,500 to 3,000. In the 1970s, there were about 900. In a census (count of the population) done in 1990 by the U.S. Bureau of the Census, people who said they were Cahuilla identified themselves this way:

Agua Caliente Cahuilla	50
Cahuilla	888
Soboba	201
Torres-Martinez	129
Other Cahuilla	26

Language family

Uto-Aztecan.

Origins and group affiliations

Centuries ago, three groups of Cahuilla occupied different regions: the Palm Springs, Pass, and Desert Cahuilla. Today the three groups are intermingled on the different reservations. The Cahuilla have a long history of cultural contact, trade, and intermarriage with their neighbors, the Serrano, the Gabrieliño, and the Luiseño (see entry). The Cahuilla are sometimes called Mission Indians, along with several tribes that lived near San Diego when the Spanish began building Catholic missions there in the eighteenth century (see the Luiseño entry). Although the Cahuilla shared many customs with the Mission Indians, they had less contact with the missions than the other tribes did.

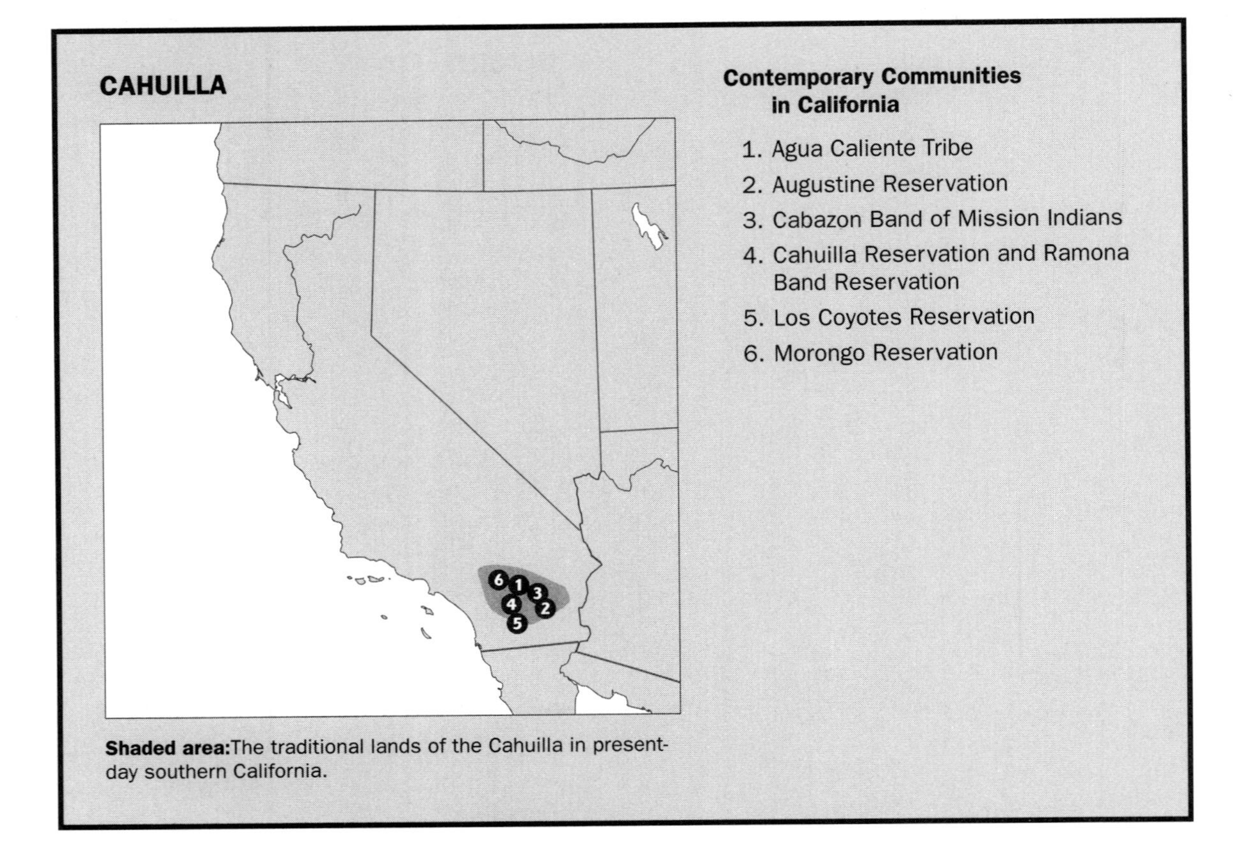

Shaded area: The traditional lands of the Cahuilla in present-day southern California.

The Cahuilla lived in a region of unpredictable weather extremes, where heavy rains one year could be replaced by drought the next, and earthquakes and fires could suddenly strike. They learned to adapt and take advantage of their environment in all its moods. They were a friendly and generous people, who would happily give away excess possessions, certain that if they were ever in need, their generosity would be repaid. Today they live in reservations near their traditional homeland. As always, they have adapted to their new circumstances but still continue to hold on to traditional customs.

HISTORY

Move to the desert

Archaeologists (they study the remains of ancient civilizations) say the Cahuilla originated in the parts of present-day Nevada and Colorado called the Great Basin. The Cahuilla still sing what they call "bird songs" that tell of their creation and their move to southern

California some 2,000 to 3,000 years ago. They settled near Lake Cahuilla, which dried up hundreds of years ago and was replaced by the Salton Sea. The Cahuilla adapted to the area and found beauty in a land that many would consider harsh and barren.

IMPORTANT DATES

1774: The Cahuilla first meet Spanish explorers.

1863: Smallpox epidemic strikes the Cahuilla.

1891: The Act for the Relief of Mission Indians establishes reservations for the Cahuilla.

Because they lived inland, the Cahuilla initially had little contact with the Spanish who were taking control of California in the late eighteenth century. The Cahuilla's first direct meeting with Europeans took place in 1774. An expedition headed by Juan Bautista de Anza passed through Cahuilla territory, looking for a land route from Mexico to the Monterey Peninsula. A Catholic mission had already been established there. The Spanish at the mission hoped Anza would find a way to bring supplies overland from Mexico rather than by the sea route, which took a long time.

Cahuilla bands guarded their territory closely, especially the vital watering holes. They objected to Spanish trespassers and fired at them with bows and arrows. Meeting similar hostility from other tribes along their land route, the Spanish gave up their search. The Cahuilla had no more contact with them for a time but heard tales about the Spanish from Indians who did have contact. They had heard stories of Spanish ill-treatment of Mission Indians, but they had also heard about Spanish goods and were very interested in them.

Contact with Spanish missions, settlers

In the early 1800s, the Cahuilla began to visit some of the Spanish missions near the coast. There they learned Spanish, adopted European clothing, and learned new technologies like ironworking. In some cases they were forced to work for the missions and were harshly treated by those in charge. Throughout the early years, however, the Cahuilla mostly managed to retain their independence while taking advantage of European goods.

In 1822 Mexico took the mission lands away from Spain in the Mexican Revolution. Again the Cahuilla managed to remain fairly independent. They took seasonal jobs as skilled laborers on cattle ranches owned by Mexicans. In 1848, however, the United States officially took control of California, and shortly after that the California Gold Rush began. These two events caused tensions between the Cahuilla and whites, as new settlers trespassed on Cahuilla land and water sources.

ROMANTIC NOVEL AROUSES INTEREST IN CALIFORNIA INDIANS

Helen Hunt Jackson (1830–1885) was a poet and writer from Massachusetts who traveled to California in 1872. While there she became interested in the condition of western Indians. In 1881 she published *A Century of Dishonor,* a non-fiction work that attacked the U.S. Indian policy and the treatment of American Indians in U.S. Society. Because of her work, the U. S. Congress formed a special commission to investigate and suggest reforms for Indian affairs.

The U.S. government then appointed Jackson to investigate and report on the conditions of Mission Indians. In 1884 she published her popular novel *Ramona,* said to be based on an actual Cahuilla woman named Ramona Lubo, whose husband had been murdered by a white settler. The novel is mainly romantic fiction, not a true account of the Indians in the area, but it did a great deal to arouse public sympathy for the Mission Indians.

Gold fever, diseases, and reservations

Miners and settlers brought new diseases; the Cahuilla had no immunity to them. In 1863 a severe smallpox epidemic reduced the Cahuilla population to about 2,500. Settlers took over their water sources, and Cahuilla crops suffered. Then the settlers began to pressure the U.S. government to set aside reservations for the Cahuilla and other California tribes. Weakened by diseases, the tribes had no choice but to submit to the reservation system. Even then, they were cheated out of their lands by the new white settlers.

In the decades that followed, the Cahuilla grew more resentful of federal government interference in their lives and the continuous chiseling away of their lands. The 1891 Act for the Relief of Mission Indians, which formalized the reservation system, took still more of the Cahuilla's land when it made the boundaries. Government schools and American missionaries tried to suppress the Cahuilla religion, language, and political systems. The 1887 Dawes General Allotment Act divided Cahuilla lands into individual parcels and made it impossible for them to do the kind of community farming they had done before.

Resist assimilation

The Cahuilla resisted interference in their affairs. In 1934 they got back some of their independence when the Indian Reorganization Act (IRA) was passed, which put an end to the allotment system and encouraged the formation of tribal governments, although the new model government was supervised by the federal government. When a federal program cut off government funding and supervision of the reservations in the 1950s, the Cahuilla became more involved in their own health, education, and welfare. In the 1960s they received funding to allow them to manage their own affairs. Their ancestors had survived and retained their independence by blending European and traditional Cahuilla ways. Today the people continue to practice elements of their traditional culture as an important part of their American way of life.

RELIGION

The unpredictable weather of their homeland provided evidence for the Cahuilla in their belief that the world is governed by an unpredictable creative force. In their traditions, that creative force made the first two human beings, Makat and Tamaioit, who were huge and powerful beings. Makat and Tamaioit then made everything else, but with the exception of shamans (pronounced *SHAY-munz*), the creatures who came after the first two did not have the same powers.

CAHUILLA WORDS

Only a small number of Cahuilla speak their traditional language anymore (about fifty in 1991). However, many still use some Cahuilla words, such as the many Cahuilla terms for relatives—for example, *qa?* for "father's father," and *qwa?* for "mother's father." Some communities offer Cahuilla language classes. Thanks to Cahuilla speakers like Katherine Siva Saubel (1920–), a respected elder and active political leader, some books of Cahuilla grammar, stories, and vocabulary have been published. In *I'isniyatam,* her Cahuilla word book, Saubel stresses the importance of naming to the Cahuilla. She offers examples like *pal* (water), *sewet* (snake), and *huyal* (arrow), with many variations. In written Cahuilla, most letters are pronounced like English letters, with a few exceptions: a *?* sounds like a gulp; and an *x* is like a scratchy *h.*

Shamans controlled rain, created food, and conducted ceremonies, where they performed amazing feats like eating hot coals. Shamans told stories of creation in songs and dances; special rattles made from gourds supplied the music. Shamans passed their knowledge and powers on to successors who were chosen because of certain special qualities they exhibited while young.

The Cahuilla believed in a life after death. They believed that the dead were reborn and lived a life much like the one they had left behind, but in the new life only good things happened.

Although their early experiences with Spanish Catholic missionaries were not pleasant, after the Cahuilla moved to reservations, missionaries renewed their efforts. In time, many Cahuilla converted to Catholicism and others to Protestantism. Today Cahuilla still maintain elements of their traditional beliefs and practices.

LANGUAGE

The Cahuilla language belongs to the Takic branch of the Uto-Aztecan stock (sometimes called Southern Californian Shoshonean) and is very close to Cupeño.

GOVERNMENT

Traditionally, the Cahuilla lived in about a dozen independent villages, each with its own name, territory, and a male ancestor common to everyone in the village. Trails connected villages with other villages and to other tribes. Each village had a headman called a *net,* who settled minor disputes, chose hunting-gathering areas, and represented the group at meetings. The position of net passed from father to son.

The net was assisted by a *paxaa?* (see box for an explanation of the use of the question mark), who made sure people behaved properly. He oversaw rituals and ceremonies, led hunting parties, and communicated to everyone the decisions made by the headman (who made them after consulting the shaman).

Traditional Cahuilla leadership was largely male-oriented, but today women are active in Cahuilla politics. Each reservation is governed by an elected five-member business committee. The committee can make decisions without a general vote of the community.

ECONOMY

The traditional Cahuilla economy was based on a complex system of hunting and gathering, which required a complete knowledge of the local plants and animals (there were hundreds of plant varieties). The people traded plants with other tribes for gourd rattles and baskets.

The Spanish introduced cattle to the region in the 1800s. The cattle ate many local plants, and this reduced food for game animals as well as people. Unable to hunt and gather as before, some Cahuilla went to work on farms and ranches owned by the Spanish and other whites.

After the move to the reservations in the late 1800s, Cahuilla women earned money by making and selling woven baskets. This art is not as widely practiced today. Some reservations now run their own money-making enterprises for the benefit of the tribe: bingo and camping facilities and a gambling casino, for instance. While many Cahuilla are very poor, they remain on the reservations because they wish to be close to their families, and they find the rural lifestyle—with its fresh air and wide-open spaces—very appealing.

DAILY LIFE

Families

Cahuilla children are born into the clan (group of related families) of their fathers: either the Wildcat or Coyote clan. According to

A Cahuilla mother and her baby.

writers Lowell Bean and Lisa Bourgeault: "[A] typical Cahuilla community consisted of elderly men who were brothers, their wives, and their sons and nephews, together with their wives and children." All of these related people worked and played together.

Education

Children began learning their adult roles while still toddlers, by observation and through play. Boys played games that taught coordination and made their muscles strong (like footraces and kickball), so they could become quick, skilled hunters. Girls developed hand-eye coordination so they could weave baskets and pick up small seeds. Children learned their history and religion from stories handed down from generation to generation. Elders were highly respected for their knowledge of tribal history; they were also called upon to tell younger people what to do during natural disasters.

Today, Cahuilla children attend public schools, colleges, and trade schools. Some reservations also sponsor classes in Native language and culture.

A Cahuilla woman, Ramona Lugu, with bowls.

Buildings

Cahuilla homes varied widely depending on location. Some families put brush shelters over the fronts of caves; some built cone-shaped homes of cedar bark. The Cahuilla used Y-shaped supports and thatched roofs and walls, sometimes plastering the walls. Many of these homes were dome-shaped, but some were rectangular. Ruby Modesto, a twentieth-century Cahuilla healer, described visits to her grandparents' *kish,* a windowless structure that had walls made from a plant called arrowwood and a slanted roof made from palm fronds; they slept inside on the earth floor and kept a fire in a circle of rocks.

At the center of the village was the largest building, the ceremonial house; the *net* lived in it or nearby. The house usually included a small area where a bundle of sacred items was kept, and a large area for religious dances. Outside was a smaller dance area, and attached to the house was a place for preparing food for ceremonies. Nearby were granaries—large nest-like baskets used for storing food—and a communal sweathouse, where men would go for social and ritual sweatbaths, and to discuss important matters.

Cahuilla families often clustered their homes together. Unlike some tribes who had winter and summer villages, the Cahuilla had permanent villages. They built near water and food sources, often in or around canyons for protection from harsh winds. They marked the boundaries of their hunting-gathering territory with designs carved into rocks. Cahuilla homes today tend to be more spread out on plots of land large enough for farming or cattle ranching.

Food

The Cahuilla diet was well-rounded and nutritious. They used a combination of hunting, harvesting, and growing. Food was gathered from four different environments: the low and high deserts, mountains, and the area in between. Tasks were divided by gender and age—the men hunted, the women harvested plants and seeds, and children and older people cooked.

The Cahuilla knew the ripening times of hundreds of plant varieties. They even pruned and watered crops they had not planted, like pine nuts, cactus, and mesquite (pronounced *meh-SKEET*) beans. Pine nuts were roasted on coals in shallow trays or baskets; cactus was boiled or eaten fresh; and mesquite beans were dried and pounded into a fine meal.

Acorns were a staple of the Cahuilla diet. They were ground into a flour and then covered with boiling water to remove the poisonous tannic acid. The Cahuilla planted corn, beans, melons, and squash.

The Cahuilla today incorporate many traditional foods into their lives. For instance, Ruby Modesto described a twentieth-century Cahuilla breakfast of coffee, eggs, refried beans, and *sawish,* a flat bread like a tortilla. The Cahuilla still enjoy acorns and cactus buds, and they continue to eat deer and quail. Mountain sheep and antelope can no longer be hunted, but once they were highly valued for their delicious meat.

Clothing and adornment

Centuries ago, the Cahuilla wore clothing made of the natural materials of their environment. They pounded mesquite bark into a soft material for women's skirts and babies' diapers. They also used mesquite bark for sandals, and made blankets out of strips of rabbit fur. Men wore deerskin and sheepskin breechcloths (garments with front and back flaps that hung from the waist). Body paint was used for ceremonies, and facial tattooing was common.

After meeting the Spanish in the late eighteenth century, many Cahuilla began combining European-style clothing—like pants, shirts, skirts, and jackets—with traditional clothing.

Healing practices

The Cahuilla believed that when the spirits were displeased, they made people sick. Shamans were then called upon. They healed by sucking directly on the affected part of the patient's body to remove the ailment, or by blowing, spitting on, stroking, or rubbing the affected area. Sometimes herbs were used, or a pit was dug, warmed with hot rocks, and the sick person would lie down in it. Those who lived near present-day Palm Springs used the hot springs there for healing. The Cahuilla have always been very concerned with cleanliness and place great importance on regular bathing and proper cleaning of cooking tools.

Shamans are men, but older women with a knowledge of herbs can help with certain conditions like childbirth or broken bones. Ruby Modesto, a twentieth-century healer or *pul,* described her life and work in her book *Not for Innocent Ears.* She noted that while many *puls* can use power in a good way, some *puls* use their power for evil deeds like poisoning people. Modesto cured people with "soul damage;" people who had seizures, for example, were thought to have soul damage.

ARTS

Once they had mastered survival in the desert, Cahuilla women had time to devote to crafts. While men made heavy baskets for practical purposes such as gathering plants and seeds, women made beautiful coiled baskets from grasses and rushes of different colors. The baskets were decorated with designs of rattlesnakes, turtles, stars, and eagles. Gift-giving was a part of every Cahuilla ceremony, and often the gifts were baskets or gift items presented in baskets.

CUSTOMS

Ceremonies and festivals

The Cahuilla placed a special emphasis on death. When a close relative died, the person's home and belongings were burned so their spirit was set free and could enjoy the belongings in the next world. The Cahuilla's most important ritual was an annual ceremony mourning the dead. The tradition continues today with a Memorial Day fiesta, celebrating Cahuilla culture and honoring Cahuilla men who died in service during World War II (1939–45).

The Cahuilla practice other rituals like the eagle ceremony. For this they form a large circle outside the ceremonial house. In the middle of the circle the dancer, wearing an eagle feather headdress and skirt, imitates the movements of an eagle while hitting two sticks together to direct the people in singing. The ceremonial house remains an important center for culture and community, even to those Cahuilla who live and work away from the reservation.

ORIGIN OF THE BIRDS

Two important figures in Cahuilla oral stories are Mukat and his brother Tamaioit, the powerful first two beings, from whom all other creatures originated. The following story, "Origin of the Birds," was told by a man named Alexandro of Morongo to anthropologist Lucile Hooper in 1918 (anthropologists study human cultures). Hooper claimed that Alexandro gave her a short version of the tale, because it would have taken "all night to name the birds."

When Mukat died, the people who were still living at the big house did not know where to go or what to do. They went east, west, north, south, above, and below. They could not decide which direction they were intended to take. They finally reached the edge of the water and here they saw Sovalivil (pelican). He told them how to find Tamaioit. When they found him, he asked why they came to him. "I am different from all of you," he said, "so I cannot help you, I fear. There is one thing I might suggest, however. I created the willow tree, which I forgot to bring with me; get the branches of that and brush yourselves with it and perhaps you will then know what to do." So they all returned and brushed themselves with the willow, then started out once more.

A few, who became tired, stopped, and turned themselves into rocks and trees. The others reached the top of Mount San Jacinto and here they slept that night. At dawn, Isel (a bird with a yellow breast that is often seen around swamps), awoke them and made them look around. A bird which is larger than a buzzard told them not to look, that there was nothing to see. Nevertheless, they all looked around and saw many beautiful green fields. They decided to go to these. On the way, one by one, they stopped. These that stopped became birds. When the others returned that way, they named the birds.

SOURCE: Lucile Hooper. "The Cahuilla Indians." *University of California Publications in Archaeology and Ethnology,* 16 (April 10, 1920).

Marriage

Knowing who their ancestors were was very important, because the Cahuilla would not marry anyone even remotely related to them. A boy's parents chose a bride from another clan, being careful to choose someone who would be an asset to their tightly-knit, hard-working community. The boy's father then offered the girl's father a gift. If he accepted the gift, his daughter simply moved into the home of the boy's family without further ceremony.

CURRENT TRIBAL ISSUES

The Cahuilla work hard to preserve their culture. A major part of this effort can be seen at the Malki Museum on the Morongo Reservation. Cahuilla scholars and storytellers have done a great deal to educate others about Cahuilla culture and history.

The Cahuilla remain active in political issues like land and water conservation. Like so many American Indian tribes, they must continually fight the reduction of their lands by outside developers, oil companies, and highway builders.

NOTABLE PEOPLE

Ruby Modesto (1913–1980) grew up speaking Cahuilla, and because she did not learn English or attend school until after she was ten, she learned a great deal about her traditional culture. Modesto became a medicine woman sometime in her forties. In her book *Not for Innocent Ears,* she described how she became responsible for healing people possessed by demons.

Cahuilla political leader Juan Antonio (born c. 1783) fought in the 1840s and 1850s to protect Cahuilla lands from Mexican and American settlers. Rupert Costo is a late-twentieth century publisher and editor who founded such magazines as *Indian Historian* and *Wassaja.*

FURTHER READING

Bean, Lowell John, and Lisa Bourgeault. *The Cahuilla.* New York: Chelsea House Publishers, 1989.

Jackson, Helen Hunt. *Ramona.* New York: Signet, 1988.

Milanovich, Richard, "Beauty in the Desert," in *All Roads Are Good: Native Voices on Life and Culture.* Washington, D.C.: Smithsonian Institution, 1994.

Modesto, Ruby. *Not for Innocent Ears: Spiritual Traditions of a Cahuilla Medicine Woman.* Cottonwood, CA: Sweetlight Books, 1989.

Saubel, Katherine. *I'isniyatami (designs): A Cahuilla Word Book.* Banning, CA: Malki Museum Press, 1977.

Chumash

Name

The name Chumash comes from the word the Chumash used to refer to the inhabitants of one of the Santa Barbara Channel Islands. The Spanish used the name "Chumash" to refer to every group of Indians living on these islands and along the southern coast of California.

Location

The Chumash used to occupy lands stretching along 200 miles of southern California coastline, plus four of the Santa Barbara Channel Islands: Anacapa, San Miguel, Santa Rosa, and Santa Cruz. Their total territory at the time of European contact comprised about 7,000 square miles, ranging from San Luis Obispo to Malibu Canyon in the Santa Monica Mountains outside Los Angeles. In the late 1990s the Chumash owned only Santa Ynez Reservation in Santa Ynez, California, located about 32 miles north of Santa Barbara and 10 miles from the Pacific Ocean. It is only about 75 acres with a small but growing population.

Population

In 1770 between 10,000 and 22,000 Chumash people were known to exist. In 1920 the number had dwindled to 74. In 1972 there were 1,925 persons of Chumash descent. In a census (count of the population) conducted in 1990 by the U.S. Bureau of the Census, 3,114 people identified themselves as Chumash, and 94 said they were Santa Ynez Chumash.

Language family

Hokan.

Origins and group affiliations

The ancestors of the Chumash people are believed by scientists to have migrated across an ancient land bridge (it no longer exists) connecting Siberia (Russia) to Alaska between 12,000 and 27,000 years ago. Chumash creation stories, however, tell of a more local origin.

There were at least six groups of Chumash; five were given the names of the Catholic missions founded in their territory beginning in the 1700s. The largest group was called the Ynezeño. Almost nothing is known about the sixth group, the Interior Chumash.

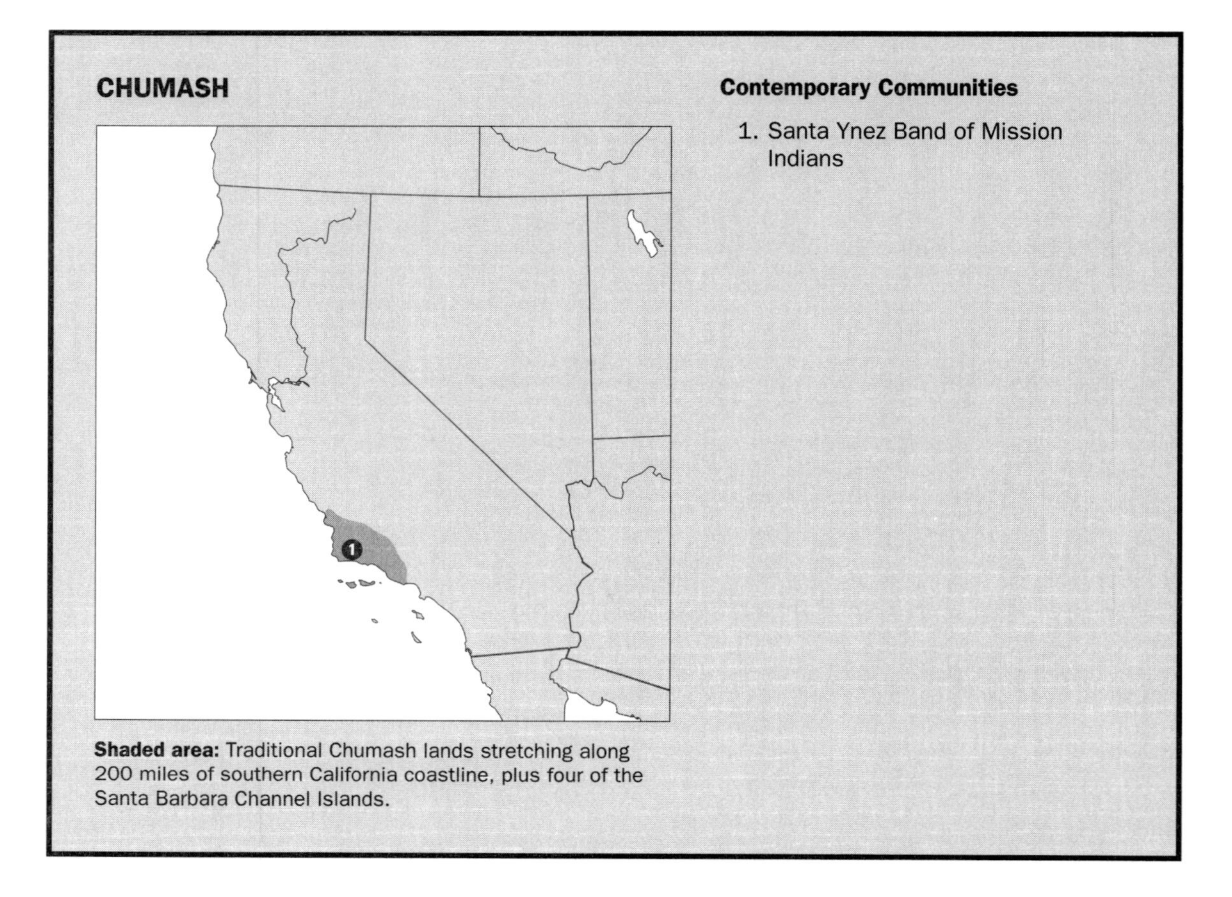

CHUMASH

Contemporary Communities

1. Santa Ynez Band of Mission Indians

Shaded area: Traditional Chumash lands stretching along 200 miles of southern California coastline, plus four of the Santa Barbara Channel Islands.

For thousands of years the Chumash sailed up and down the California coast in brightly painted cedar-plank boats that are considered marvels of engineering. They fished in the ocean and visited and traded with tribes in faraway places. After suffering at the hands of Spanish Catholic missionaries and Mexican and American settlers, the tribe was thought to have become extinct. But Chumash descendants have succeeded in keeping their culture alive. They have done so quietly, hoping to retain their privacy and protect sacred artifacts from vandals and land developers.

HISTORY

Visitors from Spain

Chumash territory has been inhabited for at least 9,000 years. Archaeologists (scientists who study the remains of ancient cultures) speculate that the Chumash had assumed control of what is now southern California by about 1000 C.E. Once one of the largest Native groups in California, the tribe carried on a lively business with its neighbors, trading soapstone (a carvable soft stone made into articles such as pipes and bowls), acorns, shells, beads, fish, and other items for animal skins, herbs, seeds, and nuts. Archaeologists have unearthed remnants of these trade objects many miles from Chumash territory, so it appears that the Chumash people engaged in trade far from their homes. There are theories that the early Chumash groups of hunter-gatherers all moved together for support during a drought. The confederacy then developed an organized and complex political and economic system. But the traditional ways of the Chumash did not interest the Spanish, Mexicans, or Americans that invaded their lands enough for anyone to record them. By the time people became interested in the group's pre-contact society, there were few Chumash left who could remember the old ways.

IMPORTANT DATES

1000–1804 C.E.: The Chumash people and other California Indians make popular the use of shell money.

1772: The first of the Spanish Catholic missions in Chumash territory is built at San Luis Obispo.

1824: In the Great Chumash Revolt led by Pacomio, 2,000 Indians rise against missionaries, holding the mission for about a month before being forced to surrender.

1978: Chumash Indians agree to end their three-day protest at the site of an ancient burial ground.

The Chumash Indians were prosperous at the time Juan Rodríguez Cabrillo, a Portuguese commander sailing for Spain, first made contact with them. He sailed along the Santa Barbara Coast in 1542, leading a small fleet of Spanish ships. Cabrillo was searching for riches and a northwest passage through North America when he happened upon the Chumash, a friendly, peaceful people said to be the first group of Native Californians ever encountered by Europeans.

The Chumash greeted Cabrillo in canoes carrying generous gifts. Cabrillo claimed the area for Spain and then left the Native people without establishing a settlement. Sixty years later, in 1602, Spanish explorer Sebastián Vizcaíno sailed through Chumash waters and named Santa Barbara Bay in honor of Saint Barbara's birthday as he explored for a port. For the next 160 years the Chumash continued to thrive without further visits by Europeans.

Spanish build missions to protect California

Spain already had a huge colonial empire in North America. By the sixteenth century Spain's colonizers had laid claim to a vast expanse of land in what is now the state of California. Over the next 200 years Russian and English adventurers arrived in the area, threatening Spain's hold on the land. In an attempt to protect their claim to the territory, the Spanish began constructing missions—sort of a combination of a fort, a plantation, and a religious center—in California in 1769. Spain expected the full cooperation of the region's Native population in this monumental task. The Spanish government embarked on a program of "Europeanization," trying to teach the Indians the Spanish language and make them into "useful" citizens. Catholic priests (*padres*) assisted in establishing the missions. The priests, who had their own goal of converting the Natives to the Catholic religion (as well as to exploit them as a free labor force), directed the construction of the missions, using unpaid and later forced Indian labor.

The first of the Spanish Catholic missions in Chumash territory was built in 1772 at San Luis Obispo. In all, twenty-one missions were constructed in California, five of them in Chumash territory. The missions became forced labor camps for the Native population. By the time the mission system came to an end more than 60 years later, the Chumash economy had been virtually destroyed and their culture critically disrupted.

Becoming "Mission Indians"

The Spanish introduced stock animals to Chumash territory. The cattle and other animals brought into the area destroyed the local plant life, greatly reducing the food supply. Game animals dependent upon the plant life became scarce. The Chumash economy was harshly disrupted, thus drawing Indians out of necessity into the colonial economy. Some Chumash sought refuge at the missions after a serious earthquake in 1812. By 1824 all of the Channel Islands Chumash who had not been killed by Russian whalers were coaxed into the mission system. Those Chumash who were not interested in joining the missions were sometimes kidnaped by Spanish soldiers and forced to join. The Chumash and other tribes who belonged to the missions are often referred to as Mission Indians.

Native Americans who had been converted to Christianity and baptized into the Catholic faith were called *neophytes* (pronounced *NEE-oh-fites*; beginners). Because Spanish law required that neophytes live near the missions, the newly baptized Indians had to leave their villages and live in camps outside the missions. At the tender age of five or six, Chumash children were taken from their families and forced to live in the filthy and disease-ridden barracks. At the mission they attended religious services, performed physical labor without pay, and were trained in carpentry, agriculture, and other occupations the Spanish considered useful.

Chumash parents were enraged by Spanish mistreatment of their children, but could do little to change things. They saw how men, women, and children were beaten, imprisoned, and sentenced to harsh physical labor for disobeying the missionaries' rules.

Mexico takes over

The mission system was still going strong 55 years after the first mission had been built. Finally, in 1824, the Chumash decided to revolt. Neophytes from several missions rose up in protest. Abandoning their own missions, they occupied La Purísima Mission for more than a month but finally surrendered after an assault by Spanish troops and artillary. Several of the Chumash who led the rebellion were executed.

In 1823 the newly independent nation of Mexico gained control of present-day California. A decade later the Mexican government took over the California missions. The neophytes were freed, and some superficial, but largely ineffective, attempts were made to help them. Mexican officials promised the Indians land—the very same land where the Chumash had hunted and built villages for thousands of years—but never delivered on the promise. Instead, Mexican settlers flooded into California, hoping to obtain some of the rich and developed former mission lands for themselves.

The people are divided

Between 1769, when the first mission was built, and 1832, just before the Mexicans took over, nearly two-thirds of the Chumash population died from disease and mission life. The survivors had few—if any—connections to their ancient villages and way of life. Some remained in positions as unpaid laborers under Mexican exploitation rather than Spanish. Others scattered to find employment in Los Angeles and other new towns that grew up along the coast. Some headed away from the coast and into the California interior to find new homes among other tribes. Many became rebels; they stole livestock from Mexican cattle ranches—or died trying.

In 1848 the United States took California from Mexico, and a year later gold was discovered in the area. Americans poured into California country, bringing terrible consequences for the Natives. The Spanish and the Mexicans had used the Indians as slaves; the Americans simply wanted them out of their way. In a matter of only a few years, American settlers killed thousands of California Natives, including many Chumash, through new disease epidemics and outright murder in terrible numbers.

A few acres are set aside for the Chumash

In 1851 the U.S. government decided to resolve California's Indian situation by setting up a reservation system. The California reservations were originally created on military reserves to protect Natives from the violence of other Californians. In reality the government reserves served fewer than 2,000 Indians at any given time. The vast majority of California Indians survived as best they could on their own.

A reservation was set aside for the Chumash in 1854, but it quickly fell apart due to the utter corruption of its administrators. The Chumash scattered. Like other California Indians, they withdrew to remote areas to stay away from settlers, but violence against them continued. Casual murder of individuals, vigilante (groups who posed as volunteer police groups, but went beyond the law) raids, and even occasional army massacres took place.

It was not until 1901 that a small group of Chumash living near the former Santa Ynez Mission was finally granted 75 acres there. The site officially became California's smallest reservation, the Santa Ynez Chumash Reservation. Seventy-five acres is not enough land to support many people. Because the reservation provides no employment, many Chumash have lived temporarily on the reservation at one time or another. They tend to come and go, living in small groups throughout their former territory.

While American settlers continued to brutalize Natives in California, the Chumash culture went underground (became secret) simply to lessen the abuse. Their withdrawal led some observers to believe that the entire tribe was extinct. Although the Chumash population was reduced to a tiny fraction of its once great size, the group and its culture managed to survive and is once again growing.

RELIGION

Traditional beliefs and practices

The Chumash believed the universe was divided into three worlds: the Sky World, the World of the People (Earth), and the Lower World (where evil beings lived). According to Chumash tradition, animals were Earth's first creatures. When death appeared on Earth, some animals rose into the sky to escape it and turned into heavenly bodies such as the Sun, Moon, Morning Star, Evening Star, Sky Coyote, and others.

The Chief of the Sky People was Eagle, who held up the sky with his wings. Eclipses were said to be a result of Eagle covering the Moon

HOW THE CHUMASH CAME TO BE

In the early 1900s an anthropologist by the name of John Peabody Harrington spent a great deal of time talking with several Chumash people and recording everything they remembered about their culture. One of these people was Maria Solares, an Ynezeño Chumash. This is her version of a Chumash creation story:

After the flood, the Coyote of the Sky, Sun, Moon, Morning Star and the Great Eagle were discussing how they were going to make man. Coyote announced that there would be people in this world and they should all be in his image since he had the finest hands. Lizard was there also, but he just listened night after night and said nothing. At last Coyote won the argument. The next day they all gathered around a beautiful table—like rock that was there in the sky, a white rock of such fine texture that whatever touched it left an exact impression. Coyote was about to stamp his hand down on the rock when Lizard, who had been standing silently just behind, quickly reached out and pressed a perfect handprint into the rock himself. Coyote was enraged and wanted to kill Lizard, but Lizard ran down into a deep crevice and so escaped. And Eagle and Sun approved of Lizard's actions, so what could Coyote do? They say that the mark is still impressed on that rock in the sky. If Lizard had not done what he did, we might have hands like a coyote today.

SOURCE: Thomas C. Blackburn. *December's Child: A Book of Chumash Oral Narratives.* Berkeley: University of California Press, 1975

with his wings. If any of the Sky People became upset, terrible storms would rain down on the World of the People. And if the two serpents who held up the World of the People became restless and moved, earthquakes and other disturbances would occur on Earth. Dead people were thought to journey through the heavenly bodies before reaching the afterworld.

A central feature of the Chumash religion was consumption of a drug called *toloache,* which is obtained from a plant called jimsonweed. The drug causes those who take it to go into a trancelike state and see visions. Chumash religious leaders were priest-astrologers, who could read meanings in the positions of the heavenly bodies. Under the influence of *toloache,* the priest-astrologers painted pictographs in sacred caves. (See "Arts.") The exact meaning of these pictographs is not known outside of the followers, but they may have been attempts to communicate with the spirit world. *Toloache* was also consumed by sons of wealthy families as part of their training for a religious society called an *antap.*

Under the mission system

Some Chumash became Catholics reluctantly and returned to their traditional religious practices when the mission system ended. Many, however, retained the Christian belief in a supreme being. Although most modern-day Chumash identify themselves as Catholic, few attend mass on a regular basis.

POVERTY: A HARSH REALITY

The Spanish came and later the Mexicans; for nearly a hundred years, the Chumash people were their slaves. Later, some Chumash worked on ranches or farms as servants or laborers. Those who fled into the interior of California faced many hardships and had to struggle just to find enough food to live. When the U.S. government finally set aside a tiny reservation for the Chumash, some families moved there, but there was never enough land to support many people.

By the 1990s the area surrounding the reservation had become a thriving tourist and farming region, but poverty remained a serious problem among the Chumash. Many families are headed by women (who tend to earn less money than men), and both women and men must look for work in nearby towns to support their families. The Chumash Tribal Business Council hopes to attract tourists to new tribal businesses such as a gaming casino and a campground.

LANGUAGE

At least six languages belonged to the Chumash language family, but the speakers of these languages were separated from each other for generations. Over time, the separated groups lost the ability to understand the other Chumash languages.

Because of the heavy Spanish influence in Chumash areas during the late eighteenth and early nineteenth centuries, most Chumash were speaking Spanish by the early 1900s. Their children, however, were taught English in public schools. The last person known to have spoken a Chumash language died in 1965.

GOVERNMENT

Under the Indian Reorganization Act (IRA) of 1934, tribes were encouraged to form tribal governments modeled after U.S. governmental systems. The Chumash decided to form a general council to govern the reservation. The council, which is composed of all members of the tribe aged 21 and over, elects five representatives to two-year terms on a special business council.

Despite the efforts of the Chumash Business Council, there are many obstacles for reservation Chumash to keep their culture alive. Because the reservation is so small, people tend not to live on the grounds for very long. Poverty necessitates looking for work away from the reservation. Off-reservation Chumash have formed groups to preserve and maintain their culture, but they have not been very successful in obtaining federal tribal recognition.

ECONOMY

Before the Spanish came, the Chumash economy revolved around gathering and trading activities. Different regions provided different resources to the Chumash groups. They processed and traded these materials with other groups. For example, the Chumash who lived on the islands collected shells, which they traded for grains and skins from the Chumash who lived on the mainland.

A two-toned Chumash basket.

Many Native American peoples worked cooperatively, with large numbers of people in a village tending fields or hunting. The Chumash people were unique in that they developed craft specialties such as fishing or basketmaking. Experts in these specialties belonged to organizations called guilds, much like the ones that operated in Europe during the Middle Ages (the period of European history before modern times, lasting roughly from about 400 to 1300 C.E.).

The guild system resulted in a surplus (too much) of certain objects, so villages began trading their excess goods. Guild members set prices for their goods and services. The most expensive items—those priced too high for most villagers—were purchased by the wealthiest families. Sometimes villages held fairs. Guild members would set up booths at a designated marketplace, and interested customers from far and wide would travel to the market to buy and trade goods.

DAILY LIFE

Families

Chumash families were large and usually consisted of a husband and wife, their married sons and their wives, their unmarried children, and other close relatives of the husband. As many as 40 to 70 people lived together in the same house.

Buildings

Most Chumash built large, dome-shaped houses—some up to 50 feet in width. These homes were situated in long neat rows separated by narrow streets. (The Chumash who lived in the interior of Califor-

ACORNS: ONCE A CALIFORNIA STAFF OF LIFE

Acorns were as vital to the California tribes as corn was to Southern tribes. A special system was developed for processing the acorns, which were extremely bitter in their natural state and contained substances called "tannins" that cause constipation. (The tannins are lost after many washings.) Acorns are high in protein and make an excellent meat substitute. According to author E. Barrie Kavasch, an authority on Native American culture and cookery, who offered this modern adaptation of a typical California acorn bread, these days we are most likely to find acorn flour and starch in Korean supermarkets.

California Pathfinder Bread

1 cup boiling water

1/4 cup maple syrup

1 Tablespoon Anaheim chili pepper, roasted and finely chopped [see note]

1 package dry yeast

1/2 teaspoon salt

3 Tablespoons hazelnut or sunflower seed oil

1 1/2 cups all-purpose flour

1/2 cup acorn meal flour or ground hazelnuts

1/2 cup buckwheat flour

1/2 cup fine yellow cornmeal

Pour the boiling water over the maple syrup and mix well with the chili pepper in a medium bread bowl. Let cool. Sprinkle the yeast over the mixture and stir in gently. Wait 5 minutes, sprinkle the salt over the surface of the mixture, add the oil, and stir well.

Carefully add the flours and cornmeal one at a time, stirring well with a wooden spoon until the dough begins to get thick. Turn the dough out onto a floured bread board. Knead for 5 to 10 minutes until no longer sticky, adding more flour as necessary.

nia built smaller, single-family homes.) The houses' willow frames were covered with mat shingles made of tule—pronounced *TOO-lee*; a type of bulrush, or North American plant—or other grasses. In the center of each home was a cooking fire, which vented smoke through a hole in the ceiling. Sleeping quarters were divided by grass mats hung from the ceiling to serve as curtains. This type of sleeping room was unusual among California tribes.

Most villages had sweat houses—secluded houses or caverns heated by steam and used for ritual cleansing, meditation, and purification. Chumash sweat houses, located partly underground, were entered by way of a hole in the roof. Men and women usually used separate sweat houses. Other buildings included houses for storing goods, a place for ceremonies, and another place for gambling. Villages might also contain dance grounds, game fields, and cemeteries.

Clothing and adornment

Because the climate in Chumash territory is mild, the people's clothing was very simple. Men generally wore nothing more than a string around the waist; from it they hung tools and food. Sometimes an animal skin was wrapped around the hips if the weather was cool.

Place dough in a lightly oiled bread bowl and turn it over once to make sure that the whole surface of the dough is glazed with oil. Cover with a clean towel. Let rest and rise in a warm place for 1 to 1 1/2 hours until nearly double in size.

Punch risen dough down and knead it for a short time on a clean, lightly floured dough board. Divide in half and shape into 2 oblong loaves. Place each in a warm, clean, well–oiled tin can (1-pound coffee cans are perfect) or 8-inch clay flowerpots. Cover again and allow to rest in a warm spot for another hour until double in size.

Preheat oven to 350° F. Bake the 2 loaves (uncovered) for about 45 minutes until the bread sounds hollow when tapped lightly on top. Breads should be a deep brown color. Remove from the oven and place on racks to cool for 10 minutes. Loosen and remove from pans or cans, then cool further on bread racks. The bread will cut best when cool, but it is so good you may want to serve it warm with hazelnut butter and fresh berry jams.

Makes 2 loaves

[Note: Fresh hot peppers can cause severe burns. When cutting them, wear rubber gloves or plastic sandwich bags to protect your hands. Always wash your hands thoroughly when you are finished. Never rub your eyes or touch your face with fingers that have been exposed to the juices of a hot pepper.

To roast a pepper, cut it in half, remove the seeds, and place skin side up on a broiler pan. Broil 2 to 3 inches from the heat under a preheated broiler until the skin blackens. Transfer to a plastic bag using tongs, seal the bag, and let the peppers steam inside the bag for 15 to 20 minutes. Then, remove the peppers from the bag and peel off the skin.]

From E. Barrie Kavasch. *Enduring Harvests: Native American Foods and Festivals for Every Season.* Old Saybrook, CT: Globe Pequot Press, 1995, p. 247.

If it was very cold, cloaks made from animal skins might be worn. Only the rich and powerful wore bear and other fur; an ankle-length fur cloak was a sign of a man's high position in the village. The poor wore clothes made from grasses and shredded bark.

Women wore two aprons—a large one hung from the waist in back and a smaller one in front. These were made of buckskin, shredded bark, or grass, and from them hung a fringe of shells. Although people usually went barefoot, sometimes deerskin socks or fiber sandals were worn. Moccasins were used only on special occasions.

Some Chumash males had pierced noses and many had pierced ears; the ear holes were large enough to hold containers for carrying tobacco. For special occasions the entire body was painted. The paint served a practical purpose, since it acted as a sunscreen. Ceremonial costumes representing animals and birds might be made from an entire bearskin or from all the plumage taken from the giant California condor.

Food

The Coastal and Island Chumash were blessed with abundant food and water. They had to move to follow the food supplies as the seasons changed, but the moves did not take them very far. Life was harder for the Chumash who lived in the rugged California interior. For the most part, Chumash women gathered food and men hunted, but sometimes widows became hunters in order to provide for their families.

By far the most important item on the Chumash menu was acorns. The Chumash encouraged the growth of oak trees by setting fires to burn out the plants with low fire resistance. This practice also encouraged large deer populations. (Since the practice of selective burning has been abandoned in California, the state's forests are no longer dominated by oak trees.) During acorn-gathering season, people from several Chumash villages joined forces, breaking up into small groups to make sure the entire region was harvested. Acorns were then ground into flour.

The Chumash also ate nuts, wild seeds, and roots. Pine nuts and wild strawberries were eaten raw; buckeyes and chia seeds were ground into flour; and nuts from the California laurel were roasted. The Chumash people hunted the abundant deer, mule deer, elk, rabbits, squirrels, ducks, and geese on their land. The rivers teemed with fish, and the ocean also supplied saltwater fish, clams, mussels, abalone (pronounced *AB-uh-LONE-ee*; a type of shellfish), crabs, and crayfish. Hunters in canoes harpooned seals, sea otters, and porpoises.

Education

Although few details are known about the education of Chumash children before the arrival of the Spanish, they probably learned mostly by observing their elders and through apprenticeships to adults. During the mission period, Indian children were taught the fundamentals of the Catholic religion. They also learned about farming, weaving, and potterymaking—trades the Spanish considered useful. The European settlers did not want to teach the Chumash to read because they feared that a young generation of educated Indians might become restless and dissatisfied with the unjust, repressive system that the missions imposed on them. In fact, teaching Indian children to read was outlawed in California until the 1920s.

The U.S. government established a school on the reservation early in the twentieth century, but it did not stay open for long. Chumash children—the majority of them speaking only broken English—then attended public schools at Santa Ynez near the reservation, where they faced racial prejudice. By the mid–1990s a little more than half of the reservation population had completed high school. The school dropout rate is high, partly because Indian youth have been

Chumash Kote Lotah and Lin-A-lul'Koy hold artifacts on an ancient Chumash site in 1992.

confronted with hostility and ignorance toward Native Americans by public school educators and the curriculum they taught, and partly because the labor of children is needed to help support families.

According to Robert O. Gibson in *The Chumash,* a new generation of Chumash people is working to save the tribe's sacred cultural sites. They have organized special education classes where historians and archaeologists are invited to teach their methods of preservation. It is particularly important to the Chumash who wish to learn more about their ancestors and traditional ways to take control of their ancient sites, because Chumash cemeteries were looted in the nienteenth century and artifacts from them were sold to art collectors

Healing practices

The Spanish who first encountered the Chumash described them as healthy; many lived to a very old age. The person responsible for curing the sick was the shaman (medicine man; pronounced *SHAY-mun*). The shaman's medical kit included herbs, charmstones (highly polished rocks believed to have great power), and a special tube for blowing or sucking out a disease-causing object. (The object was usually just a stone or even a small animal that the shaman had brought with him.) The shaman then performed a ritual that included singing and dancing over the patient. Today the people on the Santa Ynez reservation travel to Santa Barbara for modern Western medical and dental care.

ARTS

The Chumash have always had a rich artistic life. They are probably best known for the their pictographs. (See "Religion.") Historians believe these brilliantly colored images of humans, animals, and abstract circles were part of a religious ritual. The Chumash Painted Cave State Historic Park near Santa Barbara preserves samples of this art.

Beautiful bowls and animal figures were carved from a type of soft stone called steatite (pronounced *STEE-uh-TITE*; also known as soapstone). The Chumash made watertight fiber baskets interwoven with twine that they dyed black. Most of the baskets that survive date from the mission period; they were admired by the Spanish and are prized by museums and art collectors.

CUSTOMS

Class system

Chumash society had an upper, middle, and lower class. Shamans, priest-astrologers, and the brotherhood of the *tomol* (the guild that made cedar-plank canoes) belonged to the upper class. Skilled, healthy workers belonged to the middle class. The lower class consisted of people lacking special skills or those in poor health.

Festivals

Two of the most important festivals celebrated the autumn acorn harvest and the winter solstice (the longest night of the year, marking the beginning of winter). Other ceremonies honored animals, the First Beings. Men and women applied body paint for these occasions, played flutes and whistles, and scattered seeds. Descendants of the Chumash host several annual festivals; at some, they still perform the ancient Crane Dance, the Blackbird Dance, the Dolphin Dance, and the Bear Dance.

War and hunting rituals

The Chumash did not wage war often, but if a conflict could not be avoided, they would sometimes hold a mock battle. The opposing sides—dressed in full war costume—lined up facing one another. Taking turns, one member from each side shot an arrow at the other side. When one person was killed, the battle was over.

Before a hunt, men purified themselves in the sweat house. Some Chumash hunters even slept in the sweat house because sexual contact with women was believed to diminish a man's hunting abilities. The hunters rubbed their bodies with special substances to disguise their natural human scent. To keep from frightening deer, they wore deerskin headdresses and horns and made movements like those of a deer as they approached their prey.

Puberty

As Chumash girls approached puberty, they had to observe certain rules, one of which was refraining from consuming meat and grease. Both boys and girls celebrated reaching puberty by taking *toloache,* a drug that sent them into a trance, where they encountered their guardian spirit (see "Religion").

Marriage

An ordinary Chumash man chose his bride from his own village or one nearby. A wealthy man might choose a bride from a faraway village; by forming such a relationship, he helped ensure a large and united Chumash nation.

Except for the chief and his assistants, Chumash men had only one wife. After a wedding ceremony highlighted by much singing and dancing, the couple moved into the home of the groom's family.

Birth

When a pregnant Chumash woman began to feel contractions, she would dig a pit on the exact spot where she stood when the first pain came; then she would lie down in the pit. The woman went through the labor and delivery without physical help, but with a shaman present. After giving birth, the mother immediately broke her infant's nose bone because a flat nose was considered attractive. The child was named by the shaman, who consulted the stars and heavenly bodies for inspiration.

Death rituals

The Chumash were extremely respectful of the dead. After several mourners sat overnight by the body of the deceased person, it was carried to the cemetery, which was considered a sacred place.

Mourners gathered and smoked tobacco, sang, and cried. Then the body was buried face down. Sometimes a pole was placed atop the grave. From it hung objects that bore special meaning to the dead person (such as fishing gear for a fisherman). If the dead person were important enough, his pole would be painted. If he were especially important, he might be burned along with his entire house. The Chumash still observe the custom of burning a dead person's possessions. Every few years a ceremony is held to honor the souls of all the dead.

CURRENT TRIBAL ISSUES

Efforts to keep the Chumash culture alive have been hampered by technicalities. Only the Chumash who live on the reservation are "recognized" by the federal government. The government will only have relations with (recognize the rights of and give aid to) federally recognized tribes. But the small size of the Chumash people's reservation allows only 50 to 100 people to live there at any one time. Off-reservation Chumash have formed groups to preserve and maintain their culture, but they have not been very successful in obtaining federal recognition.

Preserving sacred sites against vandals and land developers is a constant concern for the Chumash. In the 1800s Chumash cemeteries were raided, and many of the artifacts found were sold to museums and art collectors. A major effort to preserve sacred sites occurred in May 1978; about 25 Chumash began a three-day protest at the site of an ancient burial ground where utility companies wanted to construct a billion-dollar facility to hold liquefied natural gas. The plant was never constructed. An agreement was worked out in which the tribe was granted access to the area for religious practices. The tribe was also granted the right to have six tribal members on hand when any future digging took place in former or current Chumash territory.

NOTABLE PEOPLE

Pacomio (Josè) Poqui (c. 1794–1844) was a Mission Indian, raised and educated as a carpenter at La Purísima Mission. Unhappy with the way his people were being treated by the Spanish, he helped lead a group of 2,000 Indians against the missionaries in an 1824 uprising. The Indians held the mission for about a month before being forced to surrender. Although he was sentenced to ten years' labor at a local prison, it is believed that Pacomio was allowed to live out the remainder of his life in Monterey, California.

F. L. Kitsepawit (c. 1804–1915) was born into a leading family in a Chumash town in what is now Santa Cruz, California. As a young man he lived in the mission at Ventura, where he was not able to speak his native language. Later, like other Chumash, he lived in remote areas, working as a ranchhand and carpenter. Toward the end of his life John Harrington, a linguist (someone who studies languages) and ethnohistorian (someone who studies the cultures of different groups) from the Smithsonian Institution sought him out as an older Chumash who could remember the Chumash culture and political systems that had been disrupted by the Spanish and Americans. Kitsepawit provided Harrington with many details remembered from his childhood. It is in part thanks to him that some of the traditions, history, and language can be brought back to the Chumash people.

FURTHER READING

Duvall, Jill. *The Chumash.* Chicago: Childrens Press, 1991.

Gibson, Robert O. *The Chumash.* New York: Chelsea House: 1991.

Grant, Campbell. *Rock Paintings of the Chumash: A Study of a California Indian Culture.* Originally published in 1965. Reprinted. Santa Barbara, CA: Santa Barbara Museum of Natural History/EZ Nature Books, 1993.

Keyworth, C. L. *California Indians.* New York: Facts on File, 1991.

Costanoan

Name

Costanoan. The name comes from the Spanish word *costeños,* which means "coast-dwellers." The Costanoan people call themselves *Ohlone,* the name of a village. Today the people are often referred to as Costanoan/Ohlone.

Location

The Costanoan inhabited the central coast of California (from San Francisco Bay to Monterey Bay) and east to the Mount Diablo mountain range. In the mid-1990s none of the Costanoan tribes was recognized by the federal government, and there was no reservation land. Most of the tribes' descendants were scattered throughout their traditional territory.

Population

Before the 1600s about 15,000 to 20,000 Costanoan people were known to exist. In 1770 the count was down to about 10,000. In 1832 fewer than 2,000 Costanoan remained. In a census (count of the population) taken in 1990 by the U.S. Bureau of the Census, 858 people identified themselves as Costanoan.

Language family

Costanoan.

Origins and group affiliations

For about a thousand years before the arrival of Europeans in North America, Costanoan settlements expanded along the coast, settling from the San Francisco Bay to the Monterrey Bay and inland. The people were divided into at least 50 independent nations.

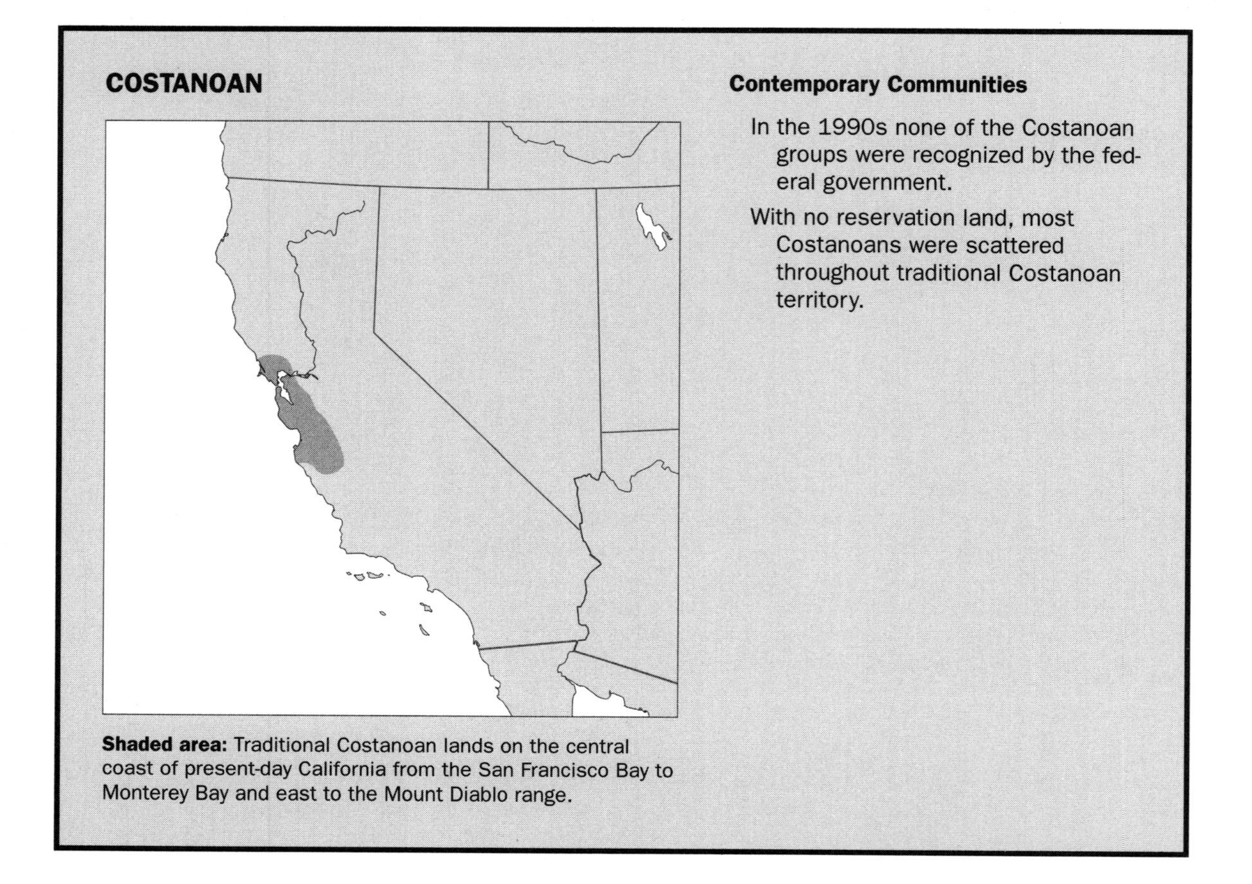

COSTANOAN

Contemporary Communities

In the 1990s none of the Costanoan groups were recognized by the federal government.

With no reservation land, most Costanoans were scattered throughout traditional Costanoan territory.

Shaded area: Traditional Costanoan lands on the central coast of present-day California from the San Francisco Bay to Monterey Bay and east to the Mount Diablo range.

The Costanoan had a comfortable life compared to many other Native American peoples. They occupied the beautiful lands of the central California coast, where the ocean teemed with fish and swimming game birds and the surrounding hills provided excellent hunting grounds. Like their Chumash neighbors (see entry), the Costanoan people suffered at the hands of Spanish Catholic missionaries and Mexican and American settlers. Eventually, they were thought to be extinct. The Costanoan people have managed to keep their culture alive despite tremendous obstacles.

HISTORY

Relationships with Indian neighbors

The Costanoan were not a united tribe. The people were divided into at least 50 separate and independent nations. They hunted, gathered, and traded with other Costanoan groups and with the Miwok (see entry) and the Yokuts. Costanoan traders exchanged shellfish, shells, salt, and bows for pine nuts and beads made from pieces of clamshell. They maintained relations with villagers from nearby and far away; sometimes men would marry the daughters of these far-off villages, thereby establishing distant friendships and trade relations that lasted a lifetime.

The people sometimes waged bow and arrow wars with other Costanoan groups. These wars usually stemmed from land rights (trespassing on another group's land), but sometimes villagers quarreled over the minerals that produced the prized red and white body paints.

IMPORTANT DATES

1692: Spanish explorer Sebastián Vizcaíno encounters some Costanoan people.

1769: The Presidio of Monterey is founded in Costanoan territory.

1770: The first Spanish Catholic mission is built in Costanoan territory.

1812: Padre Quintana is assasinated by Costanoan Mission Indians at Santa Cruz.

1960s: Costanoan people call attention to Native rights.

1980s and 1990s: Four Costanoan tribes petition the government for federal recognition.

Europeans arrive

The first contact between the Costanoan people and Europeans most likely took place in 1602, when Spanish explorer Sebastián Vizcaíno encountered a group called the Rumsen (American Indians of Monterey Bay, California). Between 1602 and 1769 the Natives and non-Natives met from time to time. European traders stopped by on their way east from the Philippines or on their way to and from the Vancouver region. Frequent contact began with the 1769 founding of the colony of Monterey by the Spanish. Much of what we now know about the Costanoan people was written down after that by Spanish explorers, soldiers, and the Catholic missionary priests—called *padres* in Spanish—who traveled with them.

One Spanish missionary, quoted by Alan K. Brown in *The Ohlone Past and Present: Native Americans of the San Francisco Bay Region,* described a trip the Spaniards took through Costanoan territory in 1772. As usual, he wrote, the visitors offered glass beads to the Costanoan in exchange for food. Initially, the Natives were unwilling to accept the beads and seemed indifferent about forming any sort of relationship with the Spanish. They were slowly won over, though, and expressed their generosity by bringing gifts of food to the European settlers. The missionary was especially impressed by the pale skin of the Costanoan people. "They are like so many Spaniards," he declared.

Spanish missions are built

By the sixteenth century the Spanish government had claimed a huge expanse of land in what is now the state of California. When Russian and English traders began showing too much interest in the

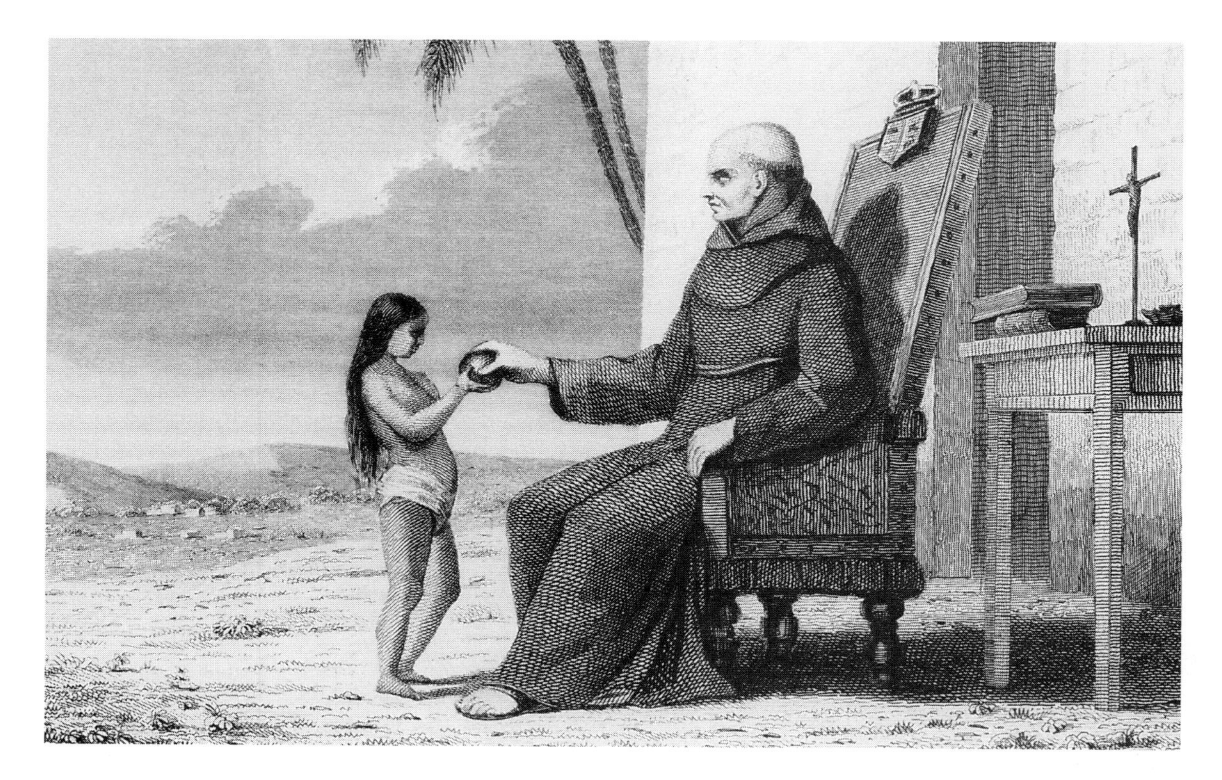

An Indian child is offered an apple by Father Francisco Durán at Mission San José de Guadalupe in this 1841 drawing. Many Indian children taken to the missions experienced terrible conditions and cruel treatment.

region, the Spanish founded the port of Monterey to protect their hold on the California coast. They relied on the muscle of the California Natives to help expand Spain's presence in the West. The Indians were taught just enough of the Spanish language to be considered "useful." Missionary priests in the region had their own goal of converting the Natives to the Catholic religion. The first Catholic mission in Costanoan territory was established in 1770; it was built with forced Indian labor. Eventually the number of missions in California reached twenty-one; seven were in Costanoan territory. Indians who joined the mission came to be known as Mission Indians.

Becoming "Mission Indians"

Most Natives did not go willingly to the missions. The Costanoan were thrust into the mission system by misfortune: their food sources were being used up by Spanish cattle, and their population was being weakened by strange new diseases brought by European traders and the Spanish colonists.

Once at the missions, the Natives were baptized into the Catholic faith and called neophytes (pronounced *NEE-oh-fites*; "beginners"). Under Spanish law, neophytes were forced to relocate to the missions.

They stayed in camps that were set up outside the missions. At the tender age of five or six, Native American children were taken from their parents and forced to live within the filthy, disease-ridden barracks. They had to attend religious services and perform physical labor without pay. The children were trained in carpentry, agriculture, and other practical occupations as dictated by the Spanish.

Conditions at the missions were appalling from the start. The Indians lived in filth. Medical care was virtually nonexistent. Many of the California Natives died from overwork, disease, and harsh treatment. They were thrown together with people from many different tribes and lost connection to their villages, their customs, or their ancient religion. Few historians consider the mission system a success: the benefits of bringing Christianity to the Native peoples is still being debated. Without question, acts of extreme cruelty were committed against the Mission Indians. Most observers agree that the establishment of the missions nearly caused the destruction of Costanoan culture. Inevitably, conflicts developed between the missionaries and those Indians who refused to convert to the Catholic religion. Rebellious Indians banded together and raided the mission's horse herds, to defy Spanish authority and cripple the economy of the colony.

Mexico takes over California

Still the mission system endured, even as the Mexican government took over California in 1834. The Mexicans freed the neophytes and made some superficial, but largely ineffective, attempts to help them. Mexican officials ordered that mission property and livestock be divided among the Natives who lived at the missions. Most of the lands and livestock, however, passed into the hands of Mexican settlers.

Some Native Americans remained at the missions, which no longer served as religious centers but had thriving farms. (Many of the mission churches still exist and have become popular tourist destinations.) Most, however, left to seek work on Mexican ranches that were being built on former Native lands. Certain Costanoan groups established Native communities with members of other tribes, but these communities grew smaller as young people left to find employment elsewhere. Many Costanoan people had died under the treatment of missionaries, and even more died at the hands of Mexican settlers. The rest became part of the larger California group of homeless and landless Natives.

California's rejected treaties

In 1848 the United States took California from Mexico; California became a state two years later. In the 1850s the U.S. government decided to resolve the country's "Indian Problem" by establishing the reservation system—setting aside pieces of land (most often undesirable ones) on which the Indians could live. Eighteen treaties were drawn up. California tribes agreed to give up most of their lands to the U.S. government in exchange for about 7.5 million acres that would be used for reservations.

Blinded by their own interests, white Californians were alarmed that so much land—about 8 percent of the state—was being "given away" to the Native peoples. They also feared that their supply of slave labor would disappear onto reservations. Such an uproar was raised that the U.S. Senate rejected the treaties.

American settlers continued to push into California, and the mistreatment of Native groups—including the Costanoan—continued. Thousands were murdered, thousands more became slaves. Others tried to make a living as best they could. Racial prejudice led many Costanoan to hide their Indian ancestry and attempt to blend in with other groups. By the early years of the twentieth century most historians believed the Costanoan people were extinct.

Costanoan people in the twentieth century

But the Costanoan were not extinct, as a man by the name of John Peabody Harrington found out. Harrington was an anthropologist, a person who studies the development of human societies. In the 1920s the Smithsonian Institution, a national research group in Washington, D.C., asked Harrington to conduct interviews with descendants of California Native groups. He found that some Costanoan were keeping their culture alive and still speaking the language.

Around the same time, the U.S. government sent a representative to study the situation of the region's homeless Indians. Based on his poorly researched report, the government determined that there was no reason to set aside land for the Costanoan people.

Several lawsuits were filed by California Natives in the twentieth century, claiming rights to lands they gave up while waiting for the 18 treaties to take effect. Costanoan people took part in two of the lawsuits but received little satisfaction. (See box titled "Costanoan Woman Sues Federal Government.")

Beginning in the 1960s various Native American groups—including the Costanoan—started calling for an end to construction

The Royal Presidio Chapel in Monterey, California.

projects that threatened cultural resources on traditional lands. By the end of the twentieth century these groups were focusing the attention of scholars and the public on the long neglected but rich culture of the Costanoan people.

RELIGION

Traditional beliefs and practices

Like other Native cultures of central California, most Costanoans believed in a Creator, an animal character called Coyote, who was one of the First People. Coyote is said to have made the world and everything in it.

Keeping the animal spirits happy was a constant concern for the Costanoan people. This was accomplished by holding frequent ceremonies and offerings. Members of a religious group called the Kuksu Society were devoted to the worship of the Creator. The Kuksu Society held dances in a large, earth-covered dance house. Dancers, who dressed in large feathered headdresses, impersonated animal spirits. During the ceremonies, boys between the ages of eight and sixteen were taught the rituals so they might one day become members.

The Costanoan believed that if the animal spirits were happy, good things would come to the people (rain, for example) and disasters would be avoided. The animal spirits were also thought to appear to people in dreams and help guide them in making major life decisions.

Under the mission system

Some of the Costanoan became Catholics under the mission system, but many were reluctant converts. The religion of their descendants blends Catholic elements with ancient spiritual beliefs and practices.

LANGUAGE

The Costanoan spoke at least eight different languages; they all belong to the language family called Costanoan. The varieties that scholars know about are called Karkin, Chocenyo, Tamyen, Ramaytush, Awaswas, Mutsun, Rumsen, and Chalon. After the 1930s there were no remaining speakers of the ancient languages.

GOVERNMENT

The Costanoan people were organized into about 50 independent groups or organizations that are sometimes called tribelets. A tribelet consisted of one main settlement surrounded by a few minor settlements. Tribelet chiefs could be either men or women, but usually the job passed from father to son. The chief was advised by a group of elders, and the chief's duties were rather broad in nature: seeing that the poor were taken care of, overseeing hunting and fishing expeditions, and the like. Apparently, the Costanoan people valued their personal freedom highly and obeyed an authority figure only during wartime.

By the twenty-first century the descendants of the Costanoan were scattered throughout California. Four groups have applied for federal recognition. As part of that process, they have organized a new kind of government.

ECONOMY

Before Europeans entered the territory, the Costanoan economy depended largely on gathering and trading activities as well as hunting and fishing. Because of their clever management of the land, the Costanoan were able to supply their own food needs and also build a surplus to trade with neighboring groups. The region also had abundant shells and the material to make dyes used for decorative items and body paints.

Under the mission system, the Costanoan were forced to become farm and ranch laborers. Later they were compelled to blend into the larger California community, which is where they find employment today.

DAILY LIFE

Families

Families usually consisted of a father, a mother, their children, and the father's relatives. From 10 to 15 people made up a household.

COSTANOAN/ OHLONE GROUPS SEEK FEDERAL RECOGNITION

Federally recognized tribes are those who have a legal relationship with the U.S. government. Without federal recognition, the tribe does not exist in the eyes of the government and is therefore not entitled to financial aid and other help or reservation lands.

In order to obtain federal recognition, a tribe must meet certain conditions. A new tribal constitution must be adopted, and a new tribal government must be formed. Five groups (sometimes called bands) of Costanoan/Ohlone have filed for federal recognition since the 1980s: the Amah/Mutsun Band, the Carmel Mission Band, the Indian Canyon Band, the Ohlone/Costanoan Esselen Nation, and the Muwekma/Ohlone Tribe. As the twentieth century drew to a close, none of the groups had yet achieved federal recognition.

Buildings

Most Costanoan built domed dwellings, although some groups constructed cone-shaped homes made from redwood. The domed structures were covered with thatch (plant material), which was attached to poles and tied at the top. A rectangular doorway led directly to a central fireplace. Homes contained beds made of bulrush mats and skins. The beds were covered with blankets that had been woven from strips of skin from sea otters, rabbits, and ducks.

Sweat houses for men and women (no children were allowed) were dug out of stream banks. The adults would retreat to sweat houses for solitude and purification rituals that helped strengthen their spiritual well-being. Dances were held either in circular enclosures or in large dome–shaped thatched structures.

Clothing and adornment

Few males wore any kind of clothing, but women were more modest. They wore tule (a kind of plant) and buckskin aprons suspended from the waist in front and back. Both sexes wore long robes in cold weather, and men sometimes covered their bodies with a special mud to keep warm. No shoes or hats were worn.

The Costanoan people had fairer hair than most of the other Native Californians, and they usually wore it long. Men tied theirs with cords decorated with feathers, while women let theirs hang loose. Many of the men had long, flowing beards.

Tattoos covered various parts of the body, and red and white paint was sometimes applied to decorate the face and body. Ornaments such as flowers or feathers hung from pierced ears, and some men had pierced noses. Both sexes wore necklaces made of shells.

Food

GATHERING Costanoan lands were so rich in food resources that the Native people did not have to farm. Even so, they lit fires as a way to clear and fertilize land for sowing the seeds of wild grasses. The grasses provided them with food and also attracted game animals.

In the spring the people moved from their villages on the coast to take advantage of the newly ripening plants, bulbs, greens, and grass seeds found further inland. A variety of berries was gathered and eaten raw or cooked. When autumn came, some villagers departed to gather acorns. These and other nuts and seeds were then processed and eaten.

HUNTING The bounty of the Pacific Coast ensured ample supplies of abalone (pronounced *AB-uh-LONE-ee*; a Rumsen word for a type of edible shellfish), crabs, mussels, oysters, sea snails, shrimp, steelhead, sturgeon, and lampreys (an eel–shaped fish). Salmon were netted and hauled aboard sturdy rafts or boats made of tule (pronounced *TOO-lee*; a type of cattail). Whales and sea lions were not hunted, but if they happened to wash ashore the people gladly roasted and ate them.

All sorts of birds were hunted. Mourning doves, quail, wild turkeys, and hawks were part of the diet, but buzzards, eagles, owls, and ravens were not eaten. Several varieties of geese were attracted by using dried and stuffed goose decoys made by skilled craftspeople. Rabbits, deer, elk, antelope, mountain lions, and grizzly bears added variety to the diet.

Education

Little is known about the education of Costanoan children prior to the arrival of European missionaries. Children probably learned by observing adults. During the mission period, children were taught the fundamentals of the Catholic religion. They also learned about farming, weaving, and potterymaking—trades the Spanish considered useful. The European settlers did not teach the Costanoan to read because they feared that a young generation of educated Indians might become restless and dissatisfied with the unjust, repressive, white-run system that had destroyed their Native ways. In fact, teaching Indian children to read was against the law until the 1920s. At the end of the twentieth century descendants of the Costanoan had organized classes in their native language, basketmaking, and folklore at Indian cultural centers in California.

Healing practices

According to Costanoan belief, diseases were caused by objects placed inside the sick person's body by angry spirits. Medicine men called shamans (pronounced *SHAY-munz*) were consulted to restore the victim's health. A shaman usually began his task by performing a ceremonial song and dance, then cured the disease by piercing the patient's skin and sucking out the disease-causing object. Shamans also used herbs as medicine, mixing them together in a special small container called a mortar. Some Costanoan doctors claimed to be able to kill their enemies by turning themselves into grizzly bears; these doctors were greatly feared.

ARTS

The California tribes—ranked among the world's best basketmakers—produced two different types of baskets: coiled and twined. The Costanoan specialty was twined baskets, made from willow, rushes, and grasses. These tightly woven baskets were both beautiful and functional; they were used for carrying, storing, and processing acorns; snaring fish; carrying and storing water; and as cooking pots and utensils.

Oral literature

The Costanoan liked to tell stories about how death came into the world. There are two common elements in these stories: a supernatural power creates death and then is sorry when a relative dies; and the decision to create death is irreversible—it cannot be changed.

CUSTOMS

Festivals and ceremonies

Shamans were the main performers at many Costanoan festivals. They organized dances to bring a good acorn crop, plentiful fish, and stranded whales. Acorn season was the most festive time of the year. The season lasts only a few weeks. After gathering all day, at night the people danced, traded, gambled, and feasted.

Puberty

Costanoan girls who had reached puberty did not eat certain foods or drink cold water during their menstrual period and went through a special ritual in a corner of the home at the onset of puberty. Menstrual blood was considered powerful and possibly even dangerous. Boys at puberty took a drug called *toloache,* obtained from a plant called jimsonweed. When consumed, the drug causes a person to go into a trancelike state and see visions.

Marriage

A class system existed among the Costanoan, and members of the elite, or highest, classes tended to marry members of their same class living in tribes throughout central California, even if they did not speak the same language.

Marriages began simply when the groom's family bestowed a small gift upon the bride's family. The newlyweds lived in the home of the husband's father. Sometimes a Costanoan man took more than one wife, usually his wife's sister. The resulting families all lived together. If a couple decided to divorce, the mother kept any children.

Childbirth

After giving birth to her baby, a new mother would undergo a ritual cleansing in the ocean or in a stream. Then, for several days, she and her newborn child would rest on a mattress in a pit lined with hot rocks. Costanoan tradition dictated the mother's diet; there were certain foods she could not eat. Shortly after birth the baby boy or girl's ears were pierced.

Death

In keeping with Costanoan tradition, a corpse was wrapped in feathers, beads, and flowers, laid out on a stack of wood, and cremated (set on fire). A deceased person who had no family members to gather firewood for the funeral fire was buried instead. The mourners chanted and expressed their wishes for the soul's easy trip to the next world. Widows and female relatives cut off their hair and beat themselves on the head and breast with pestles (the pounding and grinding implement used with a mortar). After her husband was buried, a widow would remain in mourning for a year. Memorial services for all the dead were held annually.

CURRENT TRIBAL ISSUES

Obtaining tribal recognition (see box on page 1023) and preserving sacred sites are important issues to the modern Costanoan.

Mutsun Costanoan/Ohlone tribal chairperson Ann Marie Sayers holds title to a section of Indian Canyon, a 275-mile piece of land in the San Francisco Bay area. In the nineteenth century Indian Canyon served as a refuge for Costanoan Indians fleeing the Spanish missions. From her home there, Sayers and other like-minded individuals are carrying on the struggle for federal recognition of California's nonrecognized tribes. Sayers's property is a Living Indian Heritage Area, where today Native people live and hold traditional ceremonies.

California Natives—the Costanoan among them—voice powerful opposition to major construction on their ancestral lands. A huge anti-development campaign in the late 1990s sought to prevent the building of a $100 million project around the San Bruno Mountain Indian Shell Mound (a site overlooking San Francisco Bay). The mound dates back 5,000 years and was the site of important Costanoan ceremonies and burials.

COSTANOAN WOMAN SUES FEDERAL GOVERNMENT

According to the terms of 18 treaties drawn up in the 1850s, California tribes agreed to give up most of their lands to the U.S. government in exchange for about 8 million acres that would be set aside for reservations. The treaties never became legal, but the California Natives lost their land.

In 1928 Congress passed laws that allowed California Natives to sue the federal government for the land that had been taken from them. Every California Indian who could prove they were related to an Indian alive in 1850 was entitled to participate in the lawsuit. One such person was Ann Marie Sayers, a Mutsun Costanoan/Ohlone. According to Sayers, the U.S. government finally determined that the land of her ancestors was worth 41 cents an acre. After many delays and much paperwork, in 1950 Sayers received her land settlement check—a paltry sum of $150. In 1972 she received an additional $668. Other Natives were not so fortunate; they received nothing.

NOTABLE PEOPLE

Oiyugma (dates unknown) was a Costanoan chief who led the resistance against the establishment of Mission San Jose in the late 1700s. He threatened to kill Spanish soldiers and any Indians who tried to help them build the mission.

Other notable Costanoan include: Mutsun Ohlone Ann Marie Sayers and Rumsen Ohlones Linda Yamane and Alex Ramirez, who are currently active in the movement to revive tribal traditions and bring them to the attention of a wider audience. Henry "Hank" Alvarez, a Muwekma Ohlone elder and tribal council member, and his wife, Stella, are active members of the community organization PACT (People Acting in Community Together).

FURTHER READING

Bean, Lowell John, ed. "Introduction." *The Ohlone Past and Present: Native Americans of the San Francisco Bay Region.* Menlo Park, CA: Ballena Press, 1994.

Brown, Alan K. "The European Contact of 1772 and Some Later Documentation." *The Ohlone Past and Present: Native Americans of the San Francisco Bay Region.* Edited by John Bean Lowell. Menlo Park, CA: Ballena Press, 1994.

Ohlone Costanoan Esselen Nation Home Page [Online] http://www.ucsc.edu/costano/home.html

Yamane, Linda. "Costanoan/Ohlone." *Native America in the Twentieth Century: An Encyclopedia.* Edited by Mary B. Davis. New York: Garland Publishing, 1994.

Hupa and Chilula

Names

Hupa (pronounced *HOO-pah*) and Chilula (pronounced *chee-LOO-lah*). The name "Hupa" comes from the name the Yurok Indians gave to the Hoopa Valley. One group of Hupa called themselves *Natinook-wa,* meaning "the people of the place by the river to which the trails return." A second group of Hupa called themselves *Tsnungwe,* as they still do. The valley tribe is now known as the Hoopa Valley Tribe, but the individual Native people are called Hupa.

The Chilula called themselves *Hoil'kut.* They were known to their neighbors as the Bald Hills Indians or Redwood Creek Indians.

Location

Both the Hupa and Chilula lived in northwestern California, the Hupa along the shores of the Trinity River and the Chilula in the lower section of Redwood Creek in Humboldt County. At the end of the twentieth century most of the remaining Hupa and descendants of the Chilula (who no longer use the name and have become part of the other groups on the reservation) lived on the Hoopa Valley Reservation, a 144-square-mile area that covers one-half of traditional Hupa territory. The Tsnungwe left the Hoopa Valley Reservation in the 1800s and moved back to their homeland on the south fork of the Trinity River.

Population

There were an estimated 1,000 Hupa in 1850. There were about 500–600 Chilula in the early 1800s. In a census (count of the population) conducted in 1990 by the U.S. Bureau of the Census, 2,386 people identified themselves as Hupa (or Hoopa); no one claimed to be Chilula.

Language family

Athabaskan.

Origins and group affiliations

Archaeologists and linguists believe that the Hupa and Chilula originally lived north of California, most likely in Oregon. They probably began the move south about 1,300 years ago and completed it about 300 years later. The Hupa had contact with the Yurok and Karok, and the Chilula also maintained a good relationship with the Yurok.

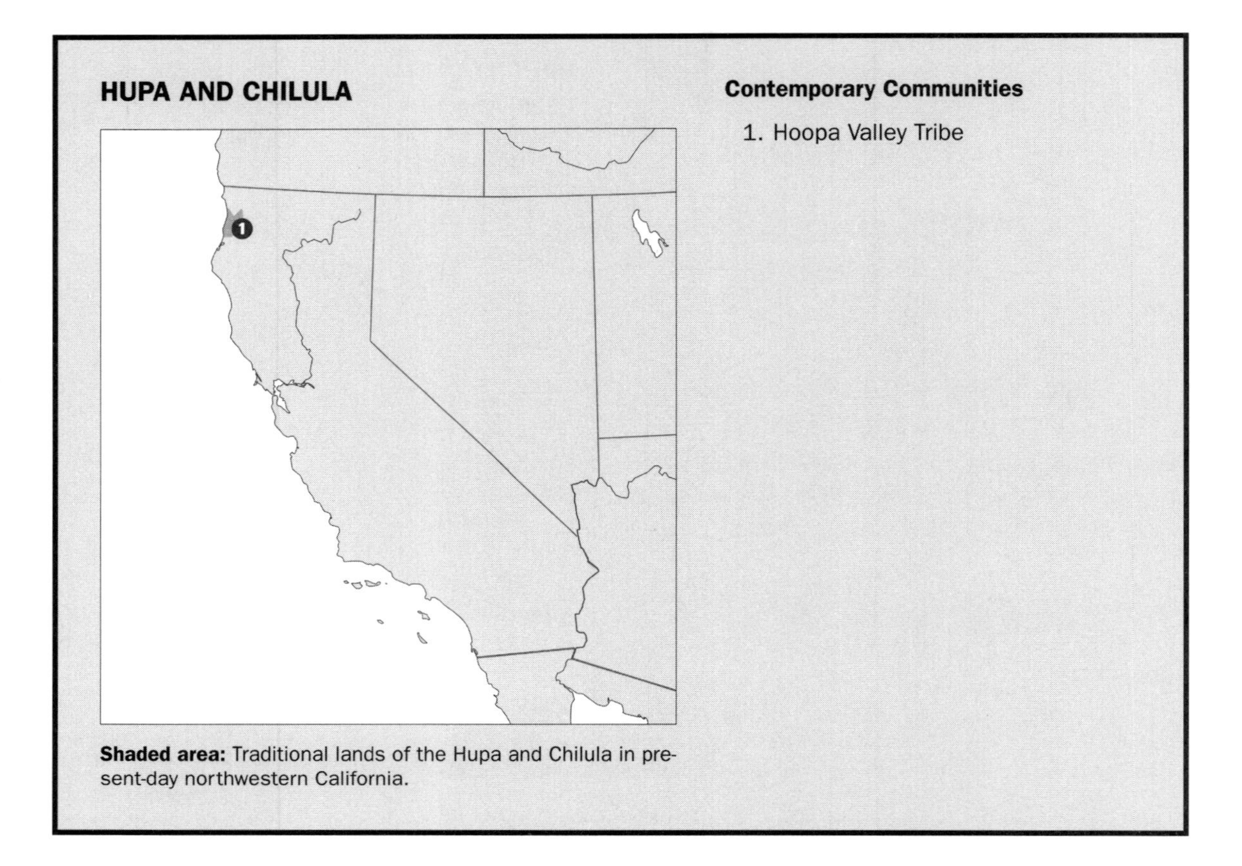

Shaded area: Traditional lands of the Hupa and Chilula in present-day northwestern California.

The Hupa are and always have been the largest of the Athabaskan-speaking tribes living in northwestern California. They were river people whose way of life depended on the runs of salmon that still occur each fall on the Trinity River. They believe their village at the heart of the Hoopa Valley is the center of the world and that all trails return to it. The Hupa shared a language and most customs with their less prosperous neighbors, the Chilula, who depended on the much smaller Redwood Creek for resources. The frequently damp, foggy climate, rocky cliffs, narrow stony beaches, and hardwood forests that surrounded the two tribes had more in common with the Pacific Northwest than with typical California locales.

HISTORY

Discovery of gold disrupts peace

Long before the coming of white fur trappers in the 1800s, the Hupa and Chilula lived in secluded and prosperous villages, where natural resources were fairly plentiful and life was comfortable. They were so secluded that they had almost no contact with whites until 1850. That year gold was discovered on the upper Trinity River, bringing a flood of miners to the Natives' lands. The gold beds quickly ran dry, but some of the miners stayed in the area and built homes and orchards.

Throughout the United States, relations between whites and Indians were far from good. In California, where white settlers and gold seekers were pouring in, rumors spread about "wild" Indians killing "innocent" whites. Fort Gaston was built in 1855 to protect white settlers from the Hupa and Chilula. U.S. troops were stationed at the fort.

IMPORTANT DATES

1828: American trappers enter the Hoopa Valley, but there is little interaction.

1850: Gold is discovered on the Trinity River; gold seekers pour onto Hupa and Chilula lands.

1859: 160 Chilula attending what they think is a peace conference are forced onto a reservation in Mendocino. Attempting to return home, most are killeded by Lassik Indians.

1864: Hoopa Valley Reservation is established.

1892: Fort Gaston is abandoned by the U.S. government.

1950: Hoopa Valley Tribe adopts a constitution, hoping to end their dependence on the U.S. Bureau of Indian Affairs.

1988: President Ronald Reagan signs the Hoopa–Yurok Settlement Act, giving the Hoopa Valley Tribe full rights to profits from timber harvested on the reservation.

Hupa resist the reservation

Seeking to end the growing violence Californians were showing toward Native Americans in the 1850s, the U.S. government began talks with the tribes, urging them to give up their homelands in exchange for other—often less desirable—lands in new reservations that were tiny and insufficient. Most California tribes were moved to stretches of land far from their traditional homelands—lands the whites didn't want. Reservation land was usually unsuitable for farming and lacking in water and game.

For five years the Hupa resisted the government's efforts to move them. Finally in 1864 a reservation was established on their ancestral land. The Hupa people who lived on the south fork of the Trinity River (they called themselves Tsnungwe) soon joined the Valley Hupa on the reservation, as did their neighbors, some Yurok. The Klamath tribe moved to the same area in the early 1880s, at which point the Tsnungwe decided to return to their homeland on the Trinity River.

Disease and war

At the time of the move to the reservation, the presence of foreigners was beginning to take its toll on the Native population. White settlers exposed the people of the Hoopa Valley to new diseases. Lacking resistance, the Hupa were hit hard by epidemics (uncontrolled outbreaks of disease) and the population fell to a mere 650 by 1864.

Between 1860 and 1872 the Hupa and other area tribes engaged in a series of Indian wars with American settlers. The whites had taken over Native territories, murdered Indians, kidnaped their children, and burned their villages. The most dramatic event occurred in 1867; it resulted in the deaths of several white law enforcement agents and one Indian who was suspected of robbery. More conflicts arose as U.S. troops tried to place non-valley Indians on the Hoopa Valley Reservation, but these disputes were relatively minor.

CHILULA RESISTANCE

The Chilula and the whites were involved in far more serious clashes. The Chilula people first met gold miners and white settlers in 1851, and the relationship between the two groups was instantly hostile. In response to the invasion of their territory by strangers who stole their resources, the Chilula ambushed the miners and took their supplies. The miners then began to shoot members of the tribe on sight. Outbreaks of violence continued throughout the 1850s, as soldiers stationed at Fort Gaston and other area sites aided the whites in their anti-Native campaign.

Chilula resistance slowed down white advancement onto Indian lands, but the tribe's skillful defense of ancestral territories fueled strong anti-Chilula feelings among the whites. Eventually, white settlers formed their own army—a particularly ruthless independent fighting force—to drive the Chilula away. On March 4, 1859, they tricked the Chilula into attending an alleged peace conference. But instead of discussing peace, the whites rounded up about 160 Chilula (one-quarter of the tribe) and forced them to move to a reservation 150 miles away in Mendocino.

Chilula warriors escaped from the reservation and headed home through unknown territory, guided by the Sun and stars. Then, near Fort Seward on the Eel River, they were attacked without warning by a Lassik (another Athabaskan-speaking California tribe) war party. All but one or two Chilula were believed to have been killed. In retaliation, the few Chilula who remained at Redwood Creek joined the Hupa and the Whilkut and raided a Lassik summer camp. Men, women, and children were killed without mercy.

Hearing of the violence, miners avoided the area. Finally, a U.S. government agent convinced the few remaining Chilula to join the Hoopa Valley Indian Reservation. Once there, the Chilula intermixed and intermarried with the other tribes on the reservation. In time, they lost the traits that made them Chilula, until ultimately they were no longer regarded as a separate tribe.

On the reservation

On the Hoopa Valley Reservation, the Indians began adapting to American ways of life: they settled down to farm and raise livestock and became self-supporting. The Hupa were more fortunate than many other California tribes. Because they were physically isolated from white communities, and because they remained on their own land and lived among the same tribes that had always been their neighbors, they were better able to preserve their traditions and their community. They did, however, encounter conflict with government agents and soldiers at Fort Gaston.

For 28 years the Hupa endured harsh treatment at the hands of occupying troops. Idle soldiers set their sights on Hupa women, randomly fathering children. In 1892 Fort Gaston was closed and the troops moved elsewhere. This change was a blessing for the Hupa. They gradually combined American and Native ways and prospered on their reservation. At the end of the twentieth century the reservation had gained recognition for its many historic sites and buildings. In spite of their adoption of American ways, the Hupa managed to retain a visible connection to their past and maintain a strong cultural identity. The Athabaskan language is still spoken, and the Hupa are making efforts to preserve their customs, arts, and traditions.

RELIGION

Much more is known about Hupa religious practices than Chilula practices. The Hupa believed that a race of Immortals (beings who would live forever) inhabited Earth prior to humans. The Immortals put the Earth in order for all humanity and formed rules for living on it. Then the ancestors of the Hupa and Chilula sprang to life. (The Chilula believed they sprang from a large hollow redwood tree.) People were only one of many important elements on Earth. Spirits were believed to be present in all things, and everything in nature was to be respected and tended.

Coping with everyday life

Everyday life was filled with uncertainty as the Hupa and Chilula people grappled with the elements, disease, fear, and the threat of war. Religion helped people cope. The Indians practiced many daily rituals to promote good health, wealth, even luck. They also performed formal rituals established by the Immortals. The rituals were an integral part of the World Renewal Cycle (see "Festivals and ceremonies"), which guaranteed world order. Village priests were in charge of the tribe's World Renewal activities.

HUPA BUILD INDIAN SHAKER CHURCH

In 1926 some Hupa built an Indian Shaker church on their reservation. The Indian Shaker religion had been established in 1881 by a Salish Indian named John Slocum (c. 1840–98) of Puget Sound, Washington. Slocum claimed that he died and returned from the dead. As he came back to life, he was seized by a fit of shaking and began to speak in words no one could understand.

Indian Shakerism is a Christian-based religion that reflects some of the practices of tribal shamans. (See "Healing practices.") For example, members who have received God's power begin to tremble or shake as the power enters them, in much the same way shamans sometimes tremble during trances.

The popularity of the Indian Shaker religion seemed to fade in the 1950s, when many Indians began to return to their traditional ways. Present-day Hupa dance in World Renewal rituals. (See "Festivals and ceremonies.")

Christian missions were established on the reservation in the late 1800s and some Native people converted to the new religion. However, their traditional rituals remained a central part of their lives.

LANGUAGE

Hupa and Chilula languages were closely related. Language was regarded as holy; nothing in the natural world was as powerful as the words used in prayers. Words could not only heal but could also do great evil. As the Chilula were absorbed into the reservation system, their language perished.

GOVERNMENT

The most important tribal unit among the northwestern California Indians was the village; there was no single chief who headed the entire Hupa or Chilula nations. Villages were composed of groups of people who shared the same family tree. Each village maintained its own version of law and order and was guided by a chief or powerful leader, usually the wealthiest or most popular man in the village. Occasionally, a group of wealthy Hupa men gathered to resolve disputes or decide on a payment for breaking rules.

After the formation of the Hoopa Valley Reservation, the Hupa became dependent on U.S. government agents—agents who were not always honest or fair in their role as mediator between the whites and the Indians. Sometimes agents of the government actually broke the very laws they were supposed to be upholding, as when they allowed whites to harvest grain planted by the Indians. (In this case, the Indians ended up experiencing a food shortage and had to ask for government handouts of food.)

A new government attitude surfaced in the mid-twentieth century, leading many tribes to become less dependent on the government. The Hoopa Valley Tribe adopted a constitution in 1950. Today, it is governed by an elected tribal council. Members represent districts that were formerly Hupa villages. The tribal council manages the large sums of money brought in by tribal businesses and serves to stimulate job creation within the tribe.

ECONOMY

Before European contact

The Hupa were primarily fishers, and the abundant resources of the Trinity River amply supplied their needs. They traveled the river in large canoes dug out of 16- to 18-foot lengths of redwood and cedar, which they received in trade from the Yurok. Often they journeyed by foot on well-used trails over the mountains to the Pacific Coast to trade, taking acorns and other foods they had gathered, plus shell money, to exchange for fish and dried seaweed. (They extracted salt from the seaweed.)

The Chilula had to rely on the less abundant resources of Redwood Creek. Because this waterway was too small for canoes to travel, the Chilula supplemented their needs with what they could obtain by hunting and gathering.

Repayment of debt was considered a pressing issue among the Hupa and Chilula. People who had borrowed from others and could not repay the debt had to go to work for the person who was owed until the debt was repaid. Records indicate that indebted men would often send their daughters to work to pay off the debt. Some historians refer to this repayment system as a form of slavery.

Unlike many Native American tribes whose hunting and gathering lands were owned by all, the Hupa and Chilula permitted individual ownership of hunting and gathering areas. In terms of fishing rights, the Hupa allowed individuals to claim certain sites; the Chilula, however, did not.

Timber and tourism

By the late 1990s the Hoopa Valley Reservation was the largest in size, population, and money earned in California. Rich timber lands on the reservation's 87,000 acres (primarily Douglas fir) supported four mills and created jobs in the timber industry.

But in spite of a thriving timber business and its standing as a historic site, a tourist destination, and a recreational center, the Hoopa Valley Reservation remains impoverished. Per capita income (income for each person in a year) is only about $6,000, compared to about $20,000 for the American population. Unemployment is high; nearly 30 percent of people who want to work cannot find a job.

A Chilula sweat house in northern California.

DAILY LIFE

Families

Northwestern California Indian families usually included a father, a mother, their children, and a few unmarried relatives. They lived in single-family homes in villages ranging in size from six to thirty homes.

Buildings

Hupa and Chilula families spent most of the year in sturdy, rectangular, redwood or cedar plank houses that lasted for generations. The wealthier the family, the bigger the house and the more desirable its location; the best sites might be on hillsides, for example, which offered better views and protection from floods.

Houses were sunk at least five feet down in a pit. A notched plank served as a staircase, leading down from the front door into the floor of the sunken dwelling. Homes often included a front porch made of rocks, where people sat and worked. In spring and fall the people moved to a gathering territory and lived in temporary shelters made of brush or bark.

Like many tribes of the West, the Hupa and Chilula built separate lodges for women who were menstruating. (The men believed that exposure to menstrual blood would ruin their good luck.) Men purified themselves before hunting and gathering by sitting in sweat houses—secluded huts or caverns heated by steam and used for ritual cleansing and meditation. Some villages also contained circular dance houses, where wealthy men hosted lavish ceremonies.

Clothing and adornment

The Hupa and Chilula dressed alike. Because the climate was mild, men usually wore only an animal-skin breechcloth (a garment with front and back flaps that hung from the waist), though many of the elderly men went nude. Women wore buckskin shirts and aprons, adding a fringed skirt threaded with shells for certain ceremonies. Sometimes Chilula women wore dresses of maplewood bark. Though the Hupa occasionally wore moccasins for long journeys and men wore leggings while hunting, they usually went barefoot. Women wore caps to protect the head while carrying baskets and cradles. In the winter the Hupa wore robes of animal skin for added warmth.

Both men and women had long hair; the Chilula wore headbands of yellow-hammer quail feathers. Men and women wore shell ornaments in their pierced ears, and women tattooed their chins with vertical bands of color.

Food

IN THE HOOPA VALLEY The Hoopa Valley had plentiful resources and a moderate climate, so the valley people did not have to travel far for food. Spared the extreme summer heat that blanketed the rest of California, the region offered a rich supply of green plants for gathering year-round. Still, the Hupa focused most of their efforts on stockpiling two main food sources—salmon and acorns—that fed them well throughout the year. These foods remain an important element in Hupa celebrations.

Each spring and fall the valley tribes harvested hordes of spawning fish in the Trinity River. They broiled fresh fish on sticks over an open fire, then sliced and smoke–dried the excess. The Hupa also fished for steelhead trout, sturgeon, eels, and an assortment of smaller fish, but hunted only rarely.

Women were responsible for gathering acorns of the tan oak. The acorns were ground to meal (into a coarsely ground state), cooked over heated stones, and served as mush. Sometimes they were cooked as cakes and mixed with other gathered foods, such as nuts, berries, fruits, roots, and various plants.

ALONG REDWOOD CREEK Chilula men were skilled hunters who depended on elk and deer—supplemented with acorns—as their main food source. The Chilula usually roasted fresh meats, and any leftovers were cut into strips, then dried or stored for winter consumption. No part of an animal was wasted. Tribal law did not allow the killing or eating of any bears; the Chilula believed bears were once their relatives.

In their temporary summer and fall camps, Chilula women gathered seeds, strawberries, huckleberries, and salmonberries. During fall they dug for wild potatoes and harvested the all-important acorns. Other key foods included Indian lettuce, clover, wild oats, wild onions, and grasses.

The Chilula fished in Redwood Creek, although it was too small to yield large catches. King salmon were taken with spears and dip nets at the base of waterfalls, and steelhead trout were caught in brushwood nets. The Chilula also developed an elaborate system of weirs (human-made dams) that slowed down eels and trout so they could be speared, harpooned, or netted. (Those Indians who helped build the dam were said to own the spot on which it stood.) A mixture of soap plant bulbs and water was used as well to drug the fish, which were then scooped out of the water in nets.

Education

Children spent most of their early years playing. They were taught religion and good manners, especially proper eating habits. Other skills were learned over time by observing adults. Young boys sometimes joined the men in the sweat houses; they listened to the adults' prayers for hunting success and learned hunting techniques, codes, and religious laws, sometimes taught through stories.

The federal government opened a day school for Indian children shortly after the Hupa and Chilula were moved onto the Hoopa Valley Reservation. The school was very unpopular among Native parents; many refused to send their children there. In an effort to force school attendance, government agents at one point withheld the government-issued clothing intended for reservation children. The school ended up closing after only a few years.

A boarding school was established on the reservation in 1893, but it, too, was unsuccessful. Funding was inadequate, help was scarce, and supplies were low. Many teachers quit. Those who stayed on treated the children poorly: students were beaten if they did not speak English, and some children were actually leased out to white families as servants.

The reservation is currently served by the Klamath-Trinity Unified School District, which operates schools in the area. There is a branch of the College of the Redwoods in nearby Hoopa, and Humboldt State University is located in the neighboring city of Arcata. In the mid-1990s about 62 percent of the adults on the reservation had completed high school or some college.

Healing practices

Like many tribes the Hupa and Chilula believed that illnesses were caused by supernatural forces; a hired doctor was called in to treat and cure them.

The Chilula had two kinds of doctors: medicine healers, who treated patients with plants, and shamans (*SHAY-munz*), who had the ability to suck the ailment out of a sick person's body. Both men and women served as doctors, but the more powerful shamans were usually men. The primary healing power came from language. A shaman could treat a person by speaking directly to his or her spirit with words that neither person understood. Sometimes the shaman prayed, danced, sang, and blew smoke over the patient. If the sick person did not recover or died shortly after treatment, the shaman refunded the payment for his services.

Shamans went through a long and difficult training period. The Chilula were considered the most skilled doctors in northwestern California. Chilula shaman trainees learned their trade at Dancing Doctor Rock, considered the tribe's most sacred site. At this rock the shaman-in-training fasted, sang, danced, and looked for a vision from a spirit. (Female shamans, though rare, always acquired their healing powers from Tan, the deer spirit.) In modern times the tribe was served by its own Hoopa Tribal Clinic and by a hospital located in the city of Hoopa.

ARTS

The Hupa have always been well known for their elaborately decorated woven baskets depicting geometric figures in red, white, and black. Examples of Hupa baskets and dance costumes are on display at the Hupa Tribal Museum, a popular tourist destination.

The Hupa also had a distinctive singing style (most music was sung), with minimal accompaniment by wooden clappers, bone whistles, and sometimes drums.

Oral literature

The most popular subject of Hupa and Chilula stories centered on how the Immortals devised the way of life followed by the people.

Hupa baskets.

Both adults and children also enjoyed humorous stories about a sly, supernatural figure called Coyote, who sometimes helped people but more often caused trouble.

CUSTOMS

Quest for riches

Being wealthy was more important to the Hupa and their neighbors than to any other Native group in California. Wealth was measured in terms of how much money a person had (they used shells for money, strung on cords and wound with strips of fish skin). Other prized possessions of the wealthy included deerskins (especially those of unusual colors) and the scalps of the red-feathered woodpecker (attached to buckskin bands). These valuable items were only used for very important purchases, such as a bride or the services of a healer. Other evidence of a person's wealth were the site of the family home and the productivity of the fishing, hunting, and gathering places a person owned.

The tribal desire to possess wealth cannot be attributed to greed. According to the Hupa belief system, everything that existed was a spiritual being. It was more to the point that a person who possessed many things would be able to harness the spirit power connected with those things. If the possessor offended the spirits, it was possible for those things—and the powers that went with them—to simply go away.

Festivals and ceremonies

The two major religious ceremonies of the northwestern California Indians were the White Deerskin Dance and the Jumping Dance, each of which could last up to 16 days. Both dances were part of the World Renewal Cycle, held in late summer or early fall to ensure that natural resources would renew themselves, that life would go on as it always had, and that disasters would be averted or prevented. The Immortals laid down the exact words and order for the ceremonies, and these instructions were followed to the letter. The White Deerskin and Jumping dances offered major opportunities for wealthy people to display their riches. Ceremonial festivities included singing, gameplaying, storytelling, and, of course, dancing.

Lesser ceremonies—conducted in strategic locations—were also associated with the cycle. For example, a village near a salmon run would host a First Salmon Ceremony. Thousands of participants from villages throughout northwestern California would gather for it, then they would move on to another village near acorn-hunting territory to take part in an Acorn Feast.

In the late 1990s these and other ceremonies were being held each year on the Hoopa Valley Reservation. All of them were open to the public. Modern additions to the ceremonial cycle included a Logging Show in May; the Whitewater Boat Race, held on Mother's Day and Father's Day; the Hoopa Open Rodeo in June; a Fourth of July Celebration; and tribe-sponsored softball and basketball tournaments.

Puberty

No special ceremony was observed for boys who reached puberty. The onset of a girl's first menstrual period was a sacred time and was celebrated with a dance. First, the girl stayed in a secluded house for 10 days, where she ate only acorn soup and salmon and bathed twice a day in a sacred pool. Her isolation provided her with time to think about the importance of cleanliness, independence, and patience. After the 10 days were up, she was considered a woman.

Courtship and marriage

Girls were considered ready for marriage at age 15 or 16, and boys were ready at 16 or 17. Courtship was basically a business transaction. A boy's family sent a representative to bargain with the girl's family, and a generous price was negotiated. Following a feast and gift exchange, the newly married couple lived in the husband's village. Poor young men might arrange a "half-marriage," paying half–price for the bride and moving in with her family.

The Immortals left a legacy of restrictions on the daily lives of the Hupa and Chilula; as a result, meditation and prayer accompanied most of their activities. Northwestern California Indians had a unique custom whereby men and women lived together only in the summer, even if they were married. Through the cold months and during the fall hunting season, men slept in sweat houses and women stayed in the family home. Some historians theorize that men avoided women because they considered them in some way inferior. Others speculate that the men were simply demonstrating self-control—the mark of a good man.

The birthing process

Pregnant women avoided certain foods and offered prayers for an easy birth. When she was ready to have her baby, the mother-to-be would go off to the menstrual house to give birth; the father remained in the sweat house. The newborn child was placed in a basket and held over steaming water that contained herbs; this ritual was thought to allow the baby's soul to enter its body.

After 10 days of isolation, mother and child rejoined their family in their home. The baby was placed sitting up in a cradle basket and, until it could walk, was allowed outside only for exercise and bathing. It was called "baby" or a similar impersonal name until receiving a real name at about age five.

Funerals

The Hupa and Chilula differed in their treatment of the dead. The bodies of Hupa dead were disposed of quickly. They were tied to boards and buried in graves lined with planks to form boxes. Relatives were expected to wail, or cry, from the time of their loved one's death until the burial process was completed. They also cut their hair in mourning, wore necklaces to ward off dreams of the dead, and were forbidden to speak the dead person's name. The Hupa believed that the dead haunted the village for four days before journeying on to the land of the dead.

When a Chilula person died, the body was covered with a deerskin blanket and remained in the house for five days. A medicine man smoked the house with herbs to ward off evil. The gravedigger was required to observe strict codes, eating only acorn soup and dried salmon while preparing the grave. After being washed, painted, and supplied with acorns and tobacco, the body was buried with its head facing south. To avoid being haunted by the spirit of the dead, the mourners would say over the body: "You are going away from me. You must not think of me." The dead person's name could not be spoken for a full year.

CURRENT TRIBAL ISSUES

Before the arrival of white settlers, the Hupa and Chilula lived in harmony with their surroundings, taking only what they needed. At the end of the twentieth century several environmental organizations were battling with logging companies to prevent the destruction of the Chilula's ancient redwood growing areas.

The Tsnungwe, Hupa people who live on the south fork of the Trinity River, have filed a petition for federal recognition, which was being considered by the U.S. government in the late 1990s. Without federal recognition, the Tsnungwe have no legal relationship with the U.S. government and are not entitled to any benefits (money and other assistance).

The 1988 passage by Congress of the Hoopa-Yurok Settlement Act has created considerable controversy. It was supposed to settle a 25-year-old dispute between the Hupa and Yurok over timber rights. The Yurok, who live on the Hoopa Valley Reservation, claimed that they were entitled to share in the profits from the reservation's old-growth Douglas fir, said to be among the most valuable trees of their kind in the world. Congress awarded timber rights to the Hupa. Under this act, too, Congress for the first time established membership standards determining who could be called a member of the Yurok tribe. Previously, the matter of tribal membership had been left to the discretion of Native Americans.

NOTABLE PEOPLE

David Risling (1921–), a Native American of Hupa, Yurok, and Karok descent, is a champion of improved education, legal rights, and economic advancement for Native Americans. He grew up on the Hoopa Valley Reservation and served in the U.S. Navy during World

War II (1939–45). Risling became director of the Native American Studies program at the University of California-Davis in 1970. In 1991 the university honored him with the Distinguished Public Service Award for his contributions to Native American education. He has written and published the *Handbook of Native American Studies* and other books.

Hupa-Yurok George Blake (1944–) is a noted ceramist, painter, and carver. He was named a National Heritage fellow by the National Endowment for the Arts (NEA) in 1991.

FURTHER READING

Davis, Susan E. "Tribal Rights, Tribal Wrongs (Hoopa, Yurok, and Congress)." In *Nation,* March 23, 1992, vol. 254, no. 11, p. 376.

Fletcher, Jill, and others, compilers. *Now You're Speaking Hupa!* Arcata, CA: Humboldt State University, 1995. Available from Center for Indian Community Development, Humboldt State University, Arcata, CA 95521 (telephone: (707) 826–3711; e–mail: njh1@axe.humboldt.edu).

Johnson, Michael. "Northwest Coast." *The Native Tribes of North America.* New York: Macmillan, 1992.

Lake, Robert G. *Chilula: People from the Ancient Redwoods.* Washington, DC: University Press of America, 1982.

Landau, Elaine. *The Chilulas.* New York: Franklin Watts, 1994.

Luiseño

Name

The Luiseño (pronounced *lew-wee-SAY-nyoh*) were named by the Spanish for the Catholic mission at San Luis Rey. The name the tribe went by before the arrival of the Spanish is not known. The Luiseño at San Juan Capistrano were called "Acjachemen." Luiseño called coastal tribal members "Payó mkawcum."

Location

The Luiseño lived along the Pacific Coast, in inland southern California, and in the Channel Islands off southern California. They inhabited a diverse 1,500-square-mile region that extended along the coast from Aliso Creek, south to Agua Hedionda Creek, and inland to include Santiago Peak, Palomar Mountain, and part of the valley of San Jose. Their territory encompassed the northwestern section of present-day San Diego County and southwestern Riverside County. At the end of the twentieth century six Luiseño bands were located on six reservations throughout the mid-southern California area (La Jolla, Pala, Pechanga, Pauma-Yuima, Rincon, and Soboba).

Population

About 10,000 Luiseño were known to exist prior to Spanish contact. In a census (count of the population) conducted in 1990 by the U.S. Bureau of the Census, 2,798 people identified themselves as Luiseño (see box on page 1053 for breakdown).

Language family

Uto-Aztecan.

Origins and group affiliations

According to archaeologists and linguists, the Luiseño may have migrated into southern California from the Great Basin (a 189,000-mile elevated region in the northwestern United States) as many as 7,000 to 8,000 years ago. Though formerly considered a separate group, the Juaneño (so named by the Spanish) are now known to have been a part of the Luiseño tribe. The Luiseño had much in common with their neighbors, the Cupeño, Gabrieliño, Cahuilla (see entry), and Yuma tribes

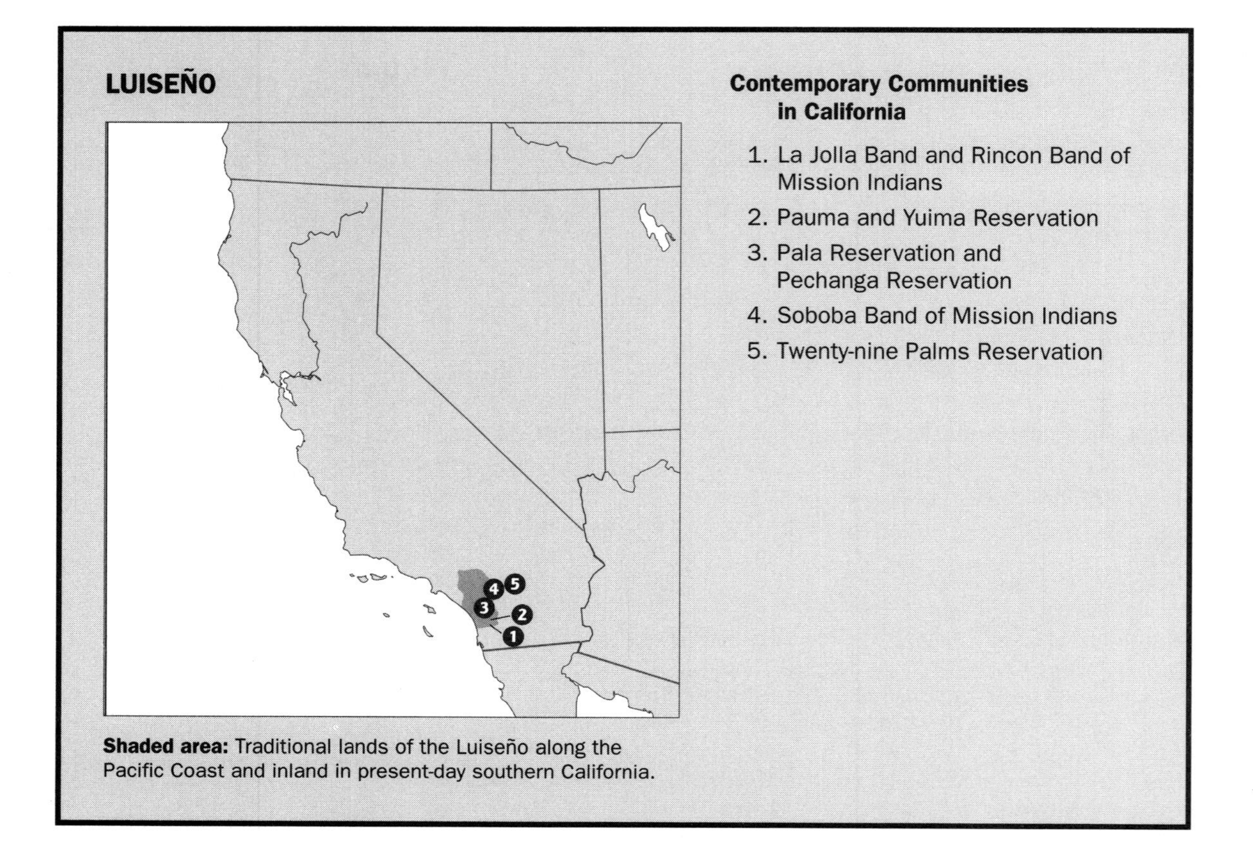

Shaded area: Traditional lands of the Luiseño along the Pacific Coast and inland in present-day southern California.

The Luiseño, like the Cahuilla and Chumash (see entries), are sometimes called Mission Indians because they became part of the Roman Catholic mission system built by the Spanish in California in the late 1700s. For centuries before, they had lived a comfortable life off the bounty of the land. They tended to keep to themselves and did not travel far to trade, although they usually married someone from outside their own villages. The Luiseño were somewhat more warlike than other California tribes, engaging in battles when their neighbors trespassed on their lands or when they could not gain access to the resources of neighboring territory through marriage.

HISTORY

Luiseño encounter Spanish

The land of the Luiseño was varied. Some groups lived along the Pacific Coast, some in the southern Channel Islands, others lived in the green valleys of the California interior or on mountain tops. The climate was mild in some parts, but other areas were subject to extreme heat and periods of drought. On the whole, though, the living was fairly easy. The tribe had fished, hunted, and gathered there for centuries before white settlers came upon their territory.

The Luiseño may have had contact with Spanish expeditions as early as 1542, when Portuguese explorer Juan Rodriguez Cabrillo sailed along the coast, leading a small fleet of Spanish ships in search of riches and a sea lane to China. The tribe's first confirmed encounter with the Spanish occurred in 1769, when a group led by Gaspar de Portollá ventured into California.

IMPORTANT DATES

1776: The mission of San Juan Capistrano is founded in Luiseño territory.

1798: The mission of San Luis Rey is founded in Luiseño territory.

1839: The first written account of Luiseño culture is written by Luiseño author Pablo Tac.

1847: The Luiseño are massacred at Temecua by the Mexican Militia and rival Cahuilla in the bloodiest battle of the Mexican period in California.

1875: The Luiseño and others sign the Treaty of Temecua with the United States, which is later rejected by the U.S. Senate.

1882: The first Luiseño reservations are established.

1891: The Act for the Relief of the Mission Indians is passed, and a system is founded to allow reservations to become self-supporting.

1950s: The Luiseño assume more control over reservation affairs.

1998: Access to and control of water sources continues to be a major issue for the tribe.

Spanish intentions

The Spanish came to establish a firm hold on California territory, but as the eighteenth century progressed England and Russia began showing interest in the North American Pacific Coast as well. In an effort to discourage further European advancement into the area, the Spanish built a series of forts on the land. Spain claimed the land as its own and actually believed that the California Indians would help protect this "Spanish" land as soon as they were "civilized" (schooled in European ways and able to follow Spanish orders). The Spanish government asked Roman Catholic priests (*padres*) to assist in the massive task of controlling the Indians. The priests had their own goal of converting the Natives to the Catholic religion, so they agreed to help and began building missions with forced Indian labor. Each mission was centered on a church and a European-style farm/ranch.

The first California mission was established in 1769. Although the mission was not situated within their territory, the Luiseño were struck hard by European diseases almost immediately. The mission of San Juan Capistrano was built in Luiseño territory in 1776, and, ravaged by the spread of disease, a weakened population found it hard to resist the padres' invitation to settle there. In 1798 Mission San Luis Rey was established on the tribe's territory, and an outpost called an

The Mission San Luis Rey de Francia, built in 1798 in Luiseño territory.

"asistencia" was erected at Pala 18 years later. The missionaries soon lured most of the Luiseño population into the mission system.

Mission Indians

Spanish settlers and missionaries worked hand in hand, manipulating the Indian people to satisfy their own goals of growth and expansion. The padres claimed their only interest was in converting the Natives to the Catholic religion, but history tells us that the missions survived on the sweat of the Indians. Disciplined Indian labor was needed to satisfy the demands of increasing numbers of Spanish settlers in California. The missionaries taught the Luiseño the basics of the Spanish language (enough so that the Natives could understand orders). They also instructed them in farming techniques and European-style trades such as carpentry and masonry (brickwork)—skills Spanish settlers valued.

Spanish treatment of the Luiseño differed somewhat from their treatment of other Mission Indians. Some Luiseño lived at the missions, but others were allowed to stay in their own communities and receive instruction from visiting padres. Still, many Luiseño became paid workers in trades such as carpentry, tanning (converting hide into leather), blacksmithing, and weaving—occupations that were far removed from their traditional lifestyle.

The Mission system takes its toll

The European-run missions were crowded and unsanitary; they acted as breeding grounds for diseases to which Native Americans had no resistance. Historians estimate that the Luiseño population declined 40 percent during the mission period.

End of the mission system

Mexico won independence from Spain in 1821 and took over the California missions in 1834. Mexican officials vowed that they would give the Mission Indians choice pieces of land, but the mission land ended up in the hands of Mexican settlers, who poured into California to claim their share of the Indian territory. Some Luiseño became unpaid laborers on Mexican-owned ranches, but others moved inland, seeking shelter among other Indian groups there. Those who worked for the Mexicans were treated poorly and staged violent rebellions from time to time. However, the Luiseño who remained in their traditional villages continued to live as they had before, but now blending Spanish and Indian economies, with the introduction of cattle raising and farming.

California became a part of the United States after the Mexican War of 1846 (a two-year war between the United States and Mexico over land that is now part of the American Southwest). Droves of American settlers rushed into California, hungry for Native land. To avoid the conflicts and to get wage labor jobs, some Luiseño migrated to Los Angeles, located in the southwestern portion of the state.

Luiseño reservations established

Tensions between the Luiseño and white settlers in California became so high that in 1875 Luiseño chief Olegario Sal went to Washington, D.C., to request that reservations be set aside for his people. That same year some Native people in California began moving onto reservation lands. Meanwhile, the U.S. government formed a committee, headed by writer Helen Hunt Jackson, whose novels *A Century of Dishonor* and *Ramona* brought the mistreatment of Native Americans to the public's attention, to investigate the condition of life among former Mission Indians and make recommendations. Jackson's report led the government to grant more land to the Luiseño in 1882 and 1883.

Luiseño Jose Pedro Losero, photographed in 1899 by C. Wharton James.

The federal government provided only minimal assistance in setting up the reservations—far less, it seems, than promised. Then, in 1891—a full 16 years after the establishment of the first Luiseño reservation—the Act for the Relief of the Mission Indians was passed. This act created five Luiseño reservations and included provisions designed to help the Native population develop an American lifestyle (a policy called "assimilation") and eventually become self-supporting. A sixth reservation, Soboba, was officially established in 1913.

Agents from the Bureau of Indian Affairs were sent to oversee the reservations. They established schools, Indian courts of law, medical clinics, and other services. But not all agents of the Bureau represented the best interests of the Native population. Corrupt agents caused so much friction among the Luiseño that the Mission Indian Federation (MIF) was founded in 1919 to resolve the problems. The MIF worked for more independence for tribal governments, full civil rights for Indians, more generous water rights (see "Current tribal issues"), and the elimination of the Bureau of Indian Affairs. (It still exists.)

The federal government continued to be involved in reservation affairs, and the Luiseño grew more and more unhappy with its methods. By the 1950s the Luiseño began to assume more control, taking active leadership roles to make sure their voices were heard when decisions affecting the reservations were made by local, state, and national governments. By the end of the 1990s most Luiseño were living on or near the reservations, and they maintained many of their old customs.

RELIGION

According to ancient Luiseño traditions, a creator called Wiyót took an empty world that already existed, filled it with all things, and gave it order. (See box titled "The Death of Wiyót, the Creator.") Later the Luiseño came to believe in a savior called *Chinigchinix,* who made the Earth, then died and went to heaven. From there he watched but seldom interfered with worldly affairs, only occasionally sending vengeful animals and other terrible punishments to those who disobeyed his teachings. Historians think the Chinigchinix religion probably developed in response to Spanish presence on tribal land.

Most Luiseño men sought membership in the Chinigchinix religion's secret society. In order to belong to the society, the males had to prove their physical endurance. The Chinigchinix religion had rigid rules that governed many aspects of peoples' lives, including hunting, warfare, harvesting, puberty, and mourning rituals. It also included many songs, dances, and *toloache* ceremonies. Toloache, a drug obtained from the jimsonweed plant, causes those who consume it to enter a trancelike state and see visions. Sacred knowledge was said to be revealed during these visions.

Catholic missionaries converted many Luiseño to Catholicism, a religion that is still practiced by most of the tribespeople. Despite the strong, centuries-long Christian presence among the Luiseño, though, traditional beliefs and practices have survived.

LANGUAGE

The Luiseño were the most southwesterly speakers of a language of the Uto-Aztecan family in the United States. By the 1970s their language was being spoken by only a few elder members of the tribe, but interest in the language was on the rise, language classes were being organized, and a language textbook had been written.

GOVERNMENT

The Luiseño lived in independent groups, each with its own clearly defined territory. At the head of each group was a powerful chief called a *nota*. This position was usually filled by a man, but a few female *notas* are known to have existed. The nota oversaw warfare, economic ventures (organizing gathering projects, for example), and the activities of religious chiefs (called *paxa*) and healers (called shamans; pronounced *SHAY-munz*).

During the mission period, Indian villages maintained the basic elements of the old style of self-government, but a new position of leadership developed—that of representative of the Luiseño to Europeans. Once the federal government began to oversee the reservations, it tried to weaken traditional authority by insisting that tribal leaders be approved by U.S. government agents.

The Luiseño objected to government interference in tribal affairs and managed to assume more control over them. In the late 1990s each reservation elected its own tribal chairperson and tribal council. To a greater extent than other California tribes, the Luiseño are involved in state and local groups that work to promote the well-being of Native Americans.

ECONOMY

Before the Spanish settled on Luiseño territory, the Native economy was rooted in hunting and gathering, usually on sites not far from home. Some property was owned by the group, and activities such as hunting, gambling, and ceremonies took place there. Other pieces of property—stands of oaks or tobacco gardens, for example—were owned by individuals or families. Groups who lived inland had special places on the coast where they went to fish and gather at a given time each year.

The Spanish missionaries taught the Native peoples how to farm and tend cattle. Although all the Luiseño engaged in these activities by the 1850s, they did not abandon their hunting and gathering practices completely.

During World War I (1914–18), Luiseño volunteers served in the U.S. armed forces or left the reservations to work in defense industries. After the war some continued to work in these industries, while others returned to the reservations and took up cattle raising and farming. Aside from those who pursue work in agriculture, the Luiseño are employed in a variety of fields, including carpentry, education, and engineering. Still, the Luiseño reservations face serious economic problems. Possible solutions to these problems are being sought through (1) the sale and leasing of land and natural resources, (2) gambling operations, and (3) various recreation-related businesses.

LUISEÑO IN THE 1990 CENSUS OF POPULATION

When a census was taken in 1990, a total of 2,798 people claimed they were Luiseño. Some identified themselves according to their reservation. This is how the Luiseño reported themselves to the U.S. Bureau of the Census:

Reservation	Population
La Jolla	162
Luiseño	1,757
Pala	549
Pauma	120
Pechanga	210
Total	**2,798**

DAILY LIFE

Buildings

The Luiseño lived in cone-shaped houses. The foundation of the house was partially underground, situated on a pit that was two to three feet deep. Construction materials included reeds, brush, and cedar bark. The only openings to the dwelling were the entrance and a smokehole. Near the house was a light, rectangular tentlike structure—called a *ramada* by the Spanish—where some household chores were performed.

Settlements also contained oval-shaped earthen sweat houses, used for purification and during some curing rituals. Each permanent settlement contained a religious enclosure, called a *wamkish,* set up in the center of the village and enclosed by a brush fence. During the acorn season, the Luiseño moved to temporary camps near stands of oak trees.

Clothing and adornment

Luiseño men usually wore no clothes in warm weather. During cold weather they wore fur capes of rabbit and deerskin; those who lived along the Pacific Coast also wore capes of sea otter skins. Women wore aprons, called *pishkwut,* which were made from plants such as dogbane (a tropical, often poisonous, plant with milky juice and big flowers) and milkweed or willow bark and cottonwood bark. Both sexes let their hair grow long. Women covered their heads with coiled caps similar to baskets; men also wore caps to protect themselves when they carried loads on their heads.

The Luiseño usually wore sandals but might put on deerskin moccasins while traveling on rough ground. They wore necklaces of bear claws, stones, and abalone (pronounced *AB-uh-LONE-ey*; a type of shellfish) shells, as well as bracelets and anklets made from human hair. Men pierced their ears and noses and wore decorations made from cane or bones. Men and women both wore tattoos and body paints.

Food

The Luiseño lived on acorns, wild plants, and small game. Usually men hunted and women gathered, but everyone pitched in to help gather the acorns produced by the six species of oak found in their territory. Acorns were stored in granaries until they were prepared and eaten. Various other kinds of seeds—such as sage, sunflower, manzanita (a type of evergreen shrub) and pine nuts—were also gathered. The seeds were heated and then ground into flour.

Women also gathered greens, such as miner's lettuce and white sage. Although not abundant in Luiseño territory, some fruits were harvested as well, including plums, manzanita berries, choke cherries, Christmas berries, and elderberries. The Luiseño practiced a custom called controlled burning (setting fire to some land), which helped some desirable crops grow better and encouraged larger rabbit populations for hunting.

Before a hunt, Luiseño men purified themselves in the sweat house, burning white sage and other herbs on the fire. They usually hunted game like rabbits, jackrabbits, and deer. They trapped woodrats, mice, quails, larks, and ducks, and took black-tailed deer and antelope with bows and arrows, snares, and nets, or by clubbing. Sometimes the hunters wore deer-head disguises so they could approach their prey without being noticed. The meat was broiled over hot coals or cooked in an earth oven.

The Luiseño who lived along the coast depended on fish and mussels as their primary source of food. They also fished for trout in the upper San Luis Rey River; a common fishing technique involved drugging the fish (by putting herbal mixtures in the water) and then scooping them into nets.

Education

While their parents and older siblings were off hunting and gathering, very young Luiseño children were taught traditional arts and crafts by elders who stayed behind. They also learned about goals and values—things essential for their growth into responsible adults.

Older men taught boys practical skills such as how to make fish nets and arrows. In addition, the older men decided which boys would be chosen to learn how to conduct ceremonies and make important decisions affecting the village. There was also formal instruction in male and female puberty rituals.

Under the mission system, children learned religion, Spanish, and skills like farming, caring for livestock, and carpentry. In the late 1800s government schools were established; their main goal was to immerse the Natives in white American culture. The schools were poorly run and finally closed in the 1930s. Luiseño children now attend nearby public schools. Because education is so highly prized by the Luiseño people, the reservations supplement public education with programs that teach children about their Native culture. And since the 1960s many Luiseño have taken advantage of opportunities to attend college.

Healing practices

Traditional Luiseño healing methods involved the use of plants to treat illnesses. Wounds were treated with wild onion and cooked and crushed tule (marsh plant) leaves, for example. Still, the tribe believed that some illnesses could only be treated by a shaman. Evil shamans could make people sick by casting a spell over a personal item such as a lock of hair or a broken fingernail, so people were very careful when disposing of such items. Only a shaman had the power to cure a sickness caused by another shaman.

Some forms of sickness were thought to be caused by foreign objects. A common method of treatment was symbolic in nature: the shaman would dramatize the healing process by "sucking out" the object that caused the illness, usually stones or beetles. Even at the dawn of the twenty-first century, some of the old medicines and healing techniques were still used. When traditional methods failed, though, assistance could be obtained from health clinics on the reservations and hospitals located in nearby cities.

ARTS

The California tribes ranked among the world's best basketmakers. Two types of baskets were made: coiled and twined. The Luiseño are best known for their beautiful coiled baskets with dark tan, red, and black geometric designs.

CUSTOMS

Ceremonies and games

Most traditional ceremonies revolved around the life cycle: birth, puberty, marriage, and death. Many present-day Luiseño celebrate Catholic feast days such as saints' days (days set aside to celebrate the lives of various saints). Catholic priests conduct rites such as baptism, confirmation, marriages, and funerals. In the 1990s traditional singers began to perform in public and at community events.

Traditional games are still played by the Luiseño. A favorite of both men and women is the peon game, a guessing game played by two teams, in which singing and magic aid the competitors.

Puberty

Complex coming-of-age ceremonies were held for boys and girls of the Luiseño tribe. Both ceremonies were conducted by a religious chief from a different village, whose role was to teach the rules of the Chinigchinix religion. Boys and girls were required to watch the religious chief create a special sand painting, depicting elements of the universe such as the Milky Way and the various animals that the Creator might send to punish people. Through these sand paintings, the religious chief taught the traditions, customs, and moral codes of Luiseño society.

BOYS' RITUAL In their puberty ritual, Luiseño boys took the drug *toloache* (see "Religion"), saw visions, and learned sacred songs and dances. They endured a number of discomforts—being lashed with nettles (prickly plants) and bitten by ants—and refrained from eating certain foods. The boys were then instructed to respect their elders and to let generosity, not greed, rule their hearts. The Luiseño believed that obeying these rules would help them to live long and well; on the other hand, disobedience would lead to sickness and death. At the end of the lecture, the boys would take a mouthful of salt mixed with white flour made from the sage plant, then spit it onto the ground. If the spit-out lump was dry, it was a sign that the boy was paying attention to the advice. A moist lump indicated that the boy had not been listening.

GIRLS' RITUAL Girls undergoing the puberty ritual assembled in the village's sacred enclosure and ate a lump of tobacco mixed with water. Any girl able to keep the tobacco down was considered virtuous; a girl who vomited up the mixture was not. Girls remained in a heated pit for three days and nights, leaving only for short periods to eat and to reheat the pit with hot rocks. Dancing and singing took place around them. At the end of the three days each girl's face was

THE DEATH OF WIYÓT, THE CREATOR

According to the Luiseño, Wiyót was one of the first beings. He took an empty world that already existed, filled it with all things, and gave it order. Everyone was supposed to live forever, but Wiyót's own death, as described in the story below, introduced death into the world.

Once Wiyót died, his people lost the knowledge of living forever (immortality). Rituals for the dead had to be invented so that the spirits of the dead could be freed from Earth. The Luiseño clothes-burning ceremony, for instance, releases the deceased's clothes from this world. These rituals keep the spirits happy.

Wiyót was the son of Túkumit [night, or night sky] and Tamáyawùt [Earth Mother]. He was called "father" by the people who lived on the Earth. Frog was the prettiest of all the women. One day Wiyót saw her swimming, and he observed that her body was thin and not beautiful. She was repulsive to him. Knowing his thoughts, she said to herself: "My father does not like me. I will kill him by magic." She secured the aid of Badger, Gopher, and other [burrowing animals], and they [cast a spell on] him. He fell sick. Four shamans were called: Wasímal [a hawk], Sakapípi [titmouse], Púipi [roadrunner], and Chaláka [horned toad]. [But they could not cure him.] And then the people knew [a spell had been cast upon] Wiyót. The other shamans tried their power in vain. Then Wiyót called Chehémal [kingbird], and told him that after death he would appear in the sky. Soon he was dead. They placed the body on a pile of wood to burn it. Then came Coyote. He seized the heart and carried it away. Three days later the Moon appeared in the sky, and Chehémal exclaimed, "Oh, there is my father, Mâila [moon] Wiyót!"

SOURCE: Edward S. Curtis. "Southern California Shoshoneans." In *The North American Indian.* Volume 15. Edited by Frederick Webb Hodge. New York: Johnson Reprint Corporation, 1970.

painted with a special design; a similar design was painted on a rock. This rite was conducted once a month for a year.

Like the boys, girls abstained from certain foods (meat and salt) for one year. At the end of the puberty rite, they listened to a lecture advising them on conduct and tradition.

Marriage

Marriages were arranged by parents, who usually helped choose mates from other villages so a family's access to their in-law's resources could be expanded. (In the late twentieth century Luiseño women often married into neighboring reservations, not to expand territory but to expand Luiseño influence.) Sometimes marriage arrangements dated back to infancy, but a couple waited at least until they had reached puberty to marry. A ceremony was performed by the religious chief, and the couple moved in with the groom's family.

Children

A special ceremony was performed when a child was born, confirming that the child belonged to its father's family.

Death

The Luiseño cremated their dead. As part of the ceremony, tribal members would blow upward three times to release the spirit of the dead person into the sky. In a mourning ceremony held a year after a person died, his or her possessions were burned. The mourning ceremony, which is still held in present times, evolved after the death of the ancient Luiseño god Wiyót. (See box on page 1057.)

CURRENT TRIBAL ISSUES

According to Luiseño expert Florence Connolly Shipek: "Water continues to be a constant concern" for the tribe. Since the late 1800s conflicts have arisen between people on the reservations and people in cities near them concerning water rights. The diversion of water away from reservations has ruined Luiseño farms and orchards, forcing people to move off the reservation to seek work elsewhere. Several lawsuits have been filed. Some Luiseño groups have received money to settle their claims; other cases had not been settled as the twentieth century drew to a close.

NOTABLE PEOPLE

Edward D. Castillo (1947–) is a university professor specializing in Native American Studies. He has a doctoral degree in anthropology and has taught and lectured about Native Americans at various universities in California. Castillo has published many articles and books on anthropology and Native American Studies, but he is probably best known for the chapters he wrote in Volume 8 of the Smithsonian Institution's massive set of reference books called *Handbook of North American Indians.*

Fritz Scholder (1937–) is a leading modern artist in the United States. His works often deal with themes relating to the Native American experience. Although his grandmother was a member of the Luiseño tribe, Scholder describes himself as "a non-Indian Indian." His critics complain that his "pop art" is shallow and casts Native American problems in a superficial light, but his work remains popular nationwide.

James Luna, Luiseño/Diegueño (1950–), is an installation and performance artist whose work explores (usually with humor) what it's like to be a Native American. His artwork, featured in museums throughout the nation, also encourages his audience to examine the ways they perceive Native Americans.

Mark Macarro, Pechanga tribal chair in the 1990s, is a spokesperson for Indians' rights in terms of operating gambling casinos in California, where legislation in the late 1990s has threatened the tribes who now run casinos with interference from the state government.

FURTHER READING

Bean, Lowell John, and Florence C. Shipek. "Luiseño." In *Handbook of North American Indians.* Vol. 8: *California.* Edited by Robert F. Heizer. Washington, DC: Smithsonian Institution, 1978.

Harvey, Herbert R. "The Luiseño." In *California Indians 11.* New York: Garland Publishing, 1974.

Shipek, Florence Connolly. "Luiseño." In *Native America in the Twentieth Century: An Encyclopedia.* Edited by Mary B. Davis. New York: Garland Publishing, 1994.

Maidu

Name

The name Maidu (pronounced *MY-doo*) comes from the tribe's term for "person." They did not use this name to refer to themselves and may not have had any name for themselves.

Location

The Maidu's traditional lands were in northeastern and north-central parts of present-day California. They live on and around the rancherias (see "History") of Auburn, Berry Creek, Chico, Enterprise, Greenville, Mooretown, and Susanville, and on the Round Valley Reservation, mostly in Plumas and Butte counties.

Population

In 1846, there were about 9,000 Maidu. In 1910, there were about 1,100. In a census (count of the population) done in 1990 by the U.S. Bureau of the Census, 2,334 people identified themselves as Maidu.

Language family

Penutian.

Origins and group affiliations

The Maidu, who have lived in California for thousands of years, consisted of three groups: the Mountain Maidu, Concow (or Konkow), and Nissenan. Today the name *Maidu* is used to refer to all three groups. The Maidu were friends with the Paiute to the east but harbored ill will toward the Washo, the Achumawi (see Pit River Indians), and the Yana (see entry).

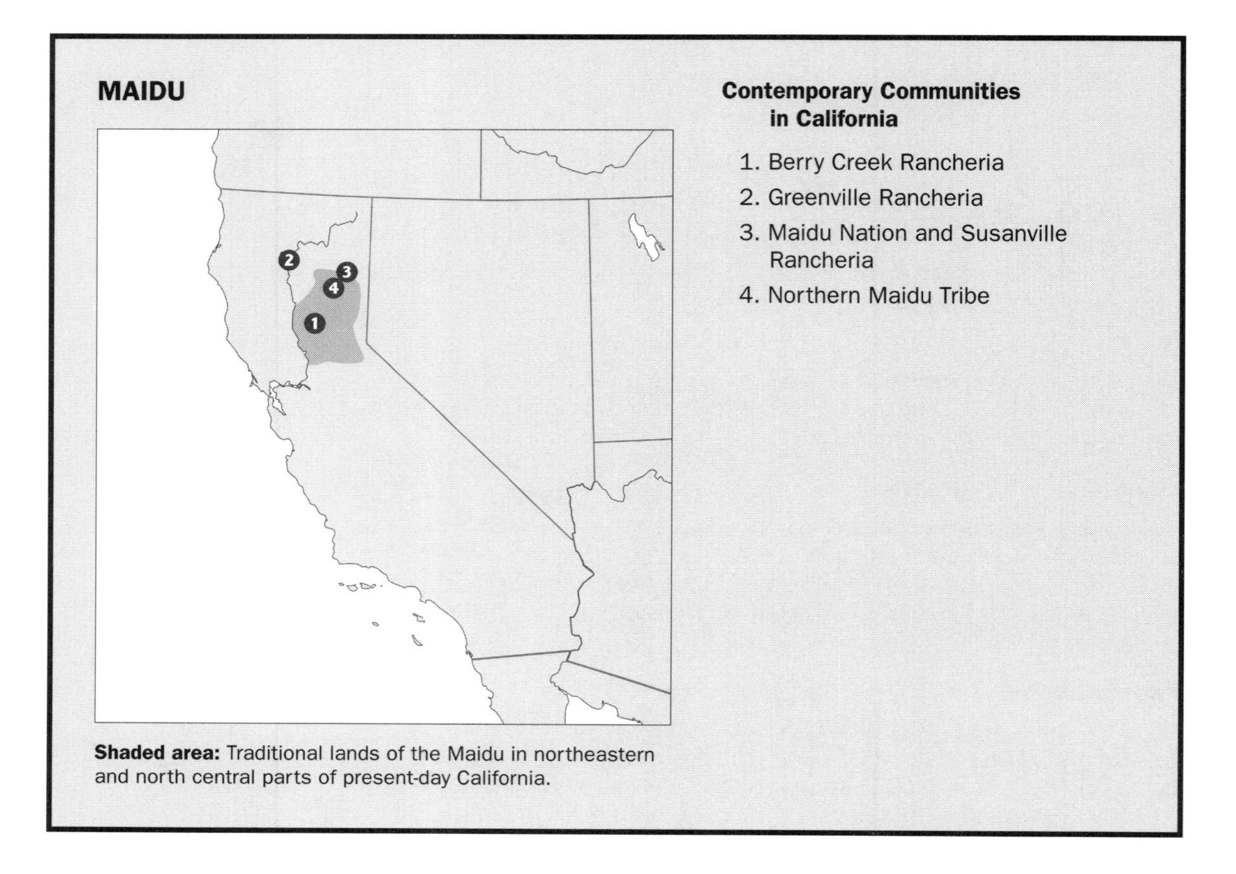

Shaded area: Traditional lands of the Maidu in northeastern and north central parts of present-day California.

In the high mountain meadows, valleys, and foothills of the Sierra Nevada range, to the floor of the Sacramento Valley and along the Sacramento River, the Maidu lived a fairly comfortable and peaceful existence of hunting, gathering, and fishing. They enjoyed a generally mild climate, plenty of food, and a rich spiritual and cultural life—until the invasion of gold miners in 1848.

HISTORY

Life before the invasion

The Maidu once controlled a large amount of territory in what is now California and were one of the most populous groups there. Their homeland in northern and central California has been inhabited by humans for at least 8,000 years, and other people probably lived there before the Maidu.

Groups of Maidu people built permanent villages because they did not have to travel far to search for food. The majority of these hardy people usually stayed in their villages to face the winter. When the season was right, they set up temporary camps near hunting and gathering areas.

Although the California tribes tended to be the least warlike of Native American tribes, the Maidu sometimes engaged in warfare with their enemies or in feuds among themselves. They fought over such issues as trespassing on hunting grounds. Sometimes they carried out sneak attacks or kidnapped or murdered hostages, but enemies often made up and resumed trading and gambling with one another.

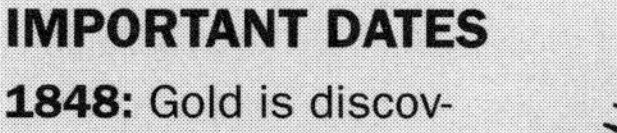

IMPORTANT DATES

1848: Gold is discovered on Maidu lands.

1851: Treaties are negotiated between the Maidu and the U.S. government to remove the Maidu to reservations. The forced relocation of the Maidu to a reservation begins.

1958: Congress passes the Rancheria Act, which results in the termination of several Maidu rancherias.

1990s: Three terminated rancherias are still seeking reversal of their terminated status.

European contact is disastrous

The Spanish were the first white people to build large-scale settlements in California, beginning in the 1700s, but the Maidu had little if any direct contact with them. They caught diseases such as smallpox and malaria from American trappers and traders who passed through their territory in the early 1800s, and many Maidu died. For the most part, whites were discouraged from exploring the land of the Maidu until the mid-1800s because it was mountainous and hard to travel.

The destruction of the Maidu way of life that began with the white man's diseases was completed after the discovery of gold in the foothills of the Sierra Nevada mountain range in 1848. The Maidu knew about the gold but considered it of no value. Far more interesting than gold were the white man's ropes, which made better bridges than the grape vines the Maidu had been using.

Gold fever

Thousands of people from all over the globe with "gold fever" poured into Maidu lands. Many merely wanted to get rich quickly and leave, giving no thought to the feelings and traditions of the native peoples whose land they were ruining. The miners regarded the Natives as hostile savages, and treated them with violence.

The discovery of gold was a disaster from which the Maidu never recovered. From an estimated population of 9,000 in 1846, just before gold was discovered, the Maidu population fell to 1,100 by 1910.

Careless gold miners polluted the streams that supplied the Maidu with food and drove away game animals. Settlers arrived, whose cattle ate local plants and whose hogs were let loose to forage for the acorns so important to the Native diet. Unable to feed themselves, some Maidu were forced to leave their villages to work in the cities or to work for whites on ranches and farms. They soon found themselves competing for jobs with disappointed gold miners.

Solving the "Indian Problem"

In 1850, only two years after the discovery of gold, discussions began over what to do about the "Indian problem" in California. The U.S. government's solution was to isolate California Natives on reservations. Government officials said that this solution would be for the Indians' protection, because it would prevent the total extinction of Native tribes by the violence of hostile white settlers.

Eighteen treaties were drawn up between the government and California tribes—including the Maidu—beginning in 1851. The tribes agreed to give up most of their lands to the U.S. government in exchange for about 7.5 million acres that would be set aside for reservations. The treaty with the Maidu gave them a large reservation on land where there was no gold. The government expected that the Maidu would learn to farm this land.

White Californians were horrified that so much land was being given away (about eight percent of the state). Such an uproar was raised that the U.S. Senate rejected the treaties. Shortly after, 1.2 million acres were set aside for reservations. The Maidu were to receive a 227-square-mile reservation away from their traditional homeland, where they would be confined with Natives from other cultures.

Maidu refuse to cooperate

Over the next several years, U.S. soldiers repeatedly escorted the Maidu people to the new reservation, which was called *Nome Lackee* by the Wintun tribe of Maidu whose land it originally was. Repeatedly the Maidu left the Nome Lackee Reservation to return to their homeland. White settlers loudly complained about the refusal of the Maidu to settle down and stay put.

In 1857, in frustration, U.S. soldiers rounded up a large group of Maidu, mostly women and children, and forced them to return to the Nome Lackee Reservation. According to Maidu who made the trip, young women had to spend the nights in trees there to protect themselves from the soldiers.

Over the next four decades, the Maidu and other California Natives faced constant violence at the hands of white settlers. In

1858, 461 Natives (including some Maidu) were rounded up and began a five-day forced walk to Round Valley Reservation in present-day Mendocino County. As many as a third of them were murdered or died on the way. Those who made it did not like the conditions under which they were expected to live. Some escaped and fled to remote areas where they tried to avoid contact with white settlers. By the beginning of the twentieth century, they found themselves landless and homeless.

Rancherias established

In 1906 a system was established to address the problem of still-homeless Natives in California. The government bought small parcels of land for them, called *rancherias,* a Spanish term for a small ranch. Much of the rancheria land was located in isolated areas, was too poor to farm, and often lacked developed water sources. Several families from the same tribe settled on each of these parcels.

Between 1906 and 1934, seven rancherias were purchased for the Maidu people. Agents from the U.S. Bureau of Indian Affairs and missionaries from various churches then tried to teach the Maidu to farm and in other ways make them more like white Americans, a policy known as assimilation. But the Maidu found it nearly impossible to support themselves in these circumstances and many people either moved away from the rancheria or became totally dependent on government handouts.

Government changes tactics

Government officials grew impatient because people on the rancherias were not assimilating fast enough. They decided assimilation would take place faster if people lived and worked in cities. So the government adopted a policy called termination. Termination would end the special relationship between the government and Native tribes and peoples, and the Natives would become subject to state laws instead. Once tribes accepted termination, they would receive no government assistance, and tribal landowners would have to pay state property taxes on their land. Since most Natives lived in poverty, taxation and no assistance meant that sooner or later they would lose their land.

Four Maidu rancherias accepted termination before the policy was changed again (see box in Miwok entry "The Rancheria Act"). Many tribal members did indeed lose their land when they could not pay property taxes. The rancheria at Mooretown became a ghost town.

A Maidu altar, a stone mound.

Modern times

The termination policy soon came under heavy criticism, and support for it died. The civil rights movement of the 1960s ushered in a new era of government programs and policies toward Native Americans. They were urged to take more responsibility for their own community and were given funds to assist them. Today the U.S. government has relations with tribal governments at four Maidu rancherias: Berry Creek in Oroville; Greenville in Redding; Maidu Mechoopda in Chico; and Susanville in Susanville, where the Maidu Nation is based. Despite the poverty and oppression they have endured, the Maidu people have preserved many ancient customs, which they have adapted to modern times.

Some traditions and landmarks of the Maidu are preserved at Plumas National Forest. They can be observed along the 67-mile Maidu Indian World Maker Route.

RELIGION

Beliefs

Among the most important of the Maidu gods was their Creator, usually called World Maker, who made a first man called *Kúksu* and a first woman called Morning Star Woman. Next World Maker created a new race of people, and told Kúksu and Morning Star Woman to teach them everything they needed to know about survival, law and order, dancing, and ceremonies. The new race of people—the Maidu—were sent out into the world, speaking many different languages and forming many tribes. Most Maidu believed they were the center of all creation.

World Maker intended for people to live easy, eternal lives, and so death did not at first exist. It was introduced by a figure called Coyote. Coyote was a fun-loving character who sometimes helped people but also made mischief. One example of the mischief he visited on the Maidu was to change the California landscape so it became more rugged, thus making life harder for the Maidu.

Most Maidu believed in individual souls, which they called the heart. When a person died, his or her heart was said to have left. The

THE FIRST GHOST DANCE MOVEMENT

The Ghost Dance of 1870 was a religious movement founded by a member of the Paiute tribe named Wodziwob. He was born in about 1844; by most accounts he died in about 1873, but some say he lived into the twentieth century. Wodzibwob was also known as Gray Hair and Fish Lake Joe, and he lived on the Walker River Reservation in Nevada.

In the late 1860s Wodziwob's people were mourning a number of calamities that had befallen them. They had lost much of their land and their way of life because of the westward expansion of American settlers. They were experiencing a drought and many were starving. Disease epidemics had greatly reduced the population.

Wodziwob brought a welcome message to these suffering people. He said that he had died and visited the spirit world, but had then come back to life and had many tales to tell of his experience. He brought messages for his people from their dead friends and relatives. He said the Indian dead were planning to come back to life and when they did, they would cause great fear among white people. He told his followers that if they performed the Ghost Dance, it would hasten the day when the Indian way of life would be restored and everyone would be happy once again.

Wodziwob's movement came to be known as the Ghost Dance. It soon spread to California tribes and the tribes of the Great Basin. Just as the movement was fading in the late 1800s, another Ghost Dance movement began; it is known as the Ghost Dance of 1890.

soul of a good person traveled along the Milky Way until it reached World Maker. The souls of bad people were reborn to live forever as rocks or bushes. The Maidu also believed that every object had a soul, which was set free when the object was destroyed.

Religious leaders and ceremonies

Maidu priests had mystical powers and could communicate with spirits. Some had both healing power and spirit power, while others had one power or the other but not both.

At their frequent religious ceremonies, the Maidu made offerings to World Maker and to earth spirits; sometimes they acted out stories about their gods. In return for their offerings, the people expected a good relationship with nature. This good relationship brought an abundance of game animals and wild foods, sufficient rain, and so on.

Some Maidu embraced the Ghost Dance religion in the 1870s, adding variations of their own (see box). Because of the efforts of missionaries to suppress Maidu religious beliefs and their expression, the people today tend to keep their beliefs to themselves.

LANGUAGE

Versions of the Penutian language were spoken by a large number of California Natives. Although all the versions were closely related, groups who spoke them often could not understand one another. Today there are very few speakers of Maidu left alive; some say that William Shipley, a professor at the University of California Berkeley, may be the last living speaker. Shipley has translated a number of Maidu myths and stories into English and published them in a book called *The Maidu Indian Myths and Stories of Hanc'ibyjim* (Heydey Books, 1991). The stories were told in 1902 to representatives of the American Museum of Natural History by Hanc'ibyjim, said to have been the last great Maidu storyteller.

GOVERNMENT

Before they had contact with white gold miners, the Maidu were organized into tribelets. In this type of organization, one main village was surrounded by a few minor outlying villages. Communities ranged in size from 100 to 500 persons and were loosely headed by a headman or chief, who lived in the large central village. He actually had very little authority except when major decisions had to be made or during ceremonies. In some tribelets, the chief (usually a man but sometimes a woman) handed down his position to his children. In other tribelets the chief was selected by the villagers or by a powerful person who had received a message from the spirits. The chief often acted with the advice of a council of elders.

The Indian Reorganization Act, passed by the U.S. Congress in 1934, encouraged tribes to form tribal governments that more closely resembled the American system of elective government. Today, Maidu rancherias elect members to a council that handles tribal government affairs.

ECONOMY

For thousands of years the Maidu economy depended on hunting, gathering, and trade. After white men came and made the traditional economy impossible, many Maidu took jobs working for them as farmers and loggers. Today, some Maidu are still employed in the forestry business and others do seasonal work in canneries. Gambling businesses provide jobs on some rancherias.

The Maidu have little land and few natural resources. Poverty is a constant presence on the rancherias. For example, at Susanville, the per capita income was $5,703 in the mid-1990s, compared to a per capita income for other Americans of about $20,000. (Per capita income is the average income one person makes in a year.) Unemployment at

Susanville hovers near 40 percent, which means that well over one-third of people at Susanville who wanted to work could not find work.

DAILY LIFE

Education

TRADITIONAL METHODS Maidu children were expected to imitate adult behavior. As soon as they learned to walk, they had the run of the village and ate and slept wherever they wished. They learned many life lessons from their grandparents, and there was a strong bond between the two generations.

When children misbehaved, their grandparents explained to them the consequences of future bad behavior. They were told, for example, that they might be kidnaped by a fearsome old lady who lurked in the woods.

Young boys in some tribelets were expected to choose a skill they wished to develop, such as fishing or hunting. Girls learned all the skills necessary to be a Maidu Indian woman, including a thorough understanding of plants, basketmaking, and gathering.

MODERN METHODS The U.S. government got involved in the education of Maidu children around the turn of the twentieth century, when they established schools like the Greenville Indian School, where boys were given a military-style education. Girls were trained to be servants. The Greenville Indian School was destroyed in a fire.

At government schools, children faced harsh treatment. They were forbidden to speak their own language and observe other Native customs. Most government schools are no longer in operation and children attend public schools in cities near the reservation. Some Maidu parents feel the public schools do not serve their children well. Susanville Rancheria supplements public school education by offering a cultural program for children during the summer months.

Buildings

WINTER HOMES The Maidu built permanent winter homes and summer shade dwellings. Winter homes, which were partly underground, were built in the spring when the ground was soft enough to dig to a depth of two to four feet. They were small cone-shaped dwellings of cedar bark covered with earth to keep them well insulated.

Inside were shelves that held large baskets full of acorns. Chairs and beds were made of a type of plant material called tule. Beds were covered with blankets made from duck and goose down. Near each dwelling were thatch-covered basketware containers for more acorns.

SUMMER HOMES AND OTHER BUILDINGS When the Maidu were on the move for hunting and gathering season, they built simple shade shelters. These were basically flat-roofed canopies made of oak branches and supported by wooden poles.

Other buildings might include a roundhouse or dance house, where ceremonies were held and the headman of the largest village often lived; sweathouses that were used by up to four or five men at a time to purify themselves; huts where women were confined during their menstrual period; and stations for butchering meat, cleaning fish, cutting wood, and storing acorns.

Food

ACORNS The climate of central California was usually mild, and in most years there was an abundance of food resources to be found within a short distance of Maidu villages. Their major source of food was acorns. Insects and worms sometimes managed to get into the acorn flour during the wintertime; these were eaten either dried or roasted. Those who were too lazy to collect a sufficient supply of acorns for winter were forced to seek shelter with relatives in other villages during the winter months.

OTHER FOODS In spring the Maidu gathered wild rye and other grass seeds in the valleys. They took to the foothills to gather pine nuts, whose shells were made into beads; the nuts were eaten as is or ground into flour. Some Maidu also gathered hazelnuts, buckeye nuts, and nutmeg. Mint tea and cider made from manzanita berries were favorite beverages. Because of their custom of digging for roots, the Maidu were called "Diggers," by gold miners; the name was used in a mean-spirited way. Other menu items included stewed eel and dried salmon.

Tobacco was the only plant grown by the Maidu. Priests offered tobacco smoke up to the spirits, and others used tobacco as a painkiller and at bedtime, because it made them sleepy.

Hunting techniques

Some Maidu left their permanent villages in the summer to hunt for deer and bear in the mountains. They had an interesting way of hunting for bears. Groups of five or six men would gather in front of the cave of a bear that was about to end its winter hibernation. First the men performed a ceremony in which they requested that the bear stand up and allow itself to be shot. Then they hid behind trees. One man at a time showed himself to the bear and shot it with an arrow or two. The bear chased the shooter, who led the bear to another hunter, who in turn shot it once or twice, until finally the bear was bristling with arrows and gave up. Some groups of Maidu would not eat the bear, but removed its hide to use as a costume in ceremonies.

Sometimes deer drives were organized with surrounding villages. One hunting technique was to entice a deer to approach by dressing like one. The hunter wore a deer mask and a rabbit-skin blanket; he smeared a substance on his body to disguise his own scent, then moved in on his prey while making movements like a feeding deer. Sometimes deer were driven into a ring of fire, then killed with bows and arrows.

A Maidu woman wearing shell money around her neck and a belt of abalone.

Clothing and adornment

Maidu men, women, and children wore little clothing year round. Men sometimes wore buckskin breechcloths (a garment with front and back flaps that hung from the waist), and younger women sometimes wore small aprons that hung from the waist in front and back and were made of buckskin, grass, or tree bark. In very cold weather they might wear deerskin leggings and ankle-length deerskin moccasins stuffed with grass. In extremely severe weather, cloaks made of feathers or the skins of rabbits, deer, or mountain lions were worn. Snowshoes were used in winter.

Hair was worn long and loose by both sexes. A hat made of tule was favored by some Maidu women. Their ears were pierced and from them hung earrings made from bone or wood decorated with woodpecker skulls or quail tips. Men preferred pierced noses. Both sexes wore necklaces made from shells and animal teeth. Tattoos and body paint added color.

Healing practices

Maidu healers, called shamans (pronounced *SHAY-munz*), could both cure and cause illness. In fact, shamans were so powerful they could make entire villages sick if they chose to.

THE HORRIBLE BEAR

The Maidu, who lived in grizzly bear country, had a great respect for bears and even had a special dance they hoped would protect them from a bear attack. While many Native American stories tell of a person marrying a bear, the story below is about a squirrel who married a bear.

There is a story told of a ground squirrel who had taken a mean old grizzly as his wife. One early morning when he had left for a day's hunting, the squirrel's home was visited by his half-brother, a bat. This creature was also very mean, and as he threw himself down on a bed of skins, he demanded to be fed. Growling with irritation, the grizzly supplied her brother-in-law with some acorn soup, jerky, and hazel nuts.

The bat began to throw the hazel nut shells into the face of his reluctant hostess, whose growls became increasingly threatening. Suddenly, she leapt at the bat. But he was ready for her attack. When the squirrel arrived home he found his wife dead from a poisoned arrow, and the bat gone.

Today's travelers into grizzly bear country are hopefully aware of additional ideas on coping with this beast. From the Maidu comes this traditional advice: if you drop a piece of meat on the ground, don't pick it up and eat it—or a "grizz" will one day eat you.

SOURCE: Donald P. Jewell. From "The Horrible Bear." *Indians of the Feather River: Tales and Legends of Concow Maidu of California.* Menlo Park, CA: Ballena Press, 1987.

Shamans cured by piercing the skin and sucking out the substances that caused diseases. Donald Jewell reported that as late as the 1950s, he saw Maidu men whose skin was scarred from having been cured this way. The sickness-causing agents were actually stones, crystals, bones, or even live animals that the shaman brought with him to the sickbed. Some Maidu groups also had female shamans. While some people believed women shamans were simply poisoners, other Maidu groups preferred them to male shamans.

Today, a high percentage of Maidu people suffer from diabetes, a disease marked by excessive urination and constant thirst. This is not uncommon among Native Americans, whose death rate for diseases such as diabetes and tuberculosis is much higher than for other Americans. The people have their health care needs attended to either at health clinics on the rancherias or in health care facilities in nearby towns.

ARTS

According to some versions of the Maidu creation story, the Creator sang the world into being. Songs and music were an important part of all Maidu festivals and ceremonies. Maidu drums imitated the sound of bears. Their rattles sounded like pebbles swishing and were sometimes made from insect cocoons attached to long wooden handles and decorated with feathers and shells. Flutes, whistles, and a type of one-stringed bow were also played.

CUSTOMS

Marriage

Marriages between Maidu often began with the couple simply moving in together, at first with the bride's family for a short time and then with the groom's family. In some groups, though, contact between a mother-in-law and a son-in-law was considered bad, so the couple lived apart from the bride's family and the husband avoided any contact with his wife's mother.

A man could choose his bride from within his own village or from another village. A husband who was a good hunter was especially prized by his wife's family, because he sometimes provided them with food. No woman had to accept a man she did not find pleasing. If either party desired a divorce, it was easily accomplished. Important men occasionally took several wives.

Pregnancy and babies

Pregnant women ate special diets that often excluded meat and fish. When her time drew near, the Maidu mother-to-be was restricted to her home, and her husband might stop hunting and fishing. An experienced older woman assisted in the birth. If a baby was stillborn, both mother and father fasted for a period ranging from one to three months. Some groups considered twins unlucky, and they sometimes killed both mother and babies.

Names were very important and were changed several times during a Maidu's lifetime. A girl at first received a baby name, such as "girl," "daughter," or "niece." The name then changed at important life events: at puberty, when she gave birth for the first time, and when she reached old age. A boy also received a baby name, such as "boy," another name at about age three, and yet another name if he joined a cult (see "Puberty"). Some examples of Maidu children names were "climbing girl" and "snoring bird."

Puberty

During her first menstrual period, a girl withdrew from the community—either to her home, to a menstrual hut, or to a place in the mountains with her mother. Afterwards, there were joyous ceremonies involving singing, dancing, bathing, face and body painting, and ear piercing.

Some very young Maidu boys were invited to join a secret religious society called the Kuksu Society. After several years spent in training, at puberty the boys took part in a secret ceremony and became members of the society.

Ceremonies and festivals

The Maidu welcomed spring with a Toto Dance. Female dancers shook beaded belts in rhythm with the music provided by the men on drums, rattles, flutes and whistles. Some groups still celebrate spring with this dance, and some still hold the bear dances that kept people safe from bear attacks.

The modern Maidu hold Maidu Indian Day in October. It features storytelling and demonstrations of traditional crafts and skills such as acorn cooking and making baskets and flint tools.

Funerals

Some Maidu groups cremated the dead. Those who buried their dead first dressed the bodies in fine clothing and wrapped them in animal skins. The bodies were buried in unmarked graves together with some of their possessions to use in the afterworld and with offerings made by mourners. What remained of a dead man's property, such as hunting and fishing equipment, canoes, and clothing, was burned.

Special mourning ceremonies were held immediately following the burial and on anniversaries thereafter. At them, women wailed and emotional speeches were given. Afterwards, much food was consumed, games were played, and songs were sung. The names of the dead were never mentioned again, but sometimes the name was passed on to a young relative.

CURRENT TRIBAL ISSUES

In common with other California tribes, the surviving Maidu face high unemployment and school dropout rates as well as poverty. The Maidu have little land, limited natural resources, and scant economic development. Migrant laborers (who travel from place to place looking for work) are taking over the jobs in the lumber and timber industries that the Maidu had been doing since the early 1900s.

In the later part of the twentieth century the Maidu displayed a renewed interest in their own culture. This led to a renewal of traditional Maidu ceremonial practices, both social and religious.

NOTABLE PEOPLE

The paintings of artist Frank Day (1902–1976) drew upon Maidu history and mythology. His father was a village headman, and Day inherited ceremonial knowledge and responsibilities from him. Day helped found a dance group called the Maidu Dancers and taught the younger dancers the songs, the meaning of the words in the songs, and the dance steps that should be used. Most of his 300 paintings are in private collections.

Artist Harry Fonseca (1946–) is probably best known for paintings and other graphics depicting Coyote, the cunning and irresponsible trickster of Maidu mythology.

Other notable Maidu include: Tobu (c. 1793), who led a group of Maidu warriors against European grave robbers; Yuki-Wailaki-Maidu dancer, basket maker, and historian of Native American Art, Frank Tuttle (1957–); and Maidu-Konkow lesbian poet Janice Gould (1949–).

FURTHER READING

Bibby, Brian. "Maidu." *Native America in the Twentieth Century: An Encyclopedia.* Editor Mary B. Davis. New York: Garland Publishing, 1994.

Burrill, Richard, *River of Sorrows: Life History of the Maidu-Nisenan Indians.* Richard Burrill; 1988.

Riddell, Francis A. "Maidu and Concow." *Handbook of North American Indians,* Vol. 8: *California.* Ed. Robert F. Heizer. Washington DC: Smithsonian Institution, 1978.

Spencer, Robert F., Jesse D. Jennings, et al. *The Native Americans.* New York: Harper & Row, 1977.

Wilson, Norman L., and Arlean H. Towne. "Nisenan." *Handbook of North American Indians,* Vol. 8: *California.* Ed. Robert F. Heizer. Washington DC: Smithsonian Institution, 1978.

Miwok

Name

Miwok (pronounced *MEE-wock*). The name derives from a Miwok word for "people." It is sometimes spelled Mewuk.

Location

Formerly, three groups lived in more than one hundred villages in a large area in central California. Their territory stretched from the Sierra Nevada mountain range in the east to the Pacific Ocean just north of San Francisco. Today they live on small, often isolated rancherias (see "History") scattered throughout their former territory.

Population

In the late 1700s, there were about 22,000 Miwok. In 1910, the population was down to about 700. In a census (count of the population) done in 1990 by the U.S. Bureau of the Census, 3,438 people identified themselves as Miwok.

Language family

Penutian.

Origins and group affiliations

Miwok groups have occupied Central California for at least 3,000 years. The three Miwok groups are Coast Miwok, Lake Miwok, and Sierra Miwok. The Coast Miwok and Lake Miwok were cut off from the Sierra Miwok and from each other by the Pomo, Patwin, and Wappo tribes. The Miwok married people of the Pomo and Maidu tribes (see entries) among other neighbors.

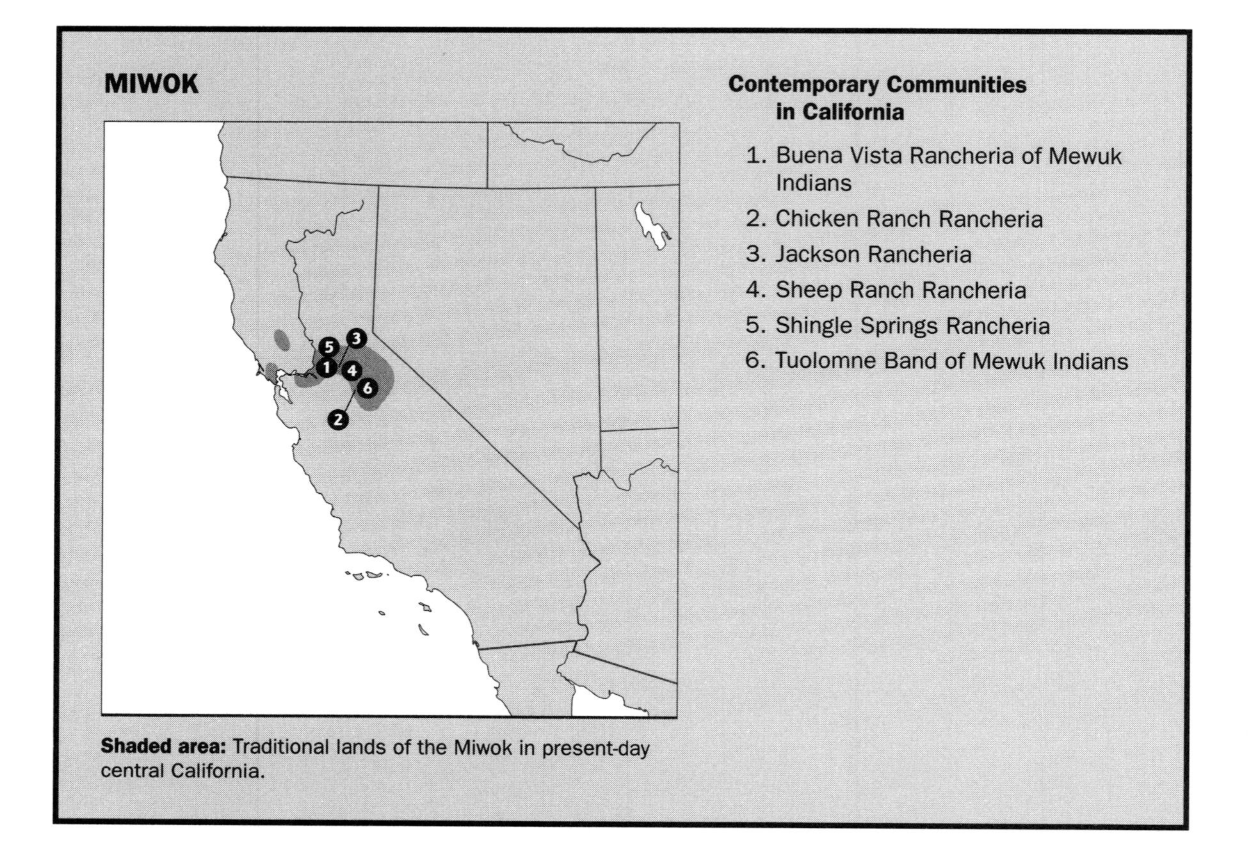

Shaded area: Traditional lands of the Miwok in present-day central California.

The Miwok were an easy-going, happy people who loved to dance. They were divided into three groups who shared a language and many customs, but there were also differences among them. The differences were related to the ecology of the region they inhabited, for a life lived in the mountains is different from a life lived by the ocean. Like other California tribes, for many years they lived a comfortable, peaceful life; then gold was discovered on their lands. The event proved to be a disaster for the Miwok.

HISTORY

Encounters with Europeans

The Coast Miwok were the first of the Miwok groups to meet Europeans. In 1579 British explorer Sir Francis Drake (1540–1596) sailed his ship, the *Golden Hind,* into Miwok waters. He spent five days there repairing the ship and wrote an account of his meeting with the Miwok. At about the same time, Spanish explorers claimed the land of California as their own, but they did not encounter the Miwok and did not build any settlements there. Two centuries were to pass before there were any further encounters between the Miwok and Europeans.

In 1769 the Spanish began to build forts and missions in California. They had decided it was time to protect the land from the British and Russians, who were showing too much interest in it. The Spanish plan was to teach Native Californians how to be "useful" to future Spanish settlers. They did this by forcing the Natives to convert to the Catholic religion, moving them into the missions, and teaching them Spanish and skills such as European-style farming and carpentry.

IMPORTANT DATES

1579: Sir Francis Drake encounters Coast Miwok.

1794: First known Miwok baptism takes place at Mission San Francisco.

1821: Mexican independence from Spain hastens settlement of Miwok territory.

1848: Gold Rush brings U.S. settlers in large numbers into Miwok country.

1900–20: Several rancherias are established for surviving Miwok.

1934–72: Most Miwok rancherias are terminated.

1972–94: Tribal status is restored to several Miwok rancherias.

Spanish subdue Miwok

The Spanish began with the Natives along the Pacific coast, and probably baptized their first Miwok convert in 1794. Soon, most of the Coast Miwok had either been converted or had died from harsh treatment at the missions or from diseases brought by Europeans. Next the missionaries turned their attention to Indians living inland. By 1811 they had reached the Sierra Miwok groups and forcibly took these people to Mission San Jose.

Miwok people who tried to flee were rounded up by Spanish soldiers. Some were killed but others joined with people from the Yokuts tribe and rebelled. During the 1820s and 1830s they learned fighting techniques from the Spanish and used them to carry out raids against the missions and to get horses from Spanish ranches. For a time they were a real threat to the Spanish.

The Miwok at the missions, like the Cahuilla, Chumash, and Costanoan (see entries), endured great hardships and the near-destruction of their culture. Many Miwok died.

Mexicans take over

Mexico won independence from Spain in 1821 and ended the mission system in 1834. But for California Natives, freedom from the missions did not mean a return to their old way of life. Although Mexico had promised them land, they never received it. Instead, they were forced to go to work for Mexican settlers who now poured into California. One Mexican rancher gathered a force of other ranchers and farmers and slaughtered large numbers of Miwok and took hundreds more as prisoners to work as slave labor to harvest his wheat crop. This type of thing happened throughout California as the Mexican settlers moved northward in force.

The United States acquires California

A third wave of settlement washed across Miwok territory after 1848. Mexico ceded California to the United States after the two nations had fought in the two-year Mexican-American War over the lands in what is now the southwest United States. Gold was discovered in the Sierras, and shortly after the war was over, the California gold rush was on. Suddenly, the Miwok of the Sierra Nevada, who had largely been spared from the troubles caused by the Mexicans, were confronted with an invasion of white prospectors and miners. White men brought fatal diseases and alcohol, which was to cause many longstanding problems for the Miwok.

Relations between the Miwok and miners were almost instantly hostile. Whites illegally took over Indian lands, leaving the Miwok with nothing but small parcels where they could live. Between 1847 and 1860, miners killed at least 200 Miwok and took their hunting and gathering grounds; no longer could they gather acorns and other plants wherever they wanted.

Treaties are signed . . . and ignored

Beginning in 1851, eighteen treaties were drawn up between the U.S. government and California tribes—including the Miwok. The tribes agreed to give up most of their lands to the U.S. government in exchange for about 7.5 million acres that would be set aside for reservations.

White Californians were horrified that so much land was being given away (about 8 percent of the state). Such an uproar was raised that the U.S. Senate rejected the treaties. Most Miwok remained in the area of their homelands, but they had no land rights. Hundreds of Miwok were enslaved or murdered by American settlers.

Rancherias for the Miwok

By 1910, the population of the Sierra Miwok had fallen to 670 from its pre-European high of 19,500. Only 41 Lake Miwok and 11 Coast Miwok were counted in a census of about the same time.

In the early part of the twentieth century, the U.S. government tried to address the problem of homeless Indians in California. The

A Miwok man at his home.

government began to buy up small parcels of land for them, called rancherias (the Spanish word for ranch). Much of this land was located in isolated areas where white people did not want to live. The land was poor and lacked developed water sources. The Lake Miwok moved onto the Middletown Rancheria of Pomo Indians with the Pomo (it is near Clear Lake). Some Sierra Miwok went to Jackson Rancheria and Tuolumne Rancheria, both in the Sierra Nevadas. Other rancherias whose residents are all or partly Miwok are: Buena Vista, Chicken Ranch, Ione, Sheep Ranch, and Shingle Springs.

Natives on the rancherias were expected to learn to farm and to assimilate—that is, to become more like white Americans. But the land was so poor that it was nearly impossible for people to support themselves. Most Miwok became totally dependent on government aid.

Government changes tactics

The government, finding that its assimilation policies were not working with Native Americans, adopted a new policy called termination. Termination would end all U.S. government relations—including government financial assistance—with Native tribes and peoples.

The Rancheria Act of 1958 forced California Natives on the rancherias to decide whether to accept or reject termination. Thirty-six of the most isolated California Indian rancherias accepted termination, including most of the Miwok rancherias. Extreme poverty was the result.

RANCHERIA ACT EXCITES CALIFORNIA TAX COLLECTORS

The Rancheria Act was passed by the U.S. Congress in 1958. It required that rancherias decide whether to accept or reject the U.S. government's new policy of termination. Termination would end the special relationship between the U.S. government and Native tribes and instead make the tribes subject to state laws and taxes. Some tribes accepted termination, but some hesitated.

State authorities, thinking they would collect tremendous sums from taxes on Indian land, visited the rancherias that were hesitating. They promised that if tribal members agreed to accept termination, the state would provide new housing, road and water system improvements, and even college scholarships for Native children. Before long, however, the state government realized that it would cost more to keep these promises than the state would collect in taxes from the rancherias.

The termination policy soon came under heavy criticism, and support for it died. However, thirty-six of the most isolated California Indian rancherias had already accepted termination. The Civil Rights Movement of the 1960s ushered in a new era of government programs and policies that were more friendly toward Native Americans, but it would be years before terminated tribes regained the special relationship they had had with the federal government.

Modern times

The termination policy soon came under heavy criticism, and support for it died. The Civil Rights Movement of the 1960s ushered in a new era of government programs and policies toward Native Americans. With more funds provided to assist them, Indian groups were able to take more responsibility for their own communities. Still, most Miwok rancherias have been too poor to devote much attention to cultural revival. On the bright side, Jackson Rancheria hopes to address this problem with profits from its casino (see "Economy"), and Tuolumne Rancheria has achieved considerable success with its active dance house and language preservation efforts.

RELIGION

The Miwok believed in a Creator, an animal god called Coyote. Other important animal gods were Coyote's son, Condor, and Condor's son, Chicken Hawk.

One of the most important figures in Miwok society was the spirit doctor, or sucking shaman (pronounced *SHAY-mun*), who could cure illnesses (see "Healing Practices") and who was in charge of sacred ceremonies (see "Festivals and ceremonies").

Secret societies were common; a major one was the Kuksu Society. Young boys who were chosen to be members underwent a long training process, in which they learned special dances and prayers. The society held ceremonies in a large, circular dance house. Members wore feathered headdresses and imitated the spirits while praying for favors like rain and an abundance of crops. The Bird Cult, another secret society, was evidence of the special feelings the Miwok had toward animals.

Some Miwok converted to Catholicism during the mission period (1769–1834), but not all conversions were sincere. Miwok who could no longer endure the disruption of their society caused by white settlers took up the Ghost Dance Religion in about 1872 (see box in Maidu entry). Those who performed the Ghost Dance believed the day would soon come when the Indian way of life would be restored and everyone would be happy once again. Some elements of the Ghost Dance Religion still survive among the Miwok.

LANGUAGE

The Miwok language has two major divisions: Eastern Miwok languages and Western Miwok languages. The two appear to have been separated about 2,500 years ago. There were many different versions of the language spoken by Miwok groups.

Under the mission system, the Miwok were forced to speak Spanish. Later, facing prejudice from American settlers, many refused to speak their language in order to conceal the fact that they were Indian. Government-run schools did not allow Miwok children to use their language. When Miwok elders died, the language began to die too. Attempts are being made by the few remaining Native speakers to teach the Miwok language to the younger generation.

GOVERNMENT

The Miwok were divided into tribelets, a type of organization in which one main settlement was surrounded by a few minor outlying settlements. Each tribelet was its own separate nation, and each was headed by a chief and one or two female leaders who were responsible for the women's ceremonial house.

The way a person became a chief differed depending on the group. In some groups, the position of chief was handed down to a male heir. If there were no male heirs, a woman could inherit the position. If the heir was too young, a woman could rule in his place until he came of age. In other groups, an old chief and four old women chose a future chief and trained him. When he was ready to take over, the old chief stepped aside. If he refused to do so, a poisoner was sometimes hired to remove him from office.

A chief's duties might include managing food resources, giving personal and legal advice, settling disputes, and making speeches. A Miwok chief was described in *The Indians of California* who had morning wake-up duty. At sunrise he made the rounds of his village, calling out: "Get up! Get up! All the people get up! Wash your face. After you wash yourself, eat breakfast. Go hunt for something. You will get hungry. After you get something, you will eat it. Get up."

Today, there is no unified Miwok nation but several separate Miwok rancherias. Each is governed by an elected tribal council.

ECONOMY

Before contact with Europeans, the Miwok economy was based on hunting and gathering, and some trading was done. Shells, which were polished and strung into necklaces, served as money.

The Miwok sense of property was very strong. Land itself was not considered private property, but the acorn-producing oaks on it, for example, could be. Payment was expected for everything. Fees were charged for the use of the dance house for a girl's puberty rite. Fees were charged for admission to dances; the fee was refunded if the audience was unhappy with the performance. Chiefs were paid for their services by hunters, who were required to turn over a portion of the meat they had caught.

After their society was disrupted by missionaries and settlers, some Miwok tried to continue supporting themselves by hunting and gathering. They had to supplement their income with the meager wages earned by performing seasonal labor. Some of this type of work was done on ranches and farms located on ancient Miwok lands. In heavily wooded former Miwok lands, some earned a living by working for white loggers; the logging industry continues to be a major employer. Yosemite National Park in the Sierra Nevada range provides employment as well.

Most Miwok lived in grinding poverty, and the situation has not changed much. One spectacular economic success story is the Jackson Miwok Rancheria Casino, one of the most profitable Indian casinos in California. It has been so successful, in fact, that in a matter of only a few years, every person living there rose from poverty to live a middle- or upper-class life. The casino is a major employer; profits from it have allowed the tribe to offer free health care and substance abuse programs, to hire a police force, build homes, and pave roads.

DAILY LIFE

Families

Miwok villages were made up of several extended families, consisting of a father, mother, children, and close relatives of the father. Usually, from six to ten people lived together in one home.

Education

Miwok children learned by observing their elders. At age six or seven, boys were trained in song and dance rites, and by adolescence they were ready to be welcomed into a variety of Miwok secret societies.

Under the mission system, children learned some Spanish and all about the Catholic religion. In modern times, Miwok children attend local public schools; some efforts are also being made to supplement the education with programs on the rancherias.

Buildings

Miwok home styles depended on where the group lived. Those in the mountains needed a sturdier house to stand up to severe weather. The most popular style had a conical shape; it often had a frame of two forked willow poles that leaned together. More poles were tied to these, and then this framework was covered with grass or bark. On the dirt floor below a smoke hole was a fire pit surrounded by stones. The rest of the floor and the entrance were covered with grass mats. Tule mats (pronounced *TOO-lee*; a type of plant material) and animal hides were used for beds.

Other buildings might include circular sweathouses, located partly underground and used by men only; ceremonial chambers or dance houses, sometimes with separate, smaller chambers for women; and cone-shaped huts for menstruating women.

Other buildings might include circular assembly houses; small, conical menstruation huts for girls; and acorn granaries constructed of an upright pole covered with brush.

Food

GATHERING The Miwok were hunter-gatherers with access to abundant foods in great variety. The acorn was a staple food for all groups (see box on page 1086). Buckeye fruits, like acorns, were gathered and prepared in a mush. Seeds and greens were gathered in season, but fruits and roots were scarce. Tobacco was both gathered and planted; it was smoked by adult males in pipes made of elderberry.

PREPARING ACORNS FOR EATING

Because acorns are bitter in their natural state, they had to be prepared for eating. After hulling and grinding the acorns into a flour, the Miwok placed the flour into a hole in the sand and covered it with several applications of hot water. The dough that was left was mixed with water in a basket and brought to a boil by adding hot stones. It was then ready to eat or to be made into bread or mush.

When the Miwok began to raid Spanish horse herds in the 1800s, they added horse meat to their diet.

COAST- AND LAKE-DWELLERS Coast Miwok built their villages close to the shore or to lagoons where fishing would be plentiful. Crabs were available year-round; in winter kelp, winter salmon runs, and late geese helped to round out the diet. Fishing began in earnest with the coming of spring; nets and small traps were used. Larger fish, such as salmon, were speared, and smaller fish were poisoned in shallow pools. Mussels and clams were important food from the sea. Small game such as rabbits and squirrels were eaten, but no sea mammals.

Lake Miwok followed much the same pattern. They too hunted deer by snaring them or tracking them until the animals were worn out. Before white settlers drove them away, elk and grizzly bears were hunted. Rabbits, squirrels, and ducks—hunted with clay pellets cast by a sling—also provided meat. Trout were caught with bare hands in larger streams or by using basket traps or dip nets. Both men and women fished, while only the men hunted game. Pine seeds were toasted and eaten, and manzanita berries were pounded into a type of candy. Seaweed was also dried and baked.

MOUNTAIN DWELLERS The Sierra Miwok gathered plants and hunted deer, elk, antelope, black and grizzly bears, quail, pigeons, woodpeckers, rabbits, squirrels, and woodrats. They would not eat dogs, coyotes, or eagles. Fishing was another important source of animal food, especially salmon and trout. Seeds were gathered with a seed beater and a burden basket; the beater dislodged seeds from the head of plants. Such plants included wild oats, balsam root, evening primrose, clarkia, gumweed, skunkweed, and California buttercup to name only a few. Manzanita and madrone berries were used in a cider drink. Wild plums, chokecherries, gooseberries, wild currants, and mushrooms were gathered.

Clothing and adornment

Clothing was fairly simple for all Miwok. Young children usually wore no clothing, while girls and women had two-piece skirts or double aprons made of deerskin or grass. Men wore animal-hide loin cloths and simple sleeveless shirts of hide or plant material.

Southern Miwok woman with sifting basket

Skin or hide robes were used for cold weather. Footwear was not common, but sock-like deerskin moccasins were worn in cold weather and for hunting.

The hair was worn long, either braided, loose, or gathered in a woven hair net. Some men also let their beards grow. Tattoos were common throughout Miwok territory for both men and women. They were made by rubbing poison oak ash into cuts in the skin. A popular design was several vertical lines at the chin and sides of the mouth; the lines might extend from chin to navel. Body paint and feathered belts and bracelets were worn on special occasions. The Miwok believed that body piercing contributed to a long life, so children had both their nose and earlobes pierced and wore flowers through their ears. Women wore shell earrings and nose sticks were made of shell or polished bone.

Healing practices

Depending on the medical situation, several types of doctors were available. A person made sick by evil spirits called a sucking doctor, who made a cut in the patient's body and sucked out the evil spirits. "Old dancers," men and women who attempted to cure the sick by dancing, singing, and playing musical instruments, were the favorite kind of doctors.

People who felt they had been treated badly and had no other way to get revenge would call upon a professional poisoner. This type of "doctor" could produce sickness in others by means of spells or by actual poison. Less serious diseases were treated by herb doctors who used plants to cure. Although the smoking of tobacco was usually done only by men, some women prescribed it for themselves to cure a bad cold.

There were doctors who took care of young girls having their first menstrual period, and there were bear doctors, whose guardian spirit was a bear. When a bear doctor put on his bear robes, he seemed to actually become a bear. He could either do harm or cure a person, and he was greatly feared.

In modern times, the Miwok and other Native Americans have faced terrible problems with alcoholism and feelings of hopelessness. Medical care has been undependable. In 1969 the Miwok and eight other California tribes took matters into their own hands by forming the California Rural Indian Health Board (CRIHB). Today the CRIHB oversees Indian health programs throughout the state. Through its efforts, health clinics have opened on the Tuolumne and Jackson reservations.

ARTS

The Miwok were gifted basket weavers, and surviving examples of their work are highly prized by modern art collectors. They were also known for their decorative use of feathers, which they used for ceremonial costumes and for weaving into the rims of baskets. Today, some Native artists have revived the basketry tradition; examples of this and contemporary arts can be seen at the Native American Invitational Art Show, held at Grinding Rock State Historical Park in conjunction with the Big Time festival (see "Ceremonies and festivals") in September.

Oral literature

Favorite Miwok stories involve the adventures and misadventures of the creator, Old Man Coyote. He displays some of the best qualities of humans, but many more of the worst ones. Also popular are tales of birds, who were believed to have magical properties. This is not surprising considering the heavily forested environment, with its many varieties of birds, in which many of the Miwok lived.

CUSTOMS

Courtship and marriage

Miwok brides were chosen not for beauty but for their love of hard work. Marriages were arranged by parents, although sometimes brides were kidnaped. Courtship began with the exchange of gifts such as beads, shells, or baskets. The bride usually moved in with her husband's family, but a poor man lived with the bride's family to show them what a good provider he could be. If a husband or wife died, the remaining spouse often married a relative of the dead mate. Marriage with members of non-Miwok tribes was common.

Pregnancy

Some groups had special small grass huts for birthing. Other groups had rules about what the mother should or should not eat during pregnancy. Among the Lake Miwok, for example, it was forbidden for a woman to eat woodpecker while pregnant; if she did, the child would cry too much after birth. Infants were named for animals or for family members or deceased relatives.

Babies

Some tribes had rules about how many children a couple could have. For example, the Coast Miwok, had a limit of three children, and any additional children were supposed to be killed. Historians do not believe this happened often, however.

Some Miwok flattened the heads of their infants, because flat heads were considered attractive. Shortly after birth, a baby was placed in a cradle and a padded board was tied to its forehead to mold the head into the flattened shape.

Puberty

Different groups had different puberty rites. The Coast Miwok celebrated a girl's first period by welcoming her into a secret society and performing a circle dance for her. Boys usually fasted for the first time at adolescence, then went on their first hunt.

Ceremonies and festivals

Religious and social dances played an important part in Miwok ceremonies, although the Miwok were so fond of dancing they often danced a few steps to celebrate minor occasions like killing a game bird. Ceremonial dancers pretended to be spirits to acquire luck, power, or good health from the spirits. Only men participated in some dances, while women and children would be included in others. Male dancers often closed the smoke hole in the dance house to make the room hot, then hours later jumped into a nearby creek to cool off.

Some popular dances included the Big Head Dance, Ghost Initiation, Old Time Dance, First Fruits ceremony, and Dance of the Dead.

Often these ceremonies would continue for many days: the Big Head Dance, for example, lasted four days and nights and would be conducted by a caretaker and a timekeeper, both trained for the purpose.

Traditional celebrations are still held at two locations: the dance house at Tuolumne Rancheria, where a September Acorn Festival is held; and Grinding Rock State Historical Park (called Chaw'se by the Miwok). People from several tribes gather at the dance house at Grinding Rock for the September Big Time celebration, where they dance and play Indian football and the traditional handgame. Jennifer Bates described the game: "It involves the singing of songs and guessing of bones; there are two marked and two unmarked bones, and two teams play against each other for the money in the 'pot.'"

Death

It was believed that at death, humans traveled toward the west to live with Coyote. Miwok were either cremated or buried along with their personal possessions. Mourners cut their hair short, and sometimes mourned for a whole year if the dead person were important enough. Some groups would not speak the name of the dead person.

CURRENT TRIBAL ISSUES

Some rancherias are still seeking recognition by the federal government, which they lost under the termination policy of the 1950s (see "History"). Without recognition, they have no official relationship with the federal government, and are entitled to no assistance.

The casino riches earned by the Jackson Miwok in recent years have had unfortunate side effects. Young people who are receiving a monthly share of the profits see no reason to attend school. The tribe finally issued a order: "No high school diploma, no money."

NOTABLE PEOPLE

Marin (d. 1834) was a Coast Miwok chief who played an important role in the early history of the San Francisco Bay area. He led his people in several successful battles against the Spanish during the years between 1815 and 1824, but was captured and imprisoned. He escaped but was recaptured. Although he was then nearly executed, priests from the mission at San Rafael intervened in his behalf. He was later converted to Catholicism and lived close to the mission until he died there in 1834. The island where he took refuge was named after him, and some years later the entire adjacent peninsula and county were also given his name.

Other notable Miwok include: Hopi/Miwok poet, artist, and educator Wendy Rose (1948–), Paiute/Miwok basketmaker Lucy Telles (1885–1955), and Pomo/Miwok professor and writer Gregory Sarris, who is also Chair of the Federated Coast Miwok Tribe.

FURTHER READING

Bates, Jennifer. "Sierra Miwok," in *Native America in the Twentieth Century: An Encyclopedia.* Ed. Mary B. Davis. New York: Garland Publishing, 1994.

"The Coastal Miwok: Marin's First Settlers," Marin County Historical Society Online, http://www.marinweb.com/marinhistory/miwok.htm

"Miwok Indians of Yosemite," by the Students of Woodland Elementary School, Mariposa County, California. [Online] http://mariposa.yosemite.net/woodland/miwok.htm

Pit River Indians

Name

The name Pit River Indians comes from the group's unique hunting technique (see box on page 1103). The tribe is made up of descendants of the Achumawi (pronounced *ah-CHOO-ma-wee*; also spelled "Achomawi") and Atsugewi (pronounced *at-SOO-gay-wee*). The name Achumawi comes from a word meaning river. The origin of the name Atsugewi is unknown; they were also called Hat Creek Indians.

Location

The Achumawi lived along the Pit River in northern California, in an area bounded by Mount Shasta to the northwest, Lassen Peak to the southwest, and the Warner range to the east. There were two Atsugewi groups: the Pine Tree People, who lived in the densely wooded area north of Mount Lassen; and the Juniper Tree People, who lived in the drier plains in and around Dixie Valley, northeast of Mount Lassen. Today both groups live, often with members of other tribes, on several rancherias (see "History") in northern California.

Population

In the early 1800s, there were about 3,000 Achumawi and 900 Atsugewi. In a census (count of the population) done in 1990, when the two groups had combined as the Pit River Indians, 1,753 people identified themselves as Pit River Indians.

Language family

Hokan.

Origins and group affiliations

The Achumawi lived in a collection of villages that were organized individually but seemed to maintain ties with one another. The Atsugewi tribe was made up of two distinct groups: the Pine Tree People and the Juniper Tree People who shared a language. The Achumawi and the Atsugewi were on good terms and frequently renewed friendship ties through marriage. Some longstanding bitterness existed between them and certain other groups. There were wars with the Modoc, Klamath, and Paiute, who sent raiding parties into Pit River territory to enslave women and children.

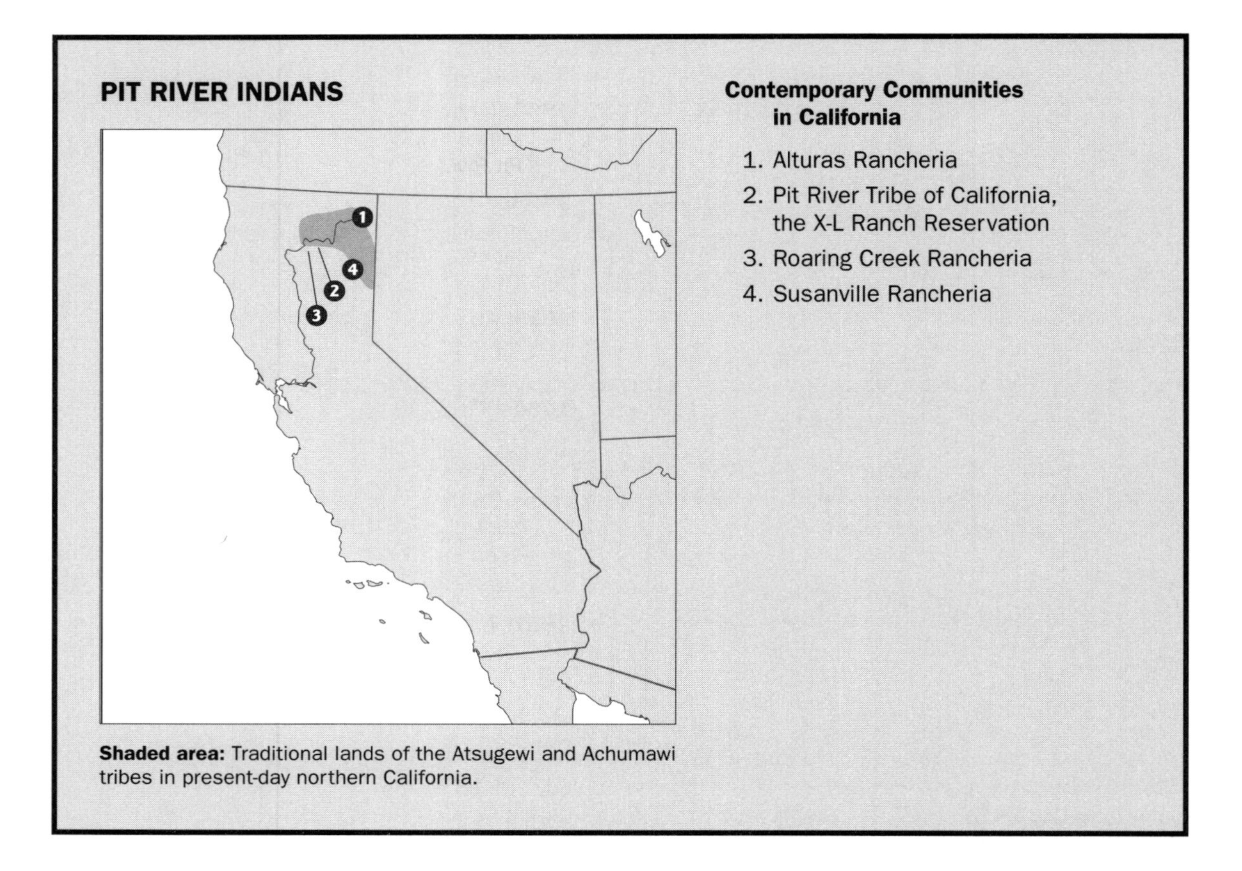

Shaded area: Traditional lands of the Atsugewi and Achumawi tribes in present-day northern California.

Although they inhabited a fairly small region, the Pit River Indians traveled every part of it, looking for food and visiting with neighbors. They rowed swiftly down California rivers in canoes they dug out of pine trees. They fished in those rivers and in countless lakes and streams. They hunted in high and low mountain regions, plains and valleys, swamps and marshes, and grasslands and meadows. Mountain groups often endured winters lasting six months. When one group fell on hard times, their neighbors were always willing to help out.

HISTORY

Unfriendly contact with Europeans

The Pit River Indians were a fairly peaceful people. They did not like to fight and usually did so only when severely provoked. When challenged, they sometimes sent a peacemaker to try and resolve issues with hostile tribes. The Modoc, Paiute, and Klamath made frequent hostile invasions into their territory and captured and enslaved their women and children. Some historians think Pit River Indian slaves may have been handed over to the Spanish in the Southwest in the early or mid-1700s, marking their actual first encounters with white people.

American fur trappers entered the Pit River region in 1827, and soon the Native population was overcome by a malaria epidemic. Further trampling on their territory occurred after Mexico gave California to the United States in 1848, and gold was discovered in 1850. Hundreds of white settlers passed through on their way to the coast, followed by gold seekers. Relations were hostile, and conflicts erupted throughout the 1850s.

IMPORTANT DATES

1833: A malaria epidemic kills many Pit River Indians.

1848: Gold is discovered in California; Native lands are overrun by gold miners.

1859: An entire friendly Atsugewi tribe is killed by whites over a misunderstanding.

1860s: Pit River Indians are forced to move to the Round Valley Reservation; most eventually leave.

1915–38: U.S. government establishes seven rancherias for Pit River Indians.

1976: Pit River Tribe is granted federal recognition.

1987: Tribal constitution is accepted by federal government.

Edward S. Curtis, in *The North American Indian,* related an eyewitness account of an encounter in the 1850s: "A band of white men from Red Bluff attacked the Fall River Achomawi in a camp at Beaver Creek and slaughtered the entire number except 30 or 40 men, who escaped. . . . About 160 were killed." In 1856 Atsugewi warriors attacked whites who had settled on their land. Three years later, an entire friendly Atsugewi group was killed by angry settlers, who mistakenly believed that their village was responsible for the murder of some whites in Hat Creek.

Outnumbered and weakened by death and diseases, the Natives were no match for the white hordes. By 1860, the surviving Atsugewi and Achumawi were removed to Round Valley Reservation in Mendocino County, where members of several other California tribes were already confined.

Allotments and rancherias

The government expected reservation Indians to give up their culture and become more like white Americans. It was not long before Pit River Indians became disenchanted with life on the reservation and made their way back to their homeland. There they made do as best they could until the Dawes General Allotment Act of 1897 was passed. This act divided some former Indian lands into small parcels, which were given to individual Indians to farm. Most of these parcels were not suitable for farming, and when the Pacific Gas and

POPULATION ON RANCHERIAS AND RESERVATIONS

Most Pit River Indians do not live on tribally-owned lands, because they cannot make a living there. In the mid-1990s, there were nine rancherias or reservations where Pit River Indians lived, usually with members of other tribes. The populations and areas of those places are shown below. A tenth parcel, the 1.32-acre Likely Rancheria, is used as a tribal cemetery.

Name	Population	Area
Alturas	3	20 acres
Big Bend	6	40 acres
Lookout	62	40 acres
Montgomery Creek	8	72 acres
Redding	72	30.89 acres
Roaring Creek	20	80 acres
Round Valley	1,181	30,537.51 acres
Susanville	491	151 acres
XL Ranch	23	9,254.86 acres

SOURCE: *American Indian Reservations and Trust Areas.* Compiled and edited by Veronica E. Velarde Tiller, Tiller Research, Inc. Prepared under an award from Economic Development Administration, U.S. Department of Commerce, 1996.

Electric Company offered to buy them up between 1917 and 1930, many Pit River Indians sold their allotments.

Between 1915 and 1938, the U.S. government purchased seven small plots of land for still-homeless Pit River Indians. These plots were called rancherias, a Spanish term for a small ranch. Like allotments, rancheria land was mostly unsuitable for farming. The largest of the rancherias, the X-L Ranch Reservation, consists of 9,255 acres of cattle-grazing land, and is now the home base of the Pit River Tribe.

Land claims

Beginning in 1919 the Pit River Indians took part in several lawsuits over land they said was taken from them illegally. A settlement was reached in 1963 between the U.S. government and all the Indians of California, in which the Indians agreed to share $29 million, which amounted to about $.47 an acre. The Pit River Indians rejected the settlement. The U.S. Bureau of Indian Affairs then sent a letter to all members of the tribe asking for their votes; based on the responses they received, the Bureau said the tribe accepted the settlement. Some tribal representatives said that those who voted yes did not fully understand the issues. The settlement went through but members of the tribe disagreed bitterly among themselves over the matter.

Some of the most unhappy members of the tribe joined in Indian protest actions during the 1960s. Protestors complained about the unjust taking of their lands and about too much government interference in tribal affairs, among other grievances.

These protests sparked a movement among Pit River Indians, who were then scattered throughout northern California. They joined together for a common goal—their recognition by the U.S. government as the Pit River Tribe. Federal recognition was granted in 1976, establishing an official relationship between the tribe and the government. Recognition entitles the tribe to certain rights and privileges not received by unrecognized tribes.

Today the Pit River Tribe is made up of eleven groups (they call themselves bands) who live in eleven areas along the Pit River and its tributaries. The Pit River Indians are an extremely private people who are unwilling to reveal details of their history or their present way of life. They seem to have retained many elements of their ancient culture, despite having their lives disrupted by whites.

RELIGION

Achumawi beliefs

This quote from an Achumawi, describing the tribe's religious beliefs, appeared in a magazine article in 1928: "All things have life in them. Trees have life, rocks have life, mountains, water, all these are full of life. You think a rock is something dead. Not at all. It is full of life."

The same magazine article described the Achumawi belief that every person has a good soul-shadow. An Achumawi shaman (pronounced *SHAY-mun*; a religious leader and doctor) by the name of Son-of-Eagle said of the soul-shadow: "You can hear it sometimes in the morning, just before you wake up. It comes from over the mountains. It comes from the East. It comes singing: 'Dawn is rising. I come. I come. Dawn is rising. I come. I come.'"

The Achumawi believed that if a person was unfortunate or angry, the soul-shadow could leave. People whose soul-shadow has left may appear to be alive, but they are really half dead.

The Achumawi believed in two creators, who laid down codes for the people to live by. These codes covered every aspect of life, including hunting, cooking, marriage, and moral conduct.

Atsugewi beliefs

The Atsugewi religion revolved around a large group of nature spirits, who appeared as people, animals, rocks, or trees. Certain people, such as shamans, could communicate with these spirits, who lived in special caves and sacred bathing areas. Old Man Spirit, for instance, lived in a cave near Lost Creek. Guardian spirits guided a person during their lifetime. They could bring a person good fortune and were often called upon in times of need. Bad fortune or sickness was blamed on unhappy guardian spirits. Information on these spirits is scant, for mentioning the name of a guardian spirit was forbidden.

Some Pit River Indians were drawn to the Ghost Dance Religion of 1890 (see box on page 1098). By the 1920s some had adopted the

GHOST DANCE OF 1890

The Ghost Dance of 1890 was a movement started by a prophet named Wovoka, a member of the Paiute tribe. A prophet is a speaker inspired by a god or supreme spirit. Wovoka was influenced by earlier prophets among his people, especially one named Wodziwob, who started the first Ghost Dance movement in 1870 (see box in Maidu entry). The first Ghost Dance movement was based on the teaching that if people performed the Ghost Dance, it would hasten the day when the Indian way of life would be restored and everyone would be happy once again. The first movement faded when hopes were dashed by more and more disruption of Native societies by white settlers.

Wovoka claimed that during an illness in 1888, he was taken to the spirit world and was taught sacred things. He then returned to his people, bringing basically the same message of hope that Wodziwob had earlier spread. People from many other western tribes heard about the movement and sent representatives to learn about it. They took the message back to their tribes, who adopted the new Ghost Dance and added their own variations.

The Ghost Dance was a circle dance during which performers often went into trances and "visited" dead friends and relatives. Government agents who oversaw Indian lands did not understand the Ghost Dance and found it threatening. When the great Sioux Chief Sitting Bull decided to take up the Ghost Dance, the government decided to stamp it out once and for all. Sitting Bull had been carrying on a feud with the U.S. military ever since he had defeated army forces at the famous Battle of the Little Bighorn in 1876. The military decision to eliminate the Ghost Dance led to the tragic massacre of men, women, and children at Wounded Knee on December 29, 1890. The Ghost Dance religion did not end, though. Some tribes continued to practice it. The Atsugewi built a dance house in 1892 to accommodate their Ghost Dancers.

Indian Mission Church, which combined elements of Christianity and traditional beliefs. While the churches have active members, the people continue to hold to the traditional beliefs.

LANGUAGE

Until a report on the languages of the Achumawi and Atsugewi was published in 1905, the two groups were commonly confused as one tribe. The distinction between the two languages showed that the Achumawi and Atsugewi were two separate tribes.

A few people in the Pit River region were reported to be speaking Achumawi in 1966, and according to the 1990 U.S. census, 81 people still spoke Achumawi at home. Thirty of those 81 Achumawi speakers were under 17 years of age, which means that the Achumawi were maintaining the language by teaching it to youngsters. On the other hand, the Atsugewi language fell out of use. According to the 1990 population census, no families spoke Atsugewi at home.

GOVERNMENT

Achumawi and Atsugewi villages were independent, each led by a chief whose position was handed down to his son (sometimes the oldest son and sometimes the most popular son). Atsugewi villages were often grouped into clusters presided over by a headman, who was usually a wealthy man and an excellent hunter.

A chief did not have to be wealthy, but he had to be wise and a hard worker. He did not rule by force but by persuading others of the rightness of his decisions. A chief set an example to his villagers, encouraging them to work hard and be alert to outside dangers. He acted as an advisor, gave instructions on when to hunt, and helped settle disputes.

When the U.S. government got involved in tribal affairs in the second half of the 1800s, many Pit River Indians complained about government interference. The Indian Reorganization Act of 1934 offered some freedom from government interference if tribes agreed to adopt a constitution like the U.S. Constitution. The Pit River Indians' constitution was finally accepted in 1987. It set up a tribal council with eleven members, each representing a Pit River group. Members are working to unify a community whose people are widely scattered and have strong and differing opinions on tribal issues.

ECONOMY

The Pit River Indian economy was based on fish and other river products, acorns, and plants. The Atsugewi traded with their neighbors, but they called it a gift exchange. A person who received a gift had to return a gift. They traded their twined baskets for Achumawi baskets and hats and exchanged more twined baskets, plus bows and furs for Maidu (see entry) skins, beads, and coiled baskets. The Yana (see entry) and Achumawi shared their acorn harvest with the Atsugewi when the crop was poor. In return the Atsugewi permitted the use of their lands for gathering root crops. The Achumawi also granted the Atsugewi use of their fishing grounds in return for access to Atsugewi root-digging areas.

Wealth was measured in terms of how many practical goods a person owned, such as pine canoes, furs, buckskins, cooking utensils, and fishing nets.

After whites began to settle in California, many Pit River Indians went to work for them on ranches and in saw mills. Some continued to gather plants in familiar territory as they always had done. In the twentieth century, the logging industry has declined in their territory, and many have sought logging work elsewhere in California. Others do seasonal work away from their homeland, picking fruits and vegetables, for example.

For the few who remain on the reservations and rancherias, some income is generated by a bingo venture run by the tribe. The tribe is also investigating ways to reap profits from tourists who visit the region's national forests and hunting and fishing areas. Among such business being considered are recreational vehicle parks, campgrounds, and gift shops.

DAILY LIFE

Families

Families consisted of a father, mother, their children, and a few relatives. Three or more families lived together in one home. The people had a great affection for children and considered them very valuable. Childless women felt shame and might consult a doctor to see what their problem was.

Education

The Atsugewi believed strongly that hard work was the way to succeed. They arose at dawn, often to the sound of their chief urging them to get up and do something for a living. A person who got little sleep was highly regarded, and was given the respected nick-name Nohalal, meaning "Going all the time."

Children were encouraged to be hard workers, and started working from the ages of eight or nine under the guidance of their parents. Young girls learned that idle chatter was not permitted while doing the important work of gathering food. Yet it was important to know just how much work was enough: Those who worked too hard were considered not very smart, because lazy people often reaped the fruits of their labor.

Children also received moral training. They were taught to display modesty in the presence of the opposite sex and to refrain from lying, fighting, and disobedience, lest they be punished by a beating with a coyote's tail.

In the late 1800s Christian missionaries and the Bureau of Indian Affairs set up religious and boarding schools for Pit River children. Since the 1930s, children have attended local public schools.

Buildings

The Atsugewi lived in two types of homes: sturdy winter structures and brush huts set up near hunting and gathering areas during the summer. Winter homes were oval in shape and were sunk about three feet into the ground. Split logs and bark covered the wooden frame, which was overlaid with earth and grass. A ladder was placed next to the central post opening, which served as both an entrance and smoke hole. The interior was very simple. A thin layer of grass covered the floor, and mats made of tule (pronounced *TOO-lee,* a plant material) hung from the dirt walls. There was no furniture, and bedding was rolled up and put aside during the daytime. These dwellings varied in size from less than 12 feet in length to as long as 20 feet.

Most Achumawi villages lined the Pit River, which at 2,000 feet above sea level was the warmest section of Achumawi territory. During the summer, the Achumawi lived in tepees covered with tule mats. Winter homes, cone-shaped and partly underground, housed several families and measured about 15 square feet. The Achumawi used trees that had been felled by nature to make the support beams. A smoke-hole in the center of the roof also served as entrance and exit by way of a ladder strapped to the central post. Tule bedding mats and skins furnished the interior. Several larger buildings—up to 20 feet by 30 feet—served as ceremonial houses.

Clothing and adornment

ATSUGEWI During the summer, Atsugewi women wore a double apron (it covered the front and back) of shredded cedar bark or fringed buckskin. Wealthier women decorated their aprons with pine nuts or bones. Basket-like caps covered their heads. Men usually wore a white coyote-skin apron, which hung down to their knees; behind hung a second apron, with the coyote's tail still attached. During the winter they wore fur or skin cloaks, leggings, mittens, hats, and waterproof moccasins. Wealthier people adopted the buckskin shirts more typical of the Great Basin and Plains tribes.

Men and women both grew their hair long. Men rolled their hair up into a hair net, while women wore pigtails wrapped in strips of mink, deerskin, or grass. Men and women groomed their hair with porcupine tail brushes, and kept their hair shiny and supple by applying deer marrow. The Atsugewi painted their bodies red, blue, and white. Young girls had their chins tattooed in vertical lines. On special occasions, tribal members wore strings of beads and shells; the chief wore eagle feathers, while others wore magpie feathers.

ACHUMAWI Achumawi clothing showed influences from east of the Rocky Mountains and the Pacific Coast. Women usually wore a fringed deerskin, shredded tule, or juniper bark apron, and a basket-like cap. On important ceremonial occasions they wore long fringed and beaded dresses, often decorated with porcupine-quill embroidery or hummingbird feathers. To protect themselves in winter they wore capes, moccasins, and deerskin leggings. They often dyed their clothes with minerals and plants that produced yellows, reds, blues, blacks, and whites. Women painted their faces with a mixture of grease and a red mineral. They wore braids or coiled their hair on top of their heads and tattooed their chins with three lines.

Men wore deerskin shirts and robes, leggings and moccasins. Badger skins were used for smaller garments, such as caps and capes. They painted their faces red on special occasions. Shells hung from their pierced noses, but unlike the women they were not tattooed.

Food

MEN'S WORK Fish and acorns were the staple foods of the tribe. Salmon was probably the most important fish, but trout was also caught. Groups who had access to salmon or acorns often invited those who did not to share in their bounty. Men were responsible for hunting and cooking meat, and for fishing, although in some groups women and children drove fish into nets held by men. They employed a number of methods for catching fish, such as drugging them with wild parsley, and hanging gill nets vertically in the water, trapping the fish as they attempted to swim through. At night, men fished from pine or cedar canoes, attracting the fish with torches and spearing them. This fishing method is still practiced today.

They hunted deer, antelope, elk, rabbits, badgers, and wood rats. Meat that was not eaten fresh was dried and partially smoked for preservation and winter storage. They also hunted fowl such as ducks, cranes, grebe, pelicans, coot, geese, swans, mudhens, grouse, meadowlarks, robins, and blackbirds. They trapped waterfowl in nets placed across rivers and swamps; once caught, fowl were clubbed to death. Some groups would not eat mink, grey fox, coyote, eagle, buzzard, magpie, or crow, either for religious reasons or because they did not taste good.

WOMEN'S WORK The Atsugewi considered women more valuable than men, because tribal survival during winter depended on the women's ability to gather sufficient supplies for storage. Acorns were pounded into flour and processed with hot water to remove their bitterness. Other foods gathered by women included various roots, pine nuts, tiger lilies, wild onions, manzanita berries, gooseberries, huckleberries, and sunflower seeds.

Food was usually boiled in baskets, roasted on hot stones, or baked. The Achumawi did not add salt to their food because they believed it caused sore eyes. They occasionally burned large areas of grass to flush out grasshoppers, which were collected and stored until winter. Grasshoppers and the larvae of yellow-jackets were considered delicacies. The only plant they grew was tobacco.

HOW THE PIT RIVER INDIANS GOT THEIR NAME

The name Pit River Indians comes from the tribe's unique hunting technique. Ten- to twelve-foot deep pits were dug along river banks for trapping game. Brushwood and grass concealed these holes, and the deer fell into them as they came down to drink. White settlers forced the Natives to abandon this hunting practice because many of their cattle and horses stumbled into the traps.

Healing practices

Illnesses were believed by the Pit River Indians to be caused by the departure of one's soul, bad blood, or by evil spirits, who were sometimes sent to them by faraway enemy tribes. Shamans, who had contact with healing spirits, were called upon to cure the afflicted one. There were three kinds of shamans: the sucking shaman, who sucked out the object that caused the disease; the singing doctor, who cured by singing to call the healing spirits; and the bear doctor. Bear doctors were men or women who could either cure or harm. Some groups believed the bear doctor could put on a grizzly bear skin and head and actually "become" a bear. This type of doctor was both respected and feared.

Village elders decided who would become a shaman-doctor. Few people wanted the job because it could be dangerous. If the shaman did not catch a disease as it left the body, it could escape and cause epidemics. To keep this from happening, a shaman who failed once too often to cure his or her patients was sometimes killed by a shaman from a neighboring tribe; the disease was then thought to die with the shaman.

Herbs and plants were also used for healing. For example, Wild parsley was a remedy for colds, coughs, and stomach aches. Snakes were warded off by rubbing one's legs with chewed angelica roots.

Long after the disruption of their society by white settlers, the Pit River Indians continued to rely on their ancient ways of healing. Even if they desired the services of modern medical doctors, they were often unable to secure them because they lived in remote areas. Things are changing slowly. The tribe now has a few medical clinics to serve its needs, and wells and other sanitary services are being installed.

AN ENCOUNTER WITH THE *TAMCÌYE*

The Atsugewi and Achumawi liked to tell creation stories. The Creator was an animal, usually either Grey Fox or Eagle. Coyote, the trouble-making trickster, also played an important role in creation stories.

Storytelling was usually meant for entertainment rather than to teach lessons, but children did hear stories of evil spirits who punished disobedience. Friendly spirits who often turned up in stories were dwarfs called tamcìye, who lived in the same way that people did. The tamcìye brought men strength and luck. The following story describes a man's encounter with the tamcìye.

One spring a lazy man went to the bench near Lost Creek to get pine nuts. Here he met two tamcìye women who asked him what he was doing. They said, "We don't eat that kind of food. You better go back with us." They took him to their house on the west side of Bald Mountain, where there was an earth lodge. He saw all the tamcìye people. The men were out hunting deer or fishing. In the evening they returned. The lazy man stayed with the tamcìye for a while, and they treated him with much hospitality. When he wanted to return home, the two tamcìye women made ready to go with him as his wives. He was given a buckskin shirt, pants, a bow and arrow, and other things. Before this he had been naked. The two women loaded themselves with dry meat and other things, and the three started to his home. But before they reached his home he made an excuse to go into the bushes, saying that he wanted to urinate, and as soon as he was out of sight he started running. He wanted to leave the women. They saw him running and were angry. They took back all the clothes and beads they had given him, so that he had nothing on when he arrived home. The man told his family what had happened. They were very angry with him for running away from the two women. He was a fool. If he had brought them back he would have made a good living.

SOURCE: Thomas R. Garth, "Atsugewi Ethnography." *Anthropological Records* 14, No. 2 (1953).

CUSTOMS

Courtship and marriage

The hardest-working woman was the most-prized bride. If she came from a wealthy family, so much the better—she was considered more valuable than a man. Once the bride's parents checked out the good reputation of the groom's family, who did some checking of their own, the families exchanged presents and the wedding took place. Often the wedding ceremony simply consisted of the groom spending the night with his bride.

A man could divorce a lazy wife by returning her to her family. If he could afford the wedding gifts, he might try out several brides before settling on one. If one partner died, his or her family "owned" the survivor, who had to marry another member of the same family.

Pregnancy and childbirth

Some pregnant women returned to the home of their parents to give birth. They were assisted by their mothers, who sometimes offered a drink made from oak bark to prevent blood poisoning. The grandmother also had the task of making the baby's first cradle.

Puberty

Although the people were usually too busy to engage in ceremonies, an exception was made for the beginning of puberty. The ritual varied from group to group, but a girl's ritual might be like this one: When her first period began, her father sent her into the hills, asking the spirits to aid her. At midnight on the first day, she began to dance. For the next four or five days she continued to dance, stopping only to dig for roots if it was summertime or to collect firewood in winter. She got little or no sleep, and the more energy she displayed, the better a worker she was believed to become. The ceremony ended with the piercing of the girl's ears or nose, which meant she was at last a woman.

When a boy's voice broke, he went on a power quest. His father or a respected village elder lectured him about his conduct and whipped him with a coyote's tail or a bow string before sending him into the mountains for two or three days. The boy fasted, lit fires, and sometimes cut his arms or legs with a sharp object. If the boy reported hearing a fawn call, he was believed to have a future of good hunting ahead of him. If he heard a groan, it was a sign that he should become a shaman.

Funerals

The dead were either buried or burned without much ceremony, together with their clothing, personal valuables, and a basket of water. Women mourners shaved their heads and covered them with soot or a sticky liquid. The dead were feared, and it was forbidden to speak their names, because they might return looking for a traveling companion on their journey through the western mountains. When an important tribal member died, his house might be burned along with two or three unpopular people who would become his traveling companions.

War and hunting rituals

In some groups, before warriors departed for battle, they carried out a mock fight against the women of the village, screaming and pretending to go after them with drawn bows. After the warriors left, the women danced war dances. Upon the warriors' return, women anointed them with roots and tea. Sometimes warriors cremated their fallen comrades in the battlefield and brought the ashes back to their village.

A skilled hunter was greatly respected, especially a man who killed grizzly bears, because he received bear powers when the bear was killed. A man who returned from a hunt empty handed, however, was ridiculed. Of all the animals hunted by the tribe, deer were the most prized. Sometimes a chief summoned a group of men to a communal deer hunt by sending round a message—knots on a piece of string, the number of knots indicating how many days until the hunt.

The night before the hunt, the men gathered in the sweat house, where they drew up a hunting scheme. Sometimes they charmed deer and antelope with singing. Sometimes they wore a deer-head disguise to get close to the animals.

Festivals and ceremonies

The Atsugewi people worked so hard that ceremonies were a rare luxury. At regular intervals, though, village chiefs ordered a day of rest, when men gambled and women cooked. Sometimes the Pit River Indians attended Maidu ceremonies (see entry) if they happened to be passing by Maidu villages at the right time.

CURRENT TRIBAL ISSUES

The Pit River Indians continue to gather plants for eating and healing. Other tribal issues remain private according to the wishes of the tribal council. A tribal representative has explained that many historical accounts about the tribe are inaccurate; however, she was unwilling to state what these inaccuracies consist of.

NOTABLE PEOPLE

Darryl "Babe" Wilson (1939–), the son of an Achumawi father and an Atsugewi mother, is a member of the Pit River tribe. He has worked to preserve the oral traditions of all Native people and has written essays, short stories, and poetry. His book *Wilma Mankiller: Principal Chief of the Cherokee Nation* was published by Modern Curriculum Press in 1995.

FURTHER READING

Boulé, Mary Null. *Atsugewi Tribe.* Vashon, WA: Merryant Publishing, 1992.

Curtis, Edward S. *The North American Indian,* Vol. 13. 1924. Reprint. New York: Johnson Reprint Corporation, 1970.

Voegelin, Erminie Wheeler. *Pit River Indians of California.* Garland Publishing, 1974.

Pomo

Name

Pomo (pronounced *PO-mo*) means "at red earth hole."

Location

The Pomo lived in northern California, near Clear Lake and the Russian River in present-day Mendocino, Sonoma, and Lake Counties. Today, they live on or near about two dozen mostly tiny, isolated rancherias and reservations located throughout their homeland.

Population

In the early 1800s, there were between 13,000 and 20,000 Pomo. In a census (count of the population) done in 1990 by the U.S. Bureau of the Census, 4,766 people identified themselves as Pomo.

Language family

Hokan.

Origins and group affiliations

The Pomo have lived in the hills and valleys north of present-day San Francisco for more than ten thousand years. Historians believe that early Pomo lived around the shores of Clear Lake, but a western branch split off from the rest, settling along the Russian River and near the Pacific Coast. There were more than seventy Pomo tribes divided into seven groups: Northern Pomo, Central Pomo, Southern Pomo, Southwestern Pomo or Kashaya, Eastern Pomo, Southeastern Pomo, and Northeastern Pomo.

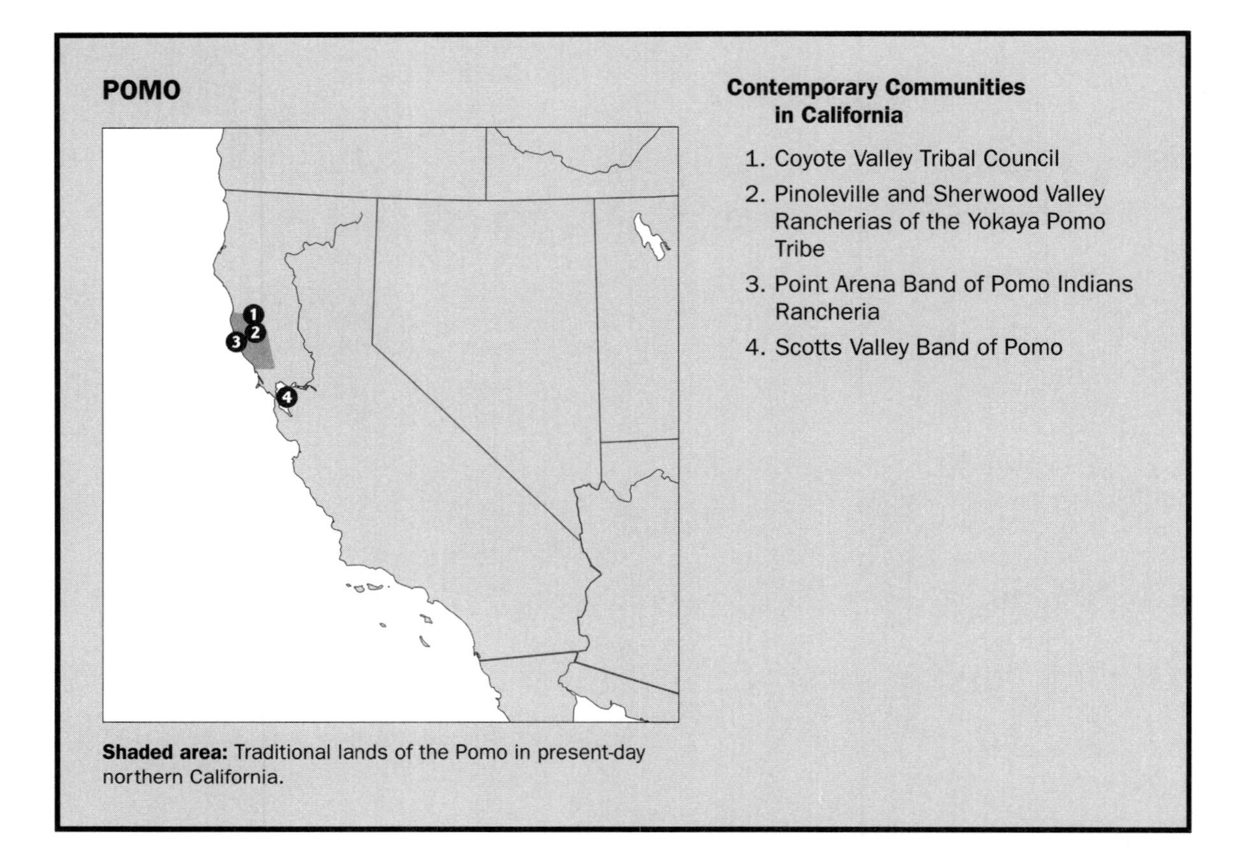

Shaded area: Traditional lands of the Pomo in present-day northern California.

For thousands of years the Pomo lived calm, well-ordered lives filled with laughter and song. Their story after contact with Europeans is a tragic one. They suffered outrageous brutality at the hands of Russians, Spanish, Mexicans, and Americans, who polluted their lands, made slaves of them, and slaughtered innocent men, women, and children. By the late nineteenth century, only a thousand or so Pomo remained, homeless in their own homeland. Federal government and private efforts of their own regained some land for the Pomo in the twentieth century, and their population began to grow.

HISTORY

Russians in Kashaya Pomo territory

There is surprisingly little information about Pomo history and ways of life before the arrival of white men in the nineteenth century. The Pomo may have had a brief encounter with British explorer

Francis Drake (1540–1596) after his 1579 landing in Coast Miwok territory (see Miwok entry) to the south of the Pomo. If there was such an encounter, it was not written down.

Groups of Pomo were spread out over a large territory, so they did not all encounter the same nationalities of white men. Each incoming group—first Russians, then Spanish, then Mexicans, and finally white Americans—played a part in the near-destruction of this large and important California tribe.

The Kashaya Pomo lived along the Pacific coast in present-day northwest Sonoma County. They were the only Pomo group who had contact with Russians, who established Fort Ross in 1811 on Bodega Bay in Kashaya Pomo territory. The Russians were there to take advantage of the big profits to be made from sea otter furs, but they also took cruel advantage of the Pomo people. They kidnaped and enslaved Pomo women and children and used them as hostages to force Pomo men to hand over furs and food.

IMPORTANT DATES

1811: The Russians establish Fort Ross in Kashaya Pomo territory.

1817: The first Spanish mission is founded in Pomo territory.

1850: U.S. Army massacres most residents of a small Pomo village.

1856: Many Pomo move to the Mendocino and Round Valley reservations.

1881: Pomo chiefs organize a fund-raising drive to buy rancherias.

1958: The state of California terminates the status of many Indian tribes, including the Pomo rancherias.

1980: Pomo woman Tillie Hardwick begins fight for federal recognition of terminated rancherias. In 1983, she wins her case and federal reservation status is restored to 17 California rancherias. In the meantime, many Indians have lost their lands.

1990s: The fight for federal recognition of all Pomo rancherias continues.

Like the Tlingit tribe to the north (see entry), the Pomo resisted the Russian invaders, but the resistance mostly consisted of a few escapes and small-scale attacks on individuals. By the time the Russians left in 1842, many of the Kashaya Pomo had died—from murder, overwork, or diseases brought by white men.

Spanish and Mexicans exploit Southern Pomo

Meanwhile, the Spanish, who claimed California as their own, feared its takeover by the Russians or British, and decided to establish forts and missions there. The forts would protect California for Spanish settlement, and the missions would convert California Natives to the Roman Catholic religion, and at the same time teach them skills so they could become slaves or laborers for the Spanish settlers.

The Southern Pomo came under the control of Spanish missionaries when a mission was built at San Rafael by 1817. About 600 Pomo people were baptized at Mission San Rafael and at Mission San Francisco de Solano.

In 1822 California became part of the Mexican Republic, and the missions were closed. Mexicans took over Pomo lands, resulting in skirmishes between the new ranchers and the Pomo people. This was especially true in the Clear Lake region. One Mexican landowner, Salvador Vallejo tried to force a group of Eastern Pomo to harvest his crops. When they refused, he sent Mexican troops after them, and the soldiers massacred some of the men who were sitting peacefully in their sweathouse. Thousands of Pomo were captured or died between 1834 and 1847 at the hands of Mexican soldiers. Trade in Indian slaves and epidemics of smallpox and cholera claimed thousands more lives.

Pomo mistreated by American settlers

The United States won California from Mexico in 1848 and California became a state in 1850. American settlers immediately poured in and began seizing Native lands. They soon reached Pomo groups who had previously had little contact with whites: the Northern Pomo, Northeastern Pomo, and Central Pomo. Hostile relations flared between these new settlers and the Pomo people, just as they had with the Mexican settlers.

Matters came to a head after two white landowners, Andrew Kelsey and Charles Stone, were killed. For three years, the pair had been forcing hundreds of Pomo to work on their ranch, even though slavery was illegal in California. Tired of being starved, beaten, and even shot, some Pomo slaves rebelled, killed both of their tormentors, and fled into the hills.

U.S. Army soldiers sent to capture those responsible for the killings came upon a peaceful group of Eastern Pomo gathered on a small island on Clear Lake. Innocent men, women, and children were slaughtered at the site, which was later renamed Bloody Island by the Pomo. The soldiers continued eastward, killing as they went, though their victims had nothing to do with the murders of Kelsey and Stone.

Pomo forced onto reservations

Hoping to end the violence that was taking place throughout California, in 1851 the U.S. government sent agents to discuss treaties with Indian tribes. In these treaties, California tribes, including the Pomo, agreed to give up most of their lands to the U.S. government in exchange for a total of about 7.5 million acres that would be set aside for reservations.

White Californians were horrified that so much land was being given away (about 8 percent of the state). They were also afraid that the

Indians they had been using as slave labor would disappear onto reservations. Such an uproar was raised that the U.S. Senate rejected the treaties. Shortly after, 1.2 million acres were set aside for reservations.

The Pomo people were rounded up and forced to move to the Mendocino Reservation and Round Valley Reservation, along with Indians from several other tribes. Pomo lands were promptly taken over by white settlers. Ten years later, in 1867, the Mendocino Reservation was abruptly closed, and many of the remaining Pomo were left completely homeless. Some returned to the area of their homeland, only to find the best land had been taken over by whites. They settled on some poor, unwanted pieces of land in the region. They watched their numbers decline as people died from diseases, and their traditions and beliefs began to disappear.

By the turn of the century, the remaining Pomo, numbering only a little over a thousand, lived a poverty-stricken existence. They survived on fish, game, and plants, in addition to the few items they could afford to buy in stores. To the dominant white culture, they were seen as second-class citizens or worse, kept apart from whites, and discriminated against.

Landowners again

But Native groups began to rally, and they united to buy pieces of their former land. Pomo groups pooled the meager sums they earned by working on white-owned ranches and the money earned by selling their beautiful feathered baskets. They bought the rancherias of Pinoleville and Yokaya. (Rancheria is a Spanish term for a small ranch.)

Religious groups and some government officials began to get involved in the rancheria movement, and the Indian Reorganization Act of 1934, which was partly designed to counteract the damage done by previous Indian policies, helped to supply funds to buy more reservations and rancherias. The Pomo bought more land. They also became skilled at using the American justice system to their advantage. In 1907, an Eastern Pomo named Ethan Anderson filed a lawsuit that resulted in the right to vote for Indian groups who had previously been denied that right. Legal actions by the Pomo and other Natives resulted in all Native Americans being granted full U.S. citizenship in 1924.

Termination

New federal government policies in the 1950s resulted in a change of status for California rancherias, including many Pomo settlements. If the rancherias agreed to terminate their special relationship with the federal government (a relationship called federal recognition), they were promised help from the Bureau of Indian Affairs in improving life on the rancherias. These promises of help were never carried out. Instead, Pomo land was divided privately among members of the rancherias, and many of the owners later lost their land because they could not make mortgage or tax payments.

In the 1970s, when it became obvious that the Bureau of Indian Affairs was not going to fulfill its promises to make improvements on the terminated rancherias, a Pomo woman named Tillie Hardwick filed a lawsuit against the United States of America. She won, and several rancherias were successful in regaining federal recognition. "Federally recognized" means the tribes and groups have a special legal relationship with the U.S. government. The relationship entitles them to certain benefits and financial assistance.

Today, the Pomo are working to keep their culture, language, and many traditional arts alive. At the same time, they continue to explore ways to work within the American system to expand their land base and to find ways to earn money from the tourists who flock to the beautiful area of their homeland.

RELIGION

The Pomo believed in many spirits, including a creator-hero who gave his name to the secret religious society called Kuksu. The Kuksu Society was open only to a small group of men, who were selected while very young to go through a long training process. Once they became members, they were responsible for carrying out many of a village's ceremonies and public affairs. At ceremonies, Kuksu dancers pretended to be spirits and wore special head pieces made of sticks with feathers at the ends. Their bodies were generally painted black. The dance rituals ensured good luck, such as abundant acorn and fruit harvests or protection against natural disaster and enemy attack.

A lesser religious society called the Ghost Society was open to all young men and, in some Pomo groups, to women too. The Ghost Society performed dances like those of the Kuksu to honor the dead. Both the Ghost and the Kuksu societies were led by professional spiritual guides, or shamans (pronounced *SHAY-munz*).

Ghost dances and dream dances

After their society was disrupted by the forced move to reservations, the Pomo adopted the Ghost Dance Religion of 1870 (see box in Maidu entry). When that religion failed to deliver on its promise to rid the world of white people, the Bole-Maru or New Ghost Dance religion was adopted.

Bole-Maru translates roughly as "spirits of the dead." The Bole-Maru religion combined elements of the old Ghost Society and the Ghost Dance Religion. Its leaders were people who had received visions in dreams; some of those visions included songs and dances, which were then taught to men and women of the tribe. The religion stressed moral behavior and belief in an afterlife and a supreme being. It opposed drinking, fighting, and stealing. The religion inspired hope in a desperate people, enough hope that the Pomo began to buy land of their own (see "History"), where they could preserve their culture. They still practice the Bole-Maru religion.

LANGUAGE

There were originally seven Pomo languages; three remain in use today. The 1990 U.S. census reported that 112 Pomo spoke their language in the home. Pomo language education programs and a growing number of published books on the subject are keeping interest in the language alive.

GOVERNMENT

At one time there were more than 70 independent Pomo tribes. They were further divided into groups called tribelets, which ranged in size from 125 to more than 500 persons. A tribelet is a type of organization in which one main village was surrounded by a few minor outlying settlements. Villages were made up of one or more family groups, who chose a group to be leaders.

Some villages had only one chief in charge, while others had as many as twenty. Women have always held a high position in Pomo society. There have been female chiefs, and among some groups, the right to become a chief passed from a chief to his sister's son, if the young man showed leadership qualities.

Today, most Pomo reservations and rancherias are governed by elected tribal councils.

ECONOMY

Traditional economy

The Pomo economy was based on hunting and gathering, and they also had a brisk trading economy that used money. Pomo money came in two forms: clamshells, which were ground into regular circles (disks), had a hole bored into them, and were strung on strings like beads; and beads made from a mineral called magnesite (pronounced *MAG-nuh-site*). When the mineral was treated with fire, it turned different shades of pink, orange, and tan.

The value of clamshell disks depended on the age of the clamshells, the thickness of the disk, and the length of the strung disks. Magnesite beads were considered more valuable and were traded individually rather than strung.

Food and non-food products were bartered at trade-feast gatherings. Direct money transactions—beads for fish, for example—were a common occurrence, allowing Pomo people to establish a surplus of goods. Magnesite beads were often used for gambling.

It is because of their use of money that the Pomo developed a reputation as great counters; they dealt in sums in the tens of thousands without using multiplication or division. Their knowledge of how money works proved useful when it came time for the Pomo to buy land from the U.S. government.

After confinement on reservations

Pomo rancherias have always been too small to support very many people. By the late nineteenth century, the people were forced to seek seasonal work on white-owned lands. They picked fruit and hops (a plant used in making beer), traveling from farm to farm to follow the crops. Women wove baskets to sell and worked doing others' laundry. Meanwhile, traditional Pomo hunting and gathering practices were all but lost.

Both World War I (1914–18) and World War II (1939–45) brought employment to Pomo men, who left to serve in the military or take jobs in cities. Women went to work in cities as maids. Today, only about a third of the population remains on the rancherias and reservations. The struggle to support themselves continues. They have opened some small businesses to cater to the region's many tourists, and other avenues of profiting from the tourist industry are being explored.

A recent major effort has been the Indian center called Ya-Ka-Ama, in Sonoma County. This all-purpose center has a Native plant nursery, which teaches modern ways of farming, among other educational projects. In addition, the Intertribal Sinkyone Wilderness Council, an organization made up of ten tribal groups including the Pomo, is restoring 3,800 acres of mountainous land along the California coast in Mendocino County as a model of how Native Americans make use of the land. Regarding the project, tribal council member Priscilla Hunter told *Sierra* magazine "We hope this project will teach all Indian people to get back to protecting Mother Earth, and to stand up and say that Indian people won't be pushed around any more. It is a blessing for each of us to come up here and be part of this land."

THE HIGH STATUS OF WOMEN IN POMO SOCIETY

Pomo women were rare among Native Americans in enjoying a fairly high status. They could be chiefs. Some became members of the tribe's secret societies, but they were barred from certain other societies, which held "devil-raising" performances carried on to frighten women.

Young couples often lived with the bride's family in homes occupied by several families. The oldest wife in the house was its owner. The modern history of the Pomo often makes mention of the many skilled women whose beautiful baskets were sold to white collectors to support the tribe during hard times and to help build up a land base for the Pomo people after they became homeless.

DAILY LIFE

Families

The Pomo placed a strong emphasis on the importance of families, as they still do. Their traditions include sharing land and homes with family members in close-knit communities.

Buildings

Three types of structures were common to all Pomo groups: dwelling houses, temporary or seasonal shelters, and sweat houses and ceremonial houses built partly underground. Building materials and shapes of houses varied, because some tribelets lived where redwood was plentiful, while others resided in the valley-foothill region.

For groups in redwood forest land, the most typical family structure was a conical house made of slabs of redwood bark. These were small, only eight to 15 feet in diameter and perhaps six feet in height. Though generally a single-family dwelling, they would house as many as 12 people. The assembly or ceremonial houses could be much larger, as big as 70 feet in diameter, supported by beams and partially covered by earth so that, from a distance, they appeared to be tiny hills.

Valley and lake Pomo groups tended to build circular, rectangular, or L-shaped structures of brush or reeds. The Clear Lake groups used the abundant tule (pronounced *TOO-lee*; a plant material) from the marshes for the construction of multi-family dwellings up to 40 feet in length and housing 20 people. Tule reeds were dried and bound together with split grape vines.

Food

All Pomo groups had abundant natural resources, and they were keenly aware of the proper times for hunting and gathering the

A Pomo man in a canoe made from tule, 1926.

various foods. Naturally, the Pomo diet varied depending on a group's environment; more seafood was eaten along the coast and more game was consumed inland.

Lake, stream, and river fish were caught by spear or basketry traps or nets by fishermen in lightweight, raft-like canoes. Clear Lake Pomo groups dried much of their catch, usually carp and blackfish, with salt that they acquired through trade with the Northeastern Pomo. Deer, elk, and antelope were hunted. Deer might be stalked by one person wearing a deer-head mask, or by groups. They hunted with bows and arrows, spears, and even clubs for bears. Some birds were also hunted, but others, such as the crow and owl, were not, because they had an important place in Pomo religious life.

Insects such as grasshoppers and caterpillars were also gathered and eaten. Various grasses, roots, berries, nuts, bulbs, and edible greens were eaten while in season, but the favorite vegetable food was the acorn. Ground acorn meal was eaten daily, generally served as a mush along with dried blackfish. While their methods of obtaining food may have changed somewhat over time, the Pomo continue to eat traditional foods.

Education

Older Pomo men and women were respected by the young, with whom they spent a great deal of time. Elders tended the fires and the home, allowing the younger members to hunt and gather. Special bonds formed between elders and youngsters. In some groups, for example, a young boy slept with his grandfather. He kept the old man warm at night, and in return, the grandfather taught the boy tribal history.

After they moved to reservations, Pomo children faced many hardships. Nearby towns refused to allow them to attend public schools. Pomo parents filed lawsuits challenging this practice. In one instance, the local school board established a separate school for Indian children. In 1923 a Pomo man named Stephen Knight took action on behalf of his daughter; his lawsuit resulted in the end of school segregation in Mendocino County. Segregation is a policy of separating a race or class of people from the rest of society.

Pomo woman with children and baby carrier.

Clothing and adornment

Pomo men usually wore no clothing but might sometimes put on a breechcloth, a garment with front and back flaps that hung from the waist. Women wore long skirts of shredded bark or tule. Both sexes sometimes wore mantles, cape-like garments consisting of long pieces of hide or woven plant fibers that tied at the neck and were belted around the waist. Wealthy people kept warm with blankets made of rabbit hides or other skins. The poor had to make do with shredded willow bark or other fiber.

Generally, the Pomo went barefoot, but for special occasions they might put on deer-hide boots and tule moccasins, as well as finely shredded skirts for the women and hide mantles and feather headdresses for the men.

Hair was worn long by both sexes, either loose or tied at the nape of the neck. Women wore ear ornaments decorated with beads and feathers. Clamshell beads, abalone shells, and feathers were used in belts, neck bands, and wrist bands, but these were usually saved for special occasions. Some women wore dance headdresses made of fur, feathers, and beads.

Healing practices

Pomo healing was closely connected with their religion, since healers (called shamans) were also heads of the Kuksu Society (see "Religion"). Shamans set broken bones and treated ailments, such as stomach problems, with herbs. But most illnesses were thought to be caused by the patient, who had either broken some rule and angered the spirits or had earned the dislike of some other member of the group. Shamans cured these illnesses by singing or by sucking out the sick-making poison. There were also bear doctors, who paid an annual fee for their position. They wore a bear's skin and head, and were thought to have the power to both heal and cause illness.

ARTS

The Pomo were known for their many basket-weaving techniques using a large variety of roots and other fibers, as well as shells and feathers. Pomo basketry and other crafts have been kept alive by internationally known basket weavers such as Elsie Allen, Mabel MacKay, and Laura Fish Somersol.

Oral literature

Coyote the trickster played an important role in Pomo literature. Coyote brought the Pomo people the Sun and did other favors, but he could also be cruel. Pomo stories tell of Coyote flooding the world to punish people for being cruel to his children. Other stories tell of Coyote bringing food and water to the Pomo during a terrible drought. Many birds are also featured in Pomo stories.

CUSTOMS

Festivals and ceremonies

Dancing and singing have always been an important part of Pomo ceremonies and trade-feasts. The tradition continues today, and some rancherias have even built dance houses. The Pinoleville Band of Pomo Indians began hosting an annual Big Time Cultural Awareness Gathering in 1994. The Big Time, which is open to the public, gives the Pomo people an opportunity to reunite and participate in traditional songs and dances.

Courtship and marriage

Marriages were arranged by parents. Children were not forced to take suitors picked for them by their parents, but they could not marry someone else without their parents' approval. With many Pomo groups, there was a trial period of living together in the woman's dwelling before gifts were exchanged and the marriage took place. After marriage, the young couple would live for a time at one of the in-laws before settling in the home of the other. Some couples remained with the groom's or bride's parents until they had children; then a new door would be cut in the home and a new fire and sleeping area added. Young couples did not generally move out on their own; only in the case of a very full house would a new one be constructed.

Childbirth

A woman normally gave birth in her family's home. Afterwards, she was presented with gifts by both sides of the family, usually lengthy ropes of clamshell beads with up to 800 disks each. Among the Eastern Pomo, the father could not leave his home for up to eight days after the birth and was forbidden to hunt, gamble, or dance for a month. Children were given two names, one each chosen by their mother's brother and their father's brother. They were often named after deceased relatives.

Puberty

Special ceremonies were performed for boys and girls when they reached puberty. Eastern Pomo girls were purified in a steaming ceremony, in which they lay on tule mats with hot coals all around. On the fourth night the girl bathed and was given a basket of acorns. She performed the complicated acorn preparation process, then served an acorn mush to her family.

Throughout their youth, boys were given songs to learn and at age 12 were presented with a bow and a fancy beaded hair net. A few boys were chosen each year to begin the long training to become a member of the Kuksu Society (see "Religion").

Death and funerals

At death, the body lay in the house for four days so that its spirit might leave. Mourning was public and dramatic, with female relatives crying and scratching themselves deeply enough to leave scars. Hair was cut short and gifts were brought. The body was then taken outside and burned, face down and pointing toward the south. The home and its contents were often burned too. Such burning ceremonies were largely stopped by the U.S. government after 1850.

CURRENT TRIBAL ISSUES

A primary issue for the Pomo is recognition by the federal government of Pomo rancherias that were terminated in the 1950s (they lost their special relationship with the federal government; see "History"). The largest Pomo settlement, Hopland Rancheria (2,070 acres), is among those seeking "untermination." Other important issues are acquiring more land and providing housing for tribal members.

Since the 1970s, the Pomo have been battling attempts by big businesses to build on sacred grounds. The waters of Clear Lake have been polluted by wastes from old, abandoned mines, from homes and resorts built around it, and from pleasure boats that race on it.

NOTABLE PEOPLE

Elsie Allen (1899–1990) was a well-known Pomo basket weaver, scholar, educator, cultural preservationist, and writer. She not only kept the art of basket-weaving alive, she created a world-wide interest in it. Her illustrated book *Pomo Basketmaking: A Supreme Art for the Weaver,* (1972) tells her life story.

Pomo/Wintu/Patwin basket weaver, doctor, and cultural preservationist Mabel McKay (1907–1993) is the subject of a biography by Pomo/Miwok writer and professor Gregory Sarris called *Weaving the Dream.* (As the title suggests, McKay dreamed the design of her baskets.)

Pomo elder, chief, and tribal historian William Benson (1860–1930) was one of the few Pomo men who made beautiful baskets. He turned to this craft when there was no longer a need for the basketry fish traps that Pomo men usually made.

FURTHER READING

Giese, Paula. "The California Pomo People, Brief History." History of the Pomo people of California, written by Paula Giese of the Native American Books Web site. [Online] http://indy4.fdl.cc.mn.us ~isk /art/basket/pomohist.html

McAuliffe, Claudeen E. "Elsie Allen," in *Notable Native Americans.* Sharon Malinowski, ed. Detroit: Gale, 1995.

Poole, William. "Return of the Sinkyone." *Sierra.* 81 (November/ December 1996): 52–55, 72.

Yahi and Yana

Name

The word Yahi (pronounced *YAH-hee*) is a form of the word Yana; both words mean "people." White settlers called the Yahi and Yana "the Deer Creek Indians," "the Mill Creek Indians," or "the Lassen Indians."

Location

The Yahi Yana occupied the area along Deer and Mill Creeks, bordered on the west by the Sacramento River and on the east by Mt. Lassen in northern California. The Yana lived in the east section of the upper Sacramento River Valley, from Pit River in the north to perhaps as far south as Rock Creek.

Population

In the early 1800s, there may have been between 1,500 and 3,000 Yana people, of whom 200 to 300 were Yahi Yana. The last Yahi Yana, Ishi, died on March 25, 1916. There were an estimated 20 Yana in 1973, but in the 1990 census (count of the population), no one identified themselves as Yana.

Language family

Hokan.

Origins and group affiliations

The Yana (the Yahi were a smaller group of Yana who spoke a slightly different language) lived in northern California for more than 3,000 years before contact with white men. The Yahi Yana were friendly with the Yana, the Nomlaki, and the Wintun (they often hunted and camped in Wintun territory). They were enemies with the Maidu (see entry). The Yana feuded and often fought with many of their neighbors, such as the Wintun and the Achumawi (see Pit River Indians entry).

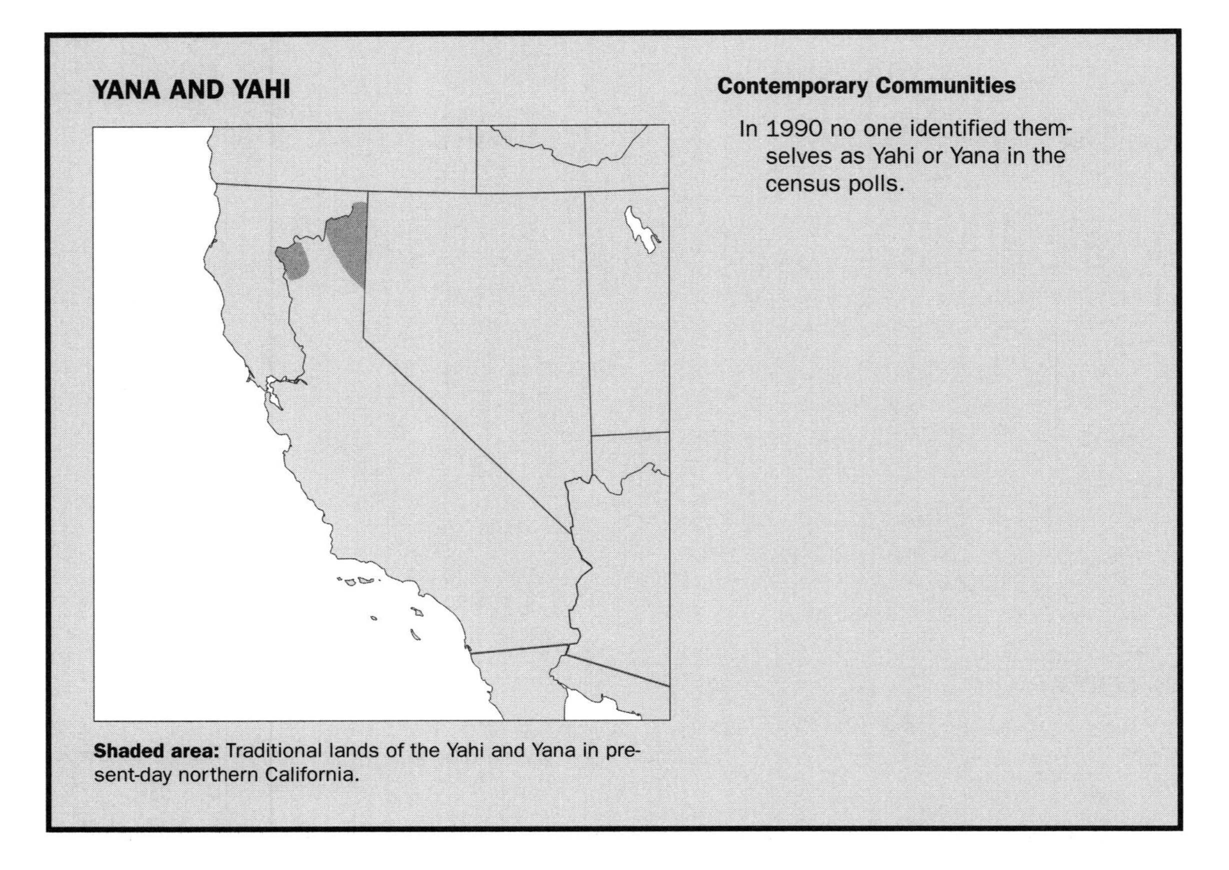

YANA AND YAHI

Shaded area: Traditional lands of the Yahi and Yana in present-day northern California.

Contemporary Communities

In 1990 no one identified themselves as Yahi or Yana in the census polls.

Yana territory in northern California has been described by historian Alfred Kroeber as "a region of endless long ridges and cliff walled canyons, of no great elevation but very rough, and covered with scrub rather than timber. The canyons contain patches of brush that is almost impenetrable [one can't get through it], and the faces of the hills are full of caves." In this rough land the Yana and Yahi long thrived but soon perished after the white men came. Their memory is preserved in the Ishi Wilderness, a rugged portion of the Lassen National Forest.

HISTORY

Settlers take over Native lands, food supplies

Little is known about Yana life prior to contact with white men. They had lived in the foothills of Mt. Lassen for many years. Some groups may have had contact with whites as early as 1821, when Spanish explorer Captain Luis Arguello journeyed eastward from San

Francisco. Between 1828 and 1846, the Yana probably encountered English fur trappers from time to time, but they had little real interaction with white people until the late 1840s. That is when non-Indians began to settle in the Yana homelands, and the theft of Yana lands and destruction of their people began.

IMPORTANT DATES

1844: White settlers begin moving into Yana territory.

1846: The first major assault against the Yana is launched.

1848: Settlers travel through the Yahi territory on the Lassen Trail. Conflicts begin.

1858–65: Hundreds of Yana are moved to reservations.

1864: Whites almost succeed in destroying the Yana.

1908: The last band of Yahi are disturbed by surveyors, who take all of their winter supplies.

1911: Ishi, the last Yahi, enters white society.

1916: Ishi dies of tuberculosis.

In 1848 Peter Lassen, a local settler, began leading new settlers over the Sierra Nevada mountains into the Sacramento Valley along the ridge between Mill Creek and Deer Creek. This route became known as the Lassen Trail and was used frequently until 1850.

Settlers' cattle ate the Natives' food, causing much hardship for Yana peoples. The Natives got even by stealing cattle—since it was grazing on their land, they believed they were entitled to it, and they needed the cattle to feed their families. Relations between the settlers and Natives grew so bad that the Natives began to hide their food. That way, if settlers chased them out of their homes, they would still have something to eat.

Massacres of Yana people begin

Whites often took violent action in response to the Yana's stealing of food. In 1846 U.S. Army Captain John Frémont led the first major attack when he surprised a peaceful Yana group on Bloody Island on the Sacramento River. The tales of other massacres of Yana people were written down by observers. Thomas Waterman wrote that the Yana's desperation in stealing food indicated that they were "very badly off at this time." Waterman related one instance where 40 to 60 Yana were killed for stealing some cattle. According to Waterman, the last 181 people of the Southern Yana were removed from their homelands in 1858 and taken to the Nome Lackee Reservation. Many of these people were very sick, and they died when the reservation was abandoned several years later.

The fighting went on and on as white men sought to destroy the entire Yana nation or remove the people to reservations. Sometime between 1858 and 1865, U.S. Army officers led 277 Yana to Round Valley Reservation in Mendocino County. Many died on the way or were too sick to finish the journey. Around 1864, white citizens killed

ISHI, THE LAST YAHI INDIAN

On August 29, 1911, a tired, starving, frightened man left the forests of his Yahi homeland and wandered into an Oroville, California, slaughterhouse in search of food. He had been living alone in hiding, terrified of the white men who had murdered his people and taken over his land. When he was discovered, the sheriff put him in jail because he did not know what to do with this man.

Local Indians were brought to speak with him but he could not communicate with any of them. He was the only person left who could speak in his Native Yahi tongue. He was taken to San Francisco by Professor Thomas Waterman of the University of California. There Alfred Kroeber, a curator at the anthropology museum that became the man's home, gave him the name Ishi, which means "man" in Yana.

Ishi had apparently gone into hiding at about the age of ten. From the year 1872 forward, he and his people had to stay completely out of the sight of white people. One of his hiding places was a concealed area called the Grizzly Bear's Hiding Place. It was occupied by Ishi, his mother, a sister, and two men. One day in 1908, a couple of surveyors happened upon Ishi while he was fishing. He fiercely scared them away. Shortly after that, a party of surveyors found the Grizzly Bear site. Ishi's mother, who was sick, was there, wrapped in a blanket. The men took all useful items, including food and implements, and left the dying woman behind. Ishi returned to move his mother, but she died a few days later. The others in his small group had disappeared, and Ishi was totally alone for a period of nearly three years.

most of the surviving Yana in response to the murder of two white women. Another terrible massacre followed, in which 300 Yana who were attending a ceremony were killed. Only a handful of Yana survived that slaughter.

The Yahi and the U.S. Army

Still the violence did not end. In 1868, white settlers appealed to the U.S. Army for assistance with their "Indian problem," and soldiers were sent out to punish the Indians for raiding white homes. Yahi Indians living on Mill Creek were considered the most troublesome, and army troops had orders to round up their leaders and send them to Alcatraz Island for imprisonment (see box). The cycle of raiding and retaliation continued. Thomas Waterman wrote that "these murders by the Indians were not one [bit] more cruel . . . than the murders of the Indians by whites. I incline wholly to believe that the whites started everything of the sort. They were certainly . . . the aggressors, pushing constantly into Indian territory."

In 1862 three children were killed by the Yahi. The settlers vowed to destroy every Yahi Indian who could be found, and by 1874 there were few Yahi left alive. Over the years they were seen from time to time by settlers, but no one was able to catch them. They lived in

After surfacing in the public world, Ishi lived for five years in the University of California's museum as a live exhibit. He demonstrated to Waterman, Kroeber, and the public his skills in making bows, arrows, harpoons, spears, and other tools. Ishi was given a job as an assistant to the head janitor, which allowed him to earn a small salary. In May 1914, Waterman, Kroeber, and Dr. Saxton Pope took Ishi on a trip back to his homeland. For three weeks Ishi displayed his intimate knowledge of the landscape and ways of survival.

Ishi had very little resistance to the diseases of the Californian settlers. He was often sick while living at the museum, and on March 26, 1916, he died of tuberculosis.

The strangeness of the world he had entered may have overwhelmed Ishi at first, but he showed remarkable adaptability and quickly made close friendships with the people involved in his life. Alfred Kroeber's wife, Theodora, who would later write a book about Ishi, wrote of his shyness and dignity, saying: "He was interested, concerned, amused, or delighted, as the case might be, with everything and everyone he knew and understood." Thomas Waterman wrote to Arthur Kroeber after Ishi's death that Ishi "was the best friend I had in the world." His doctor, Pope Saxton, wrote upon Ishi's death, "And so, stoic and unafraid, departed the last wild Indian of America. He closes a chapter of history. He looked upon us as sophisticated children—smart, but not wise. . . . His soul was that of a child, his mind that of a philosopher."

Thomas Waterman wrote in *Ishi, the Last Yahi,* that Ishi "convinced me that there is such a thing as a gentlemanliness which lies outside of all training, and is an expression of a purely inward spirit. He never learned how to shake hands but he had an innate [natural] regard for the other fellow's existence, and an inborn considerateness, that surpassed in fineness most of the civilized breeding with which I am familiar."

hiding, leaving no trace of their existence. They learned to hop among the rocks, never leaving a footprint on the earth. They practiced walking without breaking twigs or vegetation, which would provide an indication of a trail. They were spotted so rarely that by the early 1900s, it was believed that the Yahi had all been wiped out.

The last of the Yahi

In 1908 a team of surveyors (people who measure the boundaries and other features of an area) accidentally stumbled upon a hidden Yahi village. They reported that an old man and a middle-aged woman escaped. It was later learned from Ishi, the last Yahi survivor (see box), that he thought they jumped to their death. The surveyors also found a partially paralyzed elderly woman, lying on the ground, wrapped in a blanket. The surveyors helped themselves to the contents of the camp. They took bows, arrows, baskets, and blankets—everything the little band of Yahi would need to survive the winter. The surveyors visited the camp the following day to find that its inhabitants had fled. Three years after this disturbance, Ishi, the only remaining survivor of the band, emerged from his homeland to spend the rest of his life with scientists who wanted to learn about him and his culture. What is known about the Yahi and Yana is mostly due to Ishi's willingness to share his knowledge with these scientists. With his death in 1916, the Yahi ceased to exist.

Ishi, the last Yahi survivor, photographed in 1911, the year he emerged from the forest.

RELIGION

Little is known about the religious beliefs and practices of the Yana. Their religious leaders were also healers, called shamans (pronounced *SHAY-munz*), who were usually male but sometimes female. The people believed that both humans and non-humans possessed supernatural powers, which allowed them to live forever. Some historians think they had a secret religious society called the Kuksu Society (see Miwok entry), which held religious dances.

In 1871 the Northern Yana adopted the Ghost Dance Religion, which they learned about from the Maidu (see box in Maidu entry). Members believed that if they performed the Ghost Dance, the Earth would swallow up all white people and life would be as it was before whites came.

Between 1872 and 1873, some Yana became believers in the Earth Lodge Cult, an offshoot of the Ghost Dance Religion. Members of the Earth Lodge Cult danced to bring on the end of the world. When it came, believers would be protected in underground earth lodges. After the destruction was over, believers could live on in peace. Dreams, songs, and dances were important parts of the Earth Lodge Cult.

LANGUAGE

Yana groups living in different regions spoke different dialects (varieties) of the Hokan language. They could understand each other, but not perfectly.

An interesting feature of the Yana language is its division into genders. When men talked among themselves, they spoke one form of the language; women talking among themselves spoke another. However, men used the female form of speech when talking with women, although women never used the male form of speech. Both sexes understood each other's language and the differences were considered the proper way to speak.

The forms of the language used by men and women might differ in this way: Women would take the ending off the "male" form of a word. So *Yana,* meaning "person," becomes *Ya* in the mouth of a woman (or in the mouth of a man when he was talking to a woman); *auna,* "fire" and *hana* "water," become *auh* and *hah.*

In *Ishi in Two Worlds,* author Theodora Kroeber, who spent a great deal of time with Ishi, discussed how Yana people might converse with their relatives. Men did not look directly at or continue a long conversation with their mother-in-law or daughter-in-law. Women behaved the same toward their father-in-law or son-in-law. This way of speaking was considered a sign of respect and is illustrated by Ishi's behavior when visiting the home of his doctor, Saxton Pope. Pope wrote, "His attitude toward my wife or any other woman member of the household was one of quiet disinterest. Apparently his sense of [what was proper] prompted him to ignore her. If spoken to, he would reply with courtesy and brevity [few words], but otherwise he appeared not to see her."

GOVERNMENT

The Yana lived in independent groups and each group dwelled in one large village and a number of smaller surrounding settlements. Usually the chief lived in the large village. He was wealthier than other villagers and had two wives. The position of chief was passed from father to son.

Village members helped the chief by giving him items of value; for example, a successful hunter might share his deer carcass. The chief served his group by making speeches and acting as a dance leader.

ECONOMY

The economy was based on hunting and gathering and trade. In spite of feeling unfriendly toward their neighbors, the Yana actively traded with them. They got arrows, woodpecker scalps, and wildcat quivers from the Atsugewi (also called Pit River Indians; see entry) in exchange for shells and salt.

DAILY LIFE

Buildings

The shapes of houses and the materials used in constructing them depended on where a group lived. Some built cone-shaped, single-family houses, made of slabs of cedar or pine bark. They rose four to six feet above ground level over a two-foot-deep pit. Banks of earth placed around them prevented ground water from seeping into the home. The entrance faced south. Other groups had similar but larger houses that accommodated several families. There was a smokehole in the roof that some groups used as an entrance, while others built separate doorways.

Other buildings might have included earth-covered sweathouses, meeting houses, and huts where women were confined during their menstrual periods (menstrual blood was considered powerful, even dangerous). During the hot summer months, the Yana made their seasonal trip to higher and cooler elevations, where they built temporary grass and bark houses.

The housing materials and building methods of the Yahi changed after contact with white society. Ishi's village, for example, was built to hide its inhabitants, and used native and non-native materials. In *Ishi in Two Worlds,* the author described the village, called *Wowunupo mu tetha* ("Grizzly Bear's Hiding Place"). It consisted of a cookhouse, storehouse, smokehouse, and living house. The cookhouse contained a fireplace, stones for grinding acorns, cooking baskets, cooking stones, and utensils. It was covered with a brush roof to provide shelter from the sun and rain and to "diffuse the smoke," so that no one could detect their hiding place. The smokehouse, used to smoke salmon, was built of driftwood with a roof of old canvas taken from a white settler's covered wagon. The storehouse was shaped like a letter A. It had a pole framework tied together and thatched with bay branches. Inside it was separated into two rooms, for the storage of baskets, food, and tools. The living house was also an A-shaped building. It was covered with strips of bark and laurel.

Food

The Yana people got their food by hunting and gathering. Women did most of the cooking and gathering, but some Yana husbands built the roasting pits, collected the fuel, and cooked the roots and tubers (underground vegetables such as potatoes) gathered by the women.

Acorns were the staple food; if the acorn harvest was meager, people could starve. Men and women both participated in the gathering of acorns in September and October: men shook the acorns from the trees, while women collected them. They usually made the acorns into a mush. Other important foods included bulbs, buckeyes, clover, berries, sunflower seeds, hazelnuts, sugar-pine and digger-pine nuts.

They hunted large game like deer, elk, and bear, and smaller game such as rabbit, duck, quail, and goose. Some Yana groups fished in the Sacramento and Pit Rivers, but fish was considered an important food source only to the Yahi, whose Deer and Mill creeks were filled with salmon. Salmon were speared, while trout were caught with hooks, poisoned by cucumber pulp dumped in trout pools, or captured behind a wicker net. Salmon were broiled on heated rocks, roasted over a fire, or dried and stored.

Clothing and adornment

Women wore buckskin dresses and aprons or skirts made from shredded plant material. Behind the apron some wore a large piece of buckskin or plant material to cover the back of the body. Wealthier women decorated their clothing with leather fringes and braided tassels made of grass and pine-nut beads or bones, adding belts of braided human hair. Women covered their heads with basket-like caps, which were painted with black and white patterns.

Men also wore aprons and robes of deer, rabbit, wildcat, coyote, and bear skins. They tied the robes around their chests with buckskin string or wide elkskin belts. In cold weather, wealthy men wore leggings that stretched from their hips to their ankles, while poor men wore a deerhide skirt that left their legs uncovered. Sometimes a robe made of three or four deer hides sewn together was worn over the shoulders and also served as a sleeping blanket. Some groups wore a variety of shoes, including deerhide moccasins, sandals, and snowshoes.

Men and women wore their hair long. Men usually tied their hair in back or on the top of their heads. They plucked out their facial hair with a split piece of wood. Women parted their hair in the middle and wore it in two braids shaped into rolls and wrapped in mink or buckskin.

Both sexes wore necklaces made of bear claws, shells, clamshell disks, bones, juniper berries, and a type of mineral called magnesite (pronounced *MAG-na-site*). Other decorations included feather and skin headbands, woodpecker-scalp belts, leather earrings covered with beads, and shell and wood jewelry worn through their pierced noses. Tattoos were worn but they were not common.

Healing practices

Ishi described Yahi Yana healing practices to Dr. Saxton Pope. Ishi said that older women cured minor ailments with herbs, but shamans tackled major medical problems.

THE CREATION OF MEN

Yana stories explained past events and traditions; many contained moral messages. The Yana believed that animals were the creators of people. In this creation story, the place where people were created, Wama'rawi, *is near Battle Creek in the approximate center of Yana territory.*

Lizard, Gray Squirrel, and Coyote lived in a big sweat-house at Wama'rawi. They had no wives or children. Coyote wanted to make people, but the others thought that they themselves were enough. Finally Lizard agreed, "We'll make people, different kinds of people." So Lizard went out and cut three sticks like gambling sticks. The others wanted to know how he was going to make people out of these. Lizard said, "I'll show you." One stick he took for the Hat Creeks . . . one for the Wintun . . . and one for the Pit Rivers. . . . When he looked at them he said, "There is something lacking." Coyote asked, "Who has been left out?" Lizard said, "The Yana." So he took any kind of stick, broke it up into little pieces, and put them in a pile for the Yana. The stick for the Hat Creeks he placed in the east, the stick for the Wintun in the west, the stick for the Pit Rivers in the north.

All three, Lizard, Gray Squirrel, and Coyote, then made a big basket, heated rocks, put water in the basket, and heated the water by putting the hot rocks into the basket. Then Lizard put the sticks into the boiling water, put in more hot rocks to boil the sticks. All then went to sleep, after setting the basket outside on the roof and covering it up. Before they slept Lizard said, "Early in the morning you will hear some one when the basket turns over. That will be because there are people. You must keep still, must not move or snore."

Early in the morning they heard people falling down, heard the basket turn over. By and by they heard the people walking about outside. They got up, then covered the door with a large rock to keep the people out. They did not talk or answer those outside. For a long time the people were talking. One called out, "Where is the door?" Coyote said, "Keep still, that talk does not sound right." Others then spoke, asked also. Then Coyote said, "Now it sounds right," and then they opened the door. Then all the people came crowding in, all came into the sweat-house. Then the three said, "It is well. There are people."

SOURCE: Edward Sapir. "Yana Texts." *University of California Publications in American Archaeology and Ethnology* 9, No. 1 (1910).

Like many Indians of northern California, Ishi thought that most pain was caused by foreign objects in the body. These objects might be spines, thorns, bee stingers, or pins. The job of the shaman was to suck these pains out of the sick person's body or grab them from the air around the sick person. Once he got hold of the object, the shaman placed it in some type of container, often a bird carcass, that was sealed with pitch (a sticky substance obtained from pine trees) so that the sickness could not escape and cause further harm. Sometimes a shaman who did not perform his job properly, or who practiced evil or bad medicine, was killed.

Dr. Pope wrote that when Ishi was feverish he did not want to bathe with water because he believed it was important to sweat out the illness. Pope also wrote about some of Ishi's personal healing practices. Ishi had a hole in his nose, in which he wore a small piece of wood. When he had a cold, he placed a twig of juniper or baywood into this hole. When Ishi inhaled the scent of the twig, his airways opened. Ishi treated rattlesnake bites by binding a frog or toad to the bitten area.

CUSTOMS

Festivals and games

There is very little information about Yana festivals. The people are known to have been fond of dancing. They painted their faces red and white, and the men put on net caps or headdresses made of wildcat skin when dancing or on special occasions. Dancers might be accompanied by the music of rattles, flutes, and whistles.

The Yana enjoyed playing games. Jerald Jay Johnson wrote that even men enjoyed a game called double-ball shinny, usually played only by Native California women. Johnson said they took pleasure in "ring and pin, cat's cradle, throwing sticks at a stake, a child's ball game, and several forms of the grass or hand game" (a type of team gambling game).

War and hunting rituals

Although the Yana were not on friendly terms with their neighbors, they were not in the habit of waging wars. However, Yana warriors sometimes accepted payment from the Pit River Indians to join them in battle against the Wintun. Occasionally, the Yana began a war in retaliation for trespasses on their hunting grounds or the kidnaping of their women. In preparation for fighting or entering dangerous situations, they wrapped their hair around the top of the head and tied it in a topknot.

Hunting was done both by individuals and groups. Young boys were sometimes struck with their first kill to ensure good luck in future hunts.

On bear hunts, several men surrounded the animal holding flaming torches. As the bear tried to escape, the men aimed their arrows at its mouth. This went on for a long time until the animal became too exhausted to fight and was finally killed.

Ishi told Dr. Saxton Pope that Yahi men knew many animal calls and would hide and wait to ambush the animal. Deer hunters wore stuffed deer head decoys to attract the deer's attention and lure it closer so it could be killed with bows and arrows.

THE STORY OF ALCATRAZ ISLAND

Alcatraz Island is a small, barren, rocky place located in San Francisco Bay. In 1859 it was made a U.S. military prison, and some Yana people may have been imprisoned there in the 1860s. The military moved out in 1933, at a time when lawless people called gangsters were becoming a national problem. The federal government decided it needed a prison for the worst of these criminals, a remote place that would allow no escape and no communication with the outside world. Alcatraz Island, called "The Rock" by inmates, became America's first super-prison.

The prison closed in 1963, in part because Americans were rethinking many social policies, including that of imprisoning people without giving them any chance to rehabilitate (reform) themselves. At this time, policies toward Native Americans were being rethought too. Natives had become frustrated and angry at U.S. government actions that took away their lands and aimed to break up their reservations. They showed their displeasure in a number of ways, including the takeover of Alcatraz Island.

One hundred years before the takeover, the federal government had agreed that Indians who were not given reservation lands could claim abandoned forts, prisons, and other facilities no longer wanted by the government. In November 1969, 300 people, mostly college students, calling themselves the Indians of All Tribes, seized the abandoned prison on Alcatraz Island and claimed it as their own under this 100-year-

Courtship and marriage

Yana marriages were arranged by the young couple's parents. Gifts were offered by a young man's parents to the parents of the woman he desired to marry. If the gifts were accepted he had permission to marry her. Among the Yahi, if a man died his brother had to marry his wife. Men were also allowed to marry their wife's sister if their wife died.

Childbirth

Shortly before a woman gave birth, she moved to a birthing hut and stopped eating meat and salmon. The father could not hunt or fish during this time. The mother was attended by several helpers, including her own mother. If it was a difficult birth, a shaman was called in.

After giving birth, the mother lay in a shallow pit heated with hot rocks. When the child's umbilical cord dropped off, the parents purified themselves by performing a sweating ceremony and returned to normal living.

Naming

The Yana did not name a child until sometime after six years of age. Ishi said he never had a real name, because he had been all alone and

old government policy. They were led by Richard Oakes, a Mohawk Indian.

The Indians of All Tribes offered to pay the government $24 in glass beads and other trinkets. This was a mocking reference to the 1626 purchase of Manhattan Island (New York City) from the Canarsee tribe of Delaware Indians by Dutch traders for $24 in trinkets. The Indians of All Tribes offered to care for poor white people on Alcatraz Island, a mocking reference to the federal government "taking care" of Native Americans. In a biting allusion to longstanding government and missionary efforts to make Indians more like white people, the Indians of All Tribes declared: "We will offer them [white people on Alcatraz Island] our religion, our education, our life-ways, in order to help them achieve our level of civilization and thus raise them, and all their white brothers up from their savage and unhappy state."

The Indians of All Tribes occupied Alcatraz Island for nearly two years before being forcibly removed in June 1971. On the island they set up a sanitation council, day-care, a school, housing, and cooking facilities. They demanded that the federal government turn over the island to them and pay for a cultural center, a university, and a museum.

Many considered the protest a failure, but the protestors drew national attention to the problems Native Americans faced in dealing with poverty and the destruction of their cultures. During their occupation, the U.S. Senate voted to return Blue Lake, a sacred site, to the Taos Pueblo Indians of New Mexico. After the occupation, a Native American university was established near the University of California at Davis.

there had been no one to give him a name. The name Ishi was given to him by Alfred Kroeber, a caretaker of the museum of anthropology at the University of California who became a significant friend to Ishi.

Puberty

Women who were menstruating were considered bad luck. During a girl's first menstrual period, she stayed by herself in a menstrual hut and ate only acorn mush and berries. It was forbidden to touch herself with her fingers, so she used only a wooden or bone scratcher. After this ritual, every woman was required to rest in the menstrual lodge for six days each time she had her period.

Funerals

The Yana buried their dead, but the Yahi burned them. Before burial, a body was washed, dressed in fine clothing, placed in a flexed position, wrapped in a deerskin blanket, and tied with rope. The dead person's belongings were broken before being placed in the grave with the body. At the gravesite, mourners danced, cried, cut their hair short, and painted their heads with pitch. After burial, the Yana avoided saying the name of the dead person.

The Yahi cremated a body immediately after death in order to release the person's soul to begin its westward journey to the Land of the Dead. Once the soul reached its destination, it would be greeted by family and friends and directed to a place at a campfire. If the person were not cremated, his soul remained in the Land of the Living, wandering about unhappy, lonely, and causing trouble to the living. After cremation, the ashes and bones were gathered into a basket, which was buried under a rock in order to mark the grave and keep animals away.

CURRENT TRIBAL ISSUES

Steven Shackley and Jerald Johnson are archaeologists—people who study the remains of past human cultures. They have a theory that Ishi may not have been a full-blooded Yahi. During Ishi's childhood, California was in a state of turmoil; Natives were being forced onto reservations with members of other tribes. The theory is that Ishi may have been of mixed ancestry or descended from a different tribe altogether. Shackley examined arrowheads made by Ishi, and said they are more similar to those of neighboring tribes than of the Yahi type. Johnson stated that Ishi looked more like the Maidu, Wintun, or Nomlaki than the Yana.

Edward Castillo (see Luiseño entry), a historian who has studied California Natives, responded to these theories with the counter that Ishi may have learned different tool-making techniques because of his unusual lifestyle away from his own people. Or, since Ishi spent five years in the University of California's museum, surrounded by different types of arrowheads, he may have observed them closely enough to reproduce them. Ishi had shown he was able to adapt to different ways of doing things. For example, he switched to glass for making arrowheads when traditional materials became hard to get. Ishi's goods are on display at the University of California-Berkeley's Phoebe Hearst Museum.

FURTHER READING

Curtin, Jeremiah. "The Yanas." *Creation Myths of Primitive America.* Boston, MA: Little, Brown, and Company, 1903.

Johnson, Jerald Jay. "Yana." *Handbook of North American Indians,* Vol. 10: *Southwest.* Ed. Alfonso Ortiz. Washington, DC: Smithsonian Institution, 1983.

Kroeber, Alfred Louis. *Handbook of the Indians of California.* New York: Dover Publications, 1976.

Kroeber, Theodora. *Ishi in Two Worlds: A Biography of the Last Wild Indian in North America.* Berkeley: University of California Press, 1961.

Pacific Northwest

Pacific Northwest

The Pacific Northwest extends from Yakutat Bay, Alaska, in the north to roughly the California-Oregon border in the south. There are over three dozen separate identifiable groups in the Pacific Northwest culture area, representing a variety of different language groups and cultural lifeways. Living between the Pacific Ocean and the coastal mountain ranges, the Native people of the Pacific Northwest are traditionally oriented towards coastal and riverine environments. Their sustenance, oral traditions, and religious expression emphasize the importance that the resources of these environments have held in their cultures.

The Pacific Northwest culture area can be divided into five cultural regions based on similarity of culture and/or language:

In the northern area the defining characteristic is the matrilineal kinship system, in which family name and inheritance, as well as rights to property and privileges, including resource sites and ceremonial activities, are passed down through the mother's side of the family. The Tlingit (pronounced *KLINK-it*), Haida (*HIGH-da*), and Tsimshian (which includes the Nisga'a, Gitksan, coastal and southern Tsimshian) are often called the "northern matrilineal tribes."

The Wakashan area, found along the south-central coast of British Columbia and the nearby eastern shores of Vancouver Island, is composed of the Kwakwala-speaking peoples, including the Haisla, Heiltsuk (Bella Bella), Oweekeno, and Kwakwaka'wakw, as well as the Nootkan-speaking Nuu-chah-nulth, Ditidaht, and Makah.

The Salish include the contiguous tribes and bands of southwest British Columbia and western Washington, the outlying Nuxalk of the central British Columbia coast, and the Tillamook of the northern Oregon coast.

Along the Columbia River, from its mouth to the Cascade Mountains, are the several groups of Chinookan-speakers.

Along the Oregon Coast are located numerous bands of Penutian and Athabaskan speakers.

The variety of culture and experience of the Pacific Northwest tribes presents interesting comparisons. Not only is there a great deal

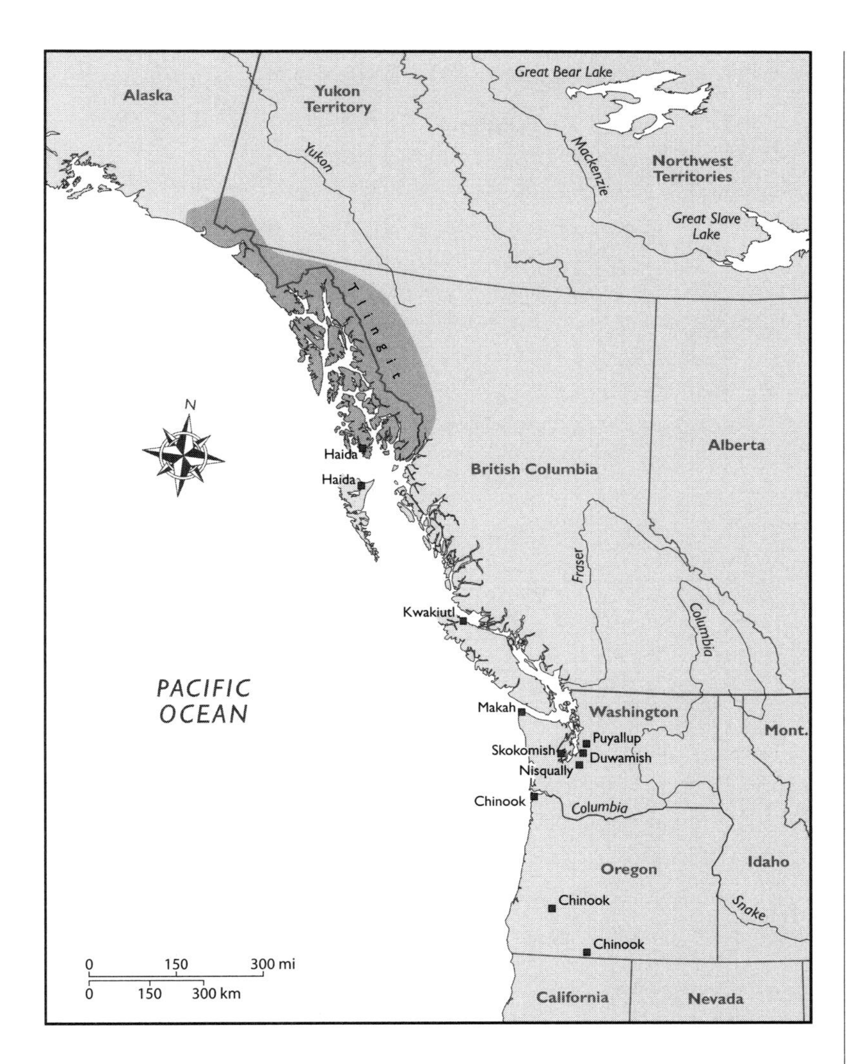

A map showing some contemporary Native American communities in the Pacific Northwest.

of difference in language and culture, but the different political boundaries have created historical and contemporary issues that differ significantly as well.

European contact

At the time of first European contact, the Native people of the Northwest Coast had well-developed political and economic systems. Abundant resources met their needs for subsistence (food, shelter, and other necessities to stay alive) and provided a surplus that contributed to trade and ceremonial life. Population estimates suggest that the Pacific Northwest was densely populated for a non-agricultural region. At the time of European contact, the northern matrilineal area probably numbered about 42,000, the Wakashan area about 34,000, the Salish about 48,000, the Chinook about 22,000, and the Oregon Coast groups about 30,000.

First contact with Europeans began with explorations in the 1700s; Pacific Northwest groups briefly encountered the Russians and the Spanish. The latter part of the eighteenth century was characterized by more brief encounters, primarily for the purpose of trade. This maritime (sea-oriented) trade was stimulated when the British Captain James Cook (1728-1779) discovered that sea otter pelts from the Pacific Northwest could bring high prices in China. After this discovery, land-based commerce was established by the Spanish at Nootka Sound in 1789, the Russians at New Archangel (Sitka) in 1799, and the Americans—who established a post at Fort Astoria at the mouth of the Columbia River—in 1811. Fort Astoria later fell to British hands, and through the early 1800s, British trading companies became well established throughout the Pacific Northwest.

At the time of, or perhaps even before, these earliest encounters, the Native people of the Pacific Northwest suffered from diseases introduced by the arriving Europeans. Infectious diseases—smallpox, measles, influenza, typhoid fever, and many others—devastated Native peoples who had no acquired resistance to them. Thousands died. Estimates suggest that there was a population decline of more than 80 percent by the late 1800s. This had a profound impact on Native culture. And it was at this time, when Native people were most vulnerable, that the European influx began.

New boundaries

In 1846 the boundary between the United States and British North America was established at 49 degrees north latitude, and in 1867 Russian America (Alaska) became a United States possession. Since these events occurred, the Native people of the Pacific Northwest have experienced somewhat different political and economic forces that have figured prominently in their lives. The Tlingit and Haida in southeast Alaska had cool relations with the Russians. While some Native people adopted the Russian Orthodox Church as their religion and most traded for Russian goods, for the most part Russian influence was minimal. When Alaska became part of the United States, interactions between Natives and non-Natives continued at a minimal level until the Yukon gold rush of 1897 brought in an influx of settlers. By 1900 the non-Native population outnumbered the Native population, bringing about a major change in political and economic life. Many Tlingit and Haida participated in wage labor in fish canneries and other economic enterprises. Political and educational systems modeled after those of other states soon became common in communities in southeast Alaska. Nevertheless, the Tlingit and Haida have maintained strong ties with their traditional culture and language.

In 1971 the Alaska Native Claims Settlement Act established Native corporations throughout the state of Alaska. A regional corporation for Alaskan Tlingit and Haida and a number of village corporations were established in southeast Alaska. The corporations were established with the intent to use Native-owned land and resources to promote economic development, but success has varied.

The Canadian province of British Columbia has established different relations with Native groups, or First Nations as they are known in Canada, than either Alaska or Washington and Oregon. Vancouver Island became a crown colony (a colony of the British Commonwealth) in 1849 and mainland British Columbia in 1858. The two were joined as British Columbia in 1866 and became part of Canada in 1871. Through the late 1800s reserves (tracts of land set apart for First Nation use, like the U.S. reservations) were established for the Native groups; today there are over 200 reserves in British Columbia. In Canada the Indian Act—which was first put into place in 1876 and has been revised five times since—defines Native rights. The Indian Act determines who can claim status as a Native, outlines the relationship between Native peoples and the Canadian government, and establishes band (tribe or Native community) government. One of the most controversial actions of the Indian Act was when the potlatch (a very important ceremony in Pacific Northwest cultures; see Customs section below) was outlawed in 1884. Although the law was repealed in 1954, the Native people of British Columbia are still angered over this government action. Today, land and resource rights have become a major issue, especially as British Columbia, the federal government of Canada, and the First Nations have entered into treaty negotiations.

The experience of Native peoples in Washington and Oregon have more in common with other Native peoples of the contiguous United States. Many of the tribes signed treaties with the United States in the 1850s that established reservations, reserved certain resource rights, and instituted relations with the federal government of the United States. Political and economic forces have played an important role in the lives of the Native peoples of Washington and Oregon—adjusting

Indian encampment, Puget Sound, Washington Territory.

to changing and often contradictory federal policy, competing with non-Native interests for land and resource rights, and struggling to maintain ties with traditional language and culture against the forces of the dominant society. Treaty issues have occupied much of the attention of Native groups in recent decades as increasing development in the Northwest decreases the resources upon which Native peoples depend for their economic and spiritual well-being.

Oral literature

Pacific Northwest oral traditions are as varied as the numerous tribes that make up this culture area. All groups have origin myths, which tell of the first people, migrations, or the origin of kin groups. All groups in the Pacific Northwest differentiate between oral traditions that tell of mythical times and those that tell of historical events. Among northern Pacific Northwest tribes, these traditions may be displayed on totem poles or in other art forms. Raven, as trickster (a culture hero), is common as a character responsible for much of the natural world. The transformer (one who can change something's outward form) also plays an important role in the oral traditions of many Pacific Northwest tribes as a sometimes benevolent teacher and sometimes harmful or evil transformer of people into natural objects.

Religion

Pacific Northwest religion is animistic, meaning that the people traditionally believe in the existence of spirits and souls in all living, and in some non-living, objects. While these beliefs are acted out in ceremony and ritual, they also find constant expression in everyday life. Winter ceremonials are an important series of events that publicize and validate the religious belief system. This may involve the expression of a personal relationship with a spiritual entity, or it may involve a community expression of supernatural understanding.

A common community event is the First Salmon Ceremony, which all Pacific Northwest groups celebrated. Honoring the first fish taken from the most important run of salmon was a way of paying respect to the resource and ensuring its continuing provision of food. The First Salmon Ceremony is still practiced by many Pacific Northwest tribes.

Language

The diversity of languages in the Pacific Northwest has been a puzzle to historical linguists (people who study languages) for over a century. The region is comprised of speakers from several not very closely related North American language groupings; several languages and language groups have no known relation to any other language.

One result of this diversity of languages was the development of Chinook Jargon, a trade language used to communicate across these language barriers. Many of the languages of the Pacific Northwest are still spoken, but many are in danger of becoming extinct. Most tribes in the Pacific Northwest culture area have instituted programs to preserve their language and to teach it to younger tribal members.

Buildings

Multi-family longhouses were the norm throughout the Pacific Northwest culture area. Built of planks split from cedar logs, these dwellings would commonly house from five to ten related families. In general, each family lived in a section of the house with the central area open for cooking and heating fires. When celebrations were held, the partitions dividing the family units would be taken down. The Pacific Northwest longhouse was no longer used as a dwelling after about 1900, but the structures continue to be built and used as community buildings and for winter ceremonials or potlatch houses.

Subsistence

The most important source of sustenance throughout the Pacific Northwest are the salmon runs, in which the fish swim up into the rivers from the ocean. Several different species of salmon are native to the west coast of North America, but not all species are available in all local areas. Fishing in the Pacific Northwest involved a variety of

A Yakima man fishing for salmon in the traditional way with a dip net.

techniques, ranging from simple spears and dip-nets to complex weirs (traps) and seines (nets). Salmon provided a staple food and also a surplus for trade and ceremony.

While salmon was important, it was by no means the only food resource. Some groups fished marine (ocean) species, such as halibut, and most groups gathered shellfish. Land mammal hunting provided food for many groups; sea mammal hunting was important for others. The Nootkan-speaking peoples were especially known as whale hunters, and many groups utilized whales that had become beached. Plant foods included tubers and berries, camas and wapato (common bulbs harvested as a starchy food), and fern roots. Plants were also used for technology and medicinal purposes.

Clothing and adornment

The traditional Pacific Northwest style of garb included cedar-bark skirts and capes and, during cold weather, a blanket worn around the shoulders. Cedar bark was either shredded or woven into material used for clothing. Leather clothing was used by some groups. Most made rain hats out of cedar bark or spruce root. Blankets were items of wealth as well as clothing and bedding. Blankets were made of cedar bark, other plant fibers, mountain goat wool, or dog wool. As trade blankets became available in the late 1700s and early 1800s they largely replaced the blankets of Native manufacture.

Ceremonial garb was quite different from daily wear. Clothing worn at ceremonials and potlatches might be highly decorated with clan or family symbols or with wealth items, such as precious shells.

One of the items of wealth often used in decoration was the dentalium shell. A small shell harvested by the Nuu-Chah-Nulth people of the west coast of Vancouver Island, the dentalia was traded north and south along the Pacific Coast and as far inland as the American Plains. During ceremonials Pacific Northwest people often painted their faces to express a spirit relationship.

Healing practices

The shaman (a traditional medical practitioner) played an important role in all Pacific Northwest tribes. Shamans could practice both good and evil medicine. While some practitioners cured with herbs or other medicines, shamans generally were called upon to cure supernatural ailments. This included removing foreign objects from a person's body that had been placed there to make them ill, or performing an elaborate ceremony designed to rescue an individual's lost soul. Often in this latter case the shaman would travel to the Land of the Dead, or some other place where the lost soul had strayed, and return it to the person's body.

Shamans still practice among many Pacific Northwest societies. Among groups from the Salish southward, the Indian Shaker Church has taken over many of the responsibilities of spiritual healing that were formerly the responsibility of shamans. The Indian Shaker Church originated with the experiences of John Slocum, a Salish man, who in the 1880s had an after-death experience which led him to form this new religion.

Customs

Of all cultural practices, the Pacific Northwest people are best known for the potlatch. A potlatch is a public ceremony that involves the giving away of accumulated wealth goods. Feasting, ceremonials, ritual, and other activities might also surround the potlatch event. The climax of the potlatch was the display and distribution of wealth goods, which demonstrated the status or inherited privilege of the giver. Potlatching was carried out for a variety of reasons, including naming a child, marriage, funerals, house raising, totem pole raising, or to show affluence.

Potlatching was banned by the Canadian government in 1884 and actively discouraged in the United States. Nevertheless, potlatching continued in secret or in a disguised form until it was revived in recent years. It has since returned as a central activity in many Pacific Northwest communities.

Natives of the Pacific Northwest preparing for a potlatch.

Other customs centered around rites of passage—including birth, naming, puberty, marriage, and death. All of these life stages were recognized by ceremony and ritual, often involving the ceremonial distribution of wealth goods—a potlatch.

CURRENT TRIBAL ISSUES

The Native peoples of the Pacific Northwest culture area are politically active on local and national levels. Because political boundaries have separated them into different jurisdictions, their actual experiences vary somewhat, but current interests tend to center around land and resource claims, tribal sovereignty (self-rule), and cultural resource control.

The Native peoples of Alaska are subject to provisions of the Alaska Native Claims Settlement Act of 1971, which established regional enterprise and made tribal members shareholders in the corporations. Generally, the Native corporations have maintained some control over certain lands and resources but are expected to use these lands and resources to generate profits in the U.S. economic system. This often conflicts with traditional uses of the land for subsistence-based resource gathering and is often at odds with Native perceptions of how development should proceed. In recent years the Tlingit and Haida in Alaska have strengthened tribal government by extending jurisdiction (their power to apply law and legislate) over certain legal matters. A tribal court system exists to hear cases and determine punishment. Current efforts include the attempt to increase the power of tribal government and strengthen the control of the clan system. As the influence of the tribes has increased in the educational system, Native language and cultural programs have been instituted in most Tlingit and Haida communities.

In British Columbia the First Nations have entered into treaty negotiations with the province and the federal government of Canada. In 1992 the British Columbia Treaty Commission was established, putting into place a negotiation procedure by which the individual bands could begin the treaty process. This is the culmination of nearly one hundred years of conflict over aboriginal (native) rights in the province. Most bands in British Columbia never entered into treaty negotiations and this process promises to be one of the most influential events in their history. Coupled with treaty negotiations is the conflict over natural resources, especially salmon. In 1990 a court ruling clarified that fishing is an aboriginal right protected by the Canadian Constitution. Since that decision, Native peoples of British Columbia have participated in the salmon fishery under provisions of the Aboriginal Fisheries Strategy, a federal action designed to avoid conflict. The AFS is highly controversial and fuels the ongoing debate over what is included in constitutional aboriginal rights in British Columbia.

The Native peoples of Washington and Oregon are embroiled in issues centered around land and resource control, tribal sovereignty, gaming, and cultural resources. As treaty tribes many of the groups have treaty-assured access to resources, such as salmon; however, the serious decline of many of these resources in recent years has often meant that the right exists but the resource does not. Tribal groups have attempted to increase the power of tribal government in the decision-making process, but with mixed success. As sovereignty issues, including gaming (running gambling casinos), emerge in the 1990s, the tribes find themselves constantly battling to maintain what control they managed to gain in the last few decades. This control often includes land and resources off-reservation as well as on-reservation and tends to center around religious or subsistence use of public lands, supposedly protected by treaty or the American Indian Religious Freedom Act (signed in 1978 "to protect and preserve for American Indians their inherent right of freedom to believe, express and exercise their traditional religions.") These issues promise to command the attention of tribal leaders into the foreseeable future.

Daniel Boxberger
Department of Anthropology
Western Washington University

FURTHER READING

Adams, John W. "Recent Ethnology of the Northwest Coast," *Annual Review of Anthropology,* Vol. 10, Palo Alto: Annual Reviews, 1981: 361–392.

Boxberger, Daniel L. *To Fish in Common: The Ethnohistory of Lummi Indian Salmon Fishing.* Lincoln: University of Nebraska Press, 1989.

Carlson, Roy L., ed. *Indian Art Traditions of the Pacific Northwest.* Burnaby: Simon Fraser University Press, 1976.

Drucker, Philip. *Cultures of the North Pacific Coast.* Scranton: Chandler Publishing, 1965.

Stewart, Hilary. *Cedar: Tree of Life to the Northwest Coast Indians.* Seattle: University of Washington Press, 1984.

Suttles, Wayne, ed. *Handbook of North American Indians,* Vol. 7: *Northwest Coast.* Washington, DC: Smithsonian Institution, 1990.

Tennant, Paul. *Aboriginal Peoples and Politics: The Indian Land Question in British Columbia, 1849–1989.* Vancouver: University of British Columbia Press, 1990.

Chinook

Name

Chinook (pronounced *shi-NOOK*).

Location

The Chinook formerly lived along the shore of the Columbia River in western Washington and Oregon. Today the Chinook are divided into three main groups: the Shoalwater Bay Chinook, who live on the Shoalwater Reservation in Pacific County, Washington; the Wahkiakum Chinook, who live on the Quinault Reservation in the southwest corner of Washington's Olympic Peninsula; and the Chinook Indian Tribe, who live in various towns and cities in Oregon and Washington.

Population

In 1825, there were approximately 720 Chinook. In 1840, there were only 280. In a census (count of the population) done in 1990 by the U.S. Bureau of the Census, 813 people identified themselves as Chinook (32 identified themselves more specifically as Clatsop and 33 as members of other Chinook groups).

Language family

Penutian.

Origins and group affiliations

The Chinook have lived in their homeland for thousands of years. The Chinook Nation was made up of many tribes, including the Cathlapotle, the Kathlamet, the Clatsop, the Clackamas, the Multnomah, and the Chinook Tribe proper, also known as the Lower Chinook.

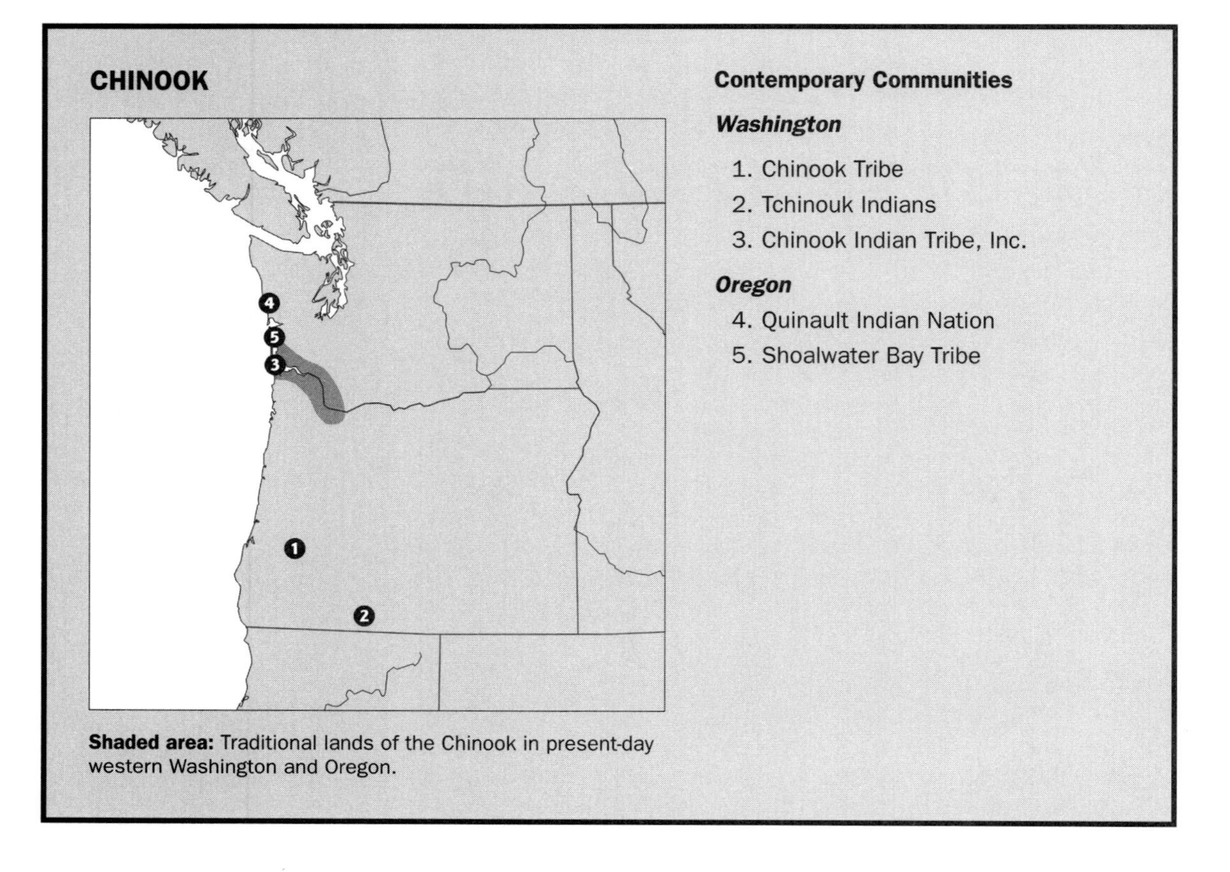

Shaded area: Traditional lands of the Chinook in present-day western Washington and Oregon.

For thousands of years, the Chinook tribe lived in Washington state along the northern shore of the Columbia River where it flows into the Pacific Ocean. The Chinook carried out extensive trade with other Native tribes and European explorers who came to the region by sea and later by land. A special trade language known as the Chinook Jargon was used by more than 100,000 people throughout the West until around 1900 (see Language Box). For more than a hundred years, the Chinook have been trying to establish a relationship with the U.S. government that would recognize them as a tribe.

HISTORY

Trading with whites

The first contact by the Chinook with non-Native peoples took place in the 1500s, when European explorers arrived on the Pacific Coast by ship. By the early 1800s, American and European trade ships regularly dropped anchor near Chinook territory to engage in trade.

In 1805, American explorers Meriwether Lewis and William Clark became the first whites to reach Chinook territory by land. By then, the fur trade had become very profitable. In 1811 John Jacob Astor, the wealthy owner of the American Fur Company, constructed a trading post called Fort Astoria on Chinook land. At first the Chinook resisted this invasion of their territory. Later, they began a productive trade relationship with the "Astorians," as the residents of the fort were called.

IMPORTANT DATES

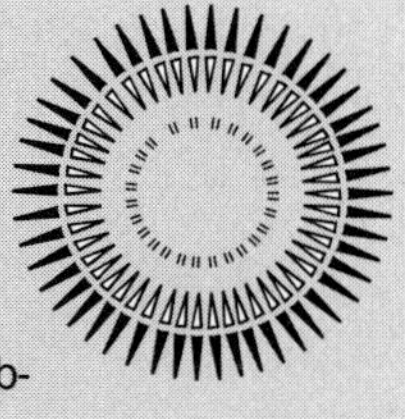

1805: Explorers Meriwether Lewis and William Clark are the first whites to reach Chinook territory by land; they establish a trading relationship.

1851: Lower Chinook sign a treaty that is never ratified by the U.S. Senate. The tribe therefore loses its chance for federal recognition and its ability to collect money for lands wrongfully taken.

1897: The Chinook become one of the first tribes to bring a successful land claims lawsuit against the United States. They receive partial compensation for their claims in 1913.

1979: Chinook Heritage Program launched to help establish legal status of tribe.

1993: The Chinook petition for federal recognition is placed on active review status.

Over the next thirty years, many traders and settlers arrived and trespassed on the tribe's lands. They brought with them diseases to which the Natives had little or no resistance. Between 1830 and 1840, nearly two-thirds of the Chinook tribe died of an illness they called the "cold sick," probably a strain of Asian flu. As the tribe struggled with this devastating epidemic, their lands were being taken. In 1851 the Chinook signed the Tansey Point Treaty, which would have assured the tribe of land and water rights in their ancestral territory. The U.S. Senate, however, failed to approve the treaty. The tribe refused another treaty set before them that would have forced them to share a reservation in central Washington with the Quinault Indians, their traditional enemies. But, with their options dwindling and their land being taken over, most Chinook did end up living with other tribes on the Warm Springs, Yakima, Chehalis, Quinault, and Grand Ronde Reservations in Washington and Oregon.

Tribe seeks money, allotments

Around 1900 the Chinook undertook the first in what would become a long series of legal battles with state and federal governments seeking to get money back for their lost lands. The tribe became one of the first to gain the right to bring a land claims lawsuit against the United States. After a lengthy court battle, the Chinook received a token settlement of $20,000 for 213,815 acres of their homeland in 1913.

Later that year, the tribe began fighting to secure allotments on an expanded Quinault Reservation that had been set aside for "fish-eating Indians." Allotments were privately owned parcels (pieces) of land into which Indian reservations were divided. During their struggle to attain allotments, the Chinook helped found an organization that involved many tribes called the Northwest Federation of American Indians.

Shoalwater Chinook gain recognition

The payments the Chinook received in legal settlements from the federal government during the twentieth century were a very small part of what they had requested to make up for the more than three-quarters of a million acres of land they had lost. Chinook people were finally granted allotments on the Quinault Reservation in 1932. The remaining Chinook lived with other Native groups or on their own in small towns and cities.

Only one of the three major groups of Chinook has gained recognition by the federal government. Without federal recognition, a tribe does not exist as far as the government is concerned, and is not entitled to financial and other help. The Chinook who share the Shoalwater Bay Reservation with Chehalis and Quinault people were federally recognized in 1979.

Efforts to attain recognition continue

The Wahkiakum Chinook, who live on the Quinault Reservation, have not won recognition. However, they did win a case against the U.S. government in 1974 that gave them the right to fish in the fishing areas used by their ancestors. It also entitled them to one-half the fish caught by Indians and non-Indians at those sites.

The third group, which is incorporated as the Chinook Indian Tribe, was recognized by the state of Washington in 1955. The federal government still refuses to acknowledge them as an American Indian nation. This is largely because of complications regarding their treaties that occurred in the last century. The lack of recognition prevents the tribe from having land claims or fishing and gambling rights, or getting money from the U.S. government.

The Chinook Indian Tribe entered the Federal Acknowledgment Program in 1978 in an effort to attain recognition from the U.S. government. Tribal elders launched the Chinook Heritage Project in 1979 to collect historical and cultural data on the tribe in order to help restore some of its traditions and establish its legal status as a tribe.

RELIGION

The Chinook were a religious people who believed in spiritual forces that guided individuals through life. Some "guardian spirits" took the form of animals while others came as invisible spirits that entered a human being's soul. At about age ten, a Chinook youngster was sent on a vision quest to meet his or her guardian spirit (see "Vision Quest" below).

The Chinook also believed that all objects contained powers. Christian missionaries were uncomfortable with the Chinook custom of worshipping sculptures and wooden objects. Both Catholic and Methodist missionaries eventually gave up their efforts to convert the Chinook.

Around 1900, many Chinook adopted the Indian Shaker religion (see Hupa and Chilula entry), which is based on a combination of traditional Native and Christian beliefs. Its followers are called "Shakers" because when they experience the power of God they shake, groan, and cry. In modern times, some members of the tribe continue to participate in the Shaker religion.

CHINOOK JARGON

The Chinook language formed the basis for the special trade language known as the Chinook Jargon, or the Oregon Trade Language. The language was widely used by traders during the eighteenth and nineteenth centuries. It began as a mixture of Native languages spoken by tribes of the Northwest who gathered to trade with the Chinook near the Columbia River. Later, when the Chinook began large-scale trading with Europeans, the Chinook Jargon incorporated words from many other languages, including Japanese and Russian. Chinook Jargon became known and used throughout the Northwest from Alaska to California. In the early 1900s English replaced the language.

Some examples of Chinook Jargon are "Hootch," meaning homemade liquor; "tzum SAM-mon," meaning spotted salmon; "PAHT-lum man," meaning drunkard; "BOS-ton il-LA-hee," meaning United States; and "TUP-so KO-pa la-ta-TAY," meaning hair.

LANGUAGE

Use of the Chinook language declined around the mid-1800s, after the loss of many members of the tribe to fatal diseases. The remaining members mixed with other tribes on reservations and adopted their languages.

In the 1890s, Franz Boas, an anthropologist (someone who studies ancient cultures), discovered two Chinook speakers living on Washington's Wilapa Bay. He recorded their accounts of Chinook legends, customs, and the authentic language. By 1900, the last fluent speakers of the language had died. Today, Chinook people are working with the information collected by Boas and with other data to reconstruct their ancestral language.

GOVERNMENT

Chiefs of Chinook villages were members of the tribe's highest social class, and the position of chief passed from father to son. Chiefs took control of the game that hunters and fishermen brought back to the village and distributed it as they liked. Chiefs could also sell orphans into slavery.

In 1925 the tribe formed a business council to help secure land allotments and protect their fishing rights, electing William Garretson as the first council president. Today, the Chinook Tribal Office in Chinook, Washington, is the site of the tribal government.

ECONOMY

The Chinook economy revolved around trade. Excess fish (especially salmon) was traded to other Natives, some from as far away as the Rocky Mountains and Alaska. The skins of sea otter, beaver, elk, deer, and bear were scraped, stretched, and smoked to make handsome hides. The hides, excess food, basket hats woven from cedar bark and spruce root, and other handmade objects were used for trade. The Chinook also specialized in the trade of blubber and canoes. Both men and women acted as traders.

Items the Chinook obtained from the Europeans, such as iron and copper goods, teapots, swords, tobacco, pots, pans, cloths, blankets, and buckets, were packed into canoes. Chinook traders then sailed as far away as 200 miles to exchange these items with other tribes, usually for furs they could trade back to the Europeans. Unfortunately, over time the number of fur-bearing animals drastically declined because of over-hunting. Other items they traded included a type of shell called *dentalium* used as money, dugout canoes, cedar boards and bark, animal horns, copper, baskets, and slaves.

Today many Chinook make their living by fishing in the Columbia River and on the Pacific Ocean. Some make yearly trips to Alaska to fish or work in canneries there.

DAILY LIFE

Families

Chinook children received a great deal of attention from their parents and grandparents and respected their elders for their wisdom. Once children learned to walk, their mothers no longer carried them about. Boys spent a lot of time swimming. Men did the fishing and hunting, while women took care of the children, sewed, wove baskets, gathered food, and made blankets. According to the accounts of Lewis and Clark, the women were "treated very badly"—they were bought, traded, or won by gambling and then put to work by their husbands so the men could purchase more wives.

A Chinook lodge, an engraving.

Buildings

The Chinook usually lived in large, rectangular houses with cedar plank walls and steeply sloped roofs thatched with cedar bark. The houses often stood about 8 feet high, and were 20 to 60 feet long and 14 to 20 feet wide. Each house might shelter up to 10 families. A Chinook village was usually made up of a long row of up to 30 such houses.

The inside of each house featured an open living area with a fire in the center, surrounded by small rooms where the different families slept. The entranceway and inner walls were decorated with colorful paintings. The floor of hard-packed earth was covered with woven mats, and beds were woven out of cedar bark or rushes. When they left the village to hunt or trade, Chinook sometimes built temporary mat shelters to protect themselves from the rain.

Clothing and adornment

Because of the constant dampness, the Chinook did not wear leather (it would soon be ruined). Instead, they wore clothing made of plant material. Men wore mat robes and wide-brimmed hats made of bear grass or cedar bark. Women wore knee-length, fringed dresses made of silk grass or cedar bark. In the winter, they covered themselves with fur blankets and robes made from the skins of dogs, muskrats, rabbits, and mountain sheep. Women sometimes twisted strips of fur together with feathers to make winter dresses. A type of body armor made of layered elkskin, called *clamons,* was a popular clothing item received in trade by the Chinook. They wore tattoos

COYOTE IN THE CEDAR TREE

Many Chinook stories centered around Coyote, who often played the role of trickster. A trickster is an animal figure that appears in stories to teach lessons by presenting the problems that humans live with. Trickster stories show reality—that the world is not perfect. They also bring out the conflicting forces at work in the world: day and night, male and female, up and down, sky and earth.

Once Coyote was traveling from the country of the Tillamooks to the country of the Clatsops. Coyote passed the mountains and the headlands of the coast. Then he followed the trail through the deep woods. As he was traveling along Coyote saw an immense cedar. The inside was hollow. He could see it through a big gap which opened and closed as the tree swayed in the wind. Coyote cried, "Open, Cedar Tree!" Then the tree opened. Coyote jumped inside. He said, "Close, Cedar Tree!" Then the tree closed. Coyote was shut inside the tree.

After a while Coyote said, "Open, Cedar Tree!" Nothing happened. Once more Coyote said, "Open, Cedar Tree!" Again nothing happened. Coyote was angry. He called to the tree, he kicked it. Then Coyote remembered that he was Coyote, the wisest and most cunning of all animals. He began to think.

After he had thought, Coyote called the birds to help him. He told them to peck a hole through the Cedar Tree. The first to try was Wren. Wren pecked and pecked at the Cedar Tree until her bill was blunted. But Wren could not even make a dent. [Here, Coyote calls other birds, but they cannot help, either. Finally the big Yellow Woodpecker makes a hole, but it is not big enough for Coyote to escape.]

and ear and nose rings made of teeth, beads, or copper, and covered their hair and skin with fish oil.

Food

Using dugout canoes up to fifty feet long, the Chinook caught fish and sea mammals near the mouth of the Columbia River. In the early spring, they used long, curved blades to rake thousands of tiny smelt into their boats. Later in the year, they probed the river bottom with long, sharp poles and caught sturgeon weighing hundreds of pounds. The highlight of the fishing season came in late spring, when the Chinook salmon made its yearly spawning run up the Columbia.

The salmon was viewed as sacred, and the people always offered the year's first several salmon to the gods during special ceremonies. They caught many fish using nets and hooks, and dried the meat for later use or for trade. Harpoons were used to hunt the sea lions and hair seals that sunned themselves near the mouth of the Columbia. The tribe also collected clams and oysters, and ate the occasional whale that washed up on shore. Bows and arrows were used to hunt deer and elk.

Women gathered edible plants and fruits including salmonberries, cranberries, currants, crab apples, cow parsnips, wild celery, cattails, skunk cabbage, and various roots.

Coyote began to think hard. After he had thought, Coyote began to take himself apart. He took himself all apart and slipped each piece through Yellowhammer's hole. First he slipped a leg through, then a paw, then his tail, then his ears, and his eyes, until he was all through the hole, and outside the Cedar Tree. Then Coyote began to put himself back together. He put his legs and paws together, then his tail, his nose, his ears, and then his body. At last Coyote had himself all together except for his eyes. He could not find his eyes. Raven had seen them on the ground and had stolen them. Coyote was blind.

But Coyote did not want the animals to know he was blind. He smelled a wild rose. He found the bush and picked two leaves. He put the rose leaves in place of his eyes. Then Coyote traveled on, feeling his way along the trail. Soon he met a squaw. The squaw began to jeer, "Oh ho, oh ho, you seem to be very blind!"

"Oh no," said Coyote. "I am measuring the ground. I can see better than you can. I can see tamanawus [spirit] rays."

The squaw was greatly ashamed. Coyote pretended to see wonderful things at a great distance.

The squaw said, "I wish I could see tamanawus rays!"

Coyote said, "Change eyes with me. Then you can see everything."

So Coyote and the squaw traded eyes. Coyote took the squaw's eyes and gave her the rose leaves. Then Coyote could see as well as ever. The squaw could see nothing. Coyote said, "For your foolishness you must always be a snail. You must creep. You must feel your way on the ground."

SOURCE: Jarold Ramsey. *Coyote Was Going There: Indian Literature in Oregon Country.* Seattle: University of Washington Press, 1977.

Education

Children in Chinook families were taught the value of hard work. Girls helped their mothers gather food, water, and wood, and learned how to make baskets and weave mats out of cattails. They also learned how to dry fish on racks or hang them from the rafters to smoke. Boys were taught how to hunt, fish, and build houses. They learned the arts of tool making, canoe building, and making nets for fishing.

Healing practices

The two types of Chinook healers were highly respected and sometimes feared by the people. Doctors called *keelalles* provided medical aid. *Etaminuas* helped the souls of dying people travel safely to the land of the spirits. Children learned during their vision quest if they were destined to be healers. The chosen few trained for about five years and then began to practice on their own.

Healers often used power sticks smeared with grease and decorated with feathers and paint to rid people of the evil spirits that were making them sick. Healers often spent several days chanting and beating the sticks on special diamond-shaped boards or on the frames of houses. Sometimes they discovered an object in a patient's body, such as a piece of wood or a stone that represented the evil spirit. These objects were destroyed in a special ceremony.

ARTS

The Chinook carved bowls and utensils from wood and animal horn. They decorated everyday items with designs of parallel lines made in wavelike or sawtooth patterns. Women created baskets from vegetation such as roots, bark, or rushes. They twined and bent several spruce root ropes into a shape, then wove in more ropes horizontally to create the sides of the basket. Designs might be animal shapes or geometric patterns. Men and women carved and painted crests (family symbols) on everyday objects, such as sticks, dance rattles, and boards.

Oral literature

Children were told to listen carefully when elders related stories about the ancient days of the tribe. Sometimes the children were asked to repeat a story exactly as it was told; no mistakes were permitted. This system ensured that the stories of Chinook life, which did not exist in written form, were preserved accurately.

CUSTOMS

Social classes

Chinook society was divided into three social classes: the upper class, commoners, and slaves. The small upper class included chiefs and their families, warriors, leading shamans (medicine men; pronounced *SHAY-munz*), and traders. While the majority, the commoners, could become wealthy by working, they rarely were allowed to rise above the class they were born into. However, sometimes an outstanding person, like a great healer, was allowed to join the upper class.

Slaves, who were usually women and children, worked at cooking, canoeing, gathering food, and cutting wood. They sometimes helped the men with hunting and fishing. Upper class Chinook purchased slaves from neighboring tribes, and seized others in raids on their enemies. Slaves could buy their freedom; some were only enslaved for a given number of years.

Head flattening

The Chinook practiced head flattening of their children, but only upper class Chinook did so. Flattened heads were considered beautiful. An infant was placed in a cradle and a padded board was tied to its forehead to mold the head into a desired shape. The Chinook were skilled in this practice, and their children did not suffer any brain damage or health risks as a result.

Vision quest

At about age ten, Chinook boys set out on a "vision quest" to find the guardian spirit who would help them get through life successfully. Taking along a special stick, a Chinook boy traveled alone to a sacred place several miles from the village. He would place the stick in the ground and fast for up to five days until his guardian spirit appeared in a vision. The guardian spirit, often in the form of an animal, told the boy what role he was expected to play as an adult member of the tribe. Sometimes the spirit taught the child a special dance or song that could be used to summon the spirit in the future. If a boy did poorly at the assigned task, it indicated that he had not been brave when his spirit first visited him.

War and hunting rituals

Although war was generally not an important aspect of Chinook life, the people occasionally used violence to respond to insults or injuries from other tribes. One description of a Chinook war dance tells of excited men shouting war threats and firing their rifles in the air. The Chinook men, wearing red, yellow and black paint, danced in a circle, yelling loudly every two or three minutes. Those with knives swiped at the air. Battles rarely resulted in any widespread loss of life. Fighting sometimes began at an agreed-upon time and continued only until the first person was killed. Then the conflict was declared over as quickly as it had begun.

Courtship and marriage

Gifts were exchanged between the families of the Chinook bride and groom. Upper class families traded beads, axes, cloth, knives, and kettles. The exchange was followed by a festive meal. Wealthy men sometimes had more than one wife. Some Chinook encouraged their daughters to marry important Indian or white men so the family could benefit from their trading business.

Funerals

Both men and women had objects that were special to them, and these items were buried with them. Sometimes bodies were placed in a canoe and suspended from a tree. Cremation and underground burial in wooden boxes became common after disease epidemics killed many Chinook.

CURRENT TRIBAL ISSUES

Today members of the Chinook Indian Tribe continue their efforts to gain recognition from the federal government, and the benefits that would come from it. They have run into problems because the treaty proposal signed by their people in 1851 never became legal and because of their refusal to sign a later treaty proposal. The tribe's petition for federal recognition was placed on active review status in 1993. At the end of the twentieth century, the Chinook were still waiting to find out whether they will finally receive the recognition from the federal government that they have sought for so long.

NOTABLE PEOPLE

Chief Comcomly (d. 1835) was a powerful Chinook leader who dominated trade along the Columbia River during the early nineteenth century. White traders held him in high regard, and Comcomly received a peace medal and American flag from explorers Lewis and Clark in 1805. After Comcomly's death during the flu epidemic in 1835, a doctor named Meredith Gairdner robbed his grave. He removed Comcomly's head and sent it to England for scientific study. After more than a century of protests by the Chinook, the head was returned to the Chinook people and reburied in 1972.

FURTHER READING

Lyons, Grant. *Pacific Coast Indians of North America.* New York: Julian Messner, 1983.

Porter, Frank W., III. *The Coast Salish People.* New York: Chelsea House Publishers, 1989.

Duwamish

Name

The name Duwamish (pronounced *dew-AH-mish*) means "inside people," referring to Native peoples living inside "the bay," or the Puget Sound (pronounced *PYEW-jit*; an arm of the Pacific Ocean that stretches up through western Washington state).

Location

Formerly in the Puget Sound area of Washington state, on the Black and Cedar rivers, and at the outlet of the Duwamish River at Lake Washington. Today the Duwamish people are scattered throughout the Puget Sound area.

Population

In 1780 about 1,200 Duwamish people were known to exist; by 1856 the number was down to 378. In a census (count of the population) conducted in 1990 by the U.S. Bureau of the Census, only 215 people identified themselves as Duwamish.

Language family

Salishan.

Origins and group affiliations

The Duwamish were one of about three dozen groups called the Coast Salish who lived in western Washington, in southwest British Columbia, and on the southeastern side of Vancouver Island. Their main ally was the Suquamish (or Squamish) tribe.

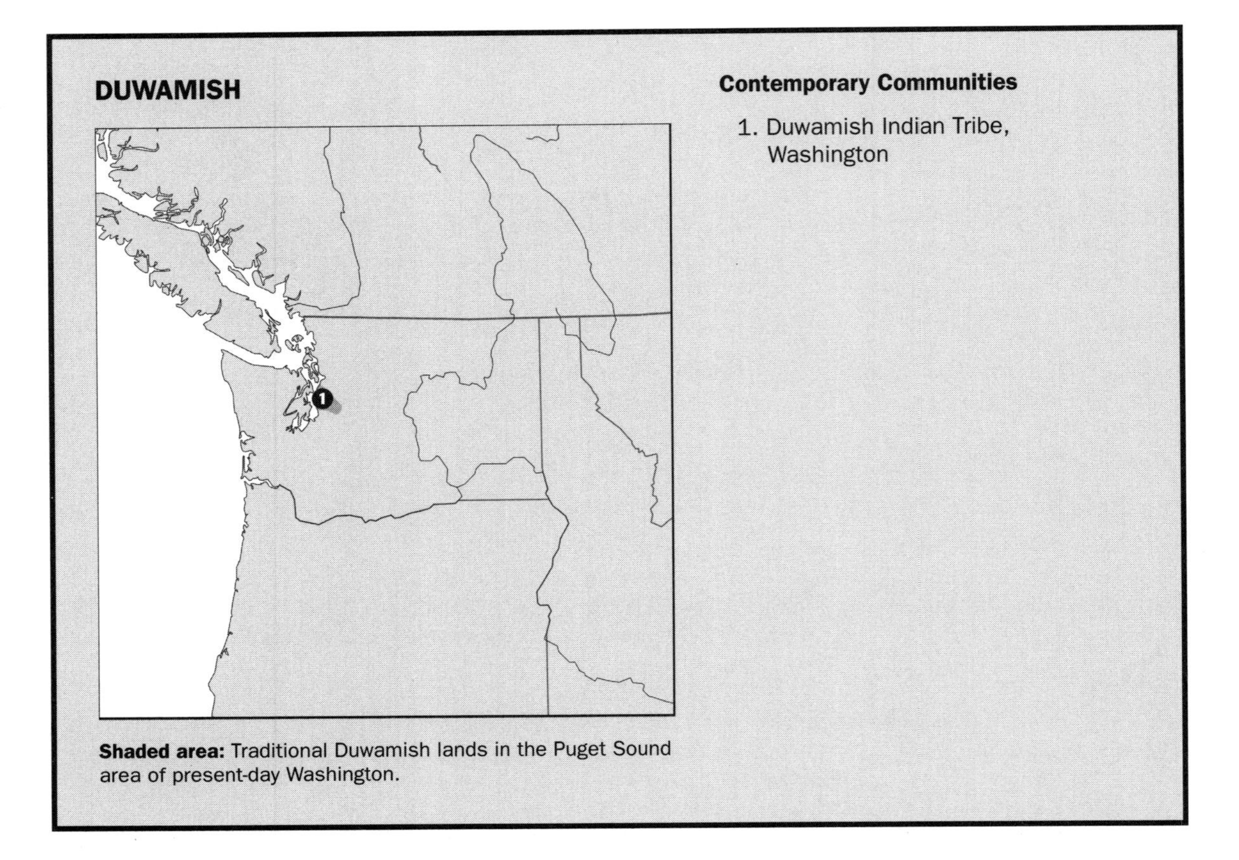

Shaded area: Traditional Duwamish lands in the Puget Sound area of present-day Washington.

The Duwamish lived in villages on the east side of the Puget Sound near present-day Seattle. The great Chief Seattle, for whom the Washington city is named, was born to a Duwamish mother. The tribe's history after contact with Europeans is a sad one: the people separated, lost all their lands, and dwindled in number, becoming nearly extinct. By the end of the twentieth century, though, the Duwamish people had started a program to reclaim and preserve their traditional tribal culture and to enhance economic development.

HISTORY

Early contact with whites

The Duwamish and other Indians of the Puget Sound first met Europeans in 1792, when British explorer George Vancouver entered the area. Europeans had little contact with the Native people in the area for the next 30 years because they were primarily interested in trade, and the Puget Sound region had few of the sea otter furs they sought.

At the time of European contact, the Duwamish were involved in ongoing wars with the Suquamish tribe under Chief Schweabe. Schweabe had a son with a Duwamish woman. This child grew up to be the famed Chief Seattle. Seattle negotiated peace among the Duwamish, the Suquamish, and other Salish-speaking tribes, but he continued warring with other tribes.

IMPORTANT DATES

1855: Chief Seattle signs Point Elliott Treaty exchanging Duwamish lands for reservation parcels.

1855–56: Some Duwamish fight in Indian Wars.

1925 The Duwamish form a government and create a constitution.

1996: Duwamish tribe is denied federal recognition.

Giving up lands

By the mid-1800s Isaac Stevens had become the governor of Washington territory (it was not yet a state) and superintendent of Indian Affairs in the region. He considered the Native tribes an "impediment to civilization"—an obstacle to the spread of U.S. power throughout the New World. Stevens believed strongly in Manifest Destiny, a popular theory of the 1840s which held that the United States was meant to dominate the entire Western Hemisphere. Beginning in 1854 he attempted to establish treaties with nearly every tribe in the region, hoping to take over as much land as possible for white settlers. His goal was to place the tribes on reservations (pieces of land set aside for the Indians) and convince the Native peoples to assimilate, or adopt the white way of life.

In 1849 the California gold rush filled the Pacific Northwest with settlers seeking the natural wealth of the area. Seattle was then the principle chief of the united Suquamish and Duwamish nations. A religious man who had been converted to Catholicism, Seattle spoke out for friendship, open trade, and the accomodation of whites. Chief Seattle agreed to sign the Point Elliott Treaty in 1855. According to the terms of the treaty, the Duwamish would give up their lands in exchange for the right to use new lands on seven reservation parcels throughout the area. No reservation lands were given to the Duwamish alone; other tribes inhabited the lands with them.

White settlers poured in and took over Indian lands. Seattle tried to maintain friendly relations with the settlers, and when they founded a city on the site of a Duwamish winter village, the grateful settlers gave it the name Seattle. Other Indians were dissatisfied because they felt the treaty had not been honored. Their anger at the loss of their lands and resources fueled the Indian War of 1855–58. Chief Seattle insisted on peace between the Native peoples and the new settlers. In accordance with the treaty he had signed, he and his people moved to the Port Madison Reservation, across the Puget Sound from the city of Seattle.

Chief Seattle of the Duwamish.

A people divided

It was not long before the Duwamish at Port Madison found themselves in conflict with the Suquamish who lived there. Many Duwamish families left and began wandering around the area. Some were pressured by the federal government to move to a reservation that had been established for the Muckleshoot tribe. By the winter of 1857 most Duwamish had gone back to living in two communities on their original homelands along the Duwamish River. From there they moved in 1897 to the growing community of Seattle. When whites in Seattle burned down their homes, the displaced Duwamish moved to Ballast Island.

Modern tribal history

In 1910 the only remaining Duwamish village was at Foster, south of Seattle. By the 1920s the Duwamish had surrendered all their land. The people scattered throughout western Washington, losing any and all sense of unity as a group. In 1925 some of the surviving Duwamish people reunited. They formed a government and wrote a constitution, hoping the U.S. government would grant them recognition. Federal recognition would make the tribe eligible for federal aid in the form of funds and programs. In 1996 their request for recognition was turned down.

Back in 1926 the tribe took legal action, seeking money from the U.S. government for lands taken from them. Nearly four decades later, in 1962, they were awarded a payment of $62,000, only $1.35 per acre. In 1974 the Duwamish joined with other tribes seeking 50 percent of the annual salmon harvest in their region. Although other tribes were granted this right, the Duwamish were excluded because they had not received federal recognition. At the end of the twentieth century the Duwamish people were scattered throughout the Puget Sound area. They owned no tribal lands. Some, however, lived as registered members on the reservations of other tribes so they could receive services and health benefits from the Bureau of Indian Affairs.

RELIGION

The tribes of the Puget Sound believed that beings with both human and animal qualities existed long ago. One such figure—

referred to as the Transformer by historians—came into the world and defeated the dangerous creatures there—creatures like the soul-stealing earth dwarves, the food-stealing forest giants, and the wife-stealing underwater people. The Transformer then taught the people the right way to live and helped them establish their customs. Like other Puget Sound tribes, the Duwamish believed in a land of the dead and in the possibility of the dead being reborn.

In the early 1800s some Duwamish, including Chief Seattle, converted to the Catholic religion, although many still retained their Native beliefs. Seattle had been converted by French missionaries and baptized as *Noah*. With his new faith, he started morning and evening church services among Native Americans that continued even after his death.

One of the traditional beliefs of the Duwamish was that speaking the name of a dead person would disturb its spirit. For this reason, when Chief Seattle agreed to give his name to the city of Seattle, he asked for a small payment to make up for the trouble his spirit would experience each time his name was mentioned.

In the early 1900s great numbers of Duwamish were converted to the Indian Shaker Church, which combined elements of both Christianity and tribal religions. (See box in Hupa and Chilula entry titled "Hupa Build Indian Shaker Church.")

LANGUAGE

The Duwamish spoke the Southern Lushoosteed dialect of the Coast Salish language family.

GOVERNMENT

There was no formal village leader among the Duwamish, but the wealthiest head of a house was usually accepted as the headman, in charge of making economic and political decisions. In the late 1990s some of the remaining Duwamish people lived on the Suquamish and the Muckleshoot reservations and participated in the governmental systems of those tribes.

ECONOMY

Before contact with Europeans, the Duwamish gathered and fished for their food. In the 1850s they were forced off their ancestral lands and onto reservations. White officials and religious leaders expected the Native people to give up their traditional ways. Their entire world—their environment, their customs, their language, their religion, their methods of gathering food, hunting, and fishing—was turned upside down by the arrival of the whites in their territory. Although the U.S. government provided some goods and food to the reservation, supplies were limited and the Indians suffered many hardships. Corrupt white officials were known to keep or sell supplies that were meant for Duwamish people. Left with no other alternatives, many Duwamish began to work for whites in sawmills, in commercial fisheries, and on farms, as some still do today.

DAILY LIFE

Families

Not much is known about the way the Duwamish people lived prior to European contact. We do know that Duwamish families were usually made up of a man and one or more wives, their children, and possibly unmarried relatives and slaves. Extended families (parents, children, and other relatives) resided together in their own section of a large house where other families also lived.

Buildings

The Duwamish built plank houses—a popular style in the Pacific Northwest. Some of the homes were open in the center, with roofs supported by posts. In the summer the tribe constructed temporary campsite structures and covered them with woven mats. A series of forts surrounded by stake-filled ditches protected the Duwamish from invaders.

After moving to the Port Madison Reservation, Chief Seattle lived in the Old Man House, a community building constructed by the Suquamish. It was 500 feet long and 50 or 60 feet wide. The Duwamish attended ceremonies at the Old Man House and may have built smaller versions of this structure prior to the twentieth century.

Clothing and adornment

In summer men went naked or wore breechcloths (pieces of material that went between the legs and fastened at the waist). Women donned aprons and skirts made of cedar bark. In cool weather both sexes wore blankets woven of mountain goat wool, adding leggings, shirts, and moccasins as it got colder. Women wore necklaces made of shells, teeth, and claws; they also tattooed their legs and chins. Both sexes wore shell earrings. Hair was usually kept long and braided. Young men plucked out their facial hair; older men let it grow. People decorated their faces and bodies with oil and paint, and wealthy people wore nose ornaments.

Queen Angeline, daughter of Duwamish Chief Seattle.

Food

The Duwamish diet was built around fish, especially salmon. The people caught and gathered many freshwater and saltwater creatures, including herring, smelt, flounder, halibut, sturgeon, clams, crabs, and oysters. Overall, the Duwamish relied more on wild foods and game than did the tribes closer to the coast or farther north. Their main prey were deer and elk, but they also hunted and trapped black bears, beavers, raccoons, and 20 kinds of waterfowl. Berries, roots, nuts, bulbs, and sprouts added variety to their diet.

Healing practices

The Duwamish believed that illnesses were caused by the loss of one's soul or by the presence of a disease-causing object within the body. Some ailments could be cured by the use of plants and herbs, but other diseases required a medicine man called a shaman (pronounced *SHAY-mun*) to either recapture the missing soul and return it to the body or remove the disease-causing foreign object through chants and rituals.

Most shamans were male, and their training started at the age of seven or eight. Ultimately, the trainee embarked on a vision quest (see "Customs")—a search for revelation and awareness about the shaman's role as healer and as mediator between humans and supernatural powers.

ARTS

Carving and basketmaking

Like other people of the Pacific Northwest, the Duwamish carved the images of mythical figures onto wooden posts that were placed in front of their houses. They also created baskets from plant fibers; these baskets were woven tightly enough to hold liquids and foods for cooking.

CUSTOMS

Class divisions

Duwamish society was made up of free people and slaves. The free population was divided into upper and lower classes. Only the wealthy upper classes were allowed to take part in ceremonial activities. Slaves were usually women and children who had been seized from enemy tribes during raids.

Secret societies

Like many other Native American tribes, the Duwamish formed secret societies. Members were wealthy adolescent boys and girls called "growling or black tamanawis" (pronounced *tah-MAN-ah-wus*; meaning power or guardian spirit). New members went through a ceremony lasting several nights. They danced and sang, were possessed by spirits, and fell into trances. On the final night of the ritual, their hosts presented them with gifts.

Festivals and ceremonies

The most important ceremonies among the Duwamish were the potlatch, the winter dance, and the soul-recovery ceremony (known among the Duwamish as the "spirit canoe ceremony"). Potlatches were gift-exchange ceremonies sometimes used as offerings of peace to other tribes. The festivities included songs, dances, and games. A winter dance was sponsored by someone who had been cured of an illness by a shaman. During the course of the evening the cured individual would perform the special song that had aided in his or her healing. The spirit canoe ceremony was especially popular among the Duwamish. Several men of the tribe—often, but not always, shamans—acted out a shaman's journey to the land of the dead to rescue living souls that had been stolen. The ceremony lasted for two nights.

Like other Coast Salish tribes, the Duwamish had ceremonies to honor the abundant salmon of the region. Similar ceremonies were held in thanksgiving for other animals, such as elk.

Childhood and puberty

No special ceremonies took place at the time of a child's birth, but within a short time parents would begin to flatten the heads of their infants with boards. Flattened heads were considered attractive among the Duwamish. Girls were separated from the rest of tribe at the time of their first menstruation, and during puberty both boys and girls were expected to embark on their own vision quests. They would set out for the forest on their own, fast, and fall into a trance-like state before receiving a vision from a guardian spirit. The vision was said to provide the youths with the power to lead successful lives. Spirits usually appeared in the form of animals but could also appear as humans, plants, and events in nature such as thunderstorms.

Courtship and marriage

Upper-class families arranged the marriages of their children, often to members of families from different villages. The families of the bride and groom exchanged goods, and the bride's people gave the new couple gifts. Divorce was uncommon in Duwamish society. Widows and widowers (people whose spouses had died) were expected to remarry within the same family to preserve the benefits they had gained from being linked by marriage.

Funerals

When a Duwamish person died, a wake (or watch over the body of a dead person prior to burial) was held and gifts were brought for the deceased. Mourners cut the dead person's hair, prepared the body, and buried it in a canoe or a box in the village cemetery. A feast was held and the deceased's personal property was distributed among friends and family.

CURRENT TRIBAL ISSUES

In 1996 the Duwamish were denied the recognition they had been seeking from the U.S. federal government since 1925. According to the Bureau of Indian Affairs, the Duwamish did not satisfy all of the requirements for federal recognition: they had not sustained a separate community over the years; they had not exercised authority over their people throughout history; and they had not had a continuous Indian identity. Therefore, the U.S. government maintained that it had no responsibility to provide benefits and other assistance to the Duwamish people.

NOTABLE PEOPLE

Chief Seattle (c. 1786–1866), also known as Seathl, was born to a Duwamish mother and a Suquamish father. He became a chief of both those tribes and of other Salish-speaking tribes in the Puget Sound area. Seattle maintained peaceful relations with white settlers. In 1854, during treaty talks with Isaac Stevens, governor of Washington territory, Seattle delivered a powerful speech on his people's future. The speech has become quite famous and remains the topic of discussion in historical circles: at least four different versions of it exist, and no one has been able to determine with certainty which of the four is the original. Seattle is regarded as the last great Native leader in the Pacific Northwest. He married twice and had six children before his death on June 7, 1866, at his home on the Port Madison Reservation.

FURTHER READING

Boxberger, Daniel L. "Duwamish." *Native America in the Twentieth Century, An Encyclopedia.* Ed. Mary B. Davis. New York: Garland Publishing, 1994.

Hodge, Frederick Webb. "Dwamish." *Handbook of American Indians North of Mexico.* New York: Pageant Books, 1959.

Johnson, Michael. "Duwamish." *The Native Tribes of North America.* New York: Macmillan, 1992.

Lyons, Grant. *Pacific Coast Indians of North America.* New York: Julian Messner, 1983.

Newsweek on Chief Seattle's controversial speech: [Online] Newsweek on http://www.synaptic.bc.ca/ejournal/newsweek.htm

"Seattle." In *Notable Native Americans.* Edited by Sharon Malinowski and George H. J. Abrams. Detroit: Gale, 1995.

Washington State Librarian on Chief Seattle's controversial speech: [Online] http://www.synaptic.bc.ca/ejournal/wslibrry.htm

Haida

Name

Haida (pronounced *HIGH-duh*). The Haida call themselves *Hidery,* which means "people."

Location

For centuries the Haida lived on the Queen Charlotte Islands (referred to by the tribe as *Haida Gwaii,* meaning "homeland") west of the Canadian province of British Columbia. Most present-day Canadian Haida, called Charlotte Haida, live in two villages on the Queen Charlotte Islands called Masset and Skidegate. Masset is located at the north end of Graham Island, outside the town of Masset, and Skidegate is located on the southeast corner of Graham Island. Alaskan Haida live on Prince of Wales Island in southeast Alaska, just north of the Queen Charlotte Islands, mostly in the village of Hydaburg. Hydaburg was formed in 1911 when five Alaskan Haida villages merged.

Population

In 1787, 10,000 Haida were known to live on Queen Charlotte Islands, Canada; in 1896, the number had dwindled to 1,600. In the 1700s, 8,000 Haida lived on Prince of Wales Island; by 1890, that number was down to 1,200. In a census (count of the population) conducted in 1990 by the U.S. Bureau of the Census, 1,936 American citizens identified themselves as Haida.

Language family

Haida.

Origins and group affiliations

The Haida probably came to the American Northwest thousands of years ago from Asia, crossing a land bridge (it no longer exists) between Alaska and Russia. They reached British Columbia around 800 C.E., making their way to the Queen Charlotte Islands a few centuries later. The Haida traded frequently with the Tsimshian, Tlingit (pronounced *KLINK-it*; see entry), and Kwakiutl (pronounced *kwak-ee-YEW-tul*; see entry) tribes, but they sometimes warred with them and the Bella Bella.

HAIDA

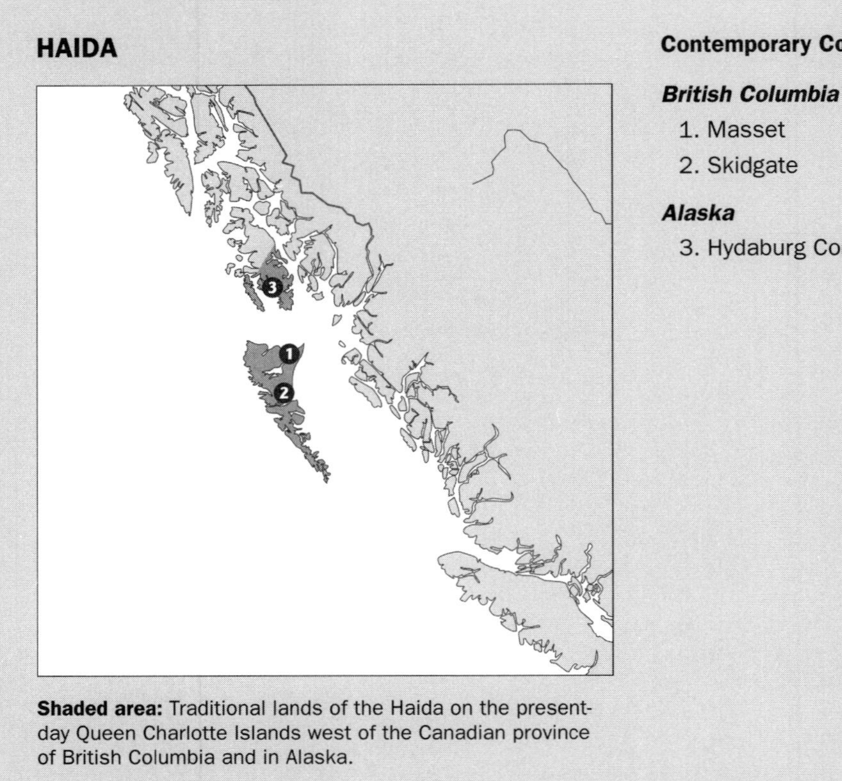

Shaded area: Traditional lands of the Haida on the present-day Queen Charlotte Islands west of the Canadian province of British Columbia and in Alaska.

Contemporary Communities

British Columbia

1. Masset
2. Skidgate

Alaska

3. Hydaburg Cooperative Association

For thousands of years the Haida people have lived on islands along the coast of the Canadian province of British Columbia and in the nearby American state of Alaska. It is a relatively warm, rainy region abundant with plant and animal life. Because they did not have to spend all their time looking for food, the Haida were able to pursue artistic and cultural interests. Considered superior among the Northwest Indian groups in terms of arts and warfare, the Haida were known for their ornately carved totem poles and powerful oceangoing canoes. They spoke a language all their own; it is said to sound like the cries of birds and the crashing of waves on a shore.

HISTORY

Ancient floods

When the Haida people first began to settle in their lands on the Pacific Coast about 10,000 years ago, the sea there was in an uproar. Its constant rising and falling rapidly changed the shoreline. People were forced to move farther inland as the waters rose and covered their homes. Haida legend recalls these events in stories of destruction and rebirth that resemble the biblical story of Noah and the Ark.

For centuries the Charlotte Haida lived a comfortable life in their villages by the sea. Endowed with a bountiful supply of food, they settled in permanent villages and developed a rich culture. From time to time the Haida set off in huge cedar canoes for the West Coast of British Columbia and into the lands of Washington and Oregon to raid or trade. Legends also tell of voyages to the southern tip of South America and of encounters with Polynesians and Maori (New Zealand Natives) in the Pacific Ocean. The Haida sometimes captured slaves or acquired them through trade.

IMPORTANT DATES

1774: First European contact between Spanish captain Juan Pérez and the Haida.

1797: Trading begins between the Haida and the British, who name the islands for Queen Charlotte.

1936: Hydaburg, Alaska, adopts a constitution. The Haida petition the U.S. government for a 905,000-acre reservation.

1968: The Alaska Haida and Tlingit tribes are finally awarded $7.2 million compensation by the U.S. Court of Claims for their land.

1985: Seventy-two Haida and their supporters are arrested while trying to prevent logging on Queen Charlotte Islands.

1987: Canadian leaders sign an agreement establishing a national park and a national marine park on the Queen Charlotte Islands.

Begin trade with Europeans

The first European ship to reach the Queen Charlotte Islands was probably the *Santiago,* piloted by Spanish captain Juan Pérez. He passed by the islands in 1774 on his way to investigate the activities of the Russians in Alaska. The French and the British also sailed through the region around the same time. In 1787 a British sea captain arrived on the islands and named them after his ship, the *Queen Charlotte.* Soon trading began between the Haida and Europeans. The British were interested in furs, especially the skins of sea otters, which brought large profits from Chinese buyers.

Haida settle in Alaska

Driven off their Native lands by warfare with neighboring tribes, one group of Haida left the Queen Charlotte Islands in the mid-1700s and established villages in southern Alaska. For the rest of the century, nearly 8,000 Haida resided in five villages at the southern end of Prince of Wales Island, just north of the Queen Charlotte Islands. Before 1867 the Haida of Alaska lived in an area claimed by Russia. Although the Russian Orthodox church converted some Haida to Christianity, Russian culture had little real impact on the Haida there. Russia sold Alaska to the United States in 1867 for $7.2 million.

The discovery of gold in Alaskan territory in 1889 ushered in a string of major life changes for the Haida. White settlers swarmed to the area in search of riches. With the coming of the whites, the Haida lost much of their land. Native people were then forced to participate in the area's growing economy as fishers and loggers, working for American companies.

The U.S. Bureau of Education and the Presbyterian church decided to "educate and civilize" the Haida. In 1911 a Presbyterian mission called Hydaburg was established in Alaska. Without support from the U.S. government, three nearby Haida villages were abandoned and the Indians from those villages reluctantly moved to Hydaburg.

The community of Hydaburg is now home to the only organized Haida group in the United States. Some Haida also make their homes in Kasaan and Ketchikan, Alaska, and in Seattle, Washington. By the 1990s many Haida had to leave Hydaburg to find employment in large cities.

Canadian Haida settle in Masset and Skidegate

In 1854 the Charlotte Haida—fearing they would lose all their land to the ever-growing number of Canadian settlers—signed a treaty that gave up most of their land, including their hunting territories, to the Canadian government. In return, they were allowed to keep their villages and farm areas, and they retained the right to hunt and fish in all their former territories.

A trading post opened in the town of Masset on the Queen Charlotte Islands in 1869. There, and at forts in the area, the Haida traded such items as meat, dried fish, and potatoes with merchants and sailors in exchange for European products. In 1871 British Columbia became part of Canada, and the government established two Haida reserves (the term Canadians use for reservations, or parcels of land set aside for the Indians) near the town of Masset and in the town of Skidegate. (See "Government.")

Impact of whites

Contact with Europeans was like a double-edged sword for the Haida who lived on the Queen Charlotte Islands: it had both a positive and negative effect on the Native way of life. The Haida traded furs with the whites for copper and iron tools, kettles, knives, and needles. The tools allowed them to make larger and more elaborate totem poles, canoes, and houses. In the early 1800s Haida artists started to sell carved objects—boxes, bowls, utensils, and the like—

Haida village and totem poles in Howkan, Alaska, 1896.

to foreign settlers, traders, and sailors. European firearms, cloths, and blankets were prized by the Haida. By the mid-nineteenth century they were trading ceremonial robes—elaborate garments decorated with copper and silver buttons—to the Europeans.

Although the Haida people benefited from the fur trade in an economic sense, the environmental repercussions of the trade were disastrous. By 1830 the sea otter was nearly extinct because of overtrapping. In addition, the salmon population was beginning to decline. Europeans then began trading with the tribe for other furs such as deer, mink, and beaver.

Contact with white settlers also brought new diseases to the Native peoples. An epidemic (an uncontrolled outbreak of disease; in this case, probably smallpox) in 1862 and 1863 led to the deaths of whole families and entire villages on the Queen Charlotte Islands. By the beginning of the twentieth century the Haida population there had fallen to nine hundred. The Haida were pressured by Canadian officials, teachers, and Christian church leaders who wanted them to assimilate (or blend in by adopting the white way of life). Large extended families no longer lived together in one big house as they had traditionally. By 1884 the Canadian government had banned

LAVINA WHITE: FIGHTING FOR TRADITION

Indian activist Lavina White is working to bring about changes in social conditions and government policies for Native Americans. Her main goal is to reverse the damage done by whites to the Haida tribal homeland. A strong critic of the Canadian government's move to create Gwaii Hanaas National Park, White claims that the benefit of the $38 million park budget was reaped solely by the white community. She also alleges that: (1) other Haida lands beyond South Moresby are being clear cut (all the trees are being cut down) by the logging industry and (2) the Canadian government is to blame for the depletion of fish stocks in Haida waters. White believes that the Haida people—indeed all Native nations—can only heal themselves by reasserting their rights to their traditional lands and resources and reestablishing their old Native ways.

potlatches (pronounced *POT-latch-ez*; gift-giving ceremonies; see "Customs") and Haida dances, and Christian missionaries were convincing the Native peoples that carving and erecting totem poles was an evil custom.

By the late 1800s many Haida families had their own gardens and kept farm animals such as horses and cows. As trade in food products and animal furs declined over the next few decades, men and women took jobs in fish-canning factories, mines, and sawmills. Some continued to fish on boats owned by Canadian firms; others had their own boats and sold their catches to Canadian companies.

The Haida in modern times

About 15 percent of the land area of the Queen Charlotte Islands—an area known as South Moresby—is home to one of the world's only remaining coastal rain forests. In the 1970s the Charlotte Haida began waging a lengthy battle with the logging industry over the use of sacred tribal lands on the islands. In one incident in 1985, Haida leaders and supporters were arrested, imprisoned, and charged with showing disrespect for the law after they blockaded a logging road. Their 13-year-long battle was resolved in 1987, when Canadian and Haida officials signed an agreement establishing a national park and marine reserve at the site. (See "Current tribal issues.") Some hailed the decision to create Canada's Gwaii Hanaas National Park a victory for the Haida. But many Natives disagree, saying all traditional tribal lands should be returned to the control of the Haida people.

RELIGION

According to Haida beliefs, the universe consists of three separate parts: the Earth itself, made up of their islands and the mainland; the area above the Earth, supported by a pillar extending from the land below; and the seawater beneath the Earth. Animals were said to have souls and were considered more intelligent than humans.

The Haida believed in *Ne-kilst-lass,* their Supreme Being who took the form of a raven. He was responsible for creation and for bringing light and order into the world. He also instructed the Haida people in their major ceremonies and taught them to establish good relations within the tribe and with other tribes. But Ne-kilst-lass had a dark side as well: he was a troublemaker responsible for all things disruptive and evil.

LANGUAGE

The Indians of the Northwest Coast spoke at least 45 languages. The Haida language was not related to any of the others. Two dialects (varieties) of the Haida language have survived at Skidegate and Masset on the Queen Charlotte Islands. The Haida who moved to Alaska beginning in the eighteenth century also spoke the Masset dialect. At the dawn of the twenty-first century, even Haida children who no longer spoke the tribe's language were being taught traditional Haida songs.

GOVERNMENT

Haida people who were related through the same female ancestor made up groups called lineages (pronounced *LIN-ee-uh-jiz*). Each lineage was led by a chief who had inherited his position. Chiefs resolved conflicts among the people, made major decisions about their welfare, and had the power to declare war.

In the 1870s the Canadian government gave its Native peoples partial control over their own land. Indian-run councils were created to govern the people in Native communities, as long as they followed Canadian law. Two Haida reserves were set up. The Masset Indian Reserve is located about 7 miles west of the village of Masset, and the Skidegate Indian Reserve is located 120 air miles from Prince Rupert, British Columbia. Even today, chiefs are said to hold considerable power in Canadian Haida communities. Hydaburg, Alaska, home of most Haida in the United States, is not a reservation but an incorporated city with its own elected government.

ECONOMY

For centuries the Haida enjoyed a life blessed with abundant natural resources and plenty of leisure time. They were able to gather their entire food supply for the year in just three months. Very little farming was necessary.

The Haida conducted a thriving canoe trade with other Native tribes. They exchanged their canoes for mountain goat wool and candlefish, a fish so oily it could be set on fire and burned like a candle.

HAIDA CANOES

One of the treasures of the American Museum of Natural History in Washington, D.C., is a 63-foot-long canoe built by Haida people on the Charlotte Islands in 1878. The canoe exhibit, created in 1910, depicts a group of Indians arriving at an important ceremonial feast. The two men with long poles at the front of the canoe and the three sets of paddlers on both sides of the canoe are captured slaves.

Haida canoes were carved from the trunks of large cedar trees. Craftspeople softened the tree trunk with boiling water, allowing it to be widened to more than 8 feet. The front of the canoe in the Natural History exhibit is decorated with the carving of a wolf and a painted killer whale. It was probably created for a chief of the nearby Bella Bella tribe. Although the identity of the creator of this particular canoe is unknown, the vessel serves as a fine example of the type of artistry that made the Haida renowned canoe builders.

The Haida were known for their unparalleled skill at canoe making. (See box titled "Haida Canoes.") Although this art was nearly lost under the influence of Europeans, attempts were being made at the end of the twentieth century to revive it. With the coming of Europeans, the Haida traded furs, food, and artwork for many European items.

In the late 1990s many Alaskan and Charlotte Haida earned their living from logging, a business that has faced opposition for causing damage to Native lands. Others made their living from fishing, an industry that has seen its share of trouble. (See "Current tribal issues.") The Queen Charlotte Islands have become a center of ecotourism (a type of tourism that features animals and vegetation in their natural habitat), and the Native peoples there provide a variety of tourist services for visitors. Haida carvers and painters create valuable artworks that are praised by art critics and sold throughout the world.

DAILY LIFE

Families

Traditional Haida society consisted of many villages of related families. For centuries Haida children were considered part of an extended family made up of a mother, her sons and daughters, her daughter's children, her granddaughter's children, and so on. (Societies that trace descent through the maternal line—or the mother's side of the family—are called *matrilineal.*) Haida families—identified as either Eagles or Ravens—owned their own property, were assigned special areas for gathering food, and, depending on their affiliation (either Eagle or Raven), lived at one of two separate ends of the village. The Eagle and Raven groupings were divided even further into a complicated system of subgroups, each with its own land, history, and customs. By the end of the nineteenth century, though, the elaborately structured Haida social system had changed a great deal: most of the Haida lived in nuclear family groups—groups made up of a father, a mother, and their children. In modern times members of the same group (Ravens, for example) were allowed to marry one another; such unions had been forbidden earlier in Haida history.

Buildings

The Haida lived in large homes called longhouses that ranged from 30 to 60 feet or more in length and 30 to 50 feet in width. The longhouses were made of cedar logs that were notched and fitted together so expertly that no pegs were needed to join them. Roofs were built of cedar bark slabs, and walls were made of planks split from standing trees. Carved log pillars supported the roof beams. At first, these pillars served merely to make the entryway more elegant; later, the carved pillars, some as tall as 50 feet, evolved into one of several kinds of totem poles. (See "Customs.")

Haida totem pole, Totem Heritage Center.

The longhouses were permanent dwellings built on seaside sites that offered protection from the weather and enemies. Several families shared the area around a central fireplace within each longhouse, but each group prepared its own meals. Family members retired at night to private sleeping quarters.

On the Queen Charlotte Islands, the longhouses were built on a narrow strip of land facing the ocean. Backed by forests of cedar trees and with large totem poles in front, they made an impressive sight when traders passed by in their canoes and ships.

When the salmon returned in spring, the Haida moved to locations along the rivers. They sometimes removed planks from their permanent homes to build temporary shelters, then carried the wood back in the fall. The planks were often tied across two canoes to serve as a platform for carrying belongings.

Other buildings were put up to house girls who were about to come of age and women about to give birth. Some buildings held the remains of the dead. Celebrations were held in large community buildings.

Clothing and adornment

The Haida were excellent weavers. Their everyday clothing was made from spruce tree roots and reeds woven into fabric and then sewn into hats, capes, and robes. Women wore bark aprons that extended from the waist to the knees. For ceremonial wear the Haida sewed garments of dog fur and mountain goat wool with thread made of bark. They also created masks representing different creatures such as the eagle and the salmon and donned headdresses decorated with fur, carvings, and sea lion whiskers.

Food

The Haida enjoyed a bountiful supply of fish and meat. Men did the fishing and hunting, and along with women gathered clams, crabs, and scallops inshore and offshore. Women also gathered berries, clover, roots, seaweed, and crab apples. Seals, sea otters, oysters, mussels, cod, herring, trout, and abalone (pronounced *AB-uh-LONE-ee*; a type of edible shellfish) were taken from the sea. The 500-pound halibut and 20-foot sturgeon caught by the Haida were so large they had to be stunned with clubs before they could be pulled on board the canoes. Nearby rivers teemed with salmon so plentiful they could be caught by hand. The Haida did not hunt whales but did make use of any stranded whales that washed ashore.

On land the Haida hunted black bears, caribou, deer, land otters, and birds' eggs. The Charlotte Islands were home to a number of species of plants and animals that are unique on this planet, such as the alpine lily, the Steller's jay, and the hairy woodpecker. Bald eagles and peregrine falcons also thrived there. Meat, such as deer or seal, was roasted or boiled, cut into strips, and preserved by drying or smoking it. An equally bountiful supply of plant and animal food was available to the Haida in Alaska.

Education

Haida children played a lot and learned songs and dances from older tribal members. By observing their elders, they learned about hunting, fishing, food gathering, and food preparation. Boys sometimes went to live with one of their mother's brothers to learn stories and ceremonies important to the tribe. They fasted and swam in cold waters to "toughen up" and develop survival skills.

In the late 1880s Methodist missionaries took over the education of Haida children on the Charlotte Islands. Unconcerned with the preservation of Haida culture, the missionaries set up boarding schools that neglected Native tradition and reinforced white ways. Later, Masset and Skidegate would open their own public schools. With the help of elder Native people, these school systems now offer studies in Haida culture, language, and dancing. The New Skills Centre in Masset blends traditional values with business management training courses. The public school in Hydaburg, Alaska, has a Haida language program and teaches classes in traditional drawing and carving.

Healing practices

Because they wore their hair long and tied it on top of their heads, Haida medicine men and women were called *skaggies,* a shortened form of the Haida words for "long-haired ones." Earlier in Haida history, skaggies served as both priests and doctors. They were believed to have the power to heal the sick, foresee the future, and bring success to hunting and fishing expeditions. When called upon for their gift of healing, skaggies usually announced their arrival on the scene by shaking a loud rattle. This same rattle—used in conjunction with a series of sharp, pointed bones that were poked into the sick person's body—served as one means of eliminating the cause of illness.

Mask called "After He Has Seen the Spirit," by Haida artist Robertson Davidson.

ARTS

Weaving and woodworking

Most Haida art stood as a lasting symbol of an artist's ancestors, status, and wealth. Traditionally, men made sculptures, carvings, and paintings, and women crafted various types of cedar and spruce baskets and woven items. Many Haida objects have great artistic value. The tribe remains well known for designing and weaving spectacular button blankets, named for the pearl buttons that outline the blankets' designs. The Haida were also very skilled in the construction of large canoes—some up to 75 feet in length and able to carry as many as 40 people and 2 tons of freight. (See box titled "Haida Canoes.")

In artistic terms, the Haida people are probably best known as master wood-carvers who covered virtually any flat surface with some kind of ornate engraving or painting. Their carvings were inspired by both realistic figures and mythical creatures, and they adorned items such as totem poles, house posts, grave markers, painted house fronts, interior screens, large dishes, and canoes. Popular smaller carved objects included rattles, cooking and serving implements, and decorative boxes. In the early 1800s the Haida gained recognition for their intricate carvings in a type of black stone called argillite (pronounced *AR-juh-lite*). They were the only Native group known to

HOW THE HAIDA GOT FIRE

The Haida believed that the Supreme Being Ne-kilst-lass, in the form of a raven, brought forth the first Haida people from a clamshell. He supplied them with fire to battle the cold and darkness on Earth. This excerpt from a Haida tale describes how Raven brought fire to the people.

Ne-kilst-lass heard that a great chief who lived on an island in the Pacific had all the fire in the world. So donning his coat of feathers he flew over to this island. Reaching the chief's island, he soon found his house. After a long conversation with him about the merits of his fire, Choo-e-ah seized a brand and with it flew over again to the mainland, letting fall, as he passed along, a few sparks amongst certain sorts of wood and stones. This sort of wood and these stones absorbed all the fire and gave it out again, when struck with a hard substance. The wood also gave it out when two pieces were quickly rubbed together. The Hidery say [that] when Choo-e-ah reached the land, part of his beak was burnt off.

SOURCE: "Of How They First Got Fire." *Tales from the Totems of the Hidery.* Volume 2. Chicago: Archives of the International Folk-Lore Association, 1899.

carve from this particular stone, and they controlled the only source from which it could be obtained.

Totem poles

The Haida were most famous for their totem poles, which were decorated with symbols of the Eagle or the Raven. Red cedar totem poles, covered entirely with carvings, often commemorated some important event in the life of the head of a family. Some poles even had little drawers that held the remains of the home's deceased owners. After the Haida acquired iron tools from the Europeans, they were able to produce much larger poles—some as tall as 50 feet. Only the upper classes could afford totem poles; commoners had to be content with images painted on their houses. In the late 1800s Christian missionaries to the Queen Charlotte Islands destroyed many totem poles. Soon after, the pole-carving tradition came to an end. It was not until the 1970s that totem poles were once again being made on the Queen Charlotte Islands, thanks to the efforts of Haida artist Bill Reid. (See "Notable people.")

CUSTOMS

Social classes

The Haida people were divided into two main social classes: commoners and the wealthy upper class. Any Haida commoner who worked hard enough could one day rise to the upper class. Slaves captured in battle made up the lowest class in Haida society. They lived in their owners' houses and were usually treated well.

Tattoos represented a person's rank in society and often included the likeness of a family's crest (a symbol of that family). Young men were tattooed on the breast. A woman's rank was reflected in the types of tattoos found on her arms and legs and in the size of her *labret* (pronounced *LAY-bret*), a kind of ornament—similar to an earring—that was inserted in the lower lip. The bigger the labret, the higher her rank.

Festivals

Most Haida ceremonies were held in the winter, the rainy season. In fact, the Haida usually held some kind of event every night from November until March.

Potlatches

Potlatches—elaborate gift-giving ceremonies common among American Indians of the Northwest Coast—were held when a tribal chief wished to celebrate an event of importance, such as the death of the chief who came before him, a marriage, a child's coming of age, or the unveiling of a new totem pole. A major potlatch required years of planning and lasted for several days. The guest list included members of the host's tribe, as well as Native peoples from neighboring villages. The host was judged by his generosity: possessions such as baskets, cloaks, shell ornaments, blankets, and canoes were given away to the guests. Guests were judged by their ability to consume huge bowls of delicacies such as seal and bear meat or berries preserved in fish oil. In fact, eating became a kind of competition at the feast. A host was usually reduced to poverty by the time the potlatch ended, but he could expect to be repaid in double on a future occasion.

The Canadian government banned potlatches in 1884. Only recently have they again become legal. Despite the longtime ban, Native peoples on the Charlotte Islands continued for many years to hold a modified form of potlatch.

Puberty and the spirit dance

When a Haida girl began to menstruate, she was taken to a special part of the family house—a part separated from the rest of the household by a screen. For a month her female relatives visited her and taught her about the traditional duties of a woman in the tribe, especially the gathering and cooking of food and the raising of children. At the end of the month the young woman took a ritual bath and a celebration was held in her honor.

Both boys and girls were treated to a spirit dance at puberty. Before the dance they embarked on a vision quest, a search for revelation and awareness. Each youth wandered alone for days through deep forests, hoping for contact with the special spirit who would serve as a guide through life. The greatest spirit power a young man (and occasionally a young woman) could receive was that of the Eagle or the Raven. Often the spirit made its presence known by singing a song to the quester. The song was then incorporated into the quester's spirit dance, a dramatization of the lesson taught by the spirit visitor. Wearing masks, face paints, and elaborate costumes during their performances, spirit dancers attempted to reenact the experience of the spirit's coming.

Courtship and marriage

Haida marriages were arranged by the couple's parents or other relatives, and young people were expected to accept their elders' choice for a partner. The bride's family hosted the marriage feast, which centered on the exchange of gifts between the two families. If a man treated his wife poorly, her family could reclaim her and her children. If he ran away and married another woman, he had to make a financial settlement with his first wife. Failure to do so could result in death. A man who abandoned his wife but did not remarry suffered no negative consequences. Historically, Haida marriages lasted a short time.

Birth

The Haida believed the spirits of the dead came back to life as newborn babies. While they welcomed all babies, girls were especially prized. At birth, children were given undesirable names and were expected to spend their formative years devoting serious energy to personal growth. Once they acquired property or wealth, a chief would reward them with a "good and honorable" name. A person could also achieve such a good name by hosting a potlatch.

Funerals

Funerals were the most important of the Haida rituals. Women washed and dressed the body of the deceased and painted his or her face. Mourners sobbed loudly and shared their sorrow. Burial in the ground was considered a horrible practice. Instead, bodies were burned. The ashes were sometimes placed inside the family totem pole, or they might rest in boxes placed in special buildings set aside for the purpose. After the cremation, a funeral potlatch was held and the dead person's possessions were distributed among the mourners.

CURRENT TRIBAL ISSUES

Commercial fishing, an important part of the economy of Haida villages in British Columbia since the 1800s, took a downturn in 1994. Canada's federal fisheries department started lowering catch limits (the amount of fish that could legally be kept) that year. Two years later, they placed a total ban on Chinook salmon fishing and further restricted other types of fishing. The Chinook salmon, known in Alaska as the king salmon, has fallen victim to decades of overfishing.

The decline of salmon fishing has greatly affected the Canadian village of Masset. While Masset's two fish processing plants once employed 90 full-time workers, by 1996 the number of employees had fallen to 22, more than half of them part-timers. That same year the catch intended for Masset's fish processing plants declined to 50,000 pounds of fish, down from about 250,000 pounds the previous year.

The outlook was a little brighter in the Haida village of Sgan Gwaii (also known as Anthony Island), abandoned since a terrible smallpox epidemic in the 1860s. In recent times a totem pole restoration project has had the village, now a Canadian national park preserve, humming with activity. Teams of professional archaeologists (scientists who study the culture and artifacts of ancient peoples) and Haida trainees are studying the area. Their discoveries indicate that humans have lived in the area for more than 9,000 years.

The Sgan Gwaii archaeological venture represents a turning point in the way Canada handles Native archaeological projects. In the past objects excavated from abandoned Native villages were removed from the scene and examined in museums. Current policy gives the Haida people complete control over Native human remains and stipulates that all artifacts be returned to the Queen Charlotte Islands Museum within six months of their release for study.

NOTABLE PEOPLE

The greatness of Haida chief Eda'nsa (c. 1810–1894; name means "Melting Ice from a Glacier"; also called Captain Douglas) is the subject of much debate. After becoming a Haida Eagle chief in 1841, he found himself at the center of considerable controversy. Eda'nsa was known by the whites as a trader in Indian slaves. (These slaves had been acquired from other Natives by barter or raid.) He also served as a guide for the whites through the difficult waters of the Queen Charlotte Islands. One of his vessels was looted and burned by a neighboring tribe. Eda'nsa became a Christian in 1884 and continued to seek new trading opportunities in the islands until his death in 1894. At that time his title passed to his nephew Charles Edenshaw (1839–1924), a skilled wood-carver and silversmith who achieved great wealth and fame and was chosen chief of the Haida village of Yatza.

Bill Reid (1920–), Edenshaw's nephew, may be the most famous Haida artist of the twentieth century. Credited with ushering in a rebirth of Haida art in the 1950s, he has many sculptures on public display throughout North America. Reid is also an accomplished author.

FURTHER READING

Bonvillain, Nancy. *People of the Northwest Coast.* Brookfield, CT: Millbrook Press, 1994.

Farnsworth, Clyde H. "Where Salmon Ruled, End of the Line." *New York Times,* August 11, 1996: 8Y.

Johnston, Moira. "Canada's Queen Charlotte Islands: Homeland of the Haida." *National Geographic,* July 1987: 102–127.

Kowinski, William Severini. "Giving New Life to Haida Art and the Culture It Expresses." *Smithsonian,* January 1995: 38.

On Haida art: [Online] http:www.uwbg.edu/~galta/mrr/haida/art.htm

Kwakiutl

Name

The name Kwakiutl (pronounced *kwak-ee-YEW-tul*) has two meanings: either "smoke of the world" or "beach at the north side of the river."

Location

Northwest Coast, British Columbia. For centuries, the Kwakiutl have lived on Queen Charlotte Sound, on northern Vancouver Island, on various small islands around Vancouver Island, and on mainland British Columbia from Douglas Channel to Bute Inlet.

Population

In 1750, there were about 5,000 to 6,000 Kwakiutl; in 1904, there were 2,173. A census (count) of the Canadian population in 1991 reported that there were 4,120 Kwakiutl living in Canada.

Language family

Wakashan.

Origins and group affiliations

Thousands of years ago, scientists believe that the ancestors of the Kwakiutl crossed a land bridge (which no longer exists) from Asia to North America, eventually settling on North America's Northwest Coast near the present-day American state of Washington. There were once about 30 Indian groups there that fell into three divisions: the Kwakiutl, the Haisla, and the Heiltsuk.

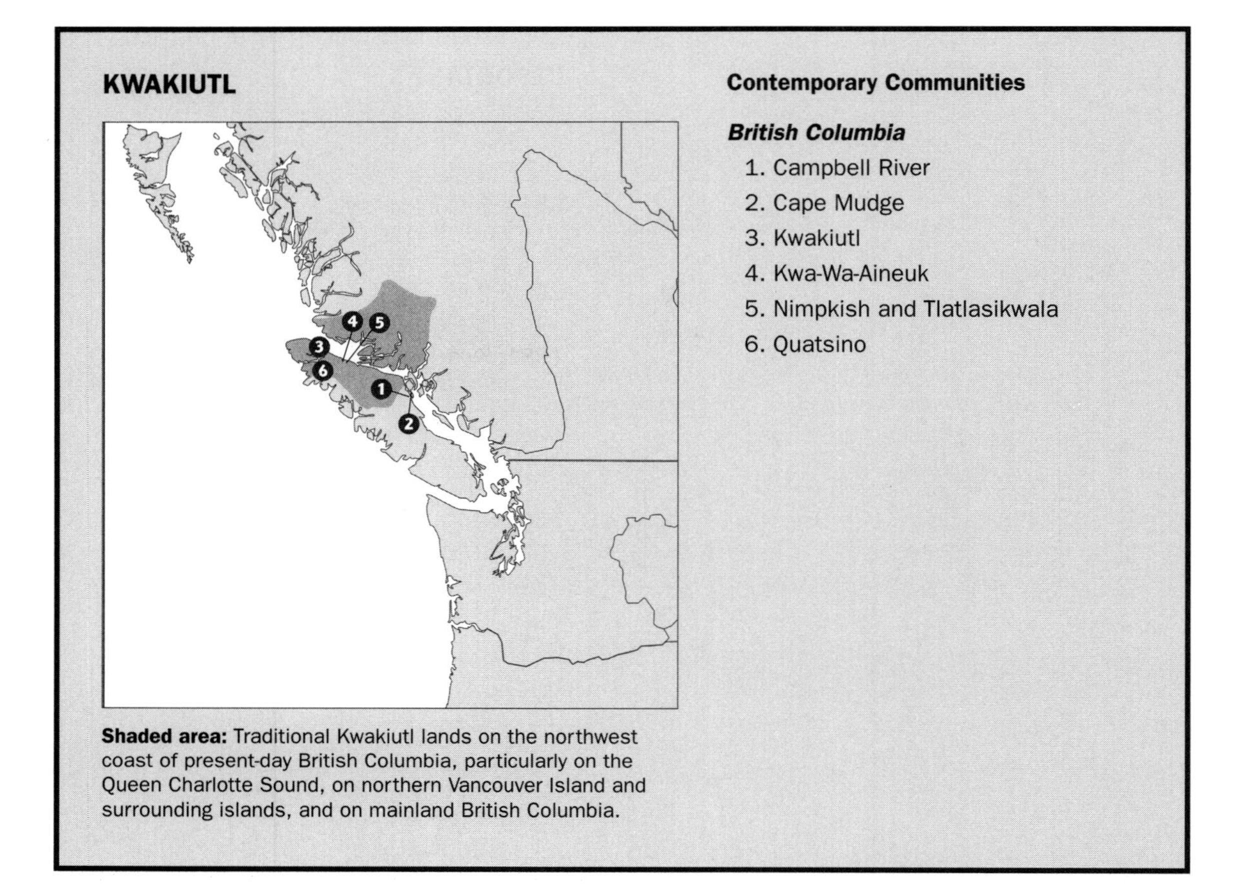

Shaded area: Traditional Kwakiutl lands on the northwest coast of present-day British Columbia, particularly on the Queen Charlotte Sound, on northern Vancouver Island and surrounding islands, and on mainland British Columbia.

For centuries the Kwakiutl enjoyed the natural bounty of the Pacific Ocean and the surrounding forests. Because their need for food was easily met, the people were able to devote much of their time to artistic pursuits and ceremonies such as potlatches (pronounced *POT-latch-ez*; major gift exchanges). The Kwakiutl were widely known for their totem poles, elaborate wooden houses, and seaworthy log canoes, as well as for dramatizing myths and performing magic tricks.

HISTORY

Before contact with whites

The many groups that made up the Kwakiutl tribe stayed apart from one other for much of their history before the coming of the whites. Those that were close neighbors were often not on friendly terms. Most historians agree that the Kwakiutl made war on their neighbors to gain slaves, territory, goods—even revenge. If a person within the tribe was killed, his or her relatives often retaliated by taking the life of someone of equal social rank or several people of lower rank. Major conflicts among Kwakiutl groups ceased by about 1865.

IMPORTANT DATES

1792: Regular trading with Europeans begins.

1849: Fort Rupert, the main Kwakiutl trading center, is established.

1865: British Navy destroys Tsahis, the largest Kwakiutl village.

1881: Kwawkewlth Agency is established to help the Natives assimilate (adopt the ways of the whites).

Trading with Europeans

The first known contact between the Kwakiutl and Europeans took place in 1786, when James Strange, a British trader, discovered the Queen Charlotte Strait, which separates northern Vancouver Island from mainland Canada. By 1792 American, Spanish, and British traders flocked to the area in search of sea-otter pelts that could be sold very profitably to the Chinese.

The Kwakiutl were described as "smart traders" by some of the first English people to make contact with them. The Natives exchanged furs with Europeans in return for iron and copper that they used to make tools, weapons, jewelry, and decorative items. They later bartered for European food items such as rice, tea, flour, and sugar, as well as tools, mirrors, cloth, and cooking pots. The Kwakiutl maintained friendly relations with the whites on their trading ships, but the two groups were known to cheat each other on occasion.

Forts established

Fort Langley was built as a trading center in 1827, and Fort McLoughlin followed in 1833, and the Kwakiutl came there to trade with whites. Fort Victoria was built in 1842 and became the major trading post for all the Indians in the area, including the Kwakiutl. Then, seven years later, Fort Rupert was established near Kwakiutl land. The Kwakiutl and three other tribes soon moved to a new village they founded nearby, which they called Tsahis. Tsahis became the largest Kwakiutl community in the region.

Settlers mean loss of land

The discovery of gold on Kwakiutl land in the mid-nineteenth century brought many settlers and gold miners to the area. Some of them claimed as their own the places where Indians had fished for centuries. By the 1860s whites greatly outnumbered the Native population, and they pressured the English officials in charge of Canada into adopting numerous illegal methods to take away Indian lands.

One 1865 law made it illegal for Indian families to own more than 10 acres; on the other hand, whites could own up to 640 acres.

Government agents, who were supposed to protect Indian rights, failed to do so. In fact, they carried out hostile actions against the Indians. In 1865 the British Navy destroyed the Kwakiutl village at Fort Rupert. It was rebuilt, but by then many of the Natives had lost all faith in the white settlers.

The coming of whites into the region had some other disastrous effects on the Native peoples. Smallpox epidemics struck in the late 1700s and again in the 1880s, and many died. Still more were killed in battles with Canadian authorities, including the battles that destroyed the village of Nahwitti in 1850 and the largest Kwakiutl village, Tsahis, in 1865.

Indians move to cities

Even when the gold rush ended in the 1860s, many whites stayed in British Columbia, which became a province (similar to an American state) of Canada in 1871. A large number of Kwakiutl settled in the capital city of Victoria and became fishers, hunters, loggers, or crewmen on whaling ships. Many poor Kwakiutl ended up in the city's Indian ghetto (an area of a city where members of a minority group live, usually because of social pressures).

The town of Alert Bay, which began as a salmon cannery in 1870, had replaced Fort Rupert as the central trading post for the people of the region by 1900. In 1881 the Canadian government established the Kwawkewlth Agency to help the Kwakiutl and other tribes to assimilate (adopt the white lifestyle) at Fort Rupert, but it was later moved to Alert Bay. In the last twenty years of the nineteenth century, a school, a sawmill, and an industrial school for boys were opened by government agents at Alert Bay to benefit the Kwakiutl and others.

Famous scholar studies tribe

In the late 1800s an anthropologist (someone who studies the cultures of different peoples) by the name of Franz Boas visited the Kwakiutl many times. He was especially interested in their art, their rituals, and their complex social system. Boas befriended members of the tribe, and they shared tribal secrets with him. He attended their potlatches and even hosted his own. Even as Boas was writing about the Kwakiutl culture, the Canadian government began to take away tribal rights and sell the Native peoples' land to whites. In time, the Indians no longer had enough land to supply them with food, and

HOW TO CURE A FISH, KWAKIUTL STYLE

The Kwakiutl were masters at preserving fish so that it could be consumed all year long. Here is a description of one method they used:

To ready a fish for curing (preserving), the fish is opened at one side of the backbone, which is then detached from the head and placed aside. The roe (eggs) are put on another pile, the innards and gills are disposed of, and the fish is rubbed inside and out with a handful of green leaves. The strip running along each side of the back is cut off and sliced into a very thin sheet. The fish, now of uniform thickness at the belly, is held open by skewers and hung up to dry. It is first placed in the sun and later put in the smoke of the house's cook fire. The thin sheets are hung on poles and partially dried in the sun, with skewers inserted so they won't curl up as they dry. Five tiers of racks are hung above the fire, and each group of salmon meat spends a day on each of the first four tiers, beginning with the lowest. After lying on the topmost shelf for five more days, the cured flesh is placed in large baskets or cedar chests. The containers are kept in dry places until it is time to eat the fish.

many went to work for whites in low-paying jobs. Laws were passed prohibiting Indians from voting or participating in potlatches.

The 1920s

In the late 1800s the Kwakiutl started to earn high incomes by becoming professional fishers. This time of wealth and prosperity declined for the tribe when powerboats used for fishing were first introduced in the 1920s. Powerboat fishers could take much larger hauls of salmon and other fish. With the number of salmon greatly reduced, salmon fishing declined rapidly and many Native Americans lost their jobs in the fishing industry.

Fight for rights begins

Most historians agree that the Canadian government overstepped its bounds in its dealings with the Kwakiutl, intruding on the traditions and the rights of tribal members. For example, when Native groups were formed in the 1930s and 1940s to fight against the illegal takeover of their lands by whites, the Canadian government made it a crime for these groups to fund any campaign that might take the government to court. Finally, in 1951, the Canadian government reformed its Indian policy. Native voting rights were restored, and potlatches were made legal.

Throughout the twentieth century many Kwakiutl moved from small villages to cities to find a better life. Those who remained on the reserves (the term Canadians use for reservations, tracts of land set aside specifically for use by Indians) faced dismal prospects for employment.

Canadian government reforms in the early 1960s provided the tribespeople with medical care, educational opportunities, and unemployment insurance. Some people were able to return to their traditional villages and take up the age-old Kwakiutl enterprise of fishing. A decline in the fishing industry in the 1990s, however, forced many Kwakiutl to seek other ways of making a living. (See "Economy.")

RELIGION

The religion of the Kwakiutl was based on a complicated system of privileges that were said to be given to certain families by supernatural powers. The Kwakiutl believed that such powers were found in all things in nature. They said daily prayers to the spirits, often asking to be granted powers of their own. Other prayers were said in thanks to the Sun, to the beaver, to a woodworking tool, to a weapon, to a plant for its curative ability, or to the wind for changing directions.

In the late nineteenth century Christian missionaries ventured to the land of the Kwakiutl and succeeded in converting some of the people to the Christian faith. The missionaries pressured the Natives to give up their traditional practices, including various ceremonies, burial rites, and even the construction of totem poles. Christian converts had to live in single-family homes rather than with larger groups of relatives. Some Indians converted to Christianity so they could obtain medical care or gain access to education. Others completely changed their beliefs but continued to take part in rituals such as potlatches (gift-giving ceremonies; see "Customs").

LANGUAGE

The Wakashan language of the Kwakiutl is only spoken on the Northwest Coast of the North American continent. Most modern-day Kwakiutl speak English as their first language, but since the 1970s the people have taught their children traditional language, mythology, art, and culture. Two tribal museums provide instruction in the Native language.

GOVERNMENT

In earlier times communities were led by the heads of the wealthiest families, who were known as *taises,* or chiefs. Some were warriors, some were medicine men called shamans, and others were in charge of trading activities with other tribes or villages.

Since 1974 a district council has governed the 15 bands (the term Canadians use for groups of Indians) that make up the Kwakiutl tribe. The district council oversees tribal affairs and makes its opinions known to the government agency that runs the Campbell River District, formerly the Kwawkewlth Indian Agency. The Kwakiutl maintain businesses, health care facilities, educational facilities, and a variety of social services.

ECONOMY

Traditionally, the Kwakiutl were fishers and gatherers. Fishing season began in spring with the capture of Chinook salmon and extended until the chum fishing season ended in the fall. In winter the people stayed in their winter village and did very little food gathering. During that time they produced such items as boxes, spoons, dishes, and canoes.

The twentieth century brought ups and downs to the Kwakiutl economy. The fishing industry boomed after World War II (1939–45). Overfishing and overcutting of trees led to a decline in the fishing and logging industries by the 1990s, and many tribal members have had to find other employment. Some have begun their own small businesses in the hotel, restaurant, and laundry industries. Others have taken jobs as janitors, clerical workers, teacher's aides, and homemaker assistants. Some Kwakiutl have college degrees and are in professional fields.

DAILY LIFE

Families

Extended families (groups of relatives who believed their ancestor was a spirit) lived together. The families shared rights to certain fishing and food gathering areas, their large houses, and the totem poles that depicted the family crest or symbol. Each family had a sacred name and its own songs and dances that told the story of its creation.

Buildings

Traditionally, the Kwakiutl lived in large houses—sometimes up to 100 feet long, 40 feet wide, and 20 feet high—that were designed to hold several families. Villages were made up of rows of such houses, sometimes built on stilts, with a large boardwalk running the entire length of the village.

Kwakiutl chief's house painted with an eagle and a whale, Watese Village, Vancouver Island.

The area where the chief and his family lived was often separated from the rest of the house by an elaborately carved screen. Other families lived along the walls in areas separated by mats. Sleeping areas were assigned according to social rank: the higher a family's rank, the more choice their sleeping area. Before slavery ended in 1850, slaves slept on blankets near the entrance of the house. A cooking fire used by everyone stood in the center of the house.

By the late nineteenth century Kwakiutl houses were being built of cedar beams and milled lumber and were decorated with elaborately painted fronts and complex carvings of family crest figures. Some houses had doorways surrounded by large carved figures; the entryway opening was cut out between the figure's legs.

Clothing and adornment

During warm weather Kwakiutl men went naked or wore a breechcloth (flaps of material at the front and rear suspended from the waist), while women wore aprons made of bark strands. As it grew colder, the Kwakiutl wrapped themselves in blankets made of bark or animal skins, which they fastened with a belt. Most Kwakiutl went barefoot. On rainy days they wore rain hats and coats made of bark mats. Men wore their long hair loose and sported long beards. Women braided their hair and wore necklaces, bracelets, and anklets made of teeth. They also wore a type of tight anklet designed to keep the feet from growing. Wealthy people wore nose and ear decorations of abalone (pronounced *AB-uh-LONE-ee*; an edible shellfish) shells. Everyone painted their faces and bodies to protect against sunburn, but they did not wear tattoos.

Food

Kwakiutl bands collected and ate whatever foods were available in their area. For example, those near Fort Rupert ate clams, while other groups ate mostly salmon. They gathered berries, roots, sea grass, and common marine food such as smelt, cod, halibut, and sea urchins. They also ate seal and sea lion. Some hunted elk, deer, wolf, bear, mink, marten, otter, whale, or mountain goat.

Families had their own territories for hunting, fishing, and food gathering. Some of the groups arranged to share sites, and some sites were considered the common property of all. The Kwakiutl dried and smoked the fish they caught in the warm months for use during the long winters.

Education

Kwakiutl children of the late twentieth century learned traditional Native customs from their elders, as their ancestors had. Organized efforts to educate children in the ways of white people began in 1881, when Anglican missionary A. J. Hall opened a school at Alert Bay and his wife began teaching homemaking skills to several young Native girls in the Hall home. In 1894 the Department of Indian Affairs established an industrial school for boys in the town; by that time Mrs. Hall's program had become a live-in school for girls. The Department of Indian Affairs school closed in 1974.

In the 1960s many Kwakiutl moved from smaller communities to larger villages that had Indian schools. Some people who believed their children were not well served by the public schools began their own schools with programs in fishing, forestry, and carpentry in addition to standardized classes in reading, mathematics, history, and the sciences.

Healing practices

Kwakiutl healers were either witches or shamans. Witches harmed people by casting spells using the hair or bodily wastes of their victims. If the victim also knew how to cast spells, he could cancel the effect of the spell cast on him.

The people used herbs to cure diseases and injuries, but they turned to shamans when traditional methods failed. Shamans drew their power from a relationship with an animal spirit, who taught special dances, songs, and magic tricks that were useful in curing the sick or in healing injuries. Some shamans also had the power to cause diseases. They used their powers to protect the chief and kill his enemies.

"Sun Mask," by Kwakiutl artist Richard Hunt.

ARTS

Woodworking

The Kwakiutl were gifted woodworkers. They used simple tools to make remarkable canoes, large food bowls, and everyday utensils. They were also known for their superb baskets and chests made from split cedar roots, spruce roots, and grasses. Both baskets and chests were so finely made that they were watertight. The people also carved elaborate masks—often adding feathers and hair—and used them in ceremonies and dances.

Kwakiutl artworks, with their realistic and geometric patterns, had their golden age between 1890 and 1921. Art critics call the works exceptional. Artwork could be found everywhere: on house fronts, on furnishings, on tools, and on totem poles. The American Museum of Natural History in New York sponsored a traveling exhibit of Kwakiutl art and culture called "Chiefly Feasts"; it toured the country from 1992 to 1994.

Totem poles

Master Kwakiutl craftspeople were in charge of carving totem poles—large wooden poles depicting the animals and family symbols believed to link a family to the spirit world. Other figures on the pole represented important incidents in the family's history. Another type of totem pole, the memorial pole, stood from 20 to 30 feet high and honored a chief who had died. Smaller totem poles, carved from large timbers, served to support the roofs of houses. Food was sometimes placed in front of the poles as an offering to the spirits.

Oral literature

Kwakiutl families told creation stories about larger-than-life supernatural ancestors who came to the people from the sky, the sea, or the Earth. One such figure was Thunderbird, who took on a human form and created his relatives, who then became the Thunderbird family.

CUSTOMS

Social classes

Each Kwakiutl family was made up of three or more groups. Each group, in turn, held property in its village—usually at least one house and various hunting, fishing, and food gathering areas. Families marked their property with special decorations, especially posts and poles that featured family crests. The family unit organized and controlled village life, directing economic activities (hunting, fishing, and so on), social relations, and ceremonial events on a daily basis.

Traditionally, a person's social rank was determined by the family into which he or she was born. People from high ranks did not perform physical labor. Instead, people called *michimis,* who cut down cedar trees, built houses, hunted game, and repaired fish traps, did such work. Sometimes people with artistic skills, such as carvers, might be permitted to join the upper class, but this was rare. This type of social organization began to disappear around 1875, when diseases reduced the Kwakiutl population and people moved away from their historic villages to live and work elsewhere.

Secret societies

The identity of a person's guardian spirits were said to be revealed through prayer and fasting. Some guardian spirits were animals, like Grizzly Bear, while others were figures such as Cannibal or Warrior. Those who shared the same guardian spirit formed secret societies like the Hamatsa or Shamans' Society or the Bear Society.

To gain membership in the Hamatsa Society, certain chosen children took part in the Hamatsa Dance. As part of the ritual, adults of the tribe abducted the children and took them to a spot in the forest. There—covered only by a few hemlock boughs and in a frenzy of

POTLATCHES REACH THE EXTREME

A person who ended up poverty-stricken after hosting a potlatch knew the condition would not last long. It was customary for a person who had received a gift of four dugout canoes at a potlatch to repay the giver eight dugout canoes at the next potlatch. By the early twentieth century, when the Kwakiutl were enjoying a fair amount of wealth, potlatches became very elaborate. Family members sometimes worked year-round at several jobs to pay for the ceremony, even pooling their life savings just to hold a single potlatch. Modern products such as sewing machines, musical instruments, boat motors, furniture, and pool tables were freely given. Families would compete to show their superiority by setting fire to large mounds of valuable goods.

An enormous potlatch took place near Alert Bay in 1921. Eighty of the three hundred guests were arrested. Without regard for the traditional significance of the ceremony, the Canadian government concluded that large-scale potlatches were bringing economic ruin to the Natives and decided to ban them. Many ceremonial items such as masks and costumes were taken by the authorities from Alert Bay and not returned to the people until the 1960s.

hunger—the youths appeared to be trying to "eat" bystanders. (Europeans who observed these ceremonies thought the participants were cannibals. In fact, the children pretended to consume pieces of flesh donated by volunteers. Later the flesh was returned to the "victim," along with an apology and a small gift.) The elder members of the tribe would then seize the youngsters and force them to control themselves. Once the children became peaceful, they took part in public and private ceremonies involving magic and became members of the Hamatsa Society.

Potlatches

The Kwakiutl held potlatches—gift-giving ceremonies—to mark births, marriages, deaths, and acceptance into secret societies. Potlatches were usually held in winter and could be simple or elaborate.

The greatest of all potlatches was called *max'wa*, meaning "doing a great thing." Visitors were invited to hear speeches, eat, dance, and marvel at their host's display of wealth. Guests were given gifts of blankets, animal furs, carved boxes, shell necklaces, fish oil, weapons, and those of greatest value—engraved metal slabs called "coppers." The more lavish the potlatch, the more honor it reflected on its host. Sometimes a chief hosting a potlatch gave away all his possessions, burned down his house, and killed his slaves. These actions were considered honorable and right.

The Winter Ceremony

One of the most significant religious events in Kwakiutl society was the annual Winter Ceremony. This event involved the entire tribe and often many visiting tribes and lasted for up to 20 days. The Kwakiutl believed that powerful spirits came and visited them during this time and granted special powers to young people. While under the spell of the spirit, the young people pretended to be insane, and the purpose of the ceremony was to "tame" them. A potlatch followed.

Head flattening

The Kwakiutl used special boards that forced the heads of their infants to take on particular shapes as they grew; some of the head shapes showed the person's rank in society. For example, the rather cone-shaped heads of the women of Vancouver Island showed their high social rank. People from a lower class were identified by their flatter and broader heads.

War and hunting rituals

The Kwakiutl believed that each living thing, whether plant or animal, had its own spirit. Animals did not mind being caught and eaten because they could return to the spirit world and take on a new body. Hunters showed great respect to the animal spirits. For example, when they caught salmon they thanked them and put their bones back into the water, believing that the bones would float back to the house of the Salmon People in the world of the spirits.

Marriage

Marriage was an opportunity to gain property and other rights and privileges, so the arrangement of a child's marriage was taken very seriously. Kwakiutl marriages might occur between two children of the same father—but of different mothers—or between a man and his younger brother's daughter.

Most present-day marriages are performed in Christian churches. They are followed by a potlatch celebration that features traditional practices such as a mock competition for the bride, a gift exchange between the families of the bride and groom, and the couple's going off to start their new life together in the groom's village (unless job demands necessitate other arrangements).

Funerals

Kwakiutl groups had different burial customs. Those of the North cremated their dead, while those to the South buried their dead in trees or caves. Important chiefs were sometimes buried in their canoes.

Kwakiutl wedding party in canoes, photo by Edward S. Curtis.

CURRENT TRIBAL ISSUES

In April 1997 the nation of Canada and the Kwakiutl First Nation, also known as the Fort Rupert Band, reached a final settlement in a land claim filed back in 1992. The Kwakiutl claimed that Deer Island and Eagle Island should have been made Kwakiutl reserves. In exchange for the land, Canada agreed to pay the Kwakiutl First Nation $500,000 for final settlement of the claim.

NOTABLE PEOPLE

Mungo Martin (c. 1879–1962; Kwakiutl name, Naka'penkim) was a chief, a sculptor, a master carver, and a leader in the campaign to preserve and restore Kwakiutl totem poles. He also carved his own totem poles, including the world's largest, which stands over 127 feet high. Martin drowned in 1962 while fishing.

James Sewid (1910–) was the chief of the Kwakiutl at Alert Bay when the ancient system of inheriting leadership positions was replaced by an election process. He had begun work for the fishing industry at age 10, married at 13, and wrote of his life in a remote Indian village in his autobiography entitled *Guests Never Leave Hungry.* Sewid has spent his later years helping to revive Kwakiutl customs. In 1955 he was selected by the National Film Board of Canada to portray his achievements in a movie called *No Longer Vanishing.*

FURTHER READING

Native American Tribes: Interesting Facts and Legends from the Reader's Digest's "Through Indian Eyes": [Online] http:www.geocities.com/Heartland/Prairie/8962/factkwak.html, pp. 3-7.

Nowell, Charles James. *Smoke from their Fires: The Life of a Kwakiutl Chief.* Hamdon, CT: Archon Books, 1968.

Prentzas, G.S. *The Kwakiutl Indians.* New York: Chelsea House, 1993.

Makah

Name

Makah (pronounced *MAH-kah*). The Makah people called themselves "kwee-DITCH-cha-uck," or "people who live by the rocks and seagulls." Neighboring tribes called them Makah, which means either "cape dwellers" (they lived on Cape Flattery) or "people generous with food."

Location

The Makah were located on the most northwestern point of Cape Flattery on the Olympic Peninsula in northwestern Washington State. In the late 1990s the Makah Indian Reservation covered 44 acres in Clallam County, Washington, and included the village of Neah Bay.

Population

In the late 1700s, there were an estimated 2,000 Makah. In 1834, they numbered about 550. In a census (count of the population) conducted in 1990 by the U.S. Bureau of the Census, 1,661 people identified themselves as Makah.

Language family

Wakashan.

Origins and group affiliations

The Makah have lived on the northwestern Pacific Coast for centuries. Long before the coming of Europeans, the Makah lived near and traded with the Nootkah and Nitinaht tribes, to whom they were sometimes friendly and sometimes hostile.

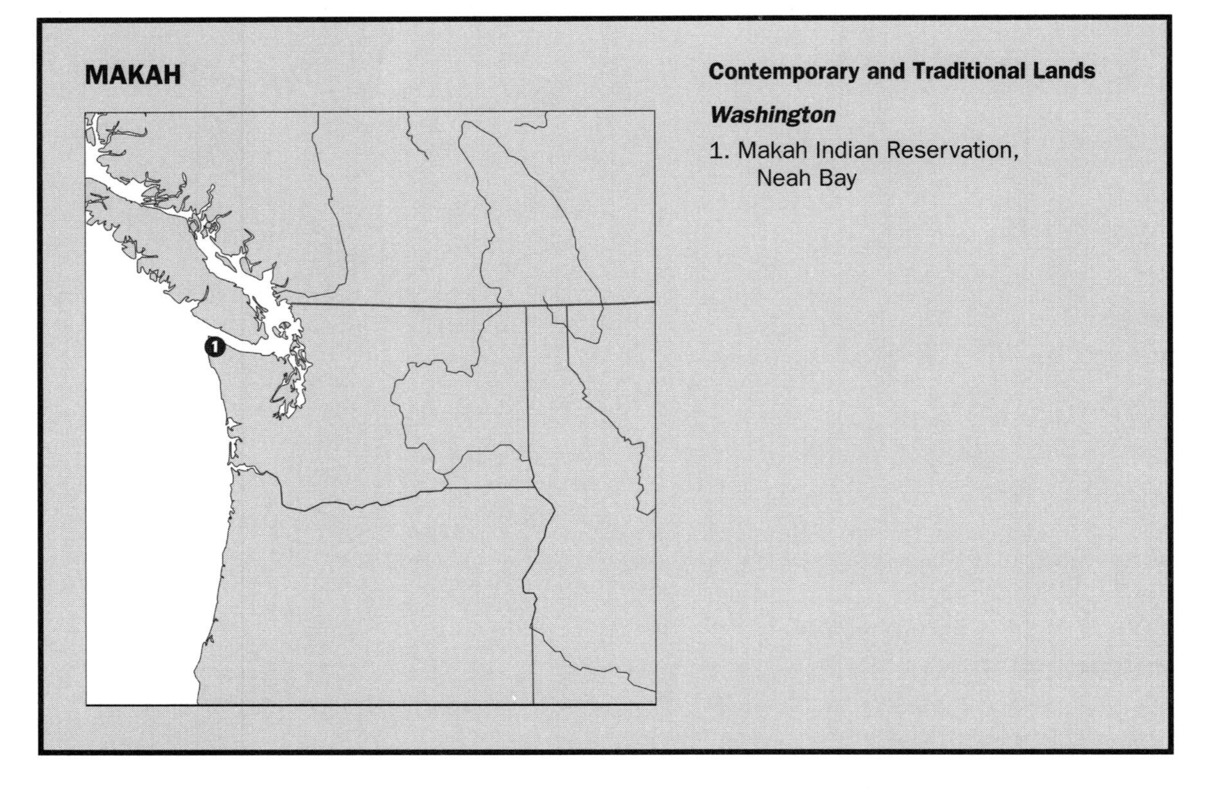

According to tribal legend, the Makah people were conceived when the stars mated with animals. Their lush forest home along the Pacific Northwest coastline is an area battered by storms, soaked with rains, and dwarfed by rugged mountains to the east. The Makah depended on the sea for their livelihood and were expert hunters of whales and seals. They survived the invasion of their homeland by white settlers and at the end of the twentieth century were the only Native American tribe with the legal right to hunt whales. The treaty guaranteeing this right has been the subject of controversy in recent years.

HISTORY

Coming of the Europeans

Before the Makah had contact with Europeans, the people lived in five villages: Bahaada, Deah (present-day Neah Bay), Waatch, Sooes, and Ozette (an excavation site). The villages were linked by similar cultures, language, and marriage.

The first recorded European contact with the Makah was made by John Meares, a British sea captain who anchored off the coast of the Makah-occupied Tatoosh Island in the spring of 1788 on a fur trading journey. Two years later Spaniards sailed into Neah Bay. They established a fort there but for unknown reasons abandoned the venture after only four months.

IMPORTANT DATES

1788: First recorded contact between the Makah and Europeans is made when John Meares moors his ship off the coast of Tatoosh Island.

1790: Spaniards establish a fort at Neah Bay but mysteriously abandon it after only four months.

1855: The Makah are forced to sign the Treaty of Neah Bay, turning all their land over to the U.S. government.

1970: Tidal erosion uncovers the ancient whaling village at Ozette. The find promotes among the Makah a renewed interest in their traditional language and culture.

1995: The Makah inform federal officials that they want to kill up to five gray whales a year for food and ceremonial uses. The whale hunt is scheduled for late 1998.

Gifted traders

The Makah were already experienced deal-makers when they began trading with Europeans in the early 1800s. Their frequent dealings with Europeans sharpened their skills and introduced them to non-Native goods.

Europeans bought sea otter and beaver pelts from the Makah to make hats and coats for the fashion-conscious people of northern Europe. Other tribes, who also became wealthy from this trade, purchased whale oil from the Makah. As the number of white settlers grew in the first half of the nineteenth century, the tribe concentrated on producing oil from whales, seals, candlefish, and dogfish to be used as machine oil in European and American factories. They took their trade items to Fort Nisqually and Fort Langley, trading centers built by the U.S. government. In 1852 alone, the Makah sold 20,000 gallons of fish and whale oil for use at sawmills in Olympia, Washington; they were, in fact, the chief suppliers of machine oil for the entire Northwest Coast.

Makah sign Treaty of Neah Bay

Isaac Stevens was the governor of Washington territory and superintendent of Indian Affairs in the mid-1800s. He considered the Native tribes of the Northwest an "impediment to civilization" (meaning they stood in the way of white advancement). Stevens believed strongly in Manifest Destiny. According to this nineteenth century philosophy, white nations—especially the United States—were meant to dominate the entire Western Hemisphere. Beginning in 1854, Stevens attempted to establish treaties with nearly every tribe in his territory (what would become the state of Washington and some of its surrounding areas). In an attempt to take over as much land as possible for white settlers, he set out to abolish Native land titles, place tribes on reservations, and persuade the Indians to adopt the white way of life.

In the mid-1800s the Makah experienced a series of epidemics that killed off significant numbers of the tribe. The weakened Makah were convinced to sign the Treaty of Neah Bay in 1855, giving up their land to the U.S. government. In return, Governor Stevens promised them access to health care. He also promised them that the U.S. government would send them oil kettles and fishing gear to make their fishing more efficient. The treaty granted them "the right of taking fish and of whaling or sealing at usual and accustomed grounds and stations," referring to family-owned patches of ocean in their old territories.

Makah refuse to farm

In keeping with the popular thinking of the mid-nineteenth century, U.S. government agents and missionaries tried to turn the Makah, who were expert whalers and fishers, into farmers—on land that was completely unsuitable for farming. The Makah ignored these efforts for the most part and continued their ocean fishing. They controlled supplies of fish oil and the halibut fish trade in the region. Late in the nineteenth century the Makah used their fleet of large whaling vessels to supply a great deal of oil for logging camps that had been established by American companies in the Northwest.

Makah involvement in the large-scale hunting of fur seals began back in 1860. It continued for 30 years, until the ever-increasing number of seal fishers and the growing use of firearms to hunt seals led to the end of the seal trade. Even so, the Makah made sure that a 1911 treaty with the U.S. government gave them and some other tribes the right to continue catching seals by the age-old method of harpooning them from canoes. The tribe continued this form of fishing for several more decades. During the twentieth century tourism and logging activities grew, replacing fishing as the major source of income for the Makah.

Ancient whaling village found

In 1970 archaeologists (scientists who study the life and culture of ancient peoples by examining the things they left behind) made an exciting discovery—a prehistoric Makah whaling village was unearthed at Ozette. Parts of the village had been covered by a mudslide more than five centuries before, and the mud had preserved skeletons of the unfortunate victims, as well as their houses and belongings, in nearly perfect condition. Ozette has been called one of the most significant archaeological discoveries ever made in North America. Many items were found there, including sculptures, har-

NATIVE AMERICAN CHURCH

The Native American church was formed in Oklahoma in 1918. It brought together several groups of Native North Americans who had been practicing the peyote religion (pronounced *pay-OH-tay*; named for a stimulant derived from mescal buttons, which are the dried tops of a small cactus) since the 1880s. The new religion was first spread by John Wilson (c. 1840–1901), a man of mixed Delaware, Caddo, and French parentage. He claimed that under the influence of peyote, he had several visions telling him the right way for Native Americans to worship Jesus Christ. (Peyote, a nonaddictive drug, brings on altered mental states and hallucinations in people who chew or consume it in the form of green tea.) Wilson preached that those who followed the Peyote Road would be set free from their sins. This was a welcome message to Indians who found themselves at the mercy of the whites—confined to reservations, stripped of the right to worship their Native religions, and seeking a way to combine their traditional beliefs with Christianity.

James Mooney (1861–1921), an employee of the Smithsonian Institution (a center for the study of American culture) in Washington, D.C., became fascinated by the peyote religion. While traveling among many Native tribes in the 1890s, Mooney came to believe that the Indians in the United States needed to be brought together through their own religion, so he drew up the legal papers forming the Native American Church. Attracting a diverse membership from numerous tribes, the church is most active in the American Northwest and Southwest. It combines Christian and Native beliefs and features an all-night ceremony of chanting, prayer, and meditation.

Peyote is considered sacred among church members, but since 1900 attempts have been made to outlaw its use in church ceremonies. In 1990 the U.S. Supreme Court ruled that the possession and use of peyote by Native American church members is not protected by the First Amendment. (The First Amendment to the U.S. Constitution guarantees Americans freedom of religion, among other freedoms.) The Supreme Court's ruling means that each state can decide whether to allow the religious use of peyote.

While the consumption of peyote has generated considerable controversy and publicity, the church's main goal is quite simple: to promote unity among its members. The Native American Church stresses brotherly love, family, self-reliance, and the avoidance of alcohol. From the beginning, it has fought to protect the First Amendment rights of its members.

Because the Native American church is so loosely organized, it is difficult to estimate its membership with accuracy. In 1922 the church claimed to have about 22,000 members; in the late 1990s it claimed more than 250,000 members.

poons, baskets, and various household utensils. The event led to the founding of the Makah Cultural and Research Center on the Makah Reservation in Neah Bay, Washington. The center highlights the history of the tribe and has helped to preserve its language and culture.

RELIGION

The Makah people believed in guardian spirits who helped individuals become successful in reaching their life goals. Shamans (pronounced *SHAY-munz*), healers who could be either male or female, helped people make contact with their guardian spirits.

At the beginning of the twentieth century some Makah people joined the Native American church, a religion that combined elements of Christianity with traditional Native beliefs and practices. (See box.)

LANGUAGE

The Makah language is similar to the language spoken by their northern neighbors, the Nootkah, Kwakiutl (see entry), and Bella Bella. With the discovery of the ancient city of Ozette, there has been a renewed interest in the teaching of the Makah language. The Makah Cultural and Research Center is home to a program that works to preserve and teach the Makah language. As a result of such efforts, the number of Makah children who spoke their native language jumped from 33 percent in 1980 to 78 percent by 1985.

GOVERNMENT

There were no Makah chiefs. The men who had the most influence in a Makah village—usually the fur seal hunters or the harpoon throwers who captured whales—were called headmen. They often displayed their wealth and power through gift-giving ceremonies called potlatches.

The Makah adopted a constitution in 1936. At the end of the twentieth century a tribal council governed the tribe. It consists of five persons who are elected to three-year terms; a new council head is chosen each year.

ECONOMY

For centuries the Makah economy was based on trade and fishing. They were among the top whale fishermen in North America until about 1860. Having gained a reputation as clever traders, they managed to control most of the money supply in the Northwest. The Makah used a type of shell called *dentalium* (pronounced *den-TAY-lee-um*; from the Latin word for "tooth") as money. The shells were polished and strung like beads.

Traditionally, the Makah hunted fur seals and whales. Each family had its own area of the ocean for fishing, and the area passed from father to son. During the nineteenth century, however, seals changed their migration patterns and almost disappeared from the tribe's homeland. Around 1866, fur seals reappeared; because sealskin was in great demand, seal hunting resumed. By the 1880s white businesspeople had started hiring Makah men to serve as seal hunters

Rallying community support for the Makah's return to gray whale hunting, Neah Bay, 1998.

aboard commercial fishing boats. (Commercial boats work for profit, not for food or an owner's personal use.) The jobs were so profitable that the Makah temporarily gave up whaling but continued seal hunting. The seal trade lasted until 1890, when seal hunting was prohibited because the supply had been so severely depleted. Many Makah then returned to whale hunting.

Commercial logging (cutting down trees for money) on Makah land began in 1926. In the 1930s the first road opened linking the mainland of Washington to the peninsula where the reservation is located. (Earlier, the peninsula could only be reached by boat.) The Makah tourist industry began to develop as more and more people discovered the beauty of the area and set out to learn about how the Natives lived. Since then, the building of a breakwater (to shelter the harbor from crashing waves) has attracted individual sailing boats and tourist boats.

Commercial fishing became important to the Makah economy later in the twentieth century, but overfishing and overcutting brought a decline in the fishing and logging industries in the 1990s. As a result, tourism has become increasingly important. It was given a boost by the opening of the Neah Bay Marina, which harbors more than 200 sailing and fishing vessels. Large and small businesses have opened at the marina and in the village to cater to tourists. (Makah Tribal Bingo, for instance, provides a considerable amount of money and jobs, but the community has rejected a full-service casino. The Makah are not interested in developing a heavy economic reliance on gambling.) The Cape Flattery Resort and Conference Facility features a lodge, camp grounds, a sweat house (a steam-heated lodge used for Native American cleansing, purification, and ritual), sports facilities, and a café. Increasing numbers of tourists visit the reservation to view wildlife, marine mammals, and birds.

DAILY LIFE

Families

The Makah family consisted of a father, mother, children, and close relatives who lived together in a large house. The bonds between grandparents and grandchildren were especially strong. Aunts and uncles were like second parents, and there was also a close association with in-laws. Members of Makah families were ranked in the society according to their relationship to the headman of the village. The closer the relationship, the more important the person. Traditionally, each Makah family owned a certain section of beach along Makah territory; they also had rights to any items that might float ashore on their property.

Buildings

Makah villages consisted of 3 to 20 flat-roofed longhouses that were set along the beaches. Each longhouse sheltered up to 20 families. The buildings had dirt floors and frames made of planks held in place by pegs. Roofs were constructed with flat wooden planks that could be shifted to let in air or removed and transported if the villagers moved to follow a spring salmon run. Moveable woven mats served as partitions to mark off each family's living area. During the winter months the partitions were taken down to provide a common place for dancing, feasting, and gambling. Although there was a central cooking fire, each family had its own smaller fire.

Clothing and adornment

Because of the mild climate, Makah men (and sometimes women) went naked or wore very little clothing year-round. The clothing they did wear consisted of woven capes, skirts made of cedar bark (soaked and pounded soft), cattail fluff, and woven down feathers. Rain gear included cone-shaped hats and bearskin robes. The Makah rarely wore shoes, but in cool weather they sometimes donned moccasins.

Food

The centerpiece of the Makah diet was sea mammals, especially whales. Both men and women participated in the butchering of whales, and every part of the whale was used for some purpose: tendons, for instance, were braided and dried for use as rope, and oil was extracted from the whale's blubber. The meat and skin were eaten immediately; the choicest piece of blubber went to the chief harpooner.

Men also fished for salmon and halibut and hunted land mammals and birds. Various fish, shrimp, small octopuses, worms, snails, and crabs added variety to the diet. The activities of women centered on gathering shellfish, plants, roots, and berries, and processing the fish and animals the men brought from the hunt. Smoked and dried meats were saved for winter or used for trade. Among the Makah people's favorite foods was a root called camas, which could only be obtained by trading with tribes from the North who were able to grow it.

Education

From their early years Makah boys learned fishing techniques and routes to their family's fishing territory. Girls learned about food gathering and preservation from adult females of the village.

After the move to the reservation, representatives of the federal government, called Indian agents, oversaw schools in Neah Bay. They showed little respect for Makah language and culture and did their best to make the children assimilate, or take on the white way of life. In 1932 the state of Washington built a public elementary and high school on the reservation.

When the Makah Cultural and Research Center opened on the Makah Reservation (see "History"), many young Makah found work there with teams who were studying the Ozette excavation site. They began to learn about their culture through formal training in anthropology (the study of human societies and cultures).

Healing practices

The Makah depended mostly on shamans to deal with illnesses. Shamans held curing ceremonies to teach the people how to use plants for healing. In the 1990s Makah health care was provided at a clinic run by the tribe and Indian Health Services.

Two Makah women weaving baskets.

ARTS

The Makah Cultural and Research Center

The Makah Cultural and Research Center, which was founded in 1979, depicts the life of the Makah people prior to European contact. It features 300- to 500-year-old articles that were uncovered from the Makah village of Ozette. (See "History.") On display are full-scale replicas of cedar-log longhouses, as well as exhibits on whaling, sealing, and how fishing canoes were made. The museum displays only about 1 percent of the 55,000 articles recovered from the Ozette site. Makah artists and craftspeople have helped revive Makah traditions and are teaching other members to make longhouses, canoes, totems, masks, baskets, clothing, and jewelry.

Oral literature

As is true with many other tribes, storytellers passed on the wisdom of the Makah tribe from one generation ro the next. One popular Makah tale describes how the Great Thunderbird, helped by the Wolf

Serpent, brought the Makah people their first whale. The Wolf Serpent, who had the head of a wolf and the body of a serpent, braced himself around the legs of the Great Thunderbird. When the bird swooped down on the whale, the Wolf Serpent wrapped itself around the whale's head and tail and helped the Great Thunderbird to lift it out of the sea. They then took the whale and presented it to the Makah people, who made use of the sea mammal for food and supplies.

CUSTOMS

Social classes

Makah society had a class system. People in the middle class could gain power by marrying into the upper classes.

Festivals and ceremonies

The Makah practiced the Wolf Ritual, a four-day winter healing ceremony. Its purpose was to welcome members into the secret Klukwalle society. Participants in the Wolf Ritual wore masks or headdresses made of thin boards.

The Doctoring Ritual was another four-day winter ceremony. It was believed to cure participants of illnesses. The ceremony was performed by a shaman, who wore yellow cedar bark robes and neck and head rings of shredded cedar bark.

In modern times a Makah Days celebration is held on the reservation each August to honor the Makah heritage. It begins with the crowning of a Makah princess, followed by nighttime fireworks and a community talent show. There are three days of salmon bakes, canoe races, and traditional dancing by children and adults.

War and hunting practices

Slaves were important to the Makah; they were captured by war parties from enemies such as the Quileute and Klallam. The wealthy owned the greatest number of slaves. Children were warned not to wander far away from camp for fear they might be taken as slaves by other tribes.

The Makah ranked among the foremost whalers in North America. Whale hunting was extremely dangerous, and preparations for a hunt went on throughout the year. To condition themselves, whale hunters bathed in cold streams or lakes when the moon was full. To toughen their skin, they rubbed their bodies with hemlock twigs until they bled. At certain times they fasted and stayed away from women.

They practiced diving underwater, holding their breath to increase their lung capacity, and they mimicked the whales' graceful swimming style. When a whale appeared in a dream to the head of the whaling group, it was time for the hunt.

Whale hunters used cedar log canoes manned by a crew of eight, who sometimes took their canoes as far as 20 miles offshore to hunt for whales. Excellent canoeing skills were needed, for whales could swim under a dugout canoe and flip or smash it with their enormous tails.

The chief whalers were known for having great spiritual powers. They stood in the front of the canoe and sang special songs to lure a whale, promising it many gifts if it let itself be killed. The songs were very valuable and were passed down through families. It was considered a crime for a whaler to "steal" another's song.

Whale hunters used harpoons tipped with sharp seashells. Seal bladders—which served as excellent flotation devices—were attached to the harpoons with whale sinew rope; after the harpoon entered the whale's flesh, the floats prevented the whale from diving. Hunters then guided the whale toward the shore to complete the kill.

Puberty

Adolescent boys went to remote places in the forest for a vision quest to find their spiritual protectors. They fasted and entered a trancelike state in which their spirits were revealed to them. Girls acquired their guardian spirits by going alone to a special place when they menstruated and by performing certain rites while wearing distinctive shell ornaments on their braids.

CURRENT TRIBAL ISSUES

A controversy erupted in 1995 when the Makah, who had not hunted whales since 1926, informed federal officials that they wanted to kill up to five gray whales a year for food and ceremonial use. The proposal met with disapproval from animal rights activists, who claimed that a sanctioned whale hunt would hamper their efforts to ban whale hunting worldwide and would push the whales closer to extinction.

Tribal members themselves are not in agreement on this issue. Several Makah elders took out a half-page ad in a local newspaper, expressing their opposition to the plan. Still, plans went forward, and the first whaling expedition was scheduled for the autumn of 1998.

NOTABLE PEOPLE

Sandra Osawa (1942–) is a successful television producer and writer, focusing primarily on Native American culture and issues. In 1980, she received an Emmy nomination (an award for excellence in television) for "I Know Who I Am," a television program on Native American cultural affairs. *The Native American Series* was the first television series ever to be produced, written, and acted exclusively by Native Americans.

FURTHER READING

Cohlene, Terri. *Clamshell Boy: A Makah Legend.* Vero Beach, FL: Rourke Corporation, 1990.

Deloria, Vince, Jr. *Indians of the Pacific Northwest.* Garden City, NY: Doubleday, 1977.

Hobbs, Will. *Ghost Canoe.* New York: Morrow Junior Books, 1997.

Lyons, Grant. *Pacific Coast Indians of North America.* New York: Julian Messner, 1983.

Nisqually

Name

Nisqually (pronounced *Nis-KWALL-ee*) is the tribe's name for themselves and comes from the word *squalli,* meaning "prairie grass."

Location

The Nisqually's traditional lands were the entire Nisqually River basin in western Washington state. Today they live on the Nisqually Reservation on the Nisqually River, in Thurston County in western Washington state. It lies on a one-mile-wide strip surrounded on both sides by America's second-largest military base, Fort Lewis.

Population

In 1780, there were about 3,600 Nisqually. At the beginning of the twentieth century, the population had fallen to 110. In a census (count of the population) done in 1990 by the U.S. Bureau of the Census, 436 people identified themselves as Nisqually.

Language family

Salishan.

Origins and group affiliations

For thousands of years, Nisqually groups lived in their homelands in what is now the state of Washington. They shared good relations with the nearby Puyallup (see entry) and the Kittitas and Yakima people who lived within the same water drainage system.

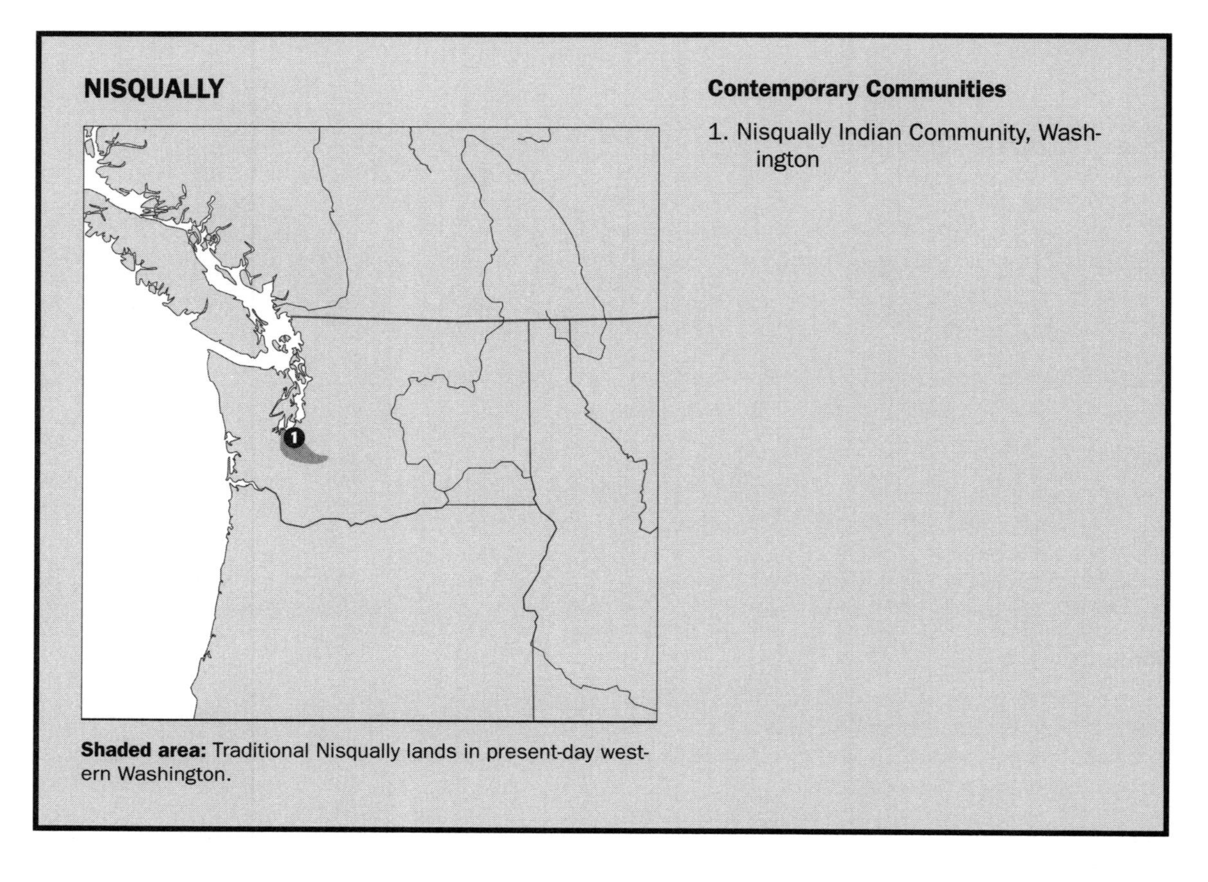

NISQUALLY

Contemporary Communities

1. Nisqually Indian Community, Washington

Shaded area: Traditional Nisqually lands in present-day western Washington.

The Nisqually thrived for thousands of years on the natural resources their vast tribal lands provided, sharing berry and hunting grounds with nearby tribes. They roamed the woodlands and coastal waters from Mt. Rainier to the Puget Sound. Their lives were ordered by finding food, feasting, and special rituals. Before the 1970s, lack of electricity and other modern resources on the reservation caused most Nisqually to move from their tribal lands. Since then, electricity has been introduced and new buildings have gone up. Hundreds of Nisqually have come back and have begun to rebuild their culture and community.

HISTORY

First contact

The first contact between Europeans and the Nisqually took place when British captain George Vancouver sailed by in 1791 exploring the Puget Sound area. The tribe was first written about in

1820, when a trading business, the Hudson Bay Company, entered the region.

George Leschi, Nisqually leader during removal.

Treaty of Medicine Creek

Before 1846 the United States and Great Britain jointly occupied the Nisqually lands. In 1846 the two countries agreed that the U.S. government would decide the Indians' fate. In 1848, U.S. officials promised the Indians that their lands would not be taken from them without their consent, but that promise was later broken.

In 1854 Isaac Stevens was appointed governor of what was called the Oregon Territory (it later became the states of Oregon, Washington, Idaho, part of Montana and northwest Wyoming), and was placed in charge of relations with the Indians. By then, the white settlers were clamoring for more land. Stevens decided the best way to get more land was to take it away from the Indians and place them on reservations. In December 1854, he made a treaty with a group of tribes including the Nisqually. Under the Treaty of Medicine Creek, the Nisqually had to give up their tribal lands. They also agreed that within one year they would move to a reservation. It was plain to Nisqually Chief George Leschi that the treaty took away the rivers where his people had always fished, and the pastures where they kept their horses. They also had to face the threat of being moved further north. Although he refused to sign the treaty, someone placed an "X" before his name on the treaty, falsely indicating his approval.

Chief Leschi leads uprising

In time, the Nisqually were forced by the U.S. government to relocate to a reservation and their life changed greatly. The people were upset to leave the grasslands they loved and move to a rocky and barren land away from their accustomed fishing sites. They became afraid when diseases brought by the whites broke out among the people. They were dismayed with U.S. government delays in putting certain plans for the tribe into action. Finally, the Nisqually enlisted the help of men from other tribes and, under the command of Chief Leschi, engaged in an uprising. However, Leschi was unsuccessful in drawing all the tribes of Western Washington in a wider war against the whites. The war was short, and the Natives lost.

IMPORTANT DATES

1854: The Treaty of Medicine Creek is signed and the Nisqually give up much of their land.

1918: Tribal land is taken by the U.S. Government for the building of Fort Lewis.

1974: The Boldt Decision affirms Nisqually off-reservation fishing rights.

1978: Nisqually Tribal Headquarters is built.

Life on the reservation

Following that incident, the Nisqually settled down to a quiet and impoverished life on the reservation. The land proved too poor for successful farming. By the beginning of the twentieth century, some of them were forced to leave the reservation to seek jobs working for whites in the lumber and agriculture industries. In time, the population of the reservation declined even further, due to disease, poor diet, and alcoholism. At the beginning of the twentieth century, the Nisqually population had fallen to 110.

Tribe organizes to fight for rights

In 1918 the U.S. War Department seized nearly two-thirds of the Nisqually Reservation land to form Fort Lewis, a military training camp for soldiers going to fight in World War I (1914–18). As the years passed, the Department took over more parcels of Nisqually land.

Protests held on fishing issues

During the 1950s, the growing number of white fishermen wanted more fishing areas for themselves. They succeeded in pressuring Washington state officials to tell the Nisqually that they would be permitted to fish only on their reservation, instead of in the much wider area they had been used to. The Nisqually defied the order and continued fishing beyond reservation lands.

In 1963 the Washington State Supreme Court upheld the state's right to impose fishing restrictions on the Native Americans. As a result, conflicts took place between the Nisqually and state police officials on the banks of the Nisqually and Puyallup rivers. In 1966, a well-known African-American comedian by the name of Dick Gregory was arrested for supporting the tribespeople during a "fish-in." The fish-in was held to protest state laws that now required hook and line fishing instead of their traditional methods that used nets anchored with rocks and that made for a larger catch. A celebrated fishing rights case resulted. The tribe claimed that, according to treaties with the federal government, it had the right to use the net-fishing procedures. A complicated series of court battles took place between the Indians and the state government.

The Boldt Decision of 1974 settled the matter. It affirmed that the 1854 Treaty of Medicine Creek permitted the tribes of western Washington to fish in their "usual and accustomed" fishing areas away from the reservation. Since this celebrated case, the input of Native peoples has been sought on fishing questions. As of the late 1990s, the Northwest Indian Fisheries Commission directed off-reservation fishing for the tribes, including the Nisqually.

Meanwhile, by 1973 the Nisqually Reservation had been reduced to only a fraction of its former size, and only a small group of Nisqually resided there. In 1974, the Nisqually people, with planning and funding aid from the federal office of Housing and Urban Development, began preparations to build a tribal headquarters on the reservation. In 1976, they purchased 53 acres of nearby land, and the new headquarters was completed in 1978. Nearby are new facilities for educational services, medical and dental care, programs for seniors and children, a police force, a library, recreational programs, and a natural resources center. In the 1990s, more than 100 homes have been built on the reservation.

RELIGION

Religion played a major role in every aspect of a person's life. Spirits gave people certain abilities, attitudes, personality traits, and preferences. Failure to cooperate with the spirits resulted in illness and death. The spirits bestowed powers that might include physical strength, artistic talent, hunting skills, long life, and wealth, among others. The powers usually were given to a person during adolescence, but they could come to anyone of any age who was physically clean and pure.

The Nisqually believed that their land was a living thing that had been created by the Great Spirit and could not be divided. Mother Earth was sacred and had to be treated with great care. The people did not accept the white concept of private property and refused to break up their land.

Today most Nisqually people are members of the Catholic Church, the Indian Shaker Church (see box in Hupa and Chilula entry), or a Nisqually division of the Assembly of God religion.

LANGUAGE

The Nisqually people spoke Southern Lushootseed, a variety of the Salish language spoken near the Puget Sound area. Today most Nisqually speak English during their everyday activities.

GOVERNMENT

There were no Nisqually chiefs in traditional times, but the advice of the head of the richest household was often sought. His main job was to sponsor feasts and potlatches (gift-giving ceremonies). When he died, a younger son or brother usually took over these duties.

Today on the Nisqually Reservation an elected business committee conducts all tribal business. It is responsible for health, social services, natural resources, accounting, and planning. The council rules according to a tribal constitution that was adopted in 1946.

ECONOMY

Before the move to the reservation, the Nisqually economy was based on fishing, hunting, gathering, and trade. Shells obtained in trade from the Nootkah of Vancouver Island were polished, strung like beads, and used as money. A person's wealth was measured by the number of blankets, fur robes, pelts, bone war clubs, canoes, and slaves he owned.

Today most of the people live in poverty, but they receive some income from the proceeds of their bingo hall and gift shop, a shellfish business, and various grants. The tribe earns additional funds from their two-acre community garden and a greenhouse, and two fish hatcheries.

DAILY LIFE

Families

In traditional times, four to eight Nisqually families shared a large house. The families usually consisted of a man, one or more of his wives, and all of his children, sometimes unmarried relatives and (in wealthy families only) one or more slaves.

Buildings

The Nisqually built solid houses out of cedar posts and planks; cedar is a strong wood that can be cut with simple tools. Houses were rectangular in shape and longer than they were wide; they usually sat in rows parallel to a body of water. The insides of the houses were lined with platforms that served as beds; the platforms were about three feet wide and had storage spaces built above them. In summer, these houses often sat empty, as most activities took place

A Nisqually woman in traditional dress placing a headdress on a young girl.

either outdoors or in square or cone-shaped summerhouses, covered with mats.

Clothing and adornment

During warm weather, Nisqually men often went naked or wore only hide or cedar bark breechcloths (garments with front and back flaps that hung from the waist). In rainy weather, they wore capes made of cedar bark strips. Women wore narrow skirts of cedar bark or full-length dresses. In winter, both men and women wore animal hides, rubbed with deer brains to soften them. They also wore hide moccasins and blankets woven of mountain goat hair or dog hair.

Nisqually women parted their hair down the middle and wore two braids, sometimes painting the part red. Men let their hair grow to neck-length, parted down the middle and combed behind their ears. Men sometimes wore rectangular fur hats and older women wore soft hats made of mountain grass. Young girls rarely wore hats.

The Nisqually did not wear body paint, but both men and women used red face paint combined with deer tallow to keep their faces from becoming weather-beaten. At ceremonial events they painted designs on the face, such as lines on the cheeks and on the chin. Both men and young girls wore headbands with shredded tassels. They wore necklaces, bracelets, earrings, and nose rings made of shells polished to look like beads.

Food

The Nisqually mainly fished and also hunted and gathered. In spring and fall men caught salmon; everyone in the tribe helped smoke and dry them. They also caught blue fish, flounder, halibut, skate, sole, and devilfish. Fish eggs and shellfish added variety to their diet. Hunters took seals by surprise and clubbed them or drove them into sharpened stakes or nets.

The meat of deer, elk, black bear, beaver, and rabbit was dried and smoked over fires. Different kinds of berries, such as blackberries, were crushed, formed into blocks, and dried in the sun or over a fire, or were boiled and made into a thick paste for later consumption. Licorice roots, wild carrots, and various bulbs were also eaten.

Food was prepared only once a day, in the late afternoon, and eating took place throughout the day. A typical evening meal might be a boiled liquid followed by steamed meat or fish.

Education

Although little is known about how the Nisqually were taught, children probably learned many of the skills needed for survival by observing their elders. In the late 1800s and early 1900s government schools were established on the reservation. Children from ages six to sixteen received a basic education in reading, writing, and arithmetic for half a day, then worked during the afternoon on farms run by the schools. Boys did repairs, and girls learned to sew clothes and keep house according to the white ways. Today, children at the Nisqually Reservation attend a public school located five miles from the reservation.

Healing Practices

When someone became ill, medicine men, called shamans (pronounced *SHAY-munz*), were consulted, but they could only cure certain diseases. After they determined what was making the person sick (often an object within his or her body), the shaman's real work began. He attempted to seize the object by using sweeping gestures, and passing his hands over the body of the patient, occasionally dipping his hands in water. Singing, dancing, and drumming accompanied the healing act. When he found the spot in the body where the object was situated, the shaman removed it. He clasped it together in his palms or bit into the patient and sucked the object out, and then transferred it to his hands. The patient's relatives helped decide whether to send the object back to its source or to have the shaman destroy it. This final part of the process often took many hours and required the aid of a second shaman.

FOLKLORE OF THE TSIATKO

The Nisqually tell stories about a group of tall Indians, called "stick" Indians, who were said to wander through the forests of the Nisqually. In the Native language they were called *tsiatko.*

The tsiatko lived like animals in hollowed-out sleeping places in the woods. They wandered on land only, never on the rivers, and usually by night. They communicated by whistling and their sounds could be heard throughout the darkness.

They played pranks on the villagers, such as stealing fish from their nets. Sometimes they played pranks on individual men, whistling to put the men into a trance and then removing their clothing and tying their legs apart.

People who interfered with them were hunted down and killed by bow and arrow. Sometimes they stole children and forced them to become wives or slaves. Women were afraid of them, and used threats of the tsiatko to keep their children in line.

One man told a story about his relatives capturing a tsiatko boy in 1850 and raising him. The boy slept all day and wandered about at night. In the morning his captors could see where he had piled up wood or caught some fish. Finally, they permitted him to go home to his people. He later returned with some of his people for a visit, then went away for good.

Many Nisqually people had a knowledge of herbs, collected or bought them, and cured themselves. Today, the staff at a small medical clinic on the reservation meets many of the people's health care needs.

CUSTOMS

Social classes

Nisqually society was divided into the upper class, the lower class, and slaves, who were usually war captives and their descendants. Villages were linked by the marriages of leading families and by participation in shared ceremonies.

Birth and babies

When a Nisqually woman was about to deliver, she went to a shelter where a specially trained woman assisted her with the birth. Following the birth, the substance expelled from a woman's womb after childbirth was wrapped and carried by a small boy to the top of a tree—the higher the better for the good luck of the baby. Parents used special boards to mold their infants' heads to form a straight line from the nose to the forehead, as this was considered an attractive feature.

Puberty and marriage

Adolescent boys took part in quests, looking for the spirit who would guide them throughout their lives. Sweat baths and fasting

A reenactment of a Nisqually wedding ceremony.

were elements of these five- to ten-day journeys. What happened on the journeys always remained a secret.

Parents arranged marriages for their children. In *People of the Totem,* writers Norman Bancroft-Hunt and Werner Forman point out that Salish Indians like the Nisqually made use of "love charms and potions which were designed to make a girl fall in love with the young man who idolized her . . . Secret formulas for 'putting names' on a girl's ears, eyes, hands, and head were used . . . to make it impossible for her to hear, see, touch, or think without being reminded of her suitor." When a woman married, she moved to her husband's village to live with his family.

Festivals and ceremonies

The Nisqually held First Salmon ceremonies, which took place when the first fish of the season was caught. The salmon was honored as if it were a visiting chief. The people presented offerings such as eagle down, and the fish was cooked and eaten with reverence. Celebrations honored other fish and creatures such as seals and elk.

War and hunting rituals

The Nisqually engaged in occasional raids but little actual warfare. They had an interesting custom associated with a potlatch. As visitors approached a village where a potlatch was being held, they pretended to be a war party and engaged in a mock battle with their hosts.

Funerals

Bodies of the dead were either buried in rocky ground or wrapped in robes, placed in a fishing canoe covered by a mat, and suspended ten to fourteen feet in the air between two trees. Cedar plank sheds marked the graves.

NOTABLE PEOPLE

Chief Leschi (1808–1858) led Native warriors in the western part of Washington during a conflict in 1855 and 1856. Leading about 1,000 troops representing various tribes, Leschi attacked the settlement of Seattle, as part of an unsuccessful resistance against Governor Isaac Stevens of Oregon. Leschi and his troops were turned back by U.S. Navy troops. Although Leschi escaped and then went to live among the Yakima tribe, in November 1856 he was taken prisoner by the U.S. Army and executed.

Billy Frank, Jr. (1931–), is a Nisqually political activist (he works to change policies that affect the lives of Native Americans). In 1991 Johns Hopkins University officials honored him for the decades he has spent fighting for the land and fishing rights of Native Americans in the Pacific Northwest.

FURTHER READING

"Chief Leschi" [Online] http://www.leschi.biz.edu/warror.htm

Deloria, Vine, Jr. *Indians of the Pacific Northwest: From the Coming of the White Man to the Present Day.* Garden City, New York: Doubleday, 1977.

Ruby, Robert H., and John A. Brown. *Indians of the Pacific Northwest.* Norman, OK: University of Oklahoma Press, 1981.

Puyallup

Name

Puyallup (pronounced *pyu-ALL-up*). The name may mean either "the mouth of the river" or "generous and welcoming behavior to all people."

Location

The Puyallup formerly lived along the Puyallup River in present-day Washington. Today they live near the Puyallup Reservation, which covers almost 100 acres near Tacoma, Washington.

Population

The Puyallup and the Nisqually (see entry) were for a long time allies and seemed enough alike that population figures often included both tribes. In 1780, the estimated total of both tribes was about 3,600 people. An 1853 estimate listed 150 Puyallup, and a count in 1854 listed only 50 people. In a census (count of the population) done in 1990 by the U.S. Bureau of the Census, 1,013 people identified themselves as Puyallup.

Language family

Coast Salish.

Origins and group affiliations

The Puyallup were part of a group called the Coast Salish peoples. The Coast Salish lived west of the Cascade Mountains between central Oregon and southern British Columbia, Canada. The Puyallup people have always been closely associated with the Nisqually people.

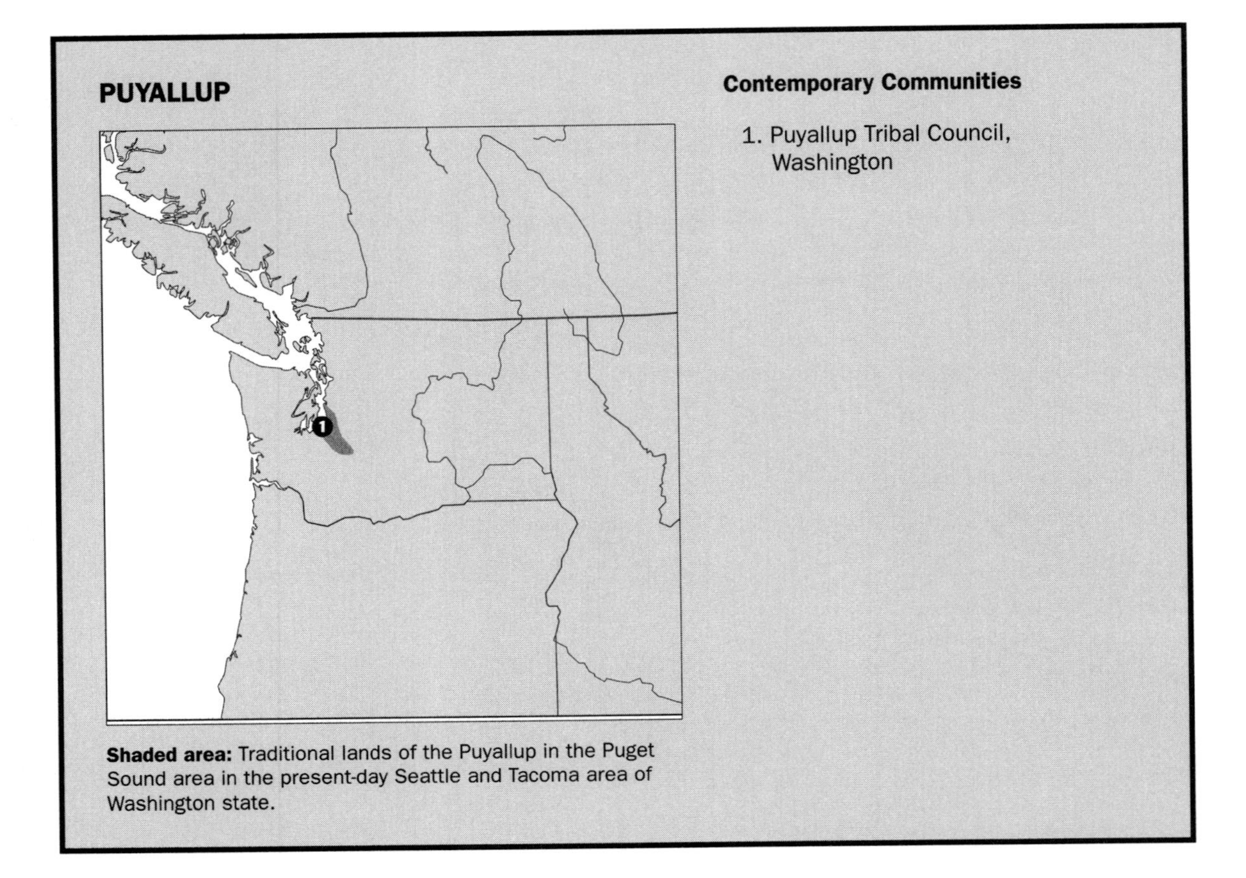

PUYALLUP

Contemporary Communities

1. Puyallup Tribal Council, Washington

Shaded area: Traditional lands of the Puyallup in the Puget Sound area in the present-day Seattle and Tacoma area of Washington state.

The Puyallup has long been an active group, looking out for and acting in its own best interests. Rather than waiting for the government to provide for them, for example, they often started projects themselves. When the U.S. government failed to build a promised bridge between the reservation and the town of Puyallup, Washington, the Puyallup proposed a compromise, and in 1887 the bridge was built. In modern times, the Puyallup have gained fame for what has been called the largest Indian land claim settlement in history.

HISTORY

Early European contact

European fishermen and explorers infected the Puyallup tribe with smallpox before the people ever saw their first white man. He was probably British explorer George Vancouver (1757–1798), who entered the Puget Sound and Hood Canal area in 1792. By then the disease had seriously reduced the tribal populations in the region.

In 1827 the Hudson's Bay Company, an important trading company, founded the Fort Langley trading post in the region where the Puyallup lived. They founded Fort Nisqually nearby six years later. Soon, many of the Southern Coast Salish tribes were trading at these sites. From these exchanges, the Puyallup got firearms and frontier-style clothing, as well as potatoes. In 1839 and 1840 Catholic missionaries entered the northwest, and were successful in converting some of the Natives.

IMPORTANT DATES

1792: British explorer George Vancouver makes first contact with the Puyallup.

1854: Medicine Creek Treaty gives Puyallup lands to the U.S. government.

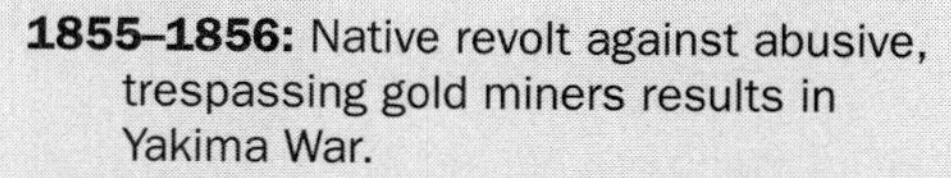

1855–1856: Native revolt against abusive, trespassing gold miners results in Yakima War.

1900: Puyallup Reservation lands are lost to railroad companies.

1936: The Puyallup form a tribal government.

1970: The Boldt Decision affirms Native fishing rights.

1996: The Chief Leschi Schools for Native-American students opens.

Trespassing settlers and miners

Isaac Stevens was the Governor of Washington Territory (it was not yet a state) and Superintendent of Indian Affairs in the mid-1800s. He considered the Native tribes an "impediment to civilization." He believed strongly in Manifest Destiny, a policy that held that the United States was meant to dominate the entire Western Hemisphere. Beginning in 1854, Stevens attempted to establish treaties with nearly every tribe in the Northwest, hoping to take over as much land as possible for white settlers. His goal was to place the tribes on reservations and convince the people to assimilate (adopt the white way of life).

In 1854, Governor Stevens convinced the Puyallup to sign the Treaty of Medicine Creek. Under this treaty, the Puyallup gave up a portion of their lands to the U.S. government. While some Indians moved to reservations, others refused. Stevens then announced that the lands formerly held by the Natives of the Washington area were available for settling, and white settlers trickled in. When gold was discovered in the area, gold seekers and more settlers poured in, trespassing on tribal lands and farms.

Conflicts among the groups erupted in the Yakima War of 1855 to1856. Some Puyallup joined the Yakima and other groups in opposing white settlements and refusing to move onto reservations. The war lasted for three years and accomplished very little for either side.

Reservation life and more land loss

Soon after the war, the Puyallup moved back along the Puyallup River onto the 17,463 acres of land that became known as the Puyallup Reservation and had been granted to them by the Treaty of

Medicine Creek. The Natives soon began to adopt a white lifestyle. They farmed, attended Christian churches, and sent their children to schools run by whites. One observer claimed that the Puyallup were "the most creditable [praiseworthy] specimens of civilized Indians to be found in the West."

In violation of their agreement, in 1893 the U.S. government authorized the sale of reservation lands to commercial fishing companies. In addition, railroad companies applied pressure to the tribe and acquired Puyallup lands in 1873 and again in 1899. The Puyallup claimed that they had been forced to give up their lands, but the sale papers bore the signatures of tribal people. By 1900 the Puyallup no longer owned any land. The few remaining Puyallup lived in poor housing located on scattered tracts of land on the banks of the Puyallup River.

State of Washington officials, who regulated hunting and fishing, began to arrest Puyallup fishermen. They argued that the Puyallup people were only permitted to fish on their reservation and that they no longer had a reservation. Tribal leaders brought a lawsuit against the United States in 1899 for loss of their lands, but they lost the case.

The twentieth century

After 1900 the Indian population of western Washington greatly diminished and Puyallup culture began to deteriorate. Marriage with whites became common and problems with alcohol became more widespread. Religious rituals such as the potlatch (a gift-exchanging ceremony) disappeared due to the disapproval of religious and other authorities outside the tribe. Children were sent to English-speaking boarding schools and older members of the tribe began speaking more English to make it easier to find work. As a result, the language spoken by the Puyallup went into decline.

Treaties dating back to the nineteenth century between the U.S. government and the Indians of Washington guaranteed them certain rights, including the "right of taking fish at all usual and accustomed grounds and stations . . . in common with all citizens of the (Washington) territory." For more than one hundred years the meaning of the phrase remained in question as non-Indian settlers and then the state of Washington fought to control access to the region's fisheries. In the 1960s one Indian leader claimed that angry whites shot him while he was fishing; the local police doubted his story.

In 1970 some Tacoma, Washington, policemen used clubs and tear gas, which causes a painful burning sensation in the eyes, to

Puyallup fishing rights protest, 1970, in Tacoma, Washington.

arrest fifty-nine protestors camped on the Puyallup River. Finally, during that same year, the century-old controversy was settled when the Natives won a federal lawsuit against the state of Washington. In 1970 federal judge George Boldt rendered the Boldt Decision, which allowed Indian fishermen half of all harvestable salmon and steelhead on their former fishing grounds.

In the fall of 1996 the Puyallup began operation of the Chief Leschi Schools. The facility was designed to serve as a model for Native American schools around the country, especially in its use of educational technology (see "Education").

RELIGION

The Puyallup believed in a creator called the Transformer, who came into the world and taught the people many things. They believed in a land of the dead and that the dead could be reborn. Puyallup looked to guardian spirits for guidance through life and help in becoming successful, but understood their own responsibility in remaining physically clean and pure. Special powers were received from the spirit world during a ceremony called the vision quest (see "Puberty" below), and they were kept secret from other people. Some powers could be obtained only in certain geographic locations, and some only came to certain people, such as the shamans (medicine men; pronounced *SHAY-munz*).

Catholic missionaries converted many Puyallup to Christianity in the early 1800s, but some retained their Native beliefs. Presbyterians came in the 1870s and some adopted their faith. The Indian Shaker Church (see Hupa and Chilula entry), a Christian religion blended with Native tradition was popular among Natives of the Northwest in the early 1900s, and found converts among the Puyallup.

LANGUAGE

All the Coast Salish tribes spoke different dialects (varieties) of the Coast Salish language, and the names of their villages came from the name of the dialect spoken by its residents. The Puyallup spoke the Southern Lushootseed dialect, although some scholars have named the tribe's dialect Nisqually.

In the late 1990s, there were only about thirty speakers of the Southern Lushootseed language, but efforts were being made to keep the language alive. For example, programs at the tribe's Chief Leschi Schools (see "Education") and other programs conducted around the Puget Sound teach English and their native language to children and adults.

GOVERNMENT

The village was the Puyallup's principal political unit. Although there was no formal village leader, the wealthiest head of a house was generally accepted as the village headman. People in different villages were linked through marriage.

The U.S. Congress passed the Indian Reorganization Act in 1934. According to that act, reservations wishing to receive certain government benefits had to form their own tribal governments and adopt a new constitution, rather than remain under the protection of the U.S. government. In 1936 the U.S. Department of the Interior approved the Puyallup constitution and its tribal government. The tribe is now governed by an elective tribal council.

ECONOMY

The Puyallup and other Coast Salish tribes kept in contact with their neighbors by canoeing from one seacoast village to another. Because of this constant interaction, they had similar lifestyles. Women and children gathered shellfish near the ocean and collected wild plants, such as camas bulbs (wild lilies), roots, and ferns. Men hunted. Wealthy people sometimes employed their poor relatives to do domestic chores. They also kept slaves captured during battles or traded for with other Indians.

After signing the Treaty of Medicine Creek in 1854 (see "History"), the Puyallup supported themselves by selling fresh salmon to the new settlements around the Puget Sound. Efforts at farming and raising cattle on the reservation also proved to be quite successful.

In the late 1980s the Puyallup tribe voted to drop the claims to some very valuable ancestral lands near the city of Tacoma, Washington, in return for a payment of $162 million in cash, land, and jobs. This historic land claim settlement provided the Puyallup with a strong base on which to further their goals for economic growth.

In modern times, human service programs that benefit the tribe employ nearly 1,500 people. Some of the programs also serve other Native Americans who have relocated to the Puyallup area. A tribal bingo operation provided jobs for more than 100 people in the mid-1990s and was a major source of income for the tribe. Riverboat gambling as a source of jobs and money was being considered in the late 1990s.

DAILY LIFE

Families

Because the culture of the Coast Salish Indians was disrupted very early after the appearance of Europeans, not much is known about how families were organized. We do know that extended families lived together (parents, children, and relatives). Each extended family had land where it held exclusive rights to hunt, fish, and gather plants and weaving material.

Buildings

The Puyallup built the common cedar plank houses of the region, sometimes called shed-roof houses. The homes were supported by carved or painted posts and were open in the center. In the summer, the people constructed temporary campsite structures with a pole frame covered by woven mats. They built sweathouses for purifying themselves.

Clothing and adornment

In summer, Puyallup men wore nothing or only breechcloths (flaps of material that covered the front and back and were suspended from the waist). Women wore cedar bark aprons and skirts. In cool weather, both sexes wore woven blankets made of mountain goat wool, and added leggings, shirts, and moccasins when it got colder.

GLACIAL MISTS COOLER

When the salmon are running in the spring, the Northwest tribes of Oregon and Washington celebrate with a salmon feast. Accompanying many such feasts is this drink offered by author E. Barrie Kavasch. The fruits may vary according to the season.

1 fresh lemon, the zest [yellow part of the skin with no white attached] grated and the rest squeezed and chopped

squeezed juice of 2 more lemons

pinch of salt

1/2 cup honey

1 teaspoon finely ground ginger root

1 teaspoon lime zest [green part of the skin with no white attached], plus the juice of the lime

1/2 cup crushed ice

Place lemon in a blender bowl. Add all other ingredients. Process for half a minute or so until you've created a fine, thoroughly slushed purée [a well-chopped mixture].

Fill 8 glasses with equal parts of crushed ice and sparkling spring water or seltzer (about 2 or 3 ounces in each glass). Add a fruity "glacial mist" to each glass. Perch a thin slice of lime or a fresh strawberry "fan" over the rim of each glass.

Serves 6 to 8

From E. Barrie Kavasch, *Enduring Harvests: Native American Foods and Festivals for Every Season.* Old Saybrook, Connecticut: Globe Pequot Press, 1995,

Women tattooed their chins and legs, and wore earrings and necklaces made of shell, teeth, and claws. Men also wore earrings, and wealthy people wore nose ornaments. The people decorated their faces and bodies with oil and paint and generally wore their hair long and braided. Young men plucked out their facial hair, though older men let it grow.

Food

Families moved from their permanent village to temporary camps in spring and summer to collect their winter supply of food. Fish, especially salmon, was the primary food. Fishing in both salt and fresh water, they caught five kinds of salmon, steelhead trout, herring, smelt, flounder, flatfish, lingcod, rockfish, halibut, and sturgeon. They gathered shellfish, such as clams, crabs, and oysters. They hunted or trapped deer, elk, black bear, beavers, raccoons, marmots, wild game, and twenty kinds of waterfowl. They also gathered berries, roots, nuts, bulbs, and sprouts.

Education

During the second half of the 1800s, the federal government opened special schools for the Puyallup. Eventually, federal funds for education were cut off, and tribal elementary schools were closed in the twentieth century.

Puyallup boys at the Indian training school in Forest Grove, Oregon, 1887.

But in the late twentieth century the tribe has been able to renew its focus on education. The Puyallup Tribe opened the Chief Leschi Tribal Schools in 1996 to serve the educational needs of Native Americans in their region, and to keep their heritage alive. The school serves nearly 800 students from thirty different tribes in kindergarten through grade twelve. Elementary school students are taught both English and the Southern Salish languages. Other programs offered by the school center on teen parenting, family and child education, and cooperative school-to-work vocational training programs.

Healing practices

The Puyallup believed that serious illnesses were caused by foreign objects in the body or by the loss of one's soul. While minor ailments could be cured by the use of herbs, more serious illnesses required drastic action. Shamans might have to recapture the missing soul and return it to the sick person's body. Or they might have to remove the object that was causing the disease.

While both men and women could become shamans, they were usually men. Training for the position began at age seven or eight. Spirits communicated to the aspiring shaman what he or she should do to invoke the spiritual powers of healing. Most villages had shamans to protect them from evil outsiders.

In recent times, the 1993 completion of the Takopid Health Center resulted in health care being offered there to over 250 tribes throughout the United States. More than 10,000 peoples of various tribal backgrounds, besides the Puyallup, living on or near the reservation, enrolled in the health center in 1990.

THE TRANSFORMER

The Puyallup believed in a creator they sometimes called Dabábet'hw or the Transformer. He created food and language and made the world less dangerous. He also taught people how to make clothes, fire, fish traps, and medicine. The following tale, told by a Puyallup, is one of the few published Puyallup myths.

Over the land Dabábet'hw traveled, everywhere banishing evil, helping the needy, and teaching the ignorant. All the arts and industries the people then learned, and their games. Men were taught how to cure the sick and to baffle evil, and all were shown the mode of acquiring magic power from the spirits.

After a while the great teacher and transformer became hungry, and seeing a salmon leaping in the water he called it ashore, [put it on a spit], and placed it beside a fire. While it was broiling he fell asleep. Then came a wanderer, who, finding a salmon cooked and its possessor asleep, ate all the fish; and before departing he rubbed a little grease on the sleeper's fingers and lips, placing also some bits of fish in his teeth. When Dabábet'hw awoke he detected instantly the trick that had been played upon him, and following rapidly he soon overtook the thief. As [the wanderer] sat gazing at his reflection in a stream, Dabábet'hw changed him to a coyote.

The news of the transformations wrought by Dabábet'hw preceded him, and caused some to fear him and wish that he might be slain. Such was a man whose occupation was the making of bone points for arrows, and who threatened that if the magic man came within his sight he would shoot him. But when Dabábet'hw actually appeared, the arrow-maker did not know him, and thought him to be an ordinary stranger. The traveler stopped to talk, and learning that he was preparing to slay the man of magic, Dabábet'hw disarmed him by thrusting the bone points into his wrists, at the same time sending him bounding away on all fours. The man, in fact, had been turned into a deer, the same as those which now roam the woods, and the pointed bones are now found in the legs of deer above the dew-claws.

Dabábet'hw now proceeded to the home of his grandmother, Toad, from whose care he had been stolen in his infancy. One of the first things to greet his eyes there was a mountain of rock, which had been formed from the coils of the fallen rope by which his mother and her sister had descended from the sky. The Earth and all its creatures had been perfected, but it occurred to him that there should be more light. He therefore ascended to the sky and traveled across it by day in the form of the Sun. But he made the days, already warm, so hot that the people could not endure it. Therefore he bade his brother, who had been made from the cradle-board, become the Sun, and Dabábet'hw himself became the night Sun. Before he finally left the Earth he announced that he would take as his wife the girl who could lift and carry his great bundle of handiwork. Only the daughter of Frog was successful and she accompanied him to the sky; and to this day Dabábet'hw, Frog, and the bag may be seen in the Moon.

SOURCE: Edward S. Curtis. *The North American Indian,* Vol. 9. 1911. Reprint. New York: Johnson Reprint Corporation, 1970.

ARTS

Puyallup woman, like others of the Salish Coast, produced outstanding textiles that had social and spiritual significance. They often carved whorls, the small wooden flywheels that control the speed of a spinning wheel. The whorls were carved with human, animal, and geometric designs. As the women did their spinning, they often stared at the whorls, which put them into a trance-like state. The Puyallup believed that this gave the spinner the ability to create textiles containing special powers. The ancient Puyallup art of weaving blankets was revived in the 1960s.

CUSTOMS

Festivals

The Puyallup held winter dances called spirit dances, first salmon ceremonies celebrating the first catch of the year, and potlatches. Potlatches were ceremonies of gift giving, especially as offers of peace to other visiting tribes. The festivities included songs, dances, and games.

Winter dances were events sponsored by an individual who had been diagnosed by a shaman with an illness brought on by the return of his guardian spirit—the spirit he had come into contact with earlier is his life on a vision quest (see "Puberty"). The spirit was lodged in his chest in the form of a song. During the evening, his friends used drumbeats and phrases to draw out the song. They painted the sponsor's face. Eventually, possessed by his power, he got up and danced and sang his song. Others joined in the performance, which was followed by a feast.

The first salmon ceremony honored the fish that made up 80 to 90 percent of the Puyallup diet. It was held at the start of the salmon-spawning season. The first salmon caught in the year was barbecued over an open fire, and small portions of the meat were given to everyone present. All the bones were saved intact. Everyone then went to the river for dancing, chanting, and singing. The salmon skeleton was placed in the water with its head pointing upstream in the direction a spawning salmon would go. This was to encourage the salmon to return in great numbers.

Today the Puyallup hold the Annual Powwow and Salmon Bake in Tacoma every Labor Day weekend. Monthly powwows at the Chief Leschi Schools, like all powwows, feature dancing and singing with drums.

Head flattening

Before Europeans came, the Puyallup, like most Coast Salish tribes, flattened the heads of infants. This was accomplished by strapping cradleboards (boards designed to mold the skull into a particular shape) to the babies' foreheads. A flattened forehead was considered an attractive feature.

Puberty

Puyallup girls were separated from the village at the time of their first menstrual period. Afterwards, a feast was held for the girl and her family. Adolsecent boys and girls were expected to embark on vision quests, sacred ceremonies in which a person goes off alone and fasts, living without food or water for a period of days. During that time, he or she hopes to learn about spiritual matters and to have a vision of a guardian spirit who will provide help and strength throughout life. These quests took place in the winter, sometimes outside tribal territory, and usually under the guidance of a trainer.

Courtship and marriage

Arranged marriages were common among the upper class, usually to a person in a different village. The families of the bride and groom exchanged gifts with one other, and the bride's family gave gifts to the young couple. Divorce was uncommon. After the death of a spouse, the surviving husband or wife was expected to remarry within the same family to preserve their alliance.

A man could have multiple wives, and men often had wives of different ages. The older wives wielded the most power. Sometimes a man would marry all the sisters in a family. He would be expected to undergo the entire marriage ceremony with each one of them. Sometimes wives were given to shamans or warriors in payment for services, and important men often received gifts of wives. Young girls were simply presented to them, without any ceremony or exchange of goods.

War and hunting

The Puyallup used an interesting method to catch ducks and other waterfowl. At night, they spread big nets across a series of tall poles that stood along the riverside. When a signal was given, the men came out of the darkness carrying lighted torches and making loud cries. The frightened birds would fly off, getting caught in the nets and falling to the ground. The stunned birds were then quickly gathered up.

Funerals

The Puyallup held wakes to which loved ones brought gifts for the deceased. Some mourners displayed their grief by biting their own hair. The body was usually buried in a box in the village cemetery, but sometimes corpses were placed in a canoe atop a cedar plank shed (in later years the sheds were made of canvas). A feast was held and the deceased's personal property was distributed among family and friends.

CURRENT TRIBAL ISSUES

In recent times, the Puyallup people are trying to strengthen their tribal government, increase their land base, develop human service programs for tribal and community members, and protect their fishing, environmental, trade, and tribal rights.

On several occasions the Puyallup have had to defend their fishing rights. They have used tactics ranging from "fish-ins" (protest rallies) to lawsuits to draw media and government attention to the issue. A recent example illustrates the problem. In 1997 the Puyallup were involved in a conflict with the state of Washington over digging clams at Titlow Beach, near the reservation. The Puyallup wanted the clams for food and ceremonial purposes. State officials objected to this attempt to harvest shellfish from a state marine preserve. As of 1998, the issue had yet to be resolved.

NOTABLE PEOPLE

Ramona Bennett (1938–) has been active in tribal government for many years, including her roles as principal administrator, controlling the budget, and chair of the Puyallup Tribal Council. She is a well-known spokesperson for Indian rights at the national level, particularly in the areas of fishing rights, Indian child welfare, and Indian health and education.

FURTHER READING

Deloria, Vine, Jr. *Indians of the Pacific Northwest: From the Coming of the White Man to the Present Day.* Garden City, NY: Doubleday, 1977.

Johnson, Michael. "Puyallup." *The Native Tribes of North America.* New York: Macmillan, 1992.

Porter, Frank W., III. *The Coast Salish Peoples.* New York: Chelsea House Publishers, 1989.

Siletz

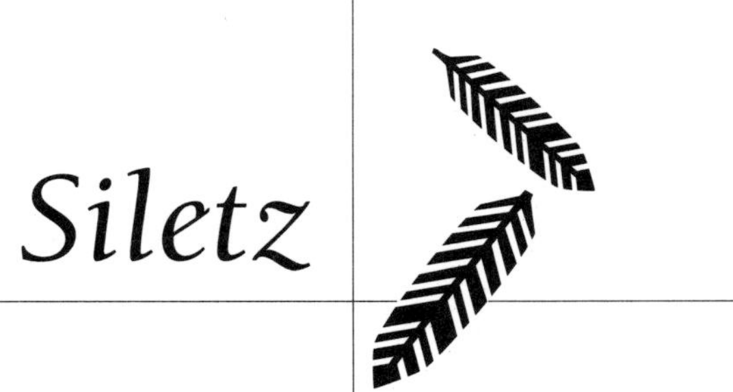

Name

The name Siletz (pronounced *SIGH-lets*) comes from the name of the river on which the Siletz tribe lived. The origin of the name is unknown. The Siletz people called themselves *Se-la-gees,* meaning "crooked river."

Location

The Siletz lived along the Pacific Coast in northern Oregon, in parts of what are now Tillamook, Lincoln, and Lane counties.

Population

In 1855, after tremendous depopulation due to epidemics and starvation, there were only 21 Siletz. A census (count of the population) taken in the area in 1934 did not identify any Siletz at all.

Language family

Salishan.

Origins and group affiliations

Some historians believe that Salishan speakers were part of the first wave of people who migrated across the Bering Strait from Russia to the New World about 10,000 years ago. The Siletz were a part of the Tillamook tribe. Little is known about friendships and conflicts, if any, between the Siletz and their neighbors.

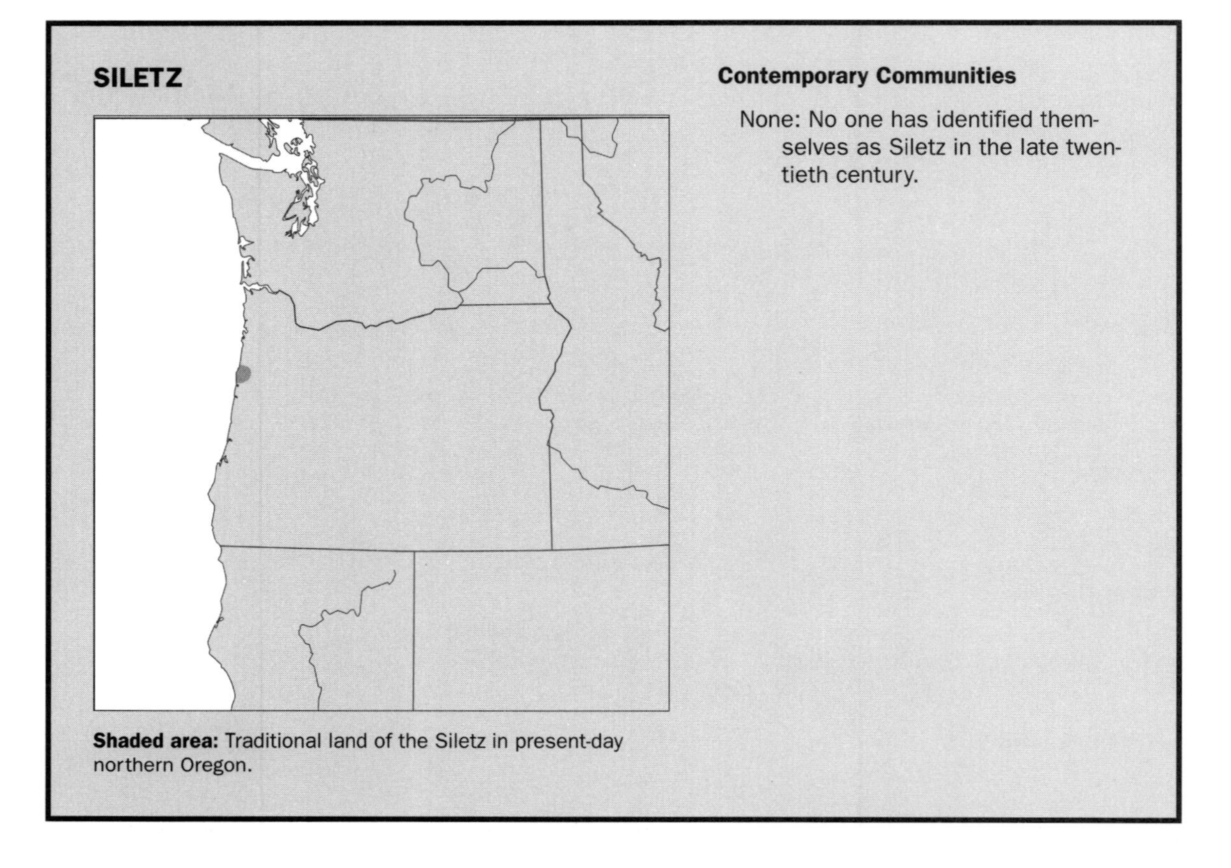

SILETZ

Contemporary Communities

None: No one has identified themselves as Siletz in the late twentieth century.

Shaded area: Traditional land of the Siletz in present-day northern Oregon.

The Siletz were a proud river people. For thousands of years they had roamed undisturbed through the western portion of present-day Oregon. By the time the U.S. government established a reservation in the heart of their territory in 1855, there were only 21 Siletz people known to be alive. The forcible relocation of the Siletz and more than a dozen other Coastal tribes proved disastrous. In the end the entire Siletz tribe perished.

HISTORY

Europeans bring suffering

Of the Pacific Northwest groups who spoke Salishan languages, the Siletz were members of the southernmost branch. They were living along the coast, next to the Siletz River in present-day Lincoln County, Oregon, when the first whites they had ever seen crossed into their territory in 1805. The men were part of the Lewis and Clark expedition (1804–6), the first navigators to make a large-scale exploration of what would become the western United States. This and other early contacts between the Siletz and whites were brief, but the consequences for the tribe were devastating.

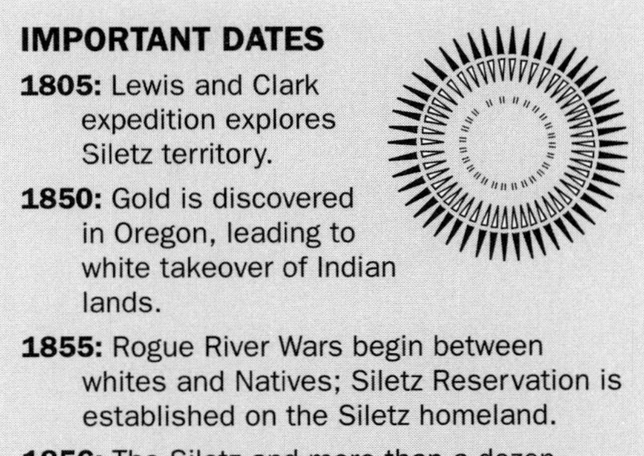

IMPORTANT DATES

1805: Lewis and Clark expedition explores Siletz territory.

1850: Gold is discovered in Oregon, leading to white takeover of Indian lands.

1855: Rogue River Wars begin between whites and Natives; Siletz Reservation is established on the Siletz homeland.

1856: The Siletz and more than a dozen other tribes are forcibly relocated to the Siletz Reservation.

European fur trappers soon followed the expedition, bringing deadly diseases to which the Siletz had no immunity. In 1828 and 1833 measles and smallpox epidemics swept through the region, killing many. A series of destructive fires compounded problems for the tribe in the late 1840s. The fires had been set by the Siletz deliberately, according to their annual practice of slashing and burning some of the land to promote better growth of food resources. But these fires burned out of control and did tremendous damage. By 1850 the Siletz tribe—weakened by diseases and starvation—had suffered a severe loss of population.

Settlers and miners bring more problems

White settlers arrived in the Oregon territory in the 1850s, drawn by the abundant furs, land suitable for plowing, and impressive forests of old growth timber. They were followed by gold miners. Relations with the Native inhabitants were hostile. The rapid growth of the white population caused serious problems for the Indians. Miners muddied the river with debris from their mining operations, game suddenly became scarce as animals were trapped for their furs, and important food sources disappeared when Native lands were fenced off for cattle farms.

Tribes such as the Rogue River Indians (who lived south of the Siletz) were the most severely affected by the arrival of settlers in Oregon. The competition for resources, combined with robbing and looting by both whites and Natives, set off the Rogue River Wars in 1855. (See box on page 1244.)

Siletz Reservation founded

The U.S. government decided the best way to stop the violence between whites and Native Americans was to establish a reservation and relocate all of the Coastal Indians there. The government chose a 150-mile stretch of the Oregon coast for the reservation, including the entire Siletz homeland, and in 1855 the Siletz Reservation was founded.

ROGUE RIVER WARS

When gold was discovered in Oregon's Rogue River Valley in the early 1850s, gold miners and settlers put pressure on the U.S. government to remove the Indians from their homelands. Hostilities erupted into war in October 1855, when a mob of miners killed more than two dozen Indians camping near the Table Rock Reservation. Many historians believe the war was started deliberately by bored and idle miners who were unable to pan for gold because of a drought. Land was not an underlying reason for the fighting; by the time the war started the Native people had already given up most of their land.

After enduring several bloody battles, the Indians who lived and fought in the mountains moved down the Rogue River to the Pacific Coast, probably to "buy time" because winter had set in and food was becoming scarce. They nearly succeeded in driving whites away from the coast, but by the following spring the white settlers were receiving extra help from reinforcements. The Indians were attacked by U.S. Army troops from California and by volunteers. Although the Natives almost won the final battle, in the end the whites emerged victorious.

The defeated Indians were forcibly removed to a new reservation constructed under the authority of the federal government in 1855. Some were taken there by steamboat; others had to walk. Although the Indians were promised sufficient land to support themselves, their acreage was eventually reduced by three-quarters; no compensation was given to them until many years later.

SOURCE: "A Brief Interpretive History of the Rogue River War and the Coast, Alsea, and Siletz Reservations to 1894." From the Native American Documents Project: http://www.cusum.edu/projects/nadp/subject.htm.

Although they had nothing to do with the Rogue River Wars, the entire Siletz tribe (population now reduced to 21) was relocated onto the Siletz Reservation, along with 2,500 Indians from more than a dozen other tribes. Many were forced to make a long overland march—in some cases walking more than 125 miles.

The Indians faced new problems adjusting to life on the reservation. Free and autonomous (independent and self-governing) tribes were suddenly obliged to live among other Native peoples. Conflicts inevitably broke out. Within 50 years of the founding of the reservation, only 483 of the original group of 2,500 Indians remained. Some died of sickness and exhaustion caused by the forced march; others were killed by the devastating effects of overcrowding and introduced diseases; still others were victims of hopelessness and despair; and another segment of the Native population simply left the reservation. A 1934 census in the region made no mention of the Siletz people. All that remains are a few artifacts, now on display at Oregon's Tillamook County Pioneer Museum.

People live on in the name of the reservation

The people who reside on the Siletz Reservation today are descendants of the many tribes who were moved there back in the

THE SILETZ RESERVATION IN THE LATE 1990S

The Siletz Reservation is located in the homeland of the Siletz people, a damp, coastal region of western Oregon in Lincoln County. There, the town of Siletz is home to the tribal headquarters of the Siletz Confederation of Tribes, which serves 2,236 people throughout an eight-county area. In 1977 the federal government restored 3,600 acres of original Siletz land to the confederations. The modern-day tribal people consist of descendants of more than twenty-four tribes who speak at least eight different languages. An elected nine-member tribal council, a general council, and an eight-member tribal court govern the confederation.

The Siletz Tribal Economic Development Commission (STEDCO) oversees economic development and manages several tribal businesses. STEDCO runs a smokehouse that sells fresh seafood and smoked salmon and tuna. The tribe's sawmill employs dozens of people. And the Siletz forestry program directs the harvesting and sale of several types of trees, including Douglas fir, western hemlock, and western red cedar. Tree sales yield more than $1 million annually for the Siletz Confederation of Tribes.

In 1996 the Siletz opened the Chinook Winds Convention and Gaming Center in Lincoln City, Oregon. The confederated tribes also run a bingo hall, a restaurant, and gift shops that employ more than 250 people. Plans for future economic development include the construction of a hotel, a year-round campground, and a tribal museum.

SOURCE: *American Indian Reservations and Trust Areas.* Compiled and edited by Veronica E. Velarde Tiller, Tiller Research, Inc. Prepared under an award from Economic Development Administration, U.S. Department of Commerce, 1996.!

mid-1850s. They are federally recognized by the U.S. government as the Confederated Tribes of Siletz. "Federal recognition" means that the tribes have a special, legal relationship with the U.S. government that entitles them to federal assistance if necessary.

RELIGION

The Siletz called their supreme being *Tk'a,* which means "Transformer." They believed he was their ancestor, the creator of the world and its people, and the being who gave them the gift of salmon. According to Siletz legend, Tk'a's soul left the land of the living, and his body assumed the form of the Medicine Rocks, a site in Siletz territory that resembles three human heads.

The Siletz believed that after death good people went to the land in the sky and bad people went to the land below the Earth. The good souls lived in a world where land, fish, and game were plentiful. The bad souls became slaves and were mistreated in the afterlife.

The Ghost Dance religion was introduced to the Siletz Reservation in the 1870s. Believers performed the Ghost Dance to bring good fortune to the Native people. They were convinced that a time would

The Chinook Winds Casino in Lincoln City, Oregon, in 1997.

come when the Earth would swallow up all whites, but Indians would be spared.

LANGUAGE

The Siletz dialect (variety) of Salishan was never written down during the people's lifetime, so not much is known about this extinct language. Franz Boas, a famous American anthropologist (someone who studies the cultures of different peoples), interviewed one of the last living members of the tribe and recorded some words. For example, the word for the carved stick or wand used by a healer is *qelqaloxten.*

GOVERNMENT

Each Siletz community had a "headman" from the upper class who coordinated major activities. He first had to prove his bravery, his speaking ability, and his capacity for settling differences among the people. The headman's leadership position was said to come from supernatural spirits.

ECONOMY

The Siletz economy was based on fishing and food gathering. Economic life revolved around the seasons. From April to June salmonberry sprouts were gathered. Camas (pronounced *KAH-muss*) roots (the edible part of certain lily plants) and lamprey (eel-like water animals) were harvested in June and July. Various berries were gathered in July and August. Chinook salmon were caught in August and September. Coho salmon were trapped in October. Elk hunting and the catching of chum salmon took place in November. December was the time for gathering lily roots and various berries, and from December to April fishers caught steelhead trout.

DAILY LIFE

Families

Three or four families often lived together in one large house. Families were made up of a man, his wife, their children, and sometimes a few other close relatives. Wealthy men often had more than one wife. The status of women was dependent on that of their parents, husbands, or other close relatives. Women enjoyed their greatest respect after their childbearing days were over.

Buildings

The tribe's permanent dwellings were rectangular winter houses made of charred cedar planks. Outside the house was a separate grass-covered structure used in the summer to store food. In warm weather temporary huts made of reed matting were erected near the sites where the Siletz gathered food.

Clothing and adornment

The Siletz wove much of their clothing, including rain capes and apronlike dresses, from plant fibers. Siletz women wore unusual woven hats that resembled baskets. Samples of these hats are on display at the Tillamook County Pioneer Museum. Both men and women pierced their ears and wore ankle and wrist bracelets.

Food

Fish and seafood—mainly salmon, mussels, and clams—were the most important parts of the Siletz diet. Freshwater fish were caught in nets or traps called weirs and were preserved by drying over a fire. Beaver, muskrat, bear, and other mammals were eaten fresh. Salt was extracted from dried seaweed and used to preserve elk meat for winter storage. Crickets, grasshoppers, and caterpillars were ground with berries and animal fat to make a nutritious winter food that would not spoil. Most foods were prepared by steaming in an earth oven or boiling in baskets or bowls on hot stones.

Healing practices

Healers called shamans (pronounced *SHAY-munz*) learned their craft from guardian spirits who appeared to them in dreams. A black

A SILETZ CREATION STORY

Franz Boas was an anthropologist who conducted interviews at the Siletz Reservation in 1890. He spoke to an old Siletz man, one of the very few survivors of the tribe who remembered the ancient language. The man told him the following story about how the Siletz were created.

The transformer Tk'a traveled all over the world. He was also called the master of salmon. He created everything and commanded the people to be good. When he came to the mouth of a river he tried to make a cascade [waterfall] at that place. When he was traveling about, he carried a bunch of arrows. When he came to a nice place he would take out some arrows, break them to pieces, and throw them down. Then he began to shout as though he were going to dance, and the arrows would be transformed into human beings and begin to dance. When day came he would take his quiver [carrying case] and the arrows would go back into it. This was his way of amusing himself; he did this every night whenever it pleased him. When he came to Siletz he called the people his relatives. When he left he transformed his body into the rock Tk'a, while his soul went to the country of the salmon from which the fish come every year.

SOURCE: Franz Boas. "Notes on the Tillamook." *University of California Publications: American Archaeology and Ethnology.* Vol. 20. Edited by A. L. Kroeber. Berkeley: University of California Press, 1923.

bear, for example, was said to teach a female shaman how to cure serious ailments with water and song. Special sweat houses—secluded huts or caverns heated by steam and used by some Native peoples for ritual cleansing, meditation, and purification—were used only to cure sickness. These healing sweat houses were made of hemlock bark and covered with dirt.

Some illnesses were believed to be caused by objects lodged within the patient's body. Shamans cured them by waving a carved wand, piercing the afflicted person's skin, and sucking out the object that caused the illness (often something brought along by the shaman). Shamans also brewed potions to ensure long life, fertility, and luck in hunting.

Being a shaman could be dangerous. Those who were unsuccessful in their healing attempts were often murdered.

CUSTOMS

Social divisions

Like other Tillamook tribes, the Siletz people were divided into classes: freeborn individuals and a small group of slaves. When work needed to be done, the people were divided into groups based on their talents. Task leaders led these groups. The task leaders might include shamans (healers), headmen, and warriors. The highest class of people included those with great wealth, professionals such as doctors, and accomplished hunters.

Festivals and ceremonies

Most Siletz festivals were held in winter, when the cold weather reduced fishing activities. The Siletz celebrated the naming of children with a special ceremony in which the new young members were welcomed into the tribe. They were often named after dead relatives. All babies had their ears pierced, and boys also had their noses pierced, usually by a shaman using a bone needle. Feasting and dancing followed. Ceremonies were also held to celebrate the onset of puberty, the beginning of salmon season, and lunar and solar eclipses.

Puberty

When a girl had her first menstrual period, she went to a secluded place for four or five days. During this time she lay on some planks of wood while her mother explained to her about becoming a woman. The girl usually cooked for herself and danced during the evenings. Later she went on an overnight trip to the nearby mountains. She was washed with decayed wood and painted with a red dye upon her return. Then she was considered a woman.

Adolescent boys were sent into the mountains to find the guardian spirit that would guide them through life. The spirit revealed to them whether they would be hunters, warriors, or shamans. The first food gathered by a young woman and the first animal caught by a young man after the puberty ritual were given as gifts of respect to the elderly of the tribe.

Courtship and marriage

The Siletz held two types of marriage ceremonies: special and common. Special marriages required that at least one of the parents be a person of some importance in the tribe, that the bride be childless, and that it be the first marriage for the groom. Many people attended these so-called special marriages, which were held outdoors and featured elaborate gift-giving rituals. Common marriages were performed by "good talkers," men with outstanding public-speaking skills. A common marriage bride was brought to the home of the groom's family, gifts were exchanged, and a feast was held.

Promises of gifts for the newlyweds' children were made—the wealthier the family, the more lavish the promises. Grooms were expected to be kind and sensitive to their new wives, and marital relations often did not occur for several nights after the marriage.

Childbirth

The birthing process was attended by women trained in birthing procedures. In early times the woman in labor sat on a board equipped with a horizontal gripping bar. Following the birth of her baby, the bar, the mother's clothing, and the floor matting were thrown into the woods. The afterbirth (material that was expelled from the womb after the baby was born) was placed at the foot of a small spruce tree so that the child would grow tall and strong. When the newborn's umbilical cord fell off, it was placed in a decorated cloth bag and was worn from the time the child was a toddler until about age six. The loss of this special bag was a bad omen, signaling that the child would become disobedient or half-witted (foolish).

Funerals

People usually had a shaman in attendance at their deathbeds. The shaman reassured the dying person that his or her belongings would be distributed properly and that the burial canoe would be prepared according to custom. After death, the body was washed and dressed, the eyes were bandaged, and the face was painted red. Then the body was wrapped in a blanket, covered with cedar bark, and laid on a plank. At the two- or three-day wake that followed, songs were sung and attendants kept each other awake so the dead person would not take their souls. The body was later placed in a canoe, which was removed through a hole in the house and placed on supports at the burial ground. Another canoe was upended and placed over the one containing the body, and goods were placed near the grave. A year later the canoe might be reopened, the bones cleaned, and new grave goods added.

FURTHER READING

Boas, Franz. "Notes on the Tillamook." *University of California Publications in American Archaeology and Ethnology.* Vol. 20. Edited by A. L. Kroeber. Berkeley: University of California Publications, 1923.

Davis, Mary, B. ed. *Native America in the Twentieth Century: An Encyclopedia.* New York: Garland Publishing, 1994.

For an online history of the Confederated Tribes of Siletz: [Online] http://ctsi.nsn.us/history.htm.

For the *Confederated Tribes of Siletz Indians Tribal Profile* from the Northwest Portland Area Indian Health Board: [Online] http://www.teleport.com/~paihb./profiles/siletz.html.

Skokomish

Name

The name Skokomish (pronounced *sko-KO-mish*) comes from the tribe's own word meaning "people of the river," probably referring to inhabitants of the villages along the Skokomish River.

Location

The Skokomish traditionally lived in the Hood Canal drainage basin west of Puget Sound, Washington. Today, they live on the Skokomish Reservation, which covers 5,000 acres on the delta of Skokomish River, where it empties into the Great Bend of the Hood Canal.

Population

In 1792, there were about 800 Skokomish. In a census (count of the population) done in 1990 by the U.S. Bureau of the Census, 737 people identified themselves as Skokomish.

Language family

Salishan.

Origins and group affiliations

The Skokomish was the largest of nine Twana Indian communities that lived near one another and shared many customs. What is now known as the Skokomish tribe is mostly made up of Twana Indians and the descendants of the other tribes who share the Skokomish Reservation. In recent years the term "Twana" has been gaining popularity as a replacement for the term "Skokomish." The closest neighbors of the Twana were the Klallam, the Squaxon, the Suquamish, and the Satsop.

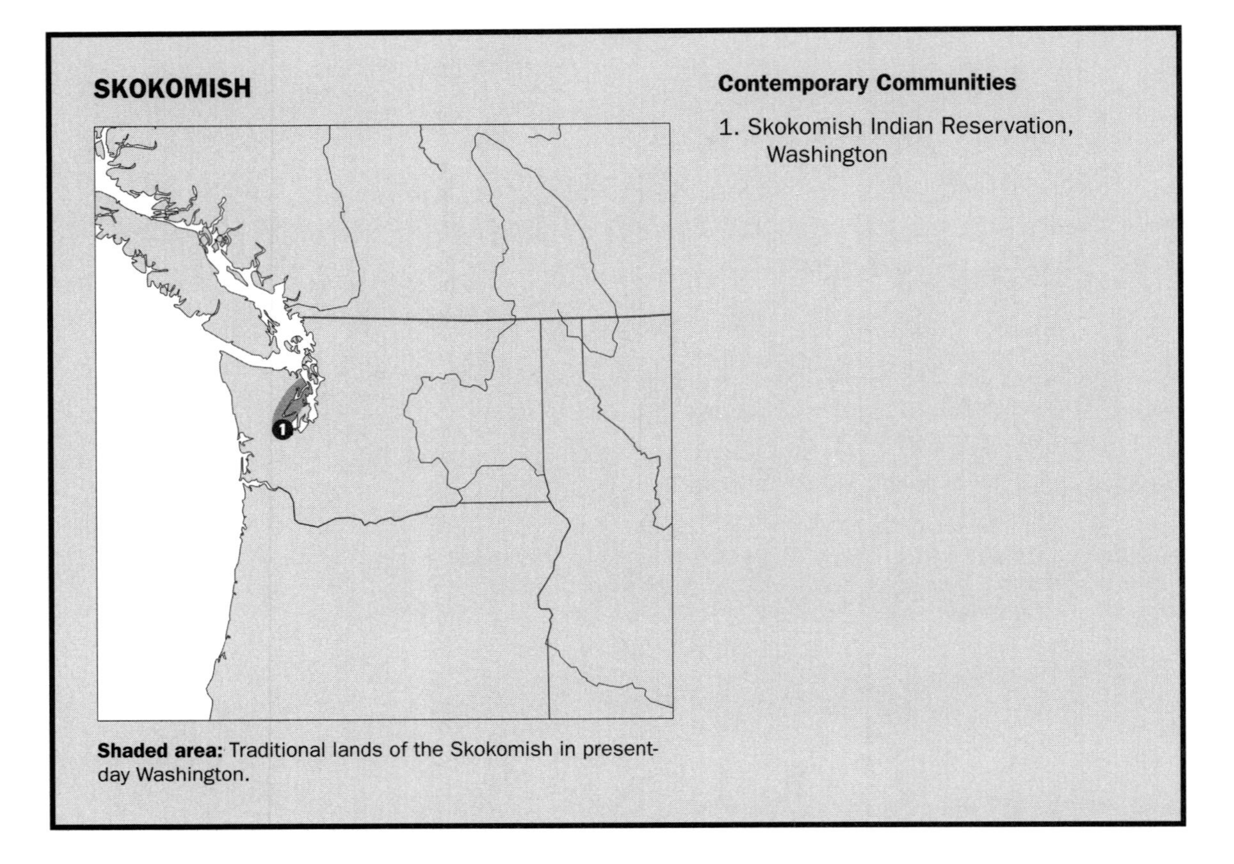

SKOKOMISH

Contemporary Communities

1. Skokomish Indian Reservation, Washington

Shaded area: Traditional lands of the Skokomish in present-day Washington.

For thousands of years, the Skokomish people have had a cultural, spiritual, and economic dependence on the Skokomish River where they make their home. Fishing has always been the backbone of their economy. In the 1990s the river was named one of the most endangered in the United States. The Skokomish are engaged in efforts to encourage the state and federal government to restore the river's natural abundance of animal and plant life.

HISTORY

Early contact with whites

The Skokomish probably had their first actual contact with Europeans in 1792, when British explorers led by Captain George Vancouver (1757–1798) explored Puget Sound and Hood Canal. The Skokomish already had experienced an epidemic of smallpox, brought to their region by Europeans, and they already owned European metal goods, probably obtained in trade from other tribes. For three decades after Vancouver's visit, there was little contact between them and Europeans.

IMPORTANT DATES

1792: Probable first contact between Skokomish and Europeans occurs.

1827: Fort Langley is founded, and Skokomish lifestyle changes as they begin to trade with whites.

1846–55: A series of treaties gives most of Skokomish homeland to the United States.

1857: The Skokomish settle on reservation land.

After trading posts were established by the British at Fort Langley in 1827 and Fort Nisqually in 1833, the Skokomish had wider contact with Europeans. They were exposed not only to European goods but also to the people who worked for Europeans, such as Iroquois Indians (see entry) and Native Hawaiians. The Skokomish traded salmon for European goods such as firearms and clothing.

The United States and Great Britain jointly occupied the Skokomish lands before 1846, around the time Americans first began arriving in the area. In that year, the two countries agreed to place all tribes in the area under the control of the U.S. government. The Skokomish signed several treaties in which they gave over their land to the United States. In a short time, new settlers started flooding into the former Skokomish lands.

Treaties strip Skokomish land

In 1854, after the Oregon Territory was organized, Governor Isaac Stevens attempted to establish treaties with nearly every tribe in what would become the state of Washington and some of its surrounding areas. He wanted to take over as much land as possible for white settlers. He hoped to accomplish this by doing away with Native land titles, placing tribes on reservations, and getting the Indians to adopt the white way of life. In 1859, as a result of the 1855 Treaty of Point No Point, the Skokomish were restricted with other tribes who spoke a similar language to a reservation located on their former lands.

Tribal rights expanded

Between 1900 and 1960 the Skokomish faced many difficulties. Around 1900 the tribe lost the sweetgrass it used to make baskets, because a white farmer was plowing and building dikes on land he bought at the mouth of the Skokomish River. At about the same time, their shellfish-gathering activities were largely restricted, because the state claimed that it controlled the tidelands. Then, in the late 1920s, the city of Tacoma built two dams on the North Fork of the Skokomish River. This resulted in the destruction of major tribal sites and restrictions on the people's ability to get to saltwater fishing sites.

A hearing on a Skokomish fisheries treaty.

Finally, Potlatch State Park was opened in 1960 on one of the best pieces of Skokomish land. The Skokomish were successful in legal cases they brought before the federal and state courts on all four of these issues.

Because the Skokomish fought for their legal rights, the wishes of white fishermen have less influence on state policies regarding the tribe's freedom to fish. The state and federal courts have affirmed Skokomish fishing rights obtained under treaties they signed in the 1850s. Once again the Skokomish people may fish in waters outside of the reservation area. Responsibility for enforcing Skokomish fishing rights now lies with tribal courts and the tribal fish patrol instead of with the state. The people have also received training in fishing management and biology, and have benefitted financially from taxes they are able to impose on non-Native fishermen.

RELIGION

The Skokomish believed that long ago there were the first beings, creatures with both animal and human qualities. A figure called the Transformer changed these first beings into objects like stones, guardian spirits, and human beings, and sent them to Earth after teaching humans the proper way to live.

The Skokomish worshiped the Sun, the Moon, and the Earth. They thought that the Sun rewarded good behavior and the Moon punished bad behavior. They believed in other spiritual beings, such as earth dwarfs who could steal souls, forest giants who stole food, and underwater creatures that took on the form of humans.

The Skokomish believed that every person possessed two souls: a life soul that caused lingering sickness when it left the body and a heart soul that died with the body. After death, the life soul went on a long journey through the land of the dead, then started life over again in a new form. Souls of dead infants did not go on this journey but became guardian spirits, who guided humans on their path through life.

People attained their guardian spirits through a vision quest (see "Customs"). Guardian spirits granted people different types of power: power for success in war, power in gambling, power in hunting on land or sea, or power in attaining wealth. They sometimes even provided protection from minor things like fleabites.

In 1839 and 1840, two Catholic priests taught the Skokomish about Christianity. Although the people seemed at first to be enthusiastic students, priests and missionaries who came later had little luck in finding converts. Today people on the reservation prefer the Indian Shaker Church (see box in Hupa and Chilula entry) and the Assemblies of God religion.

LANGUAGE

The Skokomish and other Twana people spoke a dialect (variety) of the Salishan language family. Each tribe spoke a slightly different dialect. Between 1975 and 1980 the Twana Language and Culture Project was developed to help keep the language alive. Volunteers used recordings from older members of the tribe to create a Twana language dictionary and textbooks, which are used in public schools as well as in the tribe's preschool.

GOVERNMENT

Skokomish villages had no formal government. The head of the wealthiest house in the village usually took on a leadership role in matters such as settling disputes.

The Indian Reorganization Act of 1934 encouraged American tribes to form their own elected governments modeled by the U.S. government. The Skokomish Tribal Government chose that option and was established in 1938. The tribal government is comprised of seven elected members.

"Fishing Camp—Skokomish," a photograph by Edward S. Curtis, 1912.

ECONOMY

The Skokomish economy was based mainly on gathering foods and fishing. In fact, there were three distinct types of hunters: sea hunters, land hunters, and those who caught fowl. The sea hunters used harpoons from a two-man canoe. To catch seals, hunters surprised them and clubbed them or drove them onto sharpened stakes or into nets. Seal skins were traded for European products. While fishermen were happy to make use of beached whales, they did not go out and hunt them .

Skokomish men carved objects out of wood, and women made cords and ropes, mats, and baskets out of cedar bark, and blankets of mountain goat and dog wool. The people sometimes traded these objects with people from other tribes or with whites.

Today many Skokomish people work in white-owned logging and fishing companies, but these industries are declining because of overharvesting. Since the 1970s, the tribe has been working toward the goal of supporting itself through a variety of ventures so it does not have to depend on only a few industries. With new land purchased for economic development, the tribe has created a planning department that assists in the development of businesses such as restaurants, liquor stores, and retail stores that cater to tourists. The Skokomish own a fish hatchery and a fish processing plant. The people also harvest timber and lease forest land to lumber companies. In the mid-1990s, the tribe was looking into the possibility of a cooperative farming venture using solar greenhouses and the development of a small cattle industry.

DAILY LIFE

Families

Families were made up of a man, his wife or wives, and their children, as well as one or two unmarried relatives. Wealthy people sometimes had slaves. Several families lived together in one large house, and each family had its own section of the house.

Buildings

The Skokomish built winter and summer homes. The entire community helped members of the upper class build their houses and then joined in the feasting to celebrate the home's completion.

Winter homes were large rectangular structures made of cedar planks. The roof was sloped and was supported by two main posts, painted inside with symbols of the families' guardian spirits. The dirt floors and walls were covered with mats, and walls were plugged with moss for insulation. Along the walls were bed platforms. Each family had a fireplace next to their bed space and the area underneath the bed was used for storage.

Lightweight summer shelters that could easily be moved were set up at hunting, gathering, or fishing sites. They were usually square and held a single family. The walls were made of cattail matting and covered with bark. A cooking fire was placed outside the entrance to each home.

A special building was set up for important tribal celebrations like potlatches (gift-giving ceremonies).

Clothing and adornment

In warm weather, men went naked or wore cedar bark vests and breechcloths (garments with front and back flaps that hung from the waist). Women wore only a short apron of shredded cedar bark, and upper-class women sometimes added a goatskin skirt that was short in front and long in back. During rainy weather, women covered themselves with square capes of shredded bark tied in the front.

During cooler weather, men added a knee-length buckskin shirt, buckskin trousers or leggings, or bearskin leggings with the hair left on. Fur caps of bearskin or coonskin and deerskin moccasins and mittens provided warmth in extreme cold. Fur robes and blankets were also worn, the type of fur depending on the wealth and importance of the wearer. The wealthiest people wore sea otter blankets, and robes made of mountain goat wool were also quite valuable. Deer and raccoon skins, though, were more common.

Both men and women wore ear ornaments made of pieces of shell connected to cattail fiber loops. After contact with Europeans, silver ear pendants and earrings became popular. Wealthy people often wore shell ornaments hanging from their noses. Women wore necklaces and bracelets made of shell, bone, and animal claws. Both sexes wore ankle bracelets. While women usually had their ankles, chins, and lower legs tattooed in stripes, men were rarely tattooed. Face and body painting was done only for ceremonies such as spirit dances or joining secret societies. On those occasions, the painted design depicted a person's guardian spirit or the special power a person possessed.

Men usually wore their hair shoulder length or longer, gathered in back with a thong or knot. Women wore their hair loose or in a single braid. Slaves and women in mourning wore short hair.

Food

Four different kinds of salmon made up the primary food of the Skokomish. Salmon were taken with dip nets and harpoons. The tribe also ate other sea creatures, including sea lions, seals, mollusks, and beached whales. Waterfowl were killed and eaten, and the people hunted deer, black bear, mountain beaver, beaver, and muskrat. Each year an elk hunt took place in the Olympic Mountains. Various plants were gathered for food throughout the spring, summer, and fall, so in winter the tribe could focus on social and ceremonial occasions

Healing practices

Tribal medicine men called shamans (*SHAY-munz*) got their healing powers from a guardian spirit. Two kinds of spirits appeared to shamans: a two-headed serpent-like being and an alligator-like being. Curing was a public event, and relatives and neighbors of the patient watched and participated in the healing ceremony. First the shaman sang a special power song to find out what ailed the patient. Then he cured the patient by removing the sick-making object, or by return-

"Basket Maker—Skokomish," a photograph by Edward S. Curtis, 1912.

ing to the body the life soul or guardian spirit that had been stolen. Shamans could also cause harm and even death. They were often regarded with suspicion and sometimes even killed.

ARTS

Most Skokomish art was of a religious nature. People used hard objects to peck at stone to make abstract designs. They made images of supernatural beings on objects used for ceremonial purposes, or images reflecting the owner's power, such as house posts.

Shamans were known for carving unusual wood figures out of red cedar. They were often legless torsos with oval heads that were flattened in the front and painted in red and black on a white foreground. Instead of legs they had pointed stakes that were set in the ground during ceremonies. Other common ceremonial objects were staffs topped with deer-hoof rattles that were used in healing ceremonies.

CUSTOMS

Social organization

Tribal members were divided into one of three classes based on wealth and their ancestry: the upper class; the lower class, or freemen; and slaves, who were usually war captives.

Head flattening

Members of the Skokomish upper class practiced head flattening, a common practice in the Pacific Northwest. Shortly after birth, a baby was placed in a cradle and a padded board was tied to its forehead to mold the head into a desired shape. Children were kept in these special cradles until they could walk.

Vision quests

At around the age of eight, both boys and girls began to engage in vision quests to find the guardian spirits that would guide them through life. These quests were held often both before and after puberty. They started with fasting and bathing. Older boys shaved their beard and body hair. The youngsters fell into a trance, made contact with a spirit (who might appear in animal or human form), and received their personal power and a special song. Sometimes guardian spirits were inherited from other family members.

Puberty

Menstrual blood was considered to be extremely powerful, even harmful. Upon a girl's first menstrual period, she went to an isolated hut. There she sat on a mat and was instructed on how to perform a woman's work, such as food gathering and cooking. When a girl of high social rank came out of this isolation, her parents gave a feast announcing that she was eligible for marriage.

Boys were kept away from girls in an effort to keep them focused on finding their guardian spirit. This separation led many boys to decide to marry when they were young.

Courtship and marriage

Most people chose marriage partners from outside their village. Especially in the case of upper-class families, parents usually arranged marriages. The process began with a formal request by the groom's parents to the bride's parents, and the two families exchanged gifts. While poor couples could easily obtain divorces, it was more difficult for the rich, and therefore more rare. A widow or widower was expected to marry a close relative of their deceased mate, in order to keep the children of the couple in the groom's village.

Festivals

Upper-class families, who were the only ones who could afford it, often held feasts, called potlatches, to show off their wealth. Lavish gifts were given to other members of the tribe.

In modern times, Skokomish people gather each year with other Native Americans for various celebrations, including the Treaty Day celebration in January (which is open to the public), the First Plant Ceremony in April, the First Salmon Ceremony in August, and the First Elk Ceremony in October.

Funerals

When a Skokomish person died, a series of rituals was held, beginning with a wake given by the family of the deceased. Professional undertakers prepared the body for viewing, and relatives and friends brought gifts to honor the dead person. The body was removed from the home through a hole in the wall and then taken to a cemetery, where it was placed either in a box in the ground or in a canoe on a frame. A funeral feast followed the burial. There the personal property of the deceased was given away and the widow cut her hair to show her sorrow.

CURRENT TRIBAL ISSUES

The Skokomish River has always been the social and economic focus of the Skokomish people. The river has suffered damage because of clear-cut logging (the total removal of a stand of trees) on the river's South Fork and unregulated hydroelectric development on the North Fork. Run-off of debris from the clear-cut slopes clogs the river with sediment, greatly reduces the number of salmon, and contributes to increased flooding in the Skokomish Valley. In the North Fork, the City of Tacoma's Cushman Hydroelectric Project totally blocks fish passage and pipes the waters of the North Fork out of its watershed (the area drained by the river system) to a power plant. This starves seventeen miles of river of its flows. These developments have damaged the conditions of fish and wildlife.

In 1996 the Skokomish Tribe joined with conservation groups and nearby residents in forming an action plan for restoring healthy conditions for the natural plant and animal life of the Skokomish River. The tribe has tried to influence the Federal Energy Regulatory Commission to require the City of Tacoma to restore the river to its watershed and to reduce the damage that has been done to the tribe and others who live nearby.

FURTHER READING

Porter, Frank W., III. *The Coast Salish Peoples.* New York: Chelsea House Publishers, 1989.

Paterek, Josephine. *Encyclopedia of Native American Clothing and Adornment.* Santa Barbara: ABC-CLIO, 1994.

Suttles, Wayne, and Barbara Lane. "Southern Coast Salish." *Handbook of North American Indians*, Vol. 7: *Northwest Coast*. Ed. Wayne Suttles. Washington, DC: Smithsonian Institution, 1990.

Tlingit

Name

The name Tlingit (pronounced *KLINK-ut*; sometimes *TLEENG-ut*) means "human."

Location

The Tlingit traditionally lived along the Pacific Coast in what is now southeastern Alaska and northern British Columbia. Today Tlingit communities are scattered throughout the area.

Population

The Tlingit population was about 15,000 prior to European contact. This figure may have included the Haida people (see entry), because some early European writers believed the Haida and Tlingit were the same peoples. In a census (count of the population) done in 1990 by the U.S. Bureau of the Census, 14,417 people identified themselves as Tlingit.

Language family

Tlingit.

Origins and group affiliations

The Tlingit have probably lived along the southeast coast of Alaska for thousands of years, since the time when the land was covered with large sheets of ice called glaciers. The major Tlingit tribes include the Sitka, Auk, Huna, and Tonga.

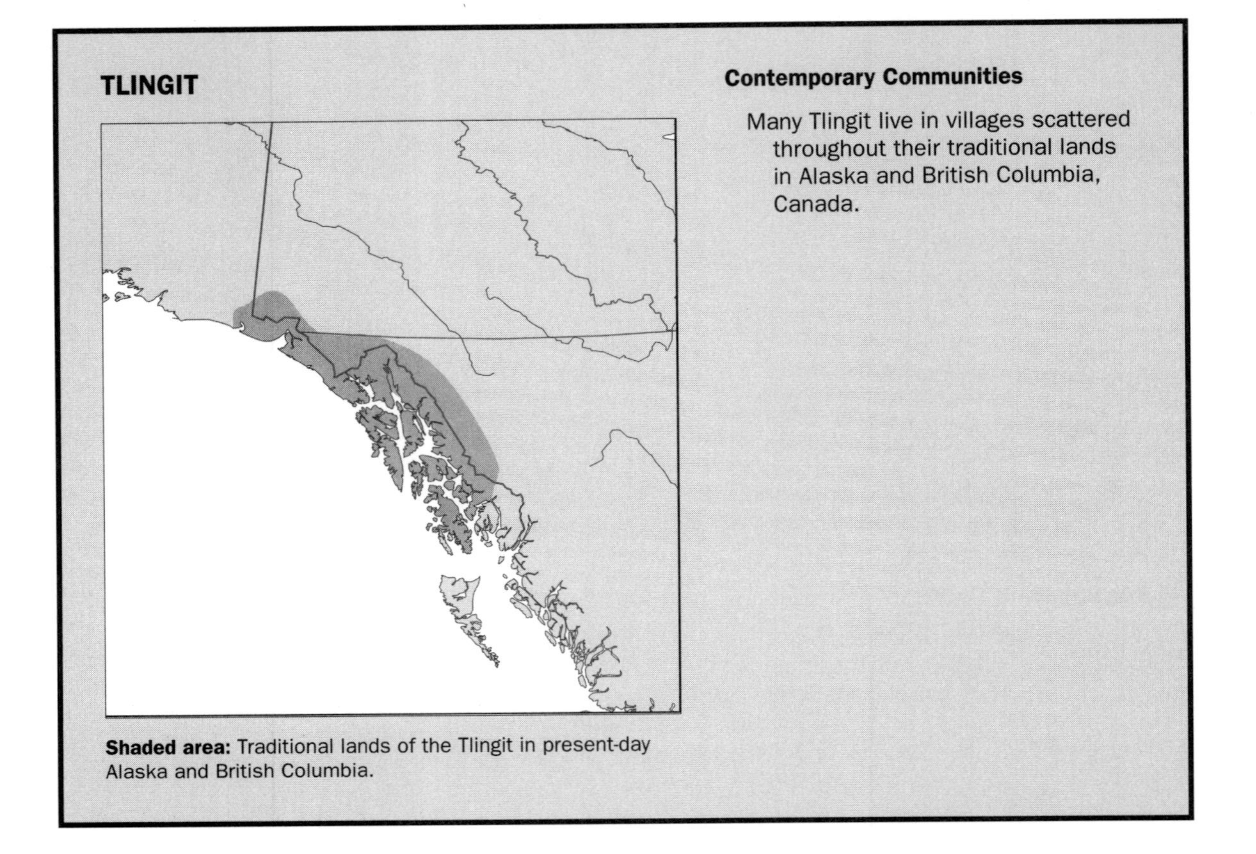

Shaded area: Traditional lands of the Tlingit in present-day Alaska and British Columbia.

Over thousands of years, the Tlingit developed a way of life that helped them survive in the rain-drenched area of Alaska known as the Panhandle. Tlingit men burned, steamed, and carved cedar wood to make canoes for fishing, as they got most of their food from the sea. Before the arrival of explorers and settlers, groups of Tlingit people would travel by canoe through treacherous waters for hundreds of miles to engage in war, attend ceremonies, trade, or marry. In recent times the Tlingit have led the fight for Native rights and have involved themselves in politics.

HISTORY

Relations with the Russians

The first Europeans in the Northwest were the Spanish, British, and Russians, who went there seeking furs in the mid-1700s. In 1741 Russian explorer Aleksey Chirikov sent two boatloads of men on a search for drinking water in Tlingit territory near the site of present-day Sitka, Alaska. Neither boat returned, and there were few if any attempts to explore Tlingit land again until well into the 1800s.

During the nineteenth century, the Tlingit people, who controlled trade in their area of southern Alaska, began trading with the Russians. Relations were friendly until the newcomers tried to settle and control trade routes. The Tlingit objected, and in 1802 Chief Katlian led a successful war party against the Russians in Sitka. The site was soon recaptured, however.

IMPORTANT DATES

1741: Russians enter deep into Tlingit territory.

1867: The United States purchases Alaska from Russia.

1912: The Tlingit organize the Alaska Native Brotherhood to establish equality.

1959: Alaska becomes a state.

1971: The Alaska Native Claims Settlement Act is passed.

United States takes control

In time, European diseases and other hardships weakened the Tlingit. Between 1836 and 1840, nearly one-half of the population living at or near Sitka was wiped out by epidemics. About this time, Americans came into Tlingit country looking for gold, and they began to occupy and control Tlingit lands. The U.S. purchase of Alaska from Russia in 1867 brought even more settlers. They established canneries (factories for canning fish), mines, and logging camps, businesses that went against Native traditions of taking only the resources necessary for survival. The Tlingit protested, but they were no match for American military strength and technology. The tribe was further weakened by the destruction of two of their villages in the late 1800s by the American military, caused by a disagreement over the deaths of two Native people.

Tlingit face threats

Over time, the American government subjected the Alaskan Natives to the same regulations and policies as American Indians in the United States (Alaska was not yet a state, but its white citizens enjoyed many U.S. citizenship rights). Natives were deprived of land, and they lost their right to deal with criminal matters according to traditional customs. By the beginning of the twentieth century, their way of life was eroding.

In response, the Tlingit people joined with other tribes in 1912 to found the Alaska Native Brotherhood (ANB). Among its goals were the same citizenship and education rights enjoyed by non-Natives in Alaska. Their wish for citizenship was granted in 1915, on condition that they became "civilized" and give up certain tribal customs. Few Alaska Natives were willing to accept these conditions and therefore did not become citizens. In the early 1900s, smallpox, influenza (flu), and tuberculosis epidemics struck some Tlingit villages.

Tlingit regain some land

At the urging of the ANB, Congress passed a law in 1935 allowing the Tlingit to sue the United States for the loss of their lands. By this time, large sections of Tlingit country had been set aside for the Tongass National Forest and Glacier Bay National Monument; further south in Tlingit country, Annette Island had been set aside as a reservation for some Canadian Indians. Some lands were returned to the Tlingit, but not enough to meet the needs of a hunting and fishing people.

Tlingit people have actively pursued the right to vote. Unlike many Alaska Native people at the time who wished to continue living as they had lived for many generations, Tlingit leaders sought increased political power.

Modern conflicts

In the first half of the twentieth century, disputes developed around such issues as Native citizenship, the right to vote, fishing methods, and discrimination. In the 1930s, 1940s, and 1950s, signs reading "No Indians Allowed" were a common sight on the doors of Alaska businesses. The ANB did much to fight prejudice and raise the social status of the Tlingit people as American citizens.

In 1959 Alaska became a state. Soon after it became a state, oil was discovered there, and oil companies wanted to build a pipeline across Native lands to carry oil south. In 1971 the Alaska Native Claims Settlement Act (ANCSA) allowed Alaska Natives to retain 44 million acres of their land and gave them $962.5 million. In exchange, they gave up all claim to other lands in Alaska—in all, nine-tenths of Alaska. The ANSCA also resulted in the formation of 12 regional corporations to be in charge of Native Alaskan economic development and land use.

Today, although Tlingit people enjoy much more acceptance, their fight for survival continues. Their ability to live off the land and sea is constantly endangered by logging, overharvesting of the waters by commercial fisheries, government regulations, and the area's increasing population.

RELIGION

Tlingit beliefs were closely tied to nature. They centered on a creator and spirit helpers who influenced the weather, hunting, and healing. Traditionally, the Tlingit believed that all members of the tribe were reborn from one of their ancestors.

Hundreds of Tlingit died in tuberculosis epidemics during the early 1900s and were buried in mass graves. Many Tlingit lost faith in the healing powers of their medicine men, called shamans (pronounced *SHAY-manz*), and traditional Native ceremonies that brought together large numbers of people nearly died out. Tlingit people turned to Christian churches for comfort. In the process of converting to Christianity, many Tlingit were given new names to replace their Tlingit names, which were an important basis of identity and status in their society.

The Russian Orthodox and Presbyterian faiths have had a great impact on Tlingit life and are well established in Tlingit communities. Smaller numbers belong to other Christian churches. People who continue to practice the old tribal religion do so privately.

THE TLINGIT LANGUAGE

Unlike the English alphabet of 26 letters, the Tlingit language has at least 32 consonants and eight vowels. The alphabet was created with not only the familiar lettering of English but also with periods, underlined letters, and apostrophes to distinguish particular sounds. For example; the word *yéil* means Raven, and *yéil'* (with the apostrophe) means elderberry.

Tlingit people do not use such greetings as hello, good-bye, good afternoon, or good evening. Some common expressions are:

Yoo xat duwasaakw	"My name is"
Gunalchéesh	"Thank you"
Yak'éi ? ixwsiteení	"It's good to see you"
Wáa sá iyatee	"How are you feeling?"
Wa.é ? ku.aa?	"Where are you going?"
Haa kaa gaa ?kuwatee	"It's good weather for us."

LANGUAGE

The Tlingit language is not closely related to any other language. Because many Tlingit sounds are made in the back of the mouth, the language sounds similar to German. It has twenty-four sounds not found in English, and the difference in meaning between words often depends entirely on the tone of the speaker's voice.

In the nineteenth century, a Russian Orthodox priest created the first Tlingit alphabet and developed a program to teach the Tlingit to read and write. In their desire to have the Tlingit adopt white ways, Americans tried to suppress the use of the Tlingit language. A Native movement to teach the language to the young began in the 1960s, when language experts created the Tlingit alphabet that is commonly used today.

GOVERNMENT

Tlingit leaders were the chiefs who headed the various clans and their close relatives (see "Tlingit social system" under "Customs"). In the early twentieth century, Tlingit leaders began to seek power in state politics. A Tlingit named William Paul was elected to the Alaska

A Chilkat robe, made from mountain goat wool and cedar bark strips, could take years to make and cost a lot of money.

Territorial House of Representatives in 1924, marking the beginning of a trend toward Native political power in the state.

Today, corporations created as a result of the Alaska Native Claims Settlement Act (see "History") have a great deal of political power. Their power comes from their ownership of valuable lands and the fact that they represent more than 16,000 Tlingit and other Natives. They use their power to influence state lawmakers to pass laws favorable to the Natives.

ECONOMY

For centuries the Tlingit economy centered on trade. They traded excess food, furs, canoes, shells, fish oil, and the beautiful woven Chilkat robes (see "Weaving") with other tribes. The price of a Chilkat robe in the mid-1800s was about $30—a very large sum at that time. Only caribou hides, copper, and later, guns, came close to the value of the Chilkat robe.

By 1900 many Tlingit worked in canneries, and their economy came to be based on work for wages and commercial fishing (fishing for profit, not food). A number of people moved from small villages to larger towns where this kind of work was more available.

Although the American way of life has greatly altered the Tlingit lifestyle, many of the people have adapted. Most Tlingit work in logging and forestry, fishing, tourism, and other business enterprises. Because the tribe emphasizes the importance of education, a number of Tlingit work in professional positions as lawyers, health-care specialists, and educators. Corporations created after the passage of the Alaska Native Claims Settlement Act provide some employment in manual labor, office work, and business management.

DAILY LIFE

Buildings

Before their first contact with Europeans, Tlingit families belonging to the same clan lived together in large homes made of spruce or cedar planks. They painted crests (family symbols) on the front of the house and decorated the interior with intricate carvings and pictures

The exterior of a Tlingit longhouse, c. 1986.

of birds and animals. The only openings were a small doorway and a hole in the center of the roof that allowed smoke to escape. Floors were made of smooth wooden planks, and platforms along the walls were used for sleeping. Large woven mats were hung from the ceiling to separate living areas. In summer, the people moved to fishing camps where they lived in temporary shelters.

Europeans influenced the Natives to build their houses on raised wooden posts, but they held on to the old custom of carving wood figures on the posts. They added windows, multiple doors, inside walls, stoves instead of fireplaces, and porches. Today, many Tlingit live in cities. Those who remain in villages live in single-family homes of various styles.

Clothing

Tlingit men and women traditionally wore loincloths (two pieces of cloth hanging from the waist in front and back) and skirts made of cedar bark. Because of the frequent rainy weather, they made raincoats from natural substances such as spruce root or cedar bark. The Tlingit wore hair ornaments and bracelets, and practiced ear and nose piercing, face painting, and tattooing. The wealth of a Tlingit woman could be determined by the size of her *labret,* a wooden disc inserted in a slit cut into the lower lip. As a woman grew older and richer, larger and large discs were inserted, until finally her lip might flap loosely on her chin.

People wore various types of highly decorated robes (see "Weaving") for ceremonies. Headdresses ranged from simple headbands to colorful carved cedar hats inlaid with pretty shells and finished with ermine fur. Today, most Tlingit people dress in modern clothes, but they often display their clan or family crest on clothing or jewelry.

Food

The traditional Tlingit diet centered on foods from the rivers and sea, including seal, seaweed, clams, herring, salmon eggs, and fish (primarily salmon, plus halibut, cod, and herring). Fish was smoked, baked, roasted, boiled, or dried for later use. Berries and deer meat were also important.

Today, the Tlingit use cooking methods learned from the Norwegians, Russians, Chinese, and Filipinos who have immigrated to Alaska, and rice has become one of their most common foods. Frybread is used for everyday meals and for special occasions, and certain fish oils are still considered a luxury.

Education

Traditionally, uncles and aunts taught Tlingit children how to survive and how to participate in society. Anyone within the clan was permitted to reprimand or guide a child. Today most Tlingit children are raised in typical American one-family homes, and the role of the aunts and uncles is not as great. But in the smaller Tlingit communities some children are still raised according to the old ways.

Beginning in 1905, two separate systems of education were set up in the Alaska Territory—one for Natives run by the federal government and one for whites run by the territorial government. It was not until 1949 that the schools in Alaska were integrated.

Many Tlingit go on to receive degrees in higher education. In addition to regular schooling, children sometimes attend dance groups, traditional survival camps, art camps, and Native education projects.

Healing practices

Glass art, "Frog," 1997, by Tlingit glassblower Preston Singletary.

The Tlingit believed that sickness was the sign of being possessed by an evil spirit, and shamans were called in to drive out the evil spirits. Shamans had spiritual helpers, called *yeks*. Each yek had its own special name and could assume both animal and human forms. A shaman's success at healing depended on the number of yeks he controlled and the quality of his relationship with them. Shamans were paid in advance for their services. If they failed to cure someone, they often claimed that bad spirits interfered with them and they needed further payment to continue their services.

Shamans never cut or combed their hair. They wore aprons made of animal hides and shoulder robes and crowns decorated with animal claws and carved bones. When engaged in their frantic healing dances, they often wore a mask that looked like one of their yeks. They shook rattles and charms, and chanted, groaned, and hissed themselves into a trance-like state.

Today, Tlingit people have access to modern medical treatment, but healing through diet and traditional local medicines still takes place.

ARTS

Dance

Dances were performed at potlatches (special gift-giving ceremonies) or around the evening fire. People told stories, made fun of people, or extended apologies through dance movements accompanied by the music of drums and carved rattles. One Tlingit dance told the story of a funeral. The "corpse" was dressed in fancy clothing with his back against the wall and another man danced the part of his widow. He would cry sorrowfully and throw himself on the "corpse" and tickle it. As the dance ended, the "corpse" sat up and grinned.

Dancers wore masks carved and painted with animals and mythical figures. They also wore headdresses made of sea lion whiskers and birdfeathers that they showered down on guests to show good wishes. Dancers sometimes put on beautiful Chilkat robes (see "Weaving") with fringe that made a wonderful visual effect as they moved.

Tlingits of the Seet-Ka-Kwaan Dance Group in tribal regalia.

Weaving

Two types of traditional ceremonial dress, the Chilkat and Raven's Tail robes, are still worn today. The intricately designed Chilkat robe is made from mountain goat wool and cedar bark strips. It can take a weaver up to five years to complete one robe. The Raven's Tail robe is woven of black and white fibers in geometric patterns. Both types of robes were signs of wealth. These art forms nearly died out, but during the twentieth century the skill revived when elderly weavers were encouraged to pass down their knowledge to younger ones. Chilkat and Raven's Tail weaving techniques are also used in leggings, medicine bags, dance purses and aprons, tunics, and shirts.

Totem poles

The Tlingit carved totem poles in the shape of animals and humans. Totems could be as high as ninety feet tall and told family stories and legends. They honored chiefs or loved ones and commemorated events such as a birth or a successful hunt. Memorial totems held the ashes of deceased loved ones. Occasionally, totems were created to make fun of someone who had wronged the clan or village.

CUSTOMS

Tlingit social system

The Tlingit social system was very complex. Each person belonged from birth to the same group as the mother, either Eagle or Raven, and was only permitted to marry a person from the other group.

The Raven and Eagle groups were divided into clans. Each clan had its own crest (an animal symbol). A person could be Eagle and belong to the Killer Whale or Brown Bear Clan, or to several other existing clans; Ravens could belong to the Frog Clan, Sea Tern Clan, Coho (salmon) Clan, and so on.

Clans were further divided into houses or extended families. Before the Tlingit had contact with Europeans, "houses" were real houses or lodges in which members of that clan or family lived. Today

THE GHOST LAND

Lacking a written language, the Tlingit used storytelling and plays that included music and dancing to pass down their history. In the following story, a young man whose wife has died does not participate in her funeral potlatch ceremony. Instead, he follows the Death Trail, and his unusual action leads to strange results.

The young wife of a chief's son died and the young man was so sorrowful he could not sleep. Early one morning he put on his fine clothes and started off. He walked all day and all night. He went through the woods a long distance, and then to a valley. The trees were very thick, but he could hear voices far away. At last he saw light through the trees and then came to a wide, flat stone on the edge of a lake.

Now all the time this young man had been walking in the Death Trail. He saw houses and people on the other side of the lake. He could see them moving around. So he shouted, "Come over and get me." But they did not seem to hear him. Upon the lake a little canoe was being paddled about by one man, and all the shore was grassy. The chief's son shouted a long while but no one answered him. At last he whispered to himself, "Why don't they hear me?"

At once a person across the lake said, "Some one is shouting." When he whispered, they heard him.

The voice said also, "Some one has come up from Dreamland. Go and bring him over."

When the chief's son reached the other side of the lake, he saw his wife. He was very happy to see her again. People asked him to sit down. They gave him something to eat, but his wife said, "Don't eat that. If you eat that you will never get back." So he did not eat it.

Then his wife said, "You had better not stay here long. Let us go right away." So they were taken back in the same canoe. It is called Ghost's Canoe and it is the only one on that lake. They landed at the broad, flat rock where the chief's son had stood calling. It is called Ghost's Rock, and is at the very end of the Death Trail. Then they started down the trail, through the valley and through the thick woods. The second night they reached the chief's house.

The chief's son told his wife to stay outside. He went in and said to his father, "I have brought my wife back."

The chief said, "Why don't you bring her in?"

The chief laid down a nice mat with fur robes on it for the young wife. The young man went out to get his wife, but when he came in with her, they could see only him. When he came very close, they saw a deep shadow following him. When his wife sat down and they put a marten skin robe [a marten is a weasel-like mammal] around her, it hung about the shadow just as if a person were sitting there. When she ate, they saw only the spoon moving up and down, but not the shadow of her hands. It looked very strange to them.

Afterward the chief's son died and the ghosts of both of them went back to Ghost Land.

SOURCE: "The Ghost Land." Katharine Berry Judson, ed. *Myths and Legends of Alaska.* Chicago: A. C. McClurg, 1911.

"houses" are one of the ways in which Tlingit people identify themselves and their relationship to others. Some examples of houses include the Snail House, Brown Bear Den House, Owl House, Crescent Moon House, Coho House, and Thunderbird House.

Beyond family and clan groupings, the Tlingit were divided into units called *kwan,* which were communities of people who lived in a mutual area, shared residence, intermarried, and lived in peace.

Tlingit in canoes attending a potlatch ceremony.

Festivals

Potlatches have always been an important part of Tlingit life. A potlatch is a great feast where people show respect, pay debts, and display their wealth. Today, potlatches are held for a variety of occasions such as funerals, adoptions, the naming of a baby, raising a totem pole, or building a lodge. They may take years of planning; in former times they could last four weeks or more, but they seldom last that long today.

War and hunting rituals

The Tlingit were a warlike people who raided neighboring tribes and other clans to seek revenge for insults or injury. Tlingit warriors wore shirts of untanned moose hide covered with armor made of wooden slats that covered the body from the neck to the knees. They sometimes took women and children as slaves, but men were considered too dangerous and were instead slain and their heads or scalps taken.

Courtship and weddings

Marriage was viewed by the Tlingit as a way to strengthen the family's social and financial position, and parents chose spouses for their children. The boy's family gave the girl's family valuable gifts. If her family found the gifts acceptable, generous gifts were given in return. Gift exchanges continued throughout the couple's married life.

Funerals

For the Tlingit, three potlatches were required to properly send a deceased person off to the spirit world. During the first, the body was prepared for cremation or burial (which is more common today), feasts were prepared, and the body was disposed of. Then a potlatch was held in honor of the deceased person's clan. The third potlatch took place about a year later; it ended with a celebration of life and happy stories and songs.

CURRENT TRIBAL ISSUES

An important issue for the Tlingit is having their own tribal courts and judges. Some progress has been made in this area since the 1970s.

Tlingit culture has undergone a rebirth that began in the 1970s. There has been a revival of dances, songs, potlatches, language, artwork, and stories. Discussions are taking place about discrimination: how it can actually make people feel sick, and what can be done to help the victims.

NOTABLE PEOPLE

Elaine Abraham (1929–), the first Tlingit to enter the nursing profession, went on to a career in education. Her accomplishments include co-founding the Alaska Native Language Center in Fairbanks, teaching the Tlingit language at the Anchorage Community College, and working as Director of Alaska Native Studies for the University of Alaska in Anchorage.

Tlingit activist Elizabeth Peratrovich made a moving plea for justice and equality for Alaska Natives in 1945 that led to the passage of an anti-discrimination bill. The State of Alaska officially recognized her efforts as a civil rights leader in 1988 with the "Annual Elizabeth Peratrovich Day."

FURTHER READING

Liptak, Karen. *North American Indian Ceremonies.* New York: Franklin Watts, 1992.

Lyons, Grant. *Pacific Coast Indians of North America.* New York: Julian Messner, 1983.

Nichols, Richard. *A Story to Tell: Traditions of a Tlingit Community.* Minneapolis: Lerner Publications Company, 1998.

Osinski, Alice. *The Tlingit.* Chicago: Childrens Press, 1990.

Steward, Hilary. *Looking at Totem Poles.* Seattle: University of Washington Press, 1993.

Bibliography

Books

Abrams, George H. J. *The Seneca People*. Phoenix, AZ: Indian Tribal Series, 1976.

The AFN Report on the Status of Alaska Natives: A Call for Action. Anchorage: Alaska Federation of Natives, 1989.

American Indian Reservations and Trust Areas. Washington, DC: U.S. Department of Commerce, 1996.

The American Indians: Algonquians of the East Coast. New York: Time-Life Books, 1995.

The American Indians: Hunters of the Northern Forest. New York: Time-Life Books, 1995.

Anderson, Gary Clayton. *Kinsmen of Another Kind: Dakota-White Relations in the Upper Mississippi Valley, 1650–1862*. Lincoln: University of Nebraska Press, 1984.

Anderson, Gary Clayton. *Little Crow: Spokesman for the Sioux*. St. Paul: Minnesota Historical Society Press, 1986.

Anderson, Gary Clayton. *Through Dakota Eyes: Narrative Accounts of the Minnesota Indian War of 1862*. St. Paul: Minnesota Historical Society Press, 1988.

Apess, William. *On Our Own Ground: The Complete Writings of William Apess, A Pequot*. Ed. Barry O'Connell. Amherst: University of Massachusetts Press, 1992.

Axtell, James. *The European and the Indian: Essays in the Ethnohistory of Colonial North America*. New York: Oxford University Press, 1981.

Ayer, Eleanor H. *The Anasazi*. New York: Walker Publishing, 1993.

Azelrod, Alan. *Chronicle of the Indian Wars*. New York: Prentice Hall, 1993.

Bahti, Tom. *Southwestern Indian Tribes.* Las Vegas: KC Publications, 1994.

Ballantine, Betty and Ian Ballantine, eds. *The Native Americans: An Illustrated History.* Atlanta: Turner Publishing, 1993.

Bamforth, Douglas B. *Ecology and Human Organization on the Great Plains.* New York: Plenum Press, 1988.

A Basic Call to Consciousness. Rooseveltown, NY: Akwesasne Notes, 1978.

Bataille, Gretchen M. *Native American Women: A Biographical Dictionary.* New York: Garland Publishing, 1993.

Beals, Ralph L. *Material Culture of the Pima, Papago, and Western Apache.* Berkeley, CA: Department of the Interior, National Park Service, 1934.

Bean, Lowell John. *Mukat's People: The Cahuilla Indians of Southern California.* Berkeley: University of California Press, 1972.

Beauchamp, William M. "Notes on Onondaga Dances." *An Iroquois Source Book,* Volume 2. Ed. Elisabeth Tooker. New York: Garland Publishing, 1985.

Beck, W. and Ynez Haas. *Historical Atlas of California.* Norman: University of Oklahoma Press, 1974.

Beckham, Stephen Dow. *Requiem for a People: The Rogue Indians and the Frontiersman.* Norman: University of Oklahoma Press, 1971.

Beckham, Stephen Dow, Kathryn Anne Toepel, and Rick Minor. *Native American Religious Practices and Uses in Western Oregon.* Eugene: University of Oregon Anthropological Papers, 1984.

Benson, Henry C. *Life Among the Choctaw Indians, and Sketches of the Southwest.* Cincinnati, OH: R. P. Thompson, 1860.

Berlainder, Jean Louis. *The Indians of Texas in 1830.* Washington, DC: Smithsonian Institution, 1969.

Berthrong, Donald J. *The Cheyenne and Arapaho Ordeal: Reservation and Agency Life in the Indian Territory.* Norman: University of Oklahoma Press, 1976.

Berthrong, Donald J. *The Southern Cheyennes.* Norman: University of Oklahoma Press, 1963.

Bieder, Robert E. *Native American Communities in Wisconsin, 1600–1960: A Study of Tradition and Change.* Madison: University of Wisconsin Press, 1995.

Biographical Dictionary of Indians of the Americas. Newport Beach, CA: American Indian Publishers, 1991.

Birket-Smith, Kaj and Frederica De Laguna. *The Eyak Indians of the Copper River Delta.* Copenhagen: Levin & Munksgaard, 1938.

Bischoff, William N. *The Indian War Diary of Plympton J. Kelly 1855–1856.* Tacoma: Washington State History Society, 1976.

Blaine, Martha Royce. *Pawnee Passage, 1870–1875.* Norman: University of Oklahoma Press, 1990.

Blaine, Martha Royce. *The Pawnees: A Critical Bibliography.* Bloomington: Indiana University Press for the Newberry Library, 1980.

Boas, Franz. *Chinook Texts.* Washington, DC: Bureau of American Ethnology Bulletin No. 20, 1894.

Boas, Franz. *Kwakiutl Ethnography.* Ed. Helen Codere. Chicago: University of Chicago Press, 1966.

Boas, Franz, ed. *Publications of the American Ethnological Society,* Vol. 1: *Fox Text,* by William Jones. Leyden: E. J. Brill, 1907.

Boas, Franz. *The Social Organization and the Secret Societies of the Kwakiutl Indians.* New York: Johnson Reprint Corporation, 1970.

Bolton, Herbert Eugene. *The Hasinais: Southern Caddoans As Seen by the Earliest Europeans.* Norman: University of Oklahoma Press, 1987.

Bourne, Russell. *Red King's Rebellion: Racial Politics in New England, 1675–1678.* New York: Atheneum Press, 1990.

Boyd, Maurice. *Kiowas Voices,* Vol. 1: *Ceremonial Dance, Ritual and Song.* Fort Worth: Texas Christian University Press, 1981.

Boyd, Maurice. *Kiowas Voices,* Vol. 2: *Myths, Legends, and Folktales.* Fort Worth: Texas Christian University Press, 1983.

Boyd, Robert. *People of the Dalles: The Indians of Wascopam Mission.* Lincoln: University of Nebraska Press, 1996.

Braund, Kathryn E. Holland. *Deerskins & Duffels: The Creek Indian Trade with Anglo-America, 1685–1815.* Lincoln: University of Nebraska Press, 1993.

Bray, Tamara L. and Thomas W. Killion. *Reckoning with the Dead: The Larsen Bay Repatriation and the Smithsonian Institution.* Washington, DC: Smithsonian Institution, 1994.

Brescia, William, Jr. "Choctaw Oral Tradition Relating to Tribal Origin." *The Choctaw Before Removal.* Ed. Carolyn Keller Reeves. Jackson: University Press of Mississippi, 1985.

Bringle, Mary. *Eskimos.* New York: Franklin Watts, 1973.

Brinton, Daniel G. *The Lenape and their Legends.* Philadelphia, 1884. Reprint. St. Clair Shores, MI: Scholarly Press, 1972.

Brown, Mark. *The Flight of the Nez Perce.* Lincoln: University of Nebraska Press, 1967.

Brown, Vinson. "Sioux, Eastern." *Dictionary of Indian Tribes of the Americas,* Vol. 3. Newport Beach, CA: American Indian Publishers, 1980.

Bruchac, Joseph. *New Voices from the Longhouse: An Anthology of Contemporary Iroquois Writing.* Greenfield Center, NY: Greenfield Review Press, 1989.

Bunte, Pamela A. and Robert J. Franklin. *From the Sands to the Mountain: Change and Persistence in a Southern Paiute Community.* Lincoln: University of Nebraska Press, 1987.

Burch, Ernest S. *The Eskimos.* Norman: University of Oklahoma Press, 1988.

Burnham, Dorothy K. *To Please the Caribou: Painted Caribou-skin Coats Worn by the Naskapi, Montagnais, and Cree Hunters of the Quebec Labrador Peninsula.* Toronto: Royal Ontario Museum, 1992.

Bushnell, David I., Jr. "The Choctaw of Bayou Lacomb, St. Tammany Parish, Louisiana (1909)." *A Choctaw Source Book. New York: Garland Publishing, 1985: pp. 1–37.*

Buskirk, Winfred. *The Western Apache.* Norman: University of Oklahoma Press, 1986.

Caduto, Michael J. *Keepers of the Earth.* Golden, CO: Fulcrum, 1988.

Cahokia. Lincoln: University of Nebraska Press, 1997.

Calloway, Colin G. *The Abenaki.* New York: Chelsea House Publishers, 1989.

Calloway, Colin G., ed. *Dawnland Encounters: Indians and Europeans in Northern New England.* Hanover, NH: University Press of New England, 1991.

Calloway, Colin G. *The World Turned Upside Down: Indian Voices from Early America.* Boston: St. Martin's Press, 1994.

Campisi, Jack. *The Mashpee Indians: Tribe on Trial.* Syracuse, NY: Syracuse University Press, 1991.

Carlisle, Richard. *The Illustrated Encyclopedia of Mankind.* New York: Marshall Cavendish, 1984.

Carlo, Poldine. *Nulato: An Indian Life on the Yukon.* Caldwell, ID: Caxton Printers, 1983.

Carlson, Richard G., ed. *Rooted Like the Ash Trees: New England Indians and the Land.* Naugatuck, CT: Eagle Wing Press, 1987.

Carter, Cecile Elkins. *Caddo Indians: Where We Come From.* Norman: University of Oklahoma Press, 1995.

Carter, Sarah. "Chapter 19—'We Must Farm to Enable Us to Live': The Plains Cree and Agriculture to 1900." *Native Peoples: The Canadian Experience.* Toronto: McClellan & Stewart, 1986.

Case, David S. *Alaska Natives and American Laws.* University of Alaska Press, 1984.

Cash, Joseph H. and Gerald W. Wolff. *The Comanche People.* Phoenix, AZ: Indian Tribal Series, 1974.

Castille, George Pierre, ed. *The Indians of Puget Sound.* Seattle: University of Washington Press, 1985.

Castillo, Edward D. and R. Jackson. *Indians, Franciscans, and Spanish Colonization: The Impact of the Mission System on California Indians.* Albuquerque: University of New Mexico Press, 1995.

Catlin, George. *Letters and Notes on the Manners, Customs, and Conditions of North American Indians.* Volume 2 (unabridged republication of the fourth [1844] edition). New York: Dover Publications, 1973.

Catlin, George. *North American Indians.* New York: Viking Press, 1989.

Chamberlain, Von Del. *When Stars Came Down to Earth: Cosmology of the Skidi Pawnee Indians of North America.* Los Altos, CA: Ballena Press and College Park: Center for Archaeoastronomy, University of Maryland, 1982.

Chalfant, William Y. *Without Quarter: The Wichita Expedition and the Fight on Crooked Creek.* Norman: University of Oklahoma Press, 1991.

Champagne, Duane, ed. *Chronology of Native North American History: From Pre-Columbian Times to the Present.* Detroit: Gale Research, 1994.

Champagne, Duane, ed. *Native America: Portrait of the Peoples.* Detroit: Visible Ink Press, 1994.

Champagne, Duane, ed. *The Native North American Almanac.* Detroit: Gale Research Inc., 1994.

Charlebois, Peter. *The Life of Louis Riel.* Toronto: New Canada Press, 1978.

Childers, Robert and Mary Kancewick. "The Gwich'in (Kutchin): Conservation and Cultural Protection in the Arctic Borderlands." Anchorage: Gwich'in Steering Committee, n.d.

Cleland, Charles E. *Rites of Conquest: The History and Culture of Michigan's Native Americans.* Ann Arbor: University of Michigan Press, 1992.

Clifton, James A. *The Prairie People: Continuity and Change in Potawatomi Indian Culture 1665–1965.* Lawrence: The Regents Press of Kansas, 1977.

Clifton, James A., *Star Woman and Other Shawnee Tales.* Lanham, MD: University Press of America, 1984.

Clifton, James A., George L. Cornell, and James M. McClurken. *People of the Three Fires: The Ottawa, Potawatomi and Ojibway of Michigan.* Grand Rapids, MI: Grand Rapids Inter-Tribal Council, 1986.

Cole, D. C. *The Chiricahua Apache 1846–1876: From War to Reservation.* Albuquerque: University of New Mexico Press, 1988.

Cole, Douglas. *Captured Heritage: The Scramble for Northwest Coast Artifacts.* Seattle: University of Washington Press, 1985.

Cook, Sherburne F. *The Conflict between the California Indian and White Civilization.* Berkeley: University of California Press, 1967.

Cordere, Helen, ed. *Kwakiutl Ethnography.* Chicago: University of Chicago Press, 1966.

Corkran, David H. *The Creek Frontier: 1540–1783.* Norman: University of Oklahoma Press, 1967.

Cotterill, R. S. *The Southern Indians: The Story of the Civilized Tribes Before Removal.* Norman: University of Oklahoma Press, 1954.

Covington, James W. *The Seminoles of Florida.* Gainsville: University of Florida Press, 1993.

Cox, Bruce Alden, ed. *Native People, Native Lands: Canadian Indians, Inuit and Métis.* Ottawa: Carleton University Press, 1987.

Crane, Verner W. *The Southern Frontier, Greenwood, CT: Greenwood Press, 1969.*

Crowder, David L. *Tendoy, Chief of the Lemhis.* Caldwell, ID: Caxton Publishers, 1969.

Crum, Steven J. *The Road On Which We Came.* Salt Lake City: University of Utah Press, 1994.

Curtis, Edward S. *The North American Indian.* Reprint. New York: Johnson Reprint Corporation, 1970.

Cushman, H. B. *History of the Choctaw, Chickasaw, and Natchez Indians.* New York: Russell & Russell, 1972.

Cvpvkke, Holátte (C. B. Clark). "'Drove Off Like Dogs'—Creek Removal." *Indians of the Lower South: Past and Present.* Ed. John K. Mahon. Pensacola, FL: Gulf Coast History and Humanities Conference, 1975.

D'Azevedo, Warren L., ed. *The Handbook of North American Indians,* Vol. 11: *Great Basin.* Washington, DC: Smithsonian Institution, 1986.

Dahl, Jens. *Indigenous Peoples of the Arctic.* Copenhagen: The Nordic Council, 1993.

Dauenhauer, Nora Marks and Richard Dauenhauer. *Haa Kusteeyí, Our Culture: Tlingit Life Stories.* Seattle: University of Washington Press; and Juneau, AK: Sealaska Heritage Foundation, 1994.

Dauenhauer, Nora Marks and Richard Dauenhauer. *Haa Tuwunáagu Yís, for Healing Our Spirit: Tlingit Oratory.* Seattle: University of Washington Press; and Juneau, AK: Sealaska Heritage Foundation, 1990.

Davis, Mary B., ed. *Native America in the Twentieth Century: An Encyclopedia.* New York: Garland Publishing, 1994.

Dawson, Dawn P. and Harvey Markowitz, eds. *Ready Reference: American Indians.* Pasadena, CA: Salem Press, 1995.

Deacon, Belle. *Engithidong Xugixudhoy: Their Stories of Long Ago: Told in Deg Hit'an Athabaskan by Belle Deacon.* Fairbanks: Alaska Native Language Center, 1987.

Deans, James. *Tales from the Totems of the Hidery,* Volume 2. Chicago: Archives of the International Folk-Lore Association, 1899.

Debo, Angie. *A History of the Indians of the United States.* Norman: University of Oklahoma Press, 1970.

Debo, Angie. *The Rise and Fall of the Choctaw Republic,* Second edition. Norman: University of Oklahoma Press, 1961.

Denig, Edwin Thompson. *Five Indian Tribes of the Upper Missouri: Sioux, Arikaras, Assiniboines, Crees, Crows.* Ed. John C. Ewers. Norman: University of Oklahoma Press, 1961.

Densmore, Frances. *Chippewa Customs.* St. Paul: Minnesota Historical Society Press, 1929; reprinted, 1979.

Densmore, Frances. *Choctaw Music* (Bulletin 136 of the Bureau of American Ethnology). DaCapo Press, 1936, reprint 1972.

Densmore, Francis. *Papago Music.* New York: Da Capo Press, 1972.

DeRosier, Arthur H. Jr. *The Removal of the Choctaw Indians.* Knoxville: University of Tennessee Press, 1970.

DeWald, Terry. *The Papago Indians and Their Basketry.* Tucson, AZ: DeWald, c. 1979.

Diedrich, Mark, *Dakota Oratory.* Rochester, MN: Coyote Books, 1989.

Dobyns, Henry F. *The Papago People.* Phoenix, Indian Tribal Series, c. 1972.

Dobyns, Henry F. *Papagos in the Cotton Fields, 1950.* Tucson, AZ: University of Arizona, Department of Anthropology, 1951.

Dockstader, Frederick J. *Great Native American Indians, Profiles in Life, and Leadership.* New York: Van Nostrand Runhold, Co., 1977.

Doherty, Robert. *Disputed Waters: Native Americans and the Great Lakes Fishery.* Lexington: University Press of Kentucky, 1990.

Doig, Ivan. *Winter Brothers.* New York: Harcourt Brace Jovanovich, 1980.

Driben, Paul. *We Are Métis.* New York: AMS Press, 1985.

Drucker, Philip and Robert F. Heizer. *To Make My Name Good: A Reexamination of the Southern Kwakiutl Potlatch.* Berkeley: University of California Press, 1967.

Duke, Philip. *Points in Time: Structure and Event in a Late Northern Plains Hunting Society.* Niwot: University Press of Colorado, 1991.

Dutton, Bertha P. *American Indians of the Southwest.* Albuquerque: University of New Mexico Press, 1983.

Dutton, Bertha P. *Indians of the American Southwest.* Englewood Cliffs, NJ: Prentice-Hall, 1975.

Eagle/Walking Turtle (Gary McLain). *Indian America: A Traveler's Companion,* Third edition. Santa Fe, NM: John Muir Publications, 1993.

Eastman, Charles A. *Old Indian Days.* Lincoln: University of Nebraska Press, 1991.

Eastman, Charles A. and Elaine Goodale Eastman. *Wigwam Evenings: Sioux Folk Tales Retold.* Lincoln: University of Nebraska Press, 1990.

Eckert, Allan W., *A Sorrow in Our Heart: The Life of Tecumseh.* New York: Bantam, 1992.

Edmunds, R. David. *The Potawatomi: Keepers of the Fire.* Norman: University of Oklahoma Press, 1978.

Edwards, R. David and Joseph L. Peyser. *The Fox Wars: The Mesquakie Challenge to New France.* Norman: University of Oklahoma Press, 1993.

Eells, Myron. *The Indians of Puget Sound: The Notebooks of Myron Eells.* Ed. George B. Castile. Seattle: University of Washington Press, 1985.

Eggan Fred. *The American Indian: Perspectives for the Study of Social Change.* New York: University of Cambridge Press, 1966.

Elliot, Michael L. *New Mexico State Monument: Jemez.* Santa Fe: Museum of New Mexico Press, 1993.

Elmendorf, W. W. *The Structure of Twana Culture.* Pullman: Washington State University, 1960.

Elmendorf, W. W. *Twana Narratives: Native Historical Accounts of a Coast Salish Culture.* Seattle: University of Washington Press, 1993.

Emmons, George Thornton. *The Tlingit Indians.* Seattle: University of Washington Press, 1991.

Erdoes, Richard. *The Rain Dance People.* New York: Alfred A. Knopf, 1976.

Ewers, John C. *Plains Indian History and Culture.* Norman: University of Oklahoma Press, 1997.

Fairbanks, Charles H. *The Florida Seminole People*. Phoenix: Intertribal Series, 1973.

Fehrenbach, T. R. *Comanches: Destruction of a People*. New York: Alfred A. Knopf, 1974.

Feit, Harvey A. "Chapter 8—Hunting and the Quest for Power: The James Bay Cree and Whitemen in the Twentieth Century." *Native Peoples: The Canadian Experience*. Toronto: McClellan & Stewart, 1986.

Fejes, Claire. *Villagers: Athabaskan Indian Life Along the Yukon*. New York: Random House, 1981.

The First Americans. Richmond, Virginia: Time-Life Books, 1992.

Fitting, James E. *The Archaeology of Michigan: A Guide to the Prehistory of the Great Lakes Region*. New York: Natural History Press for the American Museum of Natural History, 1969.

Fixico, Donald. "Tribal Leaders and the Demand for Natural Energy Resources on Reservation Lands." *The Plains Indians of the Twentieth Century. Ed. Peter Iverson. Norman: University of Oklahoma Press, 1985.*

Fontana, Bernard L. and John Paul Schaefer. *Of Earth and Little Rain: The Papago Indians*. Flagstaff, AZ: Northland Press, c. 1981.

Forbes, Jack D. *Apache, Navajo, and Spaniard*. Norman: University of Oklahoma Press, 1969, 1994.

Ford, Richard, R. *An Ecological Analysis Involving the Population of San Juan Pueblo, New Mexico*. New York: Garland Publishing, 1992.

Foreman, Grant. *The Five Civilized Tribes*. Norman: University of Oklahoma, 1934.

Fowler, Loretta. *Shared Symbols, Contested Meanings: Gros Ventre Culture and History, 1778–1984*. Ithaca, NY: Cornell University Press, 1987.

Franklin, Robert J. and Pamela A. Bunte. *The Paiute*. New York: Chelsea House, 1990.

Fredenberg, Ralph. "Indian Self-Determination." *Hearings before the Committee on Indian Affairs*, United States Senate. 73d Congress, 2d Session. On S. 2755 and S. 3645, Part 2: pp. 110–13, 1934.

Frey, Rodney. *The World of the Crow Indians: As Driftwood Lodges*. Norman: University of Oklahoma Press, 1987.

Fried, Jacob. "Aboriginal Population of Western Washington State." *Coast Salish and Western Washington Indians III.* Ed. David Agee Horr. New York: Garland Publishing, 1974.

Friesen, Gerald. *The Canadian Prairies: A History.* Lincoln: University of Nebraska Press, 1984.

Galens, Judy, Anna Sheets, and Robyn V. Young, editors. *Gale Encyclopedia of Multicultural America.* Detroit: Gale Research, 1995.

Gardener, Lion. "Lieft Lion Gardener: His Relation of the Pequot Warres (1660)." *Massachusetts Historical Society Collections,* third series, Vol. 3 (1833): pp. 131–60.

Garfield, Viola E. and Linn A. Forrest. *The Wolf and The Raven: Totem Poles of Southeastern Alaska.* Seattle: University of Washington Press, 1993.

Gibbs, George. *Indian Tribes of Washington Territory.* Fairfield, WA: Ye Galleon Press, 1972.

Gibson, Arrell M. *The Chickasaws.* Norman: University of Oklahoma, 1971.

Gifford, E. W. "Californian Kinship Terminologies." *University of California Publications in American Archaeology and Ethnology.* Vol. 18, No. 1. Reprint of Berkeley: University of California Press, 1922.

Gill, Sam D. and Irene F. Sullivan. *Dictionary of Native American Mythology.* London: Oxford University Press, 1992.

Giraud, Marcel. *The Métis in the Canadian West.* Translated by George Woodcock. Lincoln: University of Nebraska Press, 1986.

Goc, Michael J. *Land Rich Enough: An Illustrated History of Oshkosh and Winnebago County.* Northbridge, CA: Windsor Publications/Winnebago County Historical and Archaeological Society, 1988.

Goddard, Pliny Earle. "Life and Culture of the Hupa." *American Archaeology and Ethnology,* Vol. 3. Ed. Frederic Ward Putnam. Berkeley: University of California Publications, 1905. Reprint. New York: Kraus Reprint Corporation, 1964.

Goddard, Pliny Earle. "The Morphology of the Hupa Language." *American Archaeology and Ethnology,* Vol. 1. Ed. Frederic Ward Putnam. Berkeley: University of California Publications, 1903–1904. Reprint. New York: Kraus Reprint Corporation, 1964.

Goldman, Irving. *The Mouth of Heaven: An Introduction to Kwakiutl Religious Thought.* New York: John Wiley & Sons, 1975.

Goldschmidt, Walter R. and Harold E. Driver. "The Hupa White Deerskin Dance." *American Archaeology and Ethnology,* Vol. 35. Ed. A. L. Kroeber, et al. Berkeley: University of California Publications, 1943. Reprint. New York: Kraus Reprint Corporation, 1965.

Gonen, Amiram. *The Encyclopedia of the People of the World.* New York: Henry Holt and Company, 1993.

Goodwin, Glenville. *Myths and Tales of the White Mountain Apache.* New York: American Folk-lore Society, 1939.

Goodwin, Glenville. *The Social Organization of the Western Apache.* Chicago: University of Chicago Press, 1942.

Goodwin, Glenville. *Western Apache Raiding and Warfare.* Tucson: University of Arizona Press, 1971.

Grant, Bruce. *American Indians: Yesterday and Today.* New York: Dutton, 1960.

Green, Donald Edward. *The Creek People.* Phoenix: Indian Tribal Series, 1973.

Green, Michael D. *The Politics of Indian Removal.* Lincoln: University of Nebraska Press, 1982.

Gregory, H. F., ed. *The Southern Caddo: An Anthology.* New York: Garland Publishing, 1986.

Grinnell, George Bird. *Pawnee, Blackfoot and Cheyenne: History and Folklore of the Plains.* New York: Charles Scribner's Sons, 1961.

Grumet, Robert Steven. *Native Americans of the Northwest Coast: A Critical Bibliography.* Bloomington: Indiana University Press, 1979.

Haeberlin, Hermann and Erna Gunther. *The Indians of Puget Sound.* Seattle: University of Washington, 1967.

Hagan, Walter T. *The Sac and Fox Indians.* Norman: University of Oklahoma Press, 1958.

Hahn, Elizabeth. *The Creek.* Vero Beach, FL: Rourke Publications, 1992.

Hahn, Elizabeth. *The Pawnee.* Vero Beach, FL: Rourke Publications, 1992.

Haines, Francis. *The Nez Perces.* Norman: University of Oklahoma Press, 1955.

Haines, Francis. *The Plains Indians: Their Origins, Migrations, and Cultural Development.* New York: Thomas Y. Crowell Company, 1976.

Halbert, Henry S. "Courtship and Marriage Among the Choctaws of Mississippi (1882)." *A Choctaw Source Book.* New York: Garland Publishing, 1985.

Hale, Duane K. *Turtle Tales: Oral Traditions of the Delaware Tribe of Western Oklahoma.* Delaware Tribe of Oklahoma Press, 1984.

Harlow, Neal. *California Conquered: War and Peace on the Pacific, 1846–1850.* Berkeley: University of California Press, 1982.

Harrington, M. R. *Religion and Ceremonies of the Lenape.* New York: Museum of the American Indian Heye Foundation, 1921.

Harrison, Julia D. *Métis, People Between Two Worlds.* Vancouver: Glenbow-Alberta Institute, 1985.

Harrod, Howard L. *Becoming and Remaining a People: Native American Religions on the Northern Plains.* Tucson: University of Arizona Press, 1995.

Haugh, Solanus. *Papago, the Desert People.* Washington, DC: Bureau of Catholic Indian Missions, 1958.

Hauptman, Laurence M. *Tribes and Tribulations: Misconceptions About American Indians and Their Histories.* Albuquerque: University of New Mexico Press, 1995.

Hauptman, Laurence M. and James D. Wherry, eds. *The Pequots in Southern New England: The Fall and Rise of an American Indian Nation.* Norman: University of Oklahoma Press, 1990.

Haviland, William A. and Marjory W. Power. *The Original Vermonters: Native Inhabitants, Past and Present.* Hanover, NH: University Press of New England, 1981.

Heath, D. B., ed. *Mourt's Relation: A Journal of the Pilgrims at Plymouth* (1622). Reprint. Cambridge, MA: Applewood Books, 1986.

Heckewelder, John. *History, Manner, and Customs of the Indian Nations Who Once Inhabited Pennsylvania and the Neighbouring States.* Philadelphia: Historical Society of Pennsylvania, 1876.

Heizer, R. F. and M. A. Whipple, *The California Indians: A Source Book.* Berkeley: University of California Press, 1951.

Heizer, R. F. and T. Kroeber, eds. *Ishi the Last Yahi: A Documentary History.* Berkeley: University of California Press, 1979.

Heizer, Robert F., ed. *The Handbook of North American Indians,* Vol. 8: *California.* Washington, DC: Smithsonian Institution, 1978.

Helm, June, ed. *The Handbook of North American Indians,* Vol. 6: *Subarctic.* Washington, DC: Smithsonian Institution, 1981.

Hickerson, Harold. *The Chippewa and Their Neighbors: A Study in Ethnohistory.* New York: Holt, Rinehart and Winston, 1970.

Hines, Donald M. *Magic in the Mountains, the Yakima Shaman: Power & Practice.* Issaquah, WA: Great Eagle Publishing, 1993.

Hippler, Arthur E. and John R. Wood. *The Subarctic Athabascans.* Fairbanks: University of Alaska, 1974.

Hodge, Frederick Webb. *Handbook of American Indians North of Mexico.* New York: Pageant Books, 1959.

Hoig, Stan. *Tribal Wars of the Southern Plains.* Norman: University of Oklahoma Press, 1993.

Hoijer, Harry. *Apachean Culture History and Ethnology.* Eds. Keith H. Basso and Morris E. Opler. Tucson: University of Arizona Press, 1971.

Hoijer, Harry. *Chiricahua and Mescalero Apache Texts.* Chicago: University of Chicago Press, 1938.

Holt, Ronald L. *Beneath These Red Cliffs: An Ethnohistory of the Utah Paiutes.* Albuquerque: University of New Mexico Press, 1992.

Hoover, Herbert T. *The Yankton Sioux.* New York: Chelsea House, 1988.

Hornung, Rick. *One Nation Under the Gun: Inside the Mohawk Civil War.* New York: Pantheon Books, 1992.

Hothem, Lar. *Treasures of the Mound Builders: Adena and Hopewell Artifacts of Ohio.* Lancaster, Ohio: Hothem House Books, 1989.

Howard, James H., *Shawnee! The Ceremonialism of a Native American Tribe and Its Cultural Background.* Athens: Ohio University Press, 1981.

Hoxie, Frederick E. *The Crow.* New York: Chelsea House, 1989.

Hoxie, Frederick E., ed. *Encyclopedia of North American Indians.* Boston: Houghton Mifflin Company, 1996.

Hoyt, Anne Kelley. *The Bibliography of the Chickasaw.* Metuchen, New Jersey: The Scarecrow Press, 1987.

Hrdlicka, Ales. *Physical Anthropology of the Lenape or Delawares, and of the Eastern Indians in General.* Washington, DC: U.S. Government Printing Office, 1916.

Hudson, Charles. *The Southeastern Indians.* Knoxville: University of Tennessee Press, 1976.

Hudson, Peter J. "Choctaw Indian Dishes (1939)." *A Choctaw Source Book.* New York: Garland Publishing, 1985: pp. 333–35.

Hudson, Travis and Ernest Underhay. *Crystals in the Sky: An Intellectual Odyssey Involving Chumash Astronomy, Cosmology and Rock Art.* Socorro, NM: Ballena Press, 1978.

Hyde, George E. *Indians of the Woodlands: From Prehistoric Times to 1725.* Norman: University of Oklahoma Press, 1962.

Ignacio, Amera. "Her Remark Offended Me." *Native Heritage: Personal Accounts by American Indians, 1790 to the Present.* Ed. Arlene Hirschfelder. New York: Macmillan, 1995.

Indian America; A Traveler's Companion. Santa Fe: John Muir Publications, 1989.

Indian Reservations: A State and Federal Handbook. Jefferson, NC: McFarland & Co., 1974.

Iverson, Peter. *The Plains Indians of the Twentieth Century.* Norman: University of Oklahoma Press, 1986.

Ives, John, W. *A Theory of Northern Athapaskan Prehistory.* Boulder, CO: Westview Press, 1990.

Jennings, Francis. *The Invasion of America: Indians, Colonization, and the Cant of Conquest.* Chapel Hill: University of North Carolina Press, 1975.

Joe, Rita and Lynn Henry. *Song of Rita Joe: Autobiography of a Mi'kmaq Poet.* Lincoln: University of Nebraska Press, 1996.

Johansen, Bruce E. *Life and Death in Mohawk Country.* Golden, CO: North American Press, 1993.

Johnson, Elias. *Legends, Traditions and Laws of the Iroquois, or Six Nations, and History of the Tuscarora Indians* (1881). Reprint. New York: AMS Press, 1978.

Johnson, John F. C., ed. *Eyak Legends: Stories and Photographs.* Anchorage: Chugach Heritage Foundation, n.d.

Johnson, Michael G. *The Native Tribes of North America: A Concise Encyclopedia.* New York: Macmillan, 1994.

Johnston, Basil H. *Tales the Elders Told: Ojibway Legends.* Toronto: Royal Ontario Museum, 1981.

Jonaitis, Aldona. *Art of the Northern Tlingit.* Seattle, Washington: University of Washington Press, 1986.

Jonaitis, Aldona, ed. *Chiefly Feasts: The Enduring Kwakiutl Potlatch.* New York: American Museum of Natural History, 1991.

Jorgensen, Joseph G. *Salish Language and Culture.* Bloomington: Indiana University Publications, 1969.

Jorgensen, Joseph G. *The Sun Dance Religion: Power for the Powerless.* Chicago: University of Chicago Press, 1972.

Joseph, Alice, Jane Chesky, and Rosamond B. Spicer. *The Desert People: A Study of the Papago Indians.* Chicago, IL: University of Chicago Press, 1974.

Josephy, Alvin M. Jr. *500 Nations: An Illustrated History of North American Indians.* New York: Alfred A. Knopf, 1994.

Josephy, Alvin M. Jr. *The Indian Heritage of America.* New York: Alfred A. Knopf, 1968.

Josephy, Alvin M. Jr. *The Nez Perce Indians and the Opening of the Northwest.* New Haven, CT: Yale University Press, 1965.

Josephy, Alvin M. Jr. *Now That the Buffalo's Gone: A Study of Today's American Indians.* New York: Alfred A. Knopf, 1982.

Kalifornsky, Peter. *A Dena'ina Legacy: K'tl'egh'i Sukdu: The Collected Writings of Peter Kalifornsky.* Eds. James Kari and Alan Boraas. Fairbanks: Alaska Native Language Center, 1991.

Kappler, Charles J. *Indian Affairs, Laws, and Treaties,* four volumes. Washington, DC: U.S. Government Printing Office, 1929.

Kari, James, ed. *Athabaskan Stories from Anvik: Rev. John W. Chapman's "Ten'a Texts and Tales."* Fairbanks: Alaska Native Language Center, 1981.

Kari, James, translator and editor. "When They Were Killed at 'Lake That Has an Arm' (Kluane Lake)." *Tatl'ahwt'aenn Nenn': The Headwaters Peoples Country: Narratives of the Upper Ahtna Athabaskans.* Fairbanks: Alaska Native Language Center, 1985.

Kasner, Leone Leston. *Siletz: Survival for an Artifact.* Dallas OR: Itemizer-Observer, 1977.

Kennedy, Roger G. *Hidden Cities: The Discovery and Loss of Ancient American Civilization.* New York: Macmillan, 1994.

Kenner, Charles L. *A History of New Mexican-Plains Indian Relations.* Norman: University of Oklahoma Press, 1969, 1994.

Kent, Zachary, *Tecumseh.* Chicago, IL: Children's Press, 1992.

Kidwell, Clara Sue and Charles Roberts. *The Choctaws: A Critical Bibliography.* Bloomington: Indiana University Press for the Newberry Library, 1980.

Kirk, Ruth and Richard D. Daugherty. *Hunter of the Whale.* New York: William Morrow, 1974.

Klein, Barry T. *Reference Encyclopedia of the American Indian,* Seventh edition. West Nyack, NY: Todd Publications, 1995.

Klein, Laura F. and Lillian A. Ackerman. *Women and Power in Native North America.* Norman: University of Oklahoma, 1995.

Kluckhohn, Clyde and Dorothea Leighton. *The Navaho.* 1946. Revised edition. Cambridge, MA: Harvard University Press, 1974.

Korp, Maureen. *The Sacred Geography of the American Mound Builders.* New York: Edwin Mellen Press, 1990.

Kraft, Herbert C. *The Lenape: Archaeology, History, and Ethnography.* Newark: New Jersey Historical Society, 1986.

Kraft, Herbert C. *The Lenape Indians of New Jersey.* South Orange, NJ: Seton Hall University Museum, 1987.

Krech, Shepard III, ed. *Indians, Animals and the Fur Trade.* Athens: University of Georgia Press, 1981.

Kroeber, Alfred L. "The Achomawi and Atsugewi," "The Chilula.," "The Luiseño: Elements of Civilization," "The Luiseño: Organization of Civilization," "The Miwok," and "The Pomo." *Handbook of the Indians of California.* Washington, DC: U.S. Government Printing Office, 1925.

Krupp, E. C. *Beyond the Blue Horizon: Myths & Legends of the Sun, Moon, Stars, & Planets.* New York: Oxford University Press, 1991.

Lacey, Theresa Jensen. *The Pawnee.* New York: Chelsea House Publishers, 1996.

Ladd, Edmund J. "Zuñi Religion and Philosophy." *Zuñi & El Morro.* Santa Fe: SAR Press, 1983.

Langdon, Steve J. *The Native People of Alaska.* Anchorage: Greatland Graphics, 1993.

Laubin, Reginald and Gladys Laubin. *Indian Dances of North America: Their Importance to Indian Life.* Norman: University of Oklahoma Press, 1976.

Laughlin, William S. "The Aleut-Eskimo Community." *The North American Indians: A Sourcebook.* Ed. Roger C. Owen. New York: Macmillan, 1967.

Leach, Douglas E. *Flintlock and Tomahawk: New England in King Philip's War.* New York: Macmillan, 1959.

Leitch, Barbara A. *A Concise Dictionary of Indian Tribes of North America.* Algonac, MI: Reference Publications, 1979.

Lewis, Anna. *Chief Pushmataha, American Patriot: The Story of the Choctaws' Struggle for Survival.* New York: Exposition Press, 1959.

Lewis, David Rich. *Neither Wolf Nor Dog: American Indians, Environment, and Agrarian Change.* Oxford: Oxford University Press, 1994.

Liptak, Karen. *North American Indian Ceremonies.* New York: Franklin Watts, 1992.

Lowie, Robert H. *The Crow Indians.* Lincoln: University of Nebraska Press, 1983.

Lowie, Robert H. *Indians of the Plains.* Garden City, NY: Natural History Press, 1963.

Lucius, William A. and David A. Breternitz. *Northern Anasazi Ceramic Styles: A Fieldguide for Identification.* Center for Indigenous Studies in the Americas Publications in Anthropology, 1992.

Lund, Annabel. *Heartbeat: World Eskimo Indian Olympics: Alaska Native Sport and Dance Traditions.* Juneau: Fairweather Press, 1986.

Lurie, Nancy Oestreich. "Weetamoo, 1638–1676." *North American Indian Lives.* Milwaukee: Milwaukee Public Library, 1985.

MacEwan, Grant. *Métis Makers of History.* Saskatoon: Western Producer Prairie Books, 1981.

Madsen, Brigham D. *The Shoshoni Frontier and the Bear River Massacre.* Salt Lake City: University of Utah Press, 1985.

Mahon, John K. *History of the Second Seminole War 1835–1842.* Gainsville: University of Florida Press, 1967.

Maillard, Antoine Simon and Joseph M. Bellenger. *Grammaire de la Langue Mikmaque.* English translation published as *Grammar of the Mikmaque Language.* New York: AMS Press, 1970.

Mails, Thomas E. *The Cherokee People: The Story of the Cherokees from Earliest Origins to Contemporary Times.* Tulsa, OK: Council Oak Books, 1992.

Mails, Thomas E. *The Mystic Warriors of the Plains: The Culture, Arts, Crafts and Religion of the Plains Indians.* Tulsa: Council Oaks Books, 1991.

Mails, Thomas E. *Peoples of the Plains.* Tulsa, OK: Council Oak Books, 1997.

Mails, Thomas E. *The Pueblo Children of the Earth Mother.* Vol. 2. Garden City, NY: Doubleday, 1983.

Malinowksi, Sharon, ed. *Notable Native Americans.* Detroit: Gale Research, 1995.

Malinowski, Sharon and Simon Glickman, eds. *Native North American Biography.* Detroit: U•X•L, 1996.

Malone, Patrick M. *The Skulking Way of War: Technology and Tactics Among the New England Indians.* Lanham, MA: Madison Books, 1991.

Mandelbaum, David G. *The Plains Cree: An Ethnographic, Historical, and Comparative Study.* Regina, Saskatchewan: Canadian Plains Research Center, 1979.

Markowitz, Harvey, ed. *American Indians,* Pasadena, CA: Salem Press, 1995.

Marquis, Arnold. *A Guide to America's Indians: Ceremonials, Reservations, and Museums.* Norman: University of Oklahoma Press, 1974.

Marriott, Alice L. *The Ten Grandmothers.* Norman: University of Oklahoma Press, 1945.

Marriott, Alice and Carol K. Rachlin. *Plains Indian Mythology.* New York: Thomas Y. Crowell, 1975.

Martin, Calvin. *Keepers of the Game: Indian-Animal Relationships and the Fur Trade.* Berkeley: University of California Press, 1978.

Matthiessen, Peter. *In the Spirit of Crazy Horse.* New York: Viking Penguin, 1980.

Maxwell, James A., ed. *America's Fascinating Indian Heritage.* New York: The Reader's Digest Association, 1978.

Mayhall, Mildred P. *The Kiowas.* Norman: University of Oklahoma Press, 1962.

Mays, Buddy. *Indian Villages of the Southwest.* San Francisco: Chronicle Books, 1985.

McBride, Bunny. *Molly Spotted Elk: A Penobscot in Paris.* Norman and London: University of Oklahoma Press, 1995.

McFadden, Steven. *Profiles in Wisdom: Native Elders Speak About the Earth.* Sante Fe: Bear & Co., 1991.

McFee, Malcolm. *Modern Blackfeet: Montanans on a Reservation.* New York: Holt, Rinehart and Winston, 1972.

McGinnis, Anthony. *Counting Coup and Cutting Horses: Intertribal Warfare on the Northern Plains 1738–1889.* Evergreen, CO: Cordillera Press, 1990.

McKee, Jesse O. and Jon A. Schlenker. *The Choctaws: Cultural Evolution of a Native American Tribe.* Jackson: University Press of Mississippi, 1980.

McKennan, Robert, A. "The Upper Tanana Indians." *Yale University Publications in Anthropology: 55.* New Haven, CT: Yale University, 1959.

Melody, Michael E. *The Apaches: A Critical Bibliography.* Bloomington: Indiana University Press, 1977.

Merriam, C. Hart. "The Luiseño: Observations on Mission Indians." *Studies of California Indians.* Edited by the Staff of the Department of Anthropology of the University of California. Berkeley: University of California Press, 1962.

Meyer, Roy W. *History of the Santee Sioux: United States Indian Policy on Trial.* Lincoln: University of Nebraska Press, 1993.

Miller, Bruce W. *Chumash: A Picture of Their World.* Los Osos, CA: Sand River Press, 1988.

Miller, Jay. *The Delaware.* Chicago: Childrens Press, 1994.

Milliken, Randall. *A Time of Little Choice: The Disintegration of Tribal Culture in the San Francisco Bay Area, 1769–1810*. Menlo Park, CA: Ballena Press, 1995.

Milloy, John S. *The Plains Cree: Trade, Diplomacy and War, 1790 to 1870*. Winnipeg: University of Manitoba Press, 1988.

Minge, Ward Alan. *Acoma: Pueblo in the Sky*. Albuquerque: University of New Mexico Press, 1976.

Minority Rights Group. *Polar Peoples: Self Determination and Development*. London: Minority Rights Publications, 1994.

Mississippian Communities and Households. Tuscaloosa: University of Alabama Press, 1995.

Momaday, N. Scott. *The Way to Rainy Mountain*. Albuquerque: University of New Mexico Press, 1969.

Moore, John H. *The Cheyenne Nation: A Social and Demographic History*. Lincoln: University of Nebraska Press, 1987.

Moorhead, Max L. *The Apache Frontier: Jacobo Ugarte and Spanish-Indian Relations in Northern New Spain, 1769–1791*. Norman: University of Oklahoma Press, 1968.

Moquin, Wayne, ed. *Great Documents in American Indian History*. New York: Da Capo Press, 1973.

Morgan, Lewis H. *League of the Ho-de-no-sau-nee or Iroquois*. New Haven, CT: Human Relations Area Files, 1954: p. 243.

Morrison, R. Bruce and C. Roderick Wilson, eds. *Native Peoples: The Canadian Experience*. Toronto: McClellan & Stewart, 1986.

Murie, James R. *Ceremonies of the Pawnee*. Smithsonian Contributions to Anthropology, No. 27. Washington, DC: Smithsonian Institution, 1981. Reprint. Lincoln: University of Nebraska Press for the American Indian Studies Research Institute, 1989.

Murphy, Robert F. and Yolanda Murphy. "Shoshone-Bannock Subsistence and Society." *Anthropological Records*. 16:7. Berkeley: University of California Press, 1960.

Myers, Arthur. *The Pawnee*. New York: F. Watts, 1993.

Myers, William Starr, ed. *The Story of New Jersey*, Volume 1. Ed. New York: Lewis Historical Publishing Company, 1945.

Mysteries of the Ancient Americas: The New World Before Columbus. Pleasantville, NY: The Reader's Digest Association, 1986.

Nabakov, Peter and Robert Easton. *Native American Architecture.* New York: Oxford University Press, 1989.

Nairne, Thomas. *Nairne's Mushogean Journals: The 1708 Expedition to the Mississippi River.* Jackson: University Press of Mississippi, 1988.

Native Cultures in Alaska. Anchorage: Alaska Geographic Society, 1996.

Newcomb, W. W. Jr. *The Indians of Texas: From Prehistoric to Modern Times.* Austin: University of Texas Press, 1961.

Newkumet, Vynola Beaver and Howard L. Meredith. *Hasinai: A Traditional History of the Caddo Confederacy.* College Station: Texas A & M University Press, 1988.

Noble, David Grant. *Pueblos, Villages, Forts & Trails: A Guide to New Mexico's Past.* Albuquerque: University of New Mexico Press, 1994.

Northway, Walter. *Walter Northway.* Fairbanks: Alaska Native Language Center, 1987.

Norton, Jack. *Genocide in Northwestern California: When Our Worlds Cried.* San Francisco: Indian Historian Press, 1979.

O'Brien, Sharon. *American Indian Tribal Governments.* Norman: University of Oklahoma Press, 1989.

Olmsted, D. L. *Achumawi Dictionary.* Berkeley: University of California Press, 1966.

Olson, Ronald L. *The Quinault Indians.* Seattle: University of Washington Press, 1967.

O'Neill, Laurie A. *The Shawnees: People of the Eastern Woodlands.* Brookfield, CT: The Millbrook Press, 1995.

Opler, Morris Edward. *An Apache Life-Way.* New York: Cooper Square Publishers, 1965.

Orr, Charles, ed. *History of the Pequot War.* Cleveland: Helman-Taylor, 1897.

Ortiz, Alfonso, ed. *The Handbook of North American Indians,* Vol. 10: *Southwest.* Washington, DC: Smithsonian Institution, 1983.

Ortiz, Alfonso. *The Pueblo.* New York: Chelsea House Publishers, 1992.

Osgood, Cornelius. "Ingalik Mental Culture." *Yale University Publications in Anthropology: 56*. New Haven, CT: Yale University, 1959.

Oswalt, Wendell H. "The Crow: Plains Warriors and Bison Hunters." *This Land Was Theirs: A Study of North American Indians*. Mountain View, CA: Mayfield Publishing, 1988.

Owen, Roger C., James J. F. Deetz, and Anthony D. Fisher, eds. *A Guide to Indian Tribes of the Pacific Northwest*. Norman: University of Oklahoma Press, 1986.

Owen, Roger C., James J. F. Deetz, and Anthony D. Fisher, eds. *Indians of the Pacific Northwest: A History*. Norman: University of Oklahoma Press, 1981.

Owen, Roger C., James J. F. Deetz, and Anthony D. Fisher, eds. *The North American Indians: A Sourcebook*. New York: MacMillan, 1967.

Parsons, Elsie Clews. "Notes on the Caddo." *Memoirs of the American Anthropological Association*, No. 57. Menasha, WI: American Anthropological Association, 1941.

Parsons, Elsie Clews. *Pueblo Mothers and Children*. Ed. Barbara A. Babcock. Santa Fe: Ancient City Press, 1991.

Parsons, Elsie Clews. *The Social Organization of the Tewa of New Mexico*. American Anthropological Association Memoirs, Nos. 36–39. Reprint. New York: Kraus, 1964.

Patencio, Francisco. *Stories and Legends of the Palm Springs Indians As Told to Margaret Boynton*. Los Angeles: Times-Mirror Press, 1943.

Paterek, Josephine. *Encyclopedia of American Indian Costume*. Santa Barbara: ABC-CLIO, 1994.

Pauketat, Timothy R. *Temples for Cahokia Lords*. Ann Arbor: University of Michigan, Museum of Anthropology, 1993.

Peat, F. David. *Lighting the Seventh Fire: The Spiritual Ways, Healing, and Science of the Native American*. NY: Carol Publishing Group, 1994.

Penney, David W. *Art of the American Indian Frontier: The Chandler-Pohrt Collection*. Seattle: University of Washington Press, 1992.

Perdue, Theda. *The Cherokee*. New York: Chelsea House Publishers, 1989.

Peroff, N. C. *Menominee Drums: Tribal Termination and Restoration, 1954–1974*. Norman: University of Oklahoma Press, 1982.

Perry, Richard J. *Apache Reservation: Indigenous Peoples and the American State*. Austin: University of Texas Press, 1993.

Perry, Richard J. *Western Apache Heritage: People of the Mountain Corridor.* Austin: University of Texas Press, 1991.

Perttula, Timothy K. "The Caddo Nation." *Archeological and Ethnohistoric Perspectives*. Austin: University of Texas Press, 1992.

Phillips, G.H. *Indians and Indian Agents: The Origins of the Reservation System in California, 1849–1852*. Norman: University of Oklahoma Press, 1997.

Place, Ann Marie. "Putting a Face on Colonization: Factionalism and Gender Politics in the Life History of Awashunkes, the 'Squaw Sachem' of Saconet." *Northeastern Indians Lives*. Ed. Robert S. Grumet. Amherst: University of Massachusetts Press, 1996.

Pond, Samuel. *The Dakota People or Sioux in Minnesota as They Were in 1834*. St. Paul: Minnesota Historical Society Press, 1986.

Pope, Saxton T. "The Medical History of Ishi." *University of California Publications in American Archaeology and Ethnology*. Vol. 13, No. 5. Berkeley: University of California Press, 1920.

Pope, Saxton T. "Yahi Archery." *University of California Publications in American Archaeology and Ethnology*, Vol. 13, No. 3. Berkeley: University of California Press, 1923.

Porter, Frank W. III. *The Coast Salish Peoples*. New York: Chelsea House Publishers, 1989.

Powers, Stephen. "The Achomawi." *Tribes of California*. Berkeley: University of California Press, 1976. Reprinted from *Contributions to North American Ethnology*, Vol. 3. Washington, DC: U.S. Government Printing Office, 1877.

Preacher, Stephen. *Anasazi Sunrise: The Mystery of Sacrifice Rock*. El Cajon, CA: The Rugged Individualist, 1992.

Press, Margaret L. "Chemehuevi: A Grammar and Lexicon." *Linguistics*, Vol. 92. Berkeley: University of California Press, 1979.

Rand, Silas Tertius. *Dictionary of the Language of the Micmac Indians, Who Reside in Nova Scotia, New Brunswick, Prince Edward Island, Cape Breton, and Newfoundland*. Halifax, Nova Scotia: Nova Scotia Print Co., 1888. Reprint. New York, Johnson Reprint Corp., 1972.

Ray, Arthur J. *Indians in the Fur Trade: Their Role as Trappers, Hunters & Middle Man in the Lands Southwest of Hudson Bay, 1660–1860.* Toronto: University of Toronto Press, 1974.

Reddy, Marlita A. *Statistical Record of Native North Americans.* Detroit: Gale Research, 1996.

Rice, Julian, ed. *Deer Women and Elk Men: The Lakota Narratives of Ella Deloria.* Albuquerque: University of New Mexico Press, 1992.

Richardson, Rupert Norval. *The Comanche Barrier to the South Plains Settlement.* Glendale, CA: Arthur H. Clarke, 1955.

Roberts, David. *In Search of the Old Ones.* New York: Simon & Schuster, 1996.

Rockwell, Wilson. *The Utes: A Forgotten People.* Denver, CO: Alan Swallow, 1956.

Rohner, Ronald P. and Evelyn C. Rohner. *The Kwakiutl: Indians of British Columbia.* New York: Holt, Rinehart and Winston, 1970.

Rollings, Willard H. *The Osage: An Ethnohistorical Study of Hegemony on the Prairie-Plains.* Columbia: University of Missouri Press, 1992.

Rountree, Helen C., ed. *Pocahontas's People: The Powhatan Indians of Virginia through Four Centuries.* Norman: University of Oklahoma Press, 1990.

Rountree, Helen C., ed. *Powhatan Foreign Relations, 1500–1722.* Charlottesville: University Press of Virginia, 1993.

Rountree, Helen C., ed. *The Powhatan Indians of Virginia: Their Native Culture.* Norman: University of Oklahoma Press, 1989.

Ruby, Robert H. *The Chinook Indians: Traders of the Lower Columbia River.* Norman: University of Oklahoma Press, 1976.

Ruby, Robert H. and John A. Brown. *A Guide to Indian Tribes of the Pacific Northwest.* Norman: University of Oklahoma Press, 1986.

Russell, Frank. *The Pima Indians.* Tucson: University of Arizona Press, 1975.

Salisbury, Richard F. *A Homeland for the Cree: Regional Development in James Bay 1971–1981.* Kingston & Montreal: McGill-Queen's University Press, 1986.

Salzmann, Zdenek. *The Arapaho Indians: A Research Guide and Bibliography.* New York: Greenwood Press, 1988.

Samuel, Cheryl. *The Chilkat Dancing Blanket.* Seattle: Pacific Search Press, 1982.

Sando, Joe S. *Pueblo Nations: Eight Centuries of Pueblo Indian History.* Santa Fe: Clear Light Publishers, 1992.

Sauter, John and Bruce Johnson. *Tillamook Indians of the Oregon Coast.* Portland OR: Binfords and Mort, 1974.

Sawchuck, Joe. *The Métis of Manitoba: Reformulation of an Ethnic Identity.* Toronto: Peter Martin Associates, 1978.

Schlesier, Karl H. "Introduction," and "Commentary: A History of Ethnic Groups in the Great Plains A.D. 500–1550." *Plains Indians, A.D. 500–1500: The Archaeological Past of Historic Groups.* Ed. Karl H. Schlesier. Norman: University of Oklahoma Press, 1994.

Schultz, Willard James. *Blackfeet and Buffalo: Memories of Life among the Indians.* Norman: University of Oklahoma Press, 1962.

Schuster, Helen. *The Yakimas: A Critical Bibliography.* Bloomington: Indiana University Press, 1982.

Segal, Charles M. and David C. Stineback, eds. *Puritans, Indians and Manifest Destiny.* New York: Putnam, 1977.

Seger, John H. *Early Days among the Cheyenne and Arapaho Indians.* Ed. Stanley Vestal. Norman: University of Oklahoma Press, 1956.

Seiler, Hansjakob. *Cahuilla Texts with an Introduction.* Bloomington: Indiana University, 1970.

Shaffer, Lynda Norene. *Native Americans Before 1492: The Moundbuilding Centers of the Eastern Woodlands.* New York: M. E. Sharpe, 1992.

Shames, Deborah, ed. *Freedom with Reservation: The Menominee Struggle to Save Their Land and People.* Madison: National Committee to Save the Menominee People and Forests/Wisconsin Indian Legal Services, 1972.

Shawano, Marlene Miller. *Native Dress of the Stockbridge Munsee Band Mohican Indians.* Stockbridge Munsee Reservation Library, n.d.

Shipek, Florence. *Pushed into the Rocks: Southern California Indian Land Tenure, 1769–1986.* Lincoln: University of Nebraska Press, 1990.

Silverberg, Robert. *The Mound Builders.* Greenwich, CT: New York Graphic Society, Ltd., 1970.

Siy, Alexandra, *The Eeyou: People of Eastern James Bay.* New York: Dillon Press, 1993.

Slickpoo, Allen P. and Deward E. Walker Jr. *Noon Nee-Me-Poo: We, the Nez Perces.* Lapwai: Nez Perce Tribe of Idaho, 1973.

Smelcer, John. "Dotson'Sa, Great Raven Makes the World." *The Raven and the Totem: Traditional Alaska Native Myths and Tales.* Anchorage: Salmon Run, 1992: pp. 124–25.

Smith, Anne M., ed. *Shoshone Tales.* Salt Lake City: University of Utah Press, 1993.

Smith, F. Todd. *The Caddo Indians: Tribes at the Convergence of Empires, 1542–1854.* College Station: University of Texas A&M Press, 1995.

Smith, Marian W. *Indians of the Urban Northwest.* New York: AMS Press, 1949.

Smith, Marian W. *The Puyallup-Nisqually.* New York: Columbia University Press, 1940.

Snow, Dean R. *The Iroquois.* Cambridge, MA: Blackwell Publishers, 1994.

Speck, Frank G. *Penobscot Man: The Life History of a Forest Tribe in Maine.* Philadelphia: University of Pennsylvania Press, 1940.

Speck, Frank G. *A Study of the Indian Big House Ceremony.* Harrisburg: Pennsylvania Historical Commission, 1931.

Spector, Janet D. *What This Awl Means: Feminist Archaeology at a Wahpeton Dakota Village.* St. Paul: Minnesota Historical Society Press, 1993.

Spicer, Edward H. *Cycles of Conquest: The Impact of Spain, Mexico, and the United States on the Indians of the Southwest, 1533–1960.* Tucson, AZ: University of Arizona Press, 1962.

Spindler, George and Louise Spindler. *Dreamers With Power: The Menomini Indians.* New York: Holt, Rinehart & Winston, 1971.

Spittal, W. G., ed. *Iroquois Women: An Anthology.* Ohsweken, Ontario: Iroqrafts Ltd., 1990.

Spradley, James P. *Guests Never Leave Hungry: The Autobiography of James Sewid, A Kwakiutl Indian.* New Haven: Yale University Press, 1969.

Statistical Data for Planning Stockbridge Munsee Reservation. Billings, MT: U.S. Department of the Interior, Bureau of Indian Affairs, 1975.

Steele, Ian K. *Warpaths: Invasions of North America.* New York: Oxford University Press, 1994.

Steward, Julian H. *Basin-Plateau Aboriginal Sociopolitical Groups.* Washington, DC: Smithsonian Institution. *The Bureau of American Ethnology Bulletin,* No. 120. Washington, DC: U.S. Government Printing Office, 1938.

Stewart, Omer C. *Peyote Religion: A History.* Norman: University of Oklahoma, 1987.

Stevens, Susan McCullough. "Passamaquoddy Economic Development in Cultural and Historical Perspective." *World Anthropology: American Indian Economic Development.* Ed. Sam Stanley. The Hague: Mouton Publishers, 1978.

Stockel, H. Henrietta. "Ceremonies and Celebrations." *Women Of the Apache Nation: Voices of Truth.* Reno: University of Nevada Press, 1991.

Subarctic. Ed. June Helm. Washington, DC: Smithsonian Institution, 1981.

Suttles, Wayne, ed. *The Handbook of North American Indians,* Vol. 7: *Northwest Coast.* Washington, DC: Smithsonian Institution, 1990.

Swanson, Earl H, ed. *Languages and Culture of Western North America.* Pocatello: Idaho State University Press, 1970.

Swanton, John Reed. *Indian Tribes of the Lower Mississippi Valley and Adjacent Coast of the Gulf of Mexico.* Washington, DC: U.S. Government Printing Office, 1911.

Swanton, John Reed. *The Indian Tribes of North America,* Vol. 1: *Northeast.* Washington, DC: Smithsonian Institution. Reprinted from: *The Bureau of American Ethnology Bulletin,* No. 145. Washington, DC: U.S. Government Printing Office, 1953.

Swanton, John Reed. *Source Material for the Social and Ceremonial Life of the Choctaw Indians.* Bulletin No. 103. Washington, DC: U.S. Government Printing Office, 1931.

Symington, Fraser. *The Canadian Indian: The Illustrated History of the Great Tribes of Canada.* Toronto: McClelland & Stewart, 1969.

Tanner, Helen H., ed. *Atlas of Great Lakes Indian History.* Norman: University of Oklahoma Press, 1987.

Tantaquidgeon, Gladys. *Folk Medicine of the Delaware and Related Algonkian Indians*. Harrisburg: Pennsylvania Historical and Museum Commission, Anthropological Series 3, 1972.

Tantaquidgeon, Gladys. *A Study of Delaware Indian Medicine Practice and Folk Beliefs*. Harrisburg: Pennsylvania Historical Commission, 1942.

Teit, James A. "The Salishan Tribes of the Western Plateaus." *Bureau of American Ethnology Annual Report*. No. 45. Ed. Franz Boas. 1927–1928.

Tennberg, Monica, ed. *Unity and Diversity in Arctic Societies*. Rovaniemi, Finland: International Arctic Social Sciences Association, 1996.

Terrell, John Upton. *American Indian Almanac*. New York: World Publishing, 1971.

Thomas, Cyrus. *Report on the Mound Explorations of the Bureau of Ethnology*. Washington, DC: Smithsonian Institution, 1894.

Thomas, David Hurst, ed. *A Great Basin Shoshonean Source Book*. New York: Garland Publishing, 1986.

Thompson, Chad. *Athabaskan Languages and the Schools: A Handbook for Teachers*. Juneau: Alaska Department of Education, 1984.

Thompson, Judy. *From the Land: Two Hundred Years of Dene Clothing*. Hull, Quebec: Canadian Museum of Civilization, 1994.

Through Indian Eyes: The Untold Story of Native American Peoples. Pleasantville, NY: Reader's Digest Association, 1995.

Tilton, Robert S. *Pocahontas: The Evolution of an American Narrative*. New York: Cambridge University Press, 1994.

Tohono O'Odham: History of the Desert People. Arizona: Papago Tribe, c1985.

Tooker, Elisabeth, ed. *An Iroquois Source Book,* Volumes 1 and 2. New York: Garland Publishing, 1985.

"Traditional and Contemporary Ceremonies, Rituals, Festivals, Music, and Dance." *Native America: Portrait of the Peoples*. Ed. Duane Champagne. Detroit: Gale Research, 1994.

Trafzer, Clifford E. *The Chinook*. New York: Chelsea House, 1990.

Trafzer, Clifford E. *Yakima, Palouse, Cayuse, Umatilla, Walla Walla, and Wanapum Indians.* Metuchen, New Jersey: Scarecrow Press, 1992.

Trigger, Bruce G., ed. *The Handbook of North American Indians,* Vol. 15: *Northeast.* Washington, DC: Smithsonian Institution, 1978.

Trigger, Bruce G. *Natives and Newcomers: Canada's "Heroic Age" Reconsidered.* Manchester: McGill-Queen's University Press, 1985.

Trimble, Stephen. *The People: Indians of the American Southwest.* Santa Fe: NM: Sar Press, 1993.

Tyson, Carl N. *The Pawnee People.* Phoenix: Indian Tribal Series, 1976.

Underhill, Ruth. *The Autobiography of a Papago Woman.* Menasha, WI: American Anthropological Memoirs #48, 1936.

Underhill, Ruth. *Life in the Pueblos.* Santa Fe: Ancient City Press, 1991.

Underhill, Ruth. *Singing for Power.* Tucson: University of Arizona Press, 1979.

United American Indians of New England. "National Day of Mourning." *Literature of the American Indian.* Ed. Thomas E. Sanders and Walter W. Peek. Abridged edition. Beverly Hills, CA: Glencoe Press, 1976.

The Vinland Sagas: The Norse Discovery of America. Translated by Magnus Magnusson and Hermann Palsson. Baltimore: Penguin, 1965.

Vogel, Virgil J. *American Indian Medicine.* Norman: University of Oklahoma Press, 1970.

The Wabanakis of Maine and the Maritimes: A Resource Book About Penobscot, Passamaquoddy, Maliseet, Micmac, and Abenaki Indians. Philadelphia: American Friends Service Committee (AFSC), 1989.

Waldman, Carl. *Atlas of the North American Indian.* New York: Facts On File, 1985.

Waldman, Carl. *Encyclopedia of Native American Tribes.* New York: Facts on File, 1988.

Waldman, Carl. *Who Was Who in Native American History: Indians and NonIndians From Early Contacts Through 1900.* New York: Facts on File, 1990.

Waldman, Harry, ed. "Caddo." *Encyclopedia of Indians of the Americas.* St. Clair Shores, MI: Scholarly Press, 1974.

Walens, Stanley. *Feasting with Cannibals: An Essay on Kwakiutl Cosmology.* Princeton, NJ: Princeton University Press, 1981.

Wallace, Anthony F. C. *The Death and Rebirth of the Seneca: The History and Culture of the Great Iroquois Nation, Their Destruction and Demoralization, and Their Cultural Revival at the Hands of the Indian Visionary, Handsome Lake.* New York: Knopf, 1969.

Wallace, Anthony F. C. *King of the Delawares: Teedyuscung 1700–1763.* Philadelphia: University of Pennsylvania Press, 1949.

Walthall, John A. *Moundville: An Introduction to the Archaeology of a Mississippian Chiefdom.* Tuscaloosa: University of Alabama, Alabama Museum of Natural History, 1977.

Warren, William W. *History of the Ojibway People.* St. Paul: Minnesota Historical Society Press, 1885, reprint 1984.

Waterman, Thomas T. "The Yana Indians." *University of California Publications in American Archaeology and Ethnology,* Vol. 13, No. 2. Berkeley: University of California Press, 1918.

Weatherford, Jack. *Native Roots, How the Indians Enriched America.* New York: Ballantine Books, 1991.

Wedel, Waldo R. *An Introduction to Pawnee Archeology.* Bulletin of the Smithsonian Institution, Bureau of American Ethnology, No. 112. Washington, DC: U.S. Government Printing Office, 1936. Reprint. Lincoln, NE: J & L Reprint, 1977.

Wedel, Waldo R. *Prehistoric Man on the Great Plains.* Norman: University of Oklahoma Press, 1961.

Wells, Samuel J. and Roseanna Tubby, eds. *After Removal: The Choctaw in Mississippi.* Jackson: University Press of Mississippi, 1986.

Weltfish, Gene. *The Lost Universe: Pawnee Life and Culture.* Lincoln: University of Nebraska Press, 1977.

Weslager, Clinton A. *The Delaware Indian Westward Migration.* Wallingford, PA: Middle Atlantic Press, 1978.

Weslager, Clinton A. *The Delaware Indians: A History.* New Brunswick, NJ: Rutgers University Press, 1972.

White, Leslie A. *The Acoma Indians, People of the Sky City.* Originally published in *47th Annual Report of the Bureau of American Ethnology.* Washington, DC: Smithsonian Institution, 1932; Glorieta, NM: The Rio Grande Press, 1973.

White, Raymond. "Religion and Its Role Among the Luiseño." *Native Californians: A Theoretical Retrospective.* Eds. Lowell J. Bean and Thomas C. Blackburn. Socorro, NM: Ballena Press, 1976.

White, Richard. *Land Use, Environment, and Social Change.* Seattle: University of Washington Press, 1992.

Wilbur, C. Keith. *The New England Indians.* Old Saybrook, CT: Globe Pequot Press, 1978.

Wilker, Josh. *The Lenape.* New York: Chelsea House Publishers, 1994.

Wilson, Terry P. *The Underground Reservation: Osage Oil.* Lincoln: University of Nebraska Press, 1985.

Wissler, Clark. *Indians of the United States.* New York: Doubleday, 1940.

Witherspoon, Gary. *Language and Art in the Navajo Universe.* Ann Arbor: University of Michigan Press, 1977.

Wolcott, Harry F. *A Kwakiutl Village and School.* Prospect Heights, IL: Waveland Press, 1984.

Wood, Peter H., Gregory A. Waselkov, and M. Thomas Hatley, eds. *Powhatan's Mantle: Indians in the Colonial Southeast.* Lincoln: University of Nebraska Press, 1989.

Wood, W. Raymond. "Plains Trade in Prehistoric and Protohistoric Intertribal Relations." *Anthropology on the Great Plains.* Eds. Raymond Wood and Margot Liberty. Lincoln: University of Nebraska Press, 1980.

Woodward, Grace Steele. *Pocahontas.* Norman: University of Oklahoma Press, 1969.

Woodward, Susan L. and Jerry N. McDonald. *Indian Mounds of the Middle Ohio Valley: A Guide to Adena and Ohio Hopewell Sites.* Newark, OH: McDonald & Woodward Publishing Co., 1986.

Worcester, Donald E. *The Apache.* Norman: University of Oklahoma Press, 1979.

The World of the American Indians. Washington, DC: National Geographic Society, 1974.

Wright, Muriel H. *A Guide to the Indian Tribes of Oklahoma.* Norman: University of Oklahoma Press, 1951, 1986.

Yenne, Bill. *The Encyclopedia of North American Indian Tribes.* New York: Crescent Books, 1986.

Yenne, Bill and Susan Garratt. *North American Indians.* Secaucus, NJ: Chartwell Books, 1984.

Young, Mary Elizabeth. *Redskins, Ruffleshirts, and Rednecks.* Norman: University of Oklahoma Press, 1961.

Periodicals

Alexander, Don. "A First Nation Elder's Perspective on the Environment" (interview with Haida Nation activist Lavina White). *Alternatives* (March/April 1994): p. 12.

Angulo, Jaime de. "The Achumawi Life Force" (Extract, "La psychologie religieuse des Achumawi." *Anthropos* 23, 1928). *Journal of California Anthropology* 2, No. 1 (1974): pp. 60–63.

Arden, Harvey. "Living Iroquois Confederacy." *National Geographic,* Vol. 172, No. 3 (September 1987): pp. 370–403.

Barrett, Samuel A. "The Ethnogeography of the Pomo and Neighboring Indians." *University of California Publications in American Archaeology and Ethnology* 6:1 (1908): pp. 1–332.

Barrett, Samuel A., and Edward W. Gifford. "Miwok Material Culture." *Public Museum of the City of Milwaukee Bulletin* 2:4 (1933): pp. 117–376.

Capron, Lewis. "Florida's Emerging Seminoles." *National Geographic,* Vol. 136, No. 5 (November 1969): pp. 716–34.

Carlson, Paul H. "Indian Agriculture, Changing Subsistence Patterns, and the Environment on the Southern Great Plains." *Agricultural History* 66, No. 2 (1992): pp. 52–60.

Carney, Jim. "Drinking Cut Short Sockalexis' Pro Career." *Beacon Journal* (October 13, 1995).

Crisp, David. "Tribes Make Manufacturing Push: Advocates Use Network to Expand Reach." *Billings Gazette* (February 11, 1996).

Dixon, Roland B. "Achomawi and Atsugewi Tales." *Journal of American Folk-Lore* 21, No. 80 (1908): pp. 159–77.

Dixon, Roland B. "Notes on the Achomawi and Atsugewi Indians of Northern California." *American Anthropologist* 10, No. 2 (1908): pp. 208–20.

DuBois, Constance Goddard. "The Religion of the Luiseño Indians of Southern California." *University of California Publications in American Archaeology and Ethnology* 8, No. 3 (1908): pp. 69–186.

Durham, Michael S. "Mound Country." *American Heritage,* Vol. 46, No. 2 (April 1995): p. 118.

Egan, Timothy. "Tribe Stops Study of Bones That Challenges Its History." *New York Times* (September 30, 1996): A1, A10.

Euler, Robert C. "Southern Paiute Ethnohistory." *Anthropological Papers.* 78:28. University of Utah (April 1966).

Fagan, Brian. "Bison Hunters of the Northern Plains." *Archaeology* 47, No. 3 (1994): pp. 37–41.

Farrell, John Aloysius. "Cheyenne Know Cost, Perils Tied to Energy Development." *Denver Post* (November 21, 1983).

Fischman, Joshua. "California Social Climbers: Low Water Prompts High Status." *Science,* Vol. 272 (May 10, 1996): pp. 811–12.

Fontana, Bernard L. "Restoring San Xavier del Bac, 'Our Church': Tohono O'odham Work to Restore the 200-Year-Old Church Built by Their Ancestors." *Native Peoples* (Summer 1995): pp. 28–35.

French, Bob. "Seminoles: A Collision of Cultures, Independent Indians' Lifestyle Faces Scrutiny," *Sun-Sentinel* (December 24 , 1995).

Garth, Thomas R. "Atsugewi Ethnography." *Anthropological Records* 14, No. 2 (1953): pp. 129–212.

Garth, Thomas R. "Emphasis on Industriousness among the Atsugewi." *American Anthropologist* 47, No. 4 (1945): pp. 554–66.

Gifford, E. W. "Notes on Central Pomo and Northern Yana Society." *American Anthropologist* 30, No. 4 (1928): pp. 675–84.

Gifford, E. W. and A. L. Kroeber. "Culture Element Distributions, IV: Pomo." *University of California Publications in American Archaeology and Ethnology* 37(4): pp. 117–254.

Gildart, Bert. "The Mississippi Band of Choctaw: in the Shadow of Naniw Waiya." *Native Peoples* (Summer 1996): pp. 44–50.

Goddard, Pliny Earle. "Chilula Texts." *University of California Publications in American Archaeology and Ethnology* 10, No. 7 (1914): pp. 289–379.

Halbert, Henry S. "The Choctaw Creation Legend," *Publications of the Mississippi Historical Society* 2 (1901): pp. 223–34.

Halbert, Henry S. "A Choctaw Migration Legend." *American Antiquarian and Oriental Journal,* 16 (1894): pp. 215–26.

Halbert, Henry S. "Nanih Waiya, the Sacred Mound of the Choctaws," *Publications of the Mississippi Historical Society* 2 (1899): pp. 223–34.

Hanks, Christopher C. and David Pokotylo. "The Mackenzie Basin: An Alternative Approach to Dene and Metis Archaeology." *Arctic*, Vol. 42, No. 2 (1989): pp. 139–47.

Heizer, R. F. "Impact of Colonization on Native California Societies." *Journal of San Diego History,* 24:1 (1978): pp. 121–39.

Heizer, R. F. and T. Kroeber, eds. "Indians Myths of South Central California." *University of California Publications in American Archaeology and Ethnology* 4, No. 4 (1907): pp. 167–250.

Hooper, Lucile. "The Cahuilla Indians." *University of California Publications in Archaeology and Ethnology,* 16, No. 6 (April 10, 1920): pp. 315–80.

Horn, Patricia. "Polluting Sacred Ground." *Dollars and Sense* (October 1992): pp. 15–18.

"Incinerator Planned Near Pipe Spring." *National Parks* (July/August 1990).

"Indian Roots of American Democracy." *Northeast Indian Quarterly* (Winter/Spring 1987/1988).

Johnson, Kirk. "An Indian Tribe's Wealth Leads to the Expansion of Tribal Law." *New York Times* (May 22, 1994): p. 1.

Keegan, John. "Warfare on the Plains." *Yale Review 84,* No. 1 (1996): pp. 1–48.

Kelly, Isabel T. "Southern Paiute Ethnography." *Anthropological Papers.* 69:21. University of Utah (May 1964). Reprint. New York: Johnson Reprint Corporation, 1971.

Kniffen, Fred B. "Achomawi Geography." *University of California Publications in American Archaeology and Ethnology* 23, No. 5 (1928): pp. 297–332.

Koppel, Tom. "The Spirit of Haida Gwai." *Canadian Geographic* (March/April 1996): p. 2.

LaDuke, Winona. "Like Tributaries to a River," *Sierra* 81, No. 6 (November/December 1996): pp. 38–45.

LaFrance, Joan. "Essay Review." *Harvard Educational Review* (Fall 1992): pp. 388–95.

Lekson, Stephen H. "Pueblos of the Mesa Verde." *Archaeology,* Vol. 48, No. 5 (September/October 1995): pp. 56–57.

Lepper, Bradley T. "Tracking Ohio's Great Hopewell Road." *Archaeology,* Vol. 48, No. 6 (November–December 1995): p. 52.

Lincecum, Gideon. "Life of Apushimataha." *Publications of the Mississippi Historical Society* 9 (1905–06): pp. 415–85.

Linden, Eugene. "Bury My Heart at James Bay: the World's Most Extensive Hydropower Project Has Disrupted Rivers, Wildlife, and the Traditions of the Quebec Indians. Is It Really Needed?" *Time* Vol. 138, No. 2 (July 15, 1991): p. 60.

Lindgren, Kristy. "Sgt. David H. Mace Shot Wampanoag David Hendricks Eleven Times and Is Still a Free Man." *News From Indian Country,* 7, No. 4 (1993): pp. 1–2.

"Makah Tribe's Net Snares Gray Whale." *Oregonian* (July 18, 1995).

"The Makah's Case for Whale Hunting." *Seattle-Post Intelligencer* (June 8, 1995).

"Menominee Honored at UN Ceremony for Forest Practices." *News From Indian Country,* IX, No. 9 (Mid-May 1995): p. 3.

Menominee Indian Tribe of Wisconsin. "Land of the Menominee" (brochure), c. 1994.

"The Menominee Nation and Its Treaty Rights." *News From Indian Country,* IX, No. 11 (Mid-June 1995): p. 2.

Menominee Nation Treaty Rights, Mining Impact, and Communications Offices. "Protect Menominee Nation Treaty Rights." *News From Indian Country,* X, No. 10 (Late-May 1996): p. 14A.

Millin, Peggy Tabor. "Passing the Torch: Technology Saves a Culture." *Native Peoples,* 9, No. 3 (1996): pp. 48–54.

Momatiuk, Yva and John Eastcott. "*Nunavut* Means Our Land." *Native Peoples* 9, No. 1 (Fall/Winter 1995): p. 42.

Mooney, James. "Calendar History of the Kiowa Indians." *Seventeenth Annual Report of the Bureau of American Ethnology.* Washington, DC: U.S. Government Printing Office, 1898.

Morrison, Joan. "Protect the Earth Gathering Focuses Mining Opposition." *News From Indian Country,* X, No. 5 (Mid-March 1996): p. 2.

Newman, Peter C. "The Beaching of a Great Whale." *Maclean's*. (Vol. 104, No. 37): p. 38.

Norman, Geoffrey. "The Cherokee: Two Nations, One People." *National Geographic* (May 1995): pp. 72–97.

"1,000 Gather to Oppose Exxon." *News From Indian Country,* X, No. 10 (Late-May 1996): pp. 1A, 5A.

Peterson, Lindsay. "Living History: Ruby Tiger Osceola, a 100-Year-Old Seminole Indian, Is Both a Link to the Past and a Leader for the Future." *The Tampa Tribune* (March 12, 1996).

Petit, Charles. "Ishi May Not Have Been the Last Yahi Indian." *San Francisco Chronicle* (February 6, 1996).

Plungis, Jeff. "Administering Environmental Justice." *Empire State Report* (January 1995): pp. 61+.

Roberts, Chris. "Schemitzun: The Pequot People's Feast of Green Corn and Dance." *Native Peoples,* Vol. 7, No. 4 (Summer 1994): pp. 66–70.

Rossiter, William. "CSI Opposes Whaling by the Makah." *Cetacean Society International.* Vol. 5, No. 1 (January, 1996).

Sapir, Edward. "Yana Texts." *University of California Publications in American Archaeology and Ethnology* 9, No. 1 (1910): pp. 1–235.

Sapir, Edward. "The Position of Yana in the Hokan Stock." *University of California Publications in American Archaeology and Ethnology* 13, No. 1 (1917): pp. 1–34.

Sapir, Edward and Leslie Spier. "Notes on the Culture of the Yana." *Anthropological Records* 3, No. 3 (1943): pp. 239–98.

Shaw, Christopher. "A Theft of Spirit?" *New Age Journal* (July/August 1995): pp. 84+.

Sparkman, Philip Stedman. "The Culture of the Luiseño Indians." *University of California Publications in American Archaeology and Ethnology* 8, No. 4 (1908): pp. 187–234.

Spier, Leslie. "The Sun Dance of the Plains Indians: Its Development and Diffusion." *Anthropological Papers of the American Museum of Natural History* 16, No. VII (1921): pp. 459–525.

Stirling, Matthew W. "Indians of the Far West." *National Geographic* (February 1948): pp. 175–200.

Strong, W. D. "The Plains Culture in the Light of Archaeology." *American Anthropologist* 35, No. 2 (1933): pp. 271–87.

Stuart, George E, "Etowah: A Southeast Village in 1491." *National Geographic,* 180, No. 4 (October 1991): pp. 54–67.

Theimer, Sharon. "Menominee Nation Lawsuit Wins Over Motion to Dismiss." *News From Indian Country,* X, No. 5 (Mid-March 1996): p. 3A.

Thompson, Ian. "The Search for Settlements on the Great Sage Plain." *Archaeology,* Vol. 48, No. 5 (September/October 1995): pp. 57–63.

Thurston, Harry and Stephen Homer. "Power in a Land of Remembrance: Their Rivers, Lands." *Audubon.* (Vol. 93, No. 6): p. 52.

Tobias, John L. "Canada's Subjugation of the Plains Cree, 1879–1885." *Canadian Historical Review,* Vol. 64 (December 1983): p. 519.

Todhunter, Andrew. "Digging Into History." *Washington Post Book World* (May 26, 1996): pp. 9, 13.

Turner, Steve and Todd Nachowitz. "The Damming of Native Lands." *Nation,* Vol. 253, No. 13 (October 21, 1991): p. 6.

Van Natta, Don Jr. "Tribe Saw a Promise, but Party Saw a Pledge." *New York Times* (August 12, 1997): A1, C20.

"The Water Famine." *Indigenous Peoples' Literature* (January 7, 1996).

Wedel, Waldo R. "Some Aspects of Human Ecology in the Central Plains." *American Anthropologist* 55, No. 4 (1953): pp. 499–514.

"Welcome to the Land of the Menominee-Forest." *News From Indian Country,* IX, No. 14 (Late-July 1995): p. 6.

White, Raymond. "Luiseño Social Organization." *University of California Publications in American Archaeology and Ethnology* 48, No. 2 (1963): pp. 91–194.

White, Raymond. "The Luiseño Theory of 'Knowledge.'" *American Anthropologist* 59, No. 2 (1957): pp. 1–19.

White, Raymond. "Two Surviving Luiseño Indian Ceremonies." *American Anthropologist* 55, No. 4 (1953): pp. 569–78.

Williams, Lee. "Medicine Man." *New Mexico Magazine* 62 (May 1984): pp. 62–71.

Web Sites

Beckman, Tad. "The Yurok and Hupa of the Northern Coast." [Online] http://www4.hmc.edu:8001/humanities/indian/ca/ch10.htm (accessed on April 22, 1999).

The Cheyenne Indians. [Online] http://www.uwgb.edu/~galta/mrr/cheyenne (accessed on April 21, 1999).

Lawrence, Elizabeth Atwood, "The Symbolic Role of Animals in the Plains Indian Sun Dance." [Online] http://envirolink.org/arrs/psyeta/sa/sa.1/lawrence.html (accessed on April 21, 1999).

Magagnini, Stephen. "Indians find 'new buffalo' in casinos." *The Modesto Bee Online.* [Online] http://www.modbee.com/metro/story/0,1113,4447,00.html (accessed on April 22, 1999).

Powersource Consultants. *Important Dates in Cherokee History.* [Online] http://www.powersource.com:80/nation/dates.html (accessed on April 21, 1999).

Stockbridge-Munsee Home Page. [Online] http://www.pressenter.com/org/tribes/munsee.htm (accessed on April 21, 1999).

CD-ROMs

"Cherokee Language." *Microsoft Encarta 96 Encyclopedia.* Redmond, WA: Microsoft, 1993–95.

Kappler, Charles, ed. *Treaties of American Indians and the United States. Treaties with the Menominees, 1817, 1831 (February 8 and February 17), 1832, 1836, 1848, 1854, 1856. Treaty with the Chippewa, 1833. Treaty with the Stockbridge and Munsee, 1839,* version 1.00. Indianapolis: Objective Computing, 1994.

Schoolcraft, Henry R. "Archives of Aboriginal Knowledge" and "Thirty Years with the Indian Tribes," on *The Indian Question,* version 1.00. Indianapolis: Objective Computing, 1994.

Other Sources

Klasky, Philip M. "An Extreme and Solemn Relationship: Native American Perspectives: Ward Valley Nuclear Dump." A thesis submitted to the faculty of San Francisco State University in partial fulfillment of the requirements of the degree Master of Arts in Geography, May 1997.

Low, Sam. *The Ancient World* (television documentary). QED Communications, Inc./Pennsylvania State University, 1992.

Mashantucket Pequot Nation. "The Fox People." (Leaflet), c. 1994.

Mashantucket Pequot Nation. "The Mashantucket Pequots: A Proud Tradition" and "Foxwoods Resort Casino." (brochures), n.d.

Acknowledgments

Grateful acknowledgment is made to the following sources whose works appear in this volume. Every effort has been made to trace copyright, but if omissions have been made, please contact the publisher.

"Blueberry Pudding." Marx, Pamela. From *Travel-the-World Cookbook* by Pamela A. Marx. Copyright © 1996 by Pamela A. Marx. Reproduced by permission of Addison-Wesley Educational Publishers, Inc.

"The Bluebird and Coyote." *American Indian Myths and Legends* edited by Richard Erdoes and Alfonso Ortiz. Copyright © 1984 by Richard Erdoes and Alfonso Ortiz. Reproduced by permission of Pantheon Books, a division of Random House, Inc.

"Ceremony and Song." Ruoff, A. LaVonne Brown, ed. *Literatures of the American Indian.* Chelsea House Publishers, 1991. Copyright © by Chelsea House Publishers, a division of Main Line Book Co. All rights reserved. Reproduced by permission.

"Cheyenne Bread." Cox, Beverly, and Martin Jacobs. From *Spirit of the Harvest.*" Copyright © 1991 Stewart, Tabori & Chang. Reproduced by permission.

"Chippewa Wild Rice." Copyright © 1965 by Yeffe Kimball and Jean Anderson. From *The Art of American Indian Cooking* published by Doubleday. Reproduced by permission of McIntosh & Otis, Inc.

"Choctaw Acorn Biscuits." Cox, Beverly, and Martin Jacobs. From *Spirit of the Harvest.* Copyright © 1991 Stewart, Tabori & Chang. Reproduced by permission.

"Comanche Chickasaw Plum Bars." Kavasch, E. Barrie. From *Enduring Harvests: Native American Foods and Festivals for Every Season.* Copyright © 1995 Globe Pequot Press. Reproduced by permission.

"Coyote in the Cedar Tree." Ramsey, Jarold. From *Coyote Was Going There: Indian Literature in the Oregon Country.* Copyright © 1977 University of Washington Press. Reproduced by permission.

"Coyote Wants To Be Chief." Premo, Anna. From *Shoshone Tales*. Edited by Anne M. Smith. University of Utah Press, 1993. © 1993 by the University of Utah Press. All rights reserved. Reproduced by permission.

"The Death of Wiyót, the Creator." Curtis, Edward S. From *The North American Indian." Edited by Frederick Webb Hodge. Copyright © 1970 Johnson Reprint Corporation.*

"The Emergence." Tithla, Bane. From *Myths and Tales of the White Mountain Apache*. Copyright © 1939 American Folklore Society. Reproduced by permission.

"An Encounter with the Tamciye." Garth, Thomas R. From *Atsugewi Ethnography*. Copyright © 1953 Anthropological Records.

"The Girl and the Devil." Bushnell, David I. From *Choctaw Myths and Legends*. Copyright © 1985 Garland Publishing. Reproduced by permission.

"Glacial Mists Cooler." Kavasch, E. Barrie. From *Enduring Harvests: Native American Foods and Festivals for Every Season*. Copyright © 1995 Globe Pequot Press. Reproduced by permission.

"Of Glooskap and the Sinful Serpent." Leland, Charles G. From *The Alogonquin Legends of New England: or Myths and Folklore of the Micmac, Passamaquoddy, and Penobscot Tribes*. Copyright © 1884 Houghton, Mifflen. Reproduced by permission.

"High Plains Pemmican." Kavasch, E. Barrie. From *Enduring Harvests: Native American Foods and Festivals for Every Season*. Copyright © 1995 Globe Pequot Press. Reproduced by permission.

"The Horrible Bear." Jewell, Donald P. From *Indians of the Feather River: Tales and Legends of Concow Maidu of California*. Copyright © 1987 Ballena Press. Reproduced by permission.

"How the Chumash Came To Be." Blackburn, Thomas C. From *December's Child: A Book of Chumash Oral Narratives*. Copyright © 1975 Berkeley: University of California Press. Reproduced by permission.

"How the Clans Came To Be." From *Creek Lifestyles, Customs and Legends*. Ryal Public School. Reproduced by permission. [Online] http://www.edumaster.net/schools/ryal/creek.html (18 September 1998).

"How the Moon Was Made." Clay, Charles. From *Swampy Cree Legends*. The Macmillan Company of Canada Limited, 1938. Copyright, Canada 1938 by The Macmillan Company of Canada Limited. All rights reserved.

"How Youth Are Instructed by Tribal Elders." Spindler, George, and Louise Spindler. From *Dreamers with Power: The Menomini Indians.* Copyright © 1971 Holt, Rinehart & Winston. Reproduced by permission.

"Jerky." Frank, Lois Ellen. From *Native American Cooking: Foods of the Southwest Indian Nations* by Lois Ellen Frank. Copyright © 1991 by Lois Ellen Frank. Reproduced by permission of Clarkson N. Potter, a division of Crown Publishers, Inc.

"King Philip's Prophecy." William Apess. Reprinted from Barry O'Connell, ed., *On Our Own Ground: The Complete Writings of William Apess, a Pequot.* (Amherst: University of Massachusetts Press, 1992). Copyright © 1992 by the University of Massachusetts Press.

"Mary O'Brien's Apricot Blueberry Cookies." Kavasch, E. Barrie. From *Enduring Harvests: Native American Foods and Festivals for Every Season.* Copyright © 1995 Globe Pequot Press. Reproduced by permission.

"Mohawk Baked Squash." Wolfson, Evelyn. From *The Iroquois: People of the Northeast.* Copyright © 1992 The Millbrook Press. Reproduced by permission.

"The Morning Star." Lacey, Theresa Jensen. From *The Pawnee.* Chelsea House Publishers, 1995. Copyright © 1996 by Chelsea House Publishers, a division of Main Line Book Co. All rights reserved. Reproduced by permission.

"Nanabozho and Winter-Maker." Coleman, Sister Bernard, Ellen Frogner, and Estelle Eich. From *Ojibwa Myths and Legends.* Copyright © 1962 Ross and Haines.

"Navajo Peach Pudding." Frank, Lois Ellen. From *Native American Cooking: Foods of the Southwest Indian Nations* by Lois Ellen Frank. Copyright © 1991 by Lois Ellen Frank. Reproduced by permission of Clarkson N. Potter, a division of Crown Publishers, Inc.

"Pawnee Ground Roast Pound Meat with Pecans." Kavasch, E. Barrie. From *Enduring Harvests: Native American Foods and Festivals for Every Season.* Copyright © 1995 Globe Pequot Press. Reproduced by permission.

"Powhatan Hazelnut Soup" Copyright © 1965 by Yeffe Kimball and Jean Anderson. From *The Art of American Indian Cooking* published by Doubleday. Reproduced by permission of McIntosh & Otis, Inc.

"Puffballs with Wild Rice and Hazelnuts." Kavasch, E. Barrie. From *Enduring Harvests: Native American Foods and Festivals for Every Season.* Copyright © 1995 Globe Pequot Press. Reproduced by permission.

"The Rabbit Dance." Bruchac, Joseph. From *Native American Animal Stories.* Copyright © 1992 Fulcrum Publishing. Reproduced by permission.

"The Race." Grinnell, George Bird. From *Cheyenne Campfires* Copyright © 1926 Yale University Press. Reproduced by permission.

"Simi Chumbo." Kavasch, E. Barrie. From *Enduring Harvests: Native American Foods and Festivals for Every Season.* Copyright © 1995 Globe Pequot Press. Reproduced by permission.

"Sioux Plum Raisin Cakes." Kavasch, E. Barrie. From *Enduring Harvests: Native American Foods and Festivals for Every Season.* Copyright © 1995 Globe Pequot Press. Reproduced by permission.

"Southeast Native American Pecan Soup." Cox, Beverly, and Martin Jacobs. From *Spirit of the Harvest.* Copyright © 1991 Stewart, Tabori & Chang. Reproduced by permission.

"The Stolen Squashes." Reed, Evelyn Dahl. From *Coyote Tales from the Indian Pueblos.* Sunstone Press, 1988. Copyright © 1988 by Evelyn Dahl Reed. Reproduced by permission.

"Succotash." McCullough, Frances, and Barbara Witt. From *Classic American Food Without Fuss* by Barbara Witt and Frances McCullough. Copyright © 1996 by Barbara Witt and Frances McCullough. Reproduced by permission of Random House, Inc.

"The Sun Dance Wheel." Monroe, Jean Guard, and Ray A. Williamson. From *They Dance in the Sky: Native American Star Myths.* Copyright © 1987 Houghton Mifflin. Reproduced by permission.

"Wampanoag Cape Cod Cranberry Pie." Kavasch, E. Barrie. From *Enduring Harvests: Native American Foods and Festivals for Every Season.* Copyright © 1995 Globe Pequot Press. Reproduced by permission.

"Why the Bear Waddles When He Walks." Marriott, Alice, and Carol K. Rachlin. From *American Indian Mythology.* Copyright © 1968 Cromwell. Reproduced by permission.

"Windwalker Pine Nut Cookies." Kavasch, E. Barrie. From *Enduring Harvests: Native American Foods and Festivals for Every Season.* Copyright © 1995 Globe Pequot Press. Reproduced by permission.

The photographs and illustrations appearing in U•X•L Encyclopedia of Native American Tribes were received from the following sources:

Covers Volume 1: tepee, **Library of Congress;** Seminole thatched houses, **P & F Communications. David Phillips, photographer;** Volume 2: Rocky Mountains from Ute Reservation, **North Wind Picture Archives. Reproduced by permission;** Taos Pueblo scene, **Library of Congress;** Volume 3: Inuit mother and child, **National Archives and Records Administration;** Young man at Sioux powwow, **Sygma Photo News. Photograph by F. Paolini. Reproduced by permission;** Volume 4: Ramona Lugu, Cahuilla in front of home, **Los Angeles Central Library. Reproduced by permission;** Tlingit longhouse with totem poles, **Corbis. Photograph by Tom Bean. Reproduced by permission.**

© 1998 North Wind Picture Archives. Reproduced by permission: pp. 3, 133, 405; **National Anthropological Archives. Reproduced by permission:** pp. 15, 1066, 1071; **Print by M. J. Burns. North Wind Picture Archives. Reproduced by permission:** p. 21; **University of Pennsylvania Museum. Reproduced by permission:** pp. 23, 1040, 1192; **Photograph by Frank C. Wotm. Library of Congress:** pp. 24, 25; **North Wind Picture Archives. Reproduced by permission:** pp. 32, 42, 51, 90, 109, 121, 141, 160, 172, 246, 247, 290, 317, 319, 329, 346, 373, 379, 381, 400, 418, 419, 443, 463, 468, 476, 498, 527, 534, 599, 637, 687, 693, 722, 756, 766, 785, 792, 796, 814, 827, 884, 897, 975, 1140; **Library of Congress:** pp. 36, 91, 146, 166, 219, 313, 416, 582, 615, 676, 732, 769, 778, 824, 848, 856, 908, 963, 965, 1087, 1117, 1162, 1173; **Bettmann. Reproduced by permission:** pp. 39, 45, 874; **AP/Wide World Photos, Inc. Reproduced by permission:** pp. 53, 84, 118, 138, 271, 305, 424, 458, 503, 750, 841, 1009, 1246; **© 1997 N. Carter/North Wind Picture Archives. Reproduced by permission:** pp. 62, 92, 497, 499; **Photograph by Bruce M. Fritz. *The Capital Times.* Reproduced by permission:** p. 63; **CORBIS/Bettmann. Reproduced by permission:** pp. 67, 108, 188, 356, 533, 828, 832, 877, 925; **Photograph by W. H. Wessa. Library of Congress:** p. 68; **Archive Photos. Reproduced by permission:** pp. 148, 153, 192, 358, 482, 485, 526, 578, 1048; **National Archives and Records Administration:** pp. 152, 178, 296, 348, 436, 464, 538, 546, 592, 635, 641, 643, 645, 748, 793, 810, 960, 1165, 1217, 1235; **Photograph by C. M. Bell. National Archives:** p. 176; **© 1977 North Wind Picture Archives. Reproduced by permission:** p. 202; **© 1994 North Wind Picture Archives. Reproduced by permission:** p. 209; **National Archives:**

pp. 234, 807, 935; **Granger Collection. New York. Reproduced by permission:** p. 249; **© 1995. North Wind Picture Archives. Reproduced by permission:** pp. 388, 465, 492, 553, 601, 892; **© 1993 North Wind Pictures Archives:** p. 391; **Mesa Verde National Park/National Park Service. Reproduced by permission:** p. 402; **Painting by Waldo Mootzka. Photograph by Seth Rothman. Dick Howard Collection. Reproduced by permission:** p. 460; **Southwest Museum. Reproduced by permission:** pp. 477, 479, 480, 979, 991, 1050; **Photograph by Edward S. Curtis. The Library of Congress:** pp. 512, 567, 694, 1116, 1256, 1259; **Photograph by Edward S. Curtis. CORBIS. Reproduced by permission:** pp. 517, 547; **CORBIS/Arne Hodalic. Reproduced by permission:** p. 519; **© 1991 N. Carter/North Wind Picture Archives. Reproduced by permission:** p. 535; **CORBIS/E. O. Hoppe. Reproduced by permission:** p. 550; **Photograph by T. Harmon Parkhurst. Courtesy Museum of New Mexico, negative number 7454:** p. 559; **Photograph by Bluford W. Muir. CORBIS. Reproduced by permission:** p. 579; **Photograph by Orville L. Snider. CORBIS. Reproduced by permission:** p. 581; **CORBIS/Adam Woolfit. Reproduced by permission:** p. 585; **CORBIS/David G. Houser. Reproduced by permission:** pp. 606, 950; **CORBIS/Tom Bean. Reproduced by permission:** p. 610, 1269; **CORBIS. Reproduced by permission:** pp. 670, 672, 768, 922; **CORBIS/Joel Bennett. Reproduced by permission:** p. 675; **Provincial Archives of Manitoba. Reproduced by permission:** p. 714; **Photograph by Wiliam S. Soule. National Archives and Records Administration:** p. 736; **CORBIS/ Brian Vikander. Reproduced by permission:** p. 773; **Photgraph by Alexander Gardner. CORBIS. Reproduced by permission:** pp. 782, 784; **Photograph by William S. Soule. The Library of Congress:** p. 783; **Photograph by William H. Jackson. National Archives and Records Administration:** p. 840; **Buffalo Bill Historical Center, Cody, WY. Gift of Mrs. Cornelius Vanderbilt Whitney. Reproduced by permission:** p. 883; **Photograph by Eadweard Muybridge. National Archives and Records Administration:** p. 934; **Photograph by Larry Phillips. Institute of American Indian Arts Museum, Santa Fe:** p. 952; **Los Angeles Public Library. Reproduced by permission:** p. 992; **California History Section, California State Library. Reproduced by permission:** p. 1018; **CORBIS/David Muench. Reproduced by permission:** p. 1021; **Smithsonian Insititution, Bureau of American Ethnology. Reproduced by permission:** pp. 105, 1036; **CORBIS/Ed Young. Reproduced by permission:** p. 1081; **American Museum of Natural History. Reproduced by permission:** p. 1126; **CORBIS/**

Natalie Fobes. Reproduced by permission: pp. 1142, 1221, 1224; Photograph by Blankenburg Photo. CORBIS/PEMCO—Webster Stevens Collection; Museum of History & Industry, Seattle. Reproduced by permission: p. 1144; Photograph © Thomas Hoepker. Reproduced by permission of Joe Manfredini: p. 1177; Photograph by William McLennan. University of British Columbia Museum of Anthropology. Reproduced by permission: p. 1179; KWA-Gulth Arts Ltd. Reproduced by permission of Richard Hunt: p. 1194; Photograph by Edward S. Curtis. Univerversity of Pennsylvania Museum. Reproduced by permission: p. 1198; Photograph by Anthony Bolante. Reuters/Archive Photos. Reproduced by permission: p. 1207; CORBIS/Museum of History and Industry, Seattle. Reproduced by permission: p. 1210; CORBIS/Seattle Post–Intelligencer Collection. Museum of History and Industry, Seattle. Reproduced by permission: p. 1254; Courtesy Dept. of Library Services American Museum of Natural History, Neg. No. 41184. Reproduced by permission: p. 1268; Reproduced by permission of Preston Singletary: p. 1271; Photograph by Jeff Greenberg. Archive Photos. Reproduced by permission: p. 1272; Photograph by Winter and Pont. CORBIS. Reproduced by permission: p. 1274.

Index

Italic type indicates volume numbers; boldface type indicates entries and their page numbers; (ill.) indicates illustration.

A

B

C

D

E

F

G

H

I

J

K

L

M

O

P

Q

R

S

T

U

V

W

X

Y

Z